Greenhill Books

BOMBER HARRIS
HIS LIFE AND TIMES

Dedicated to Arthur Harris's 'old lags'

BOMBER HARRIS
HIS LIFE AND TIMES

The Biography of Marshal of the Royal Air Force
Sir Arthur Harris, the Wartime Chief of Bomber Command

Air Commodore Henry Probert, MBE MA

Greenhill Books, London
Stackpole Books, Pennsylvania

Bomber Harris: His Life and Times
first published 2001
by Greenhill Books, Lionel Leventhal Limited, Park House, 1 Russell Gardens,
London NW11 9NN
www.greenhillbooks.com
and
Stackpole Books, 5067 Ritter Road, Mechanicsburg, PA 17055, USA

British Library Cataloguing in Publication Data

Probert, Henry
Bomber Harris: his life and times: the biography of Marshal of the Royal Air Force
Sir Arthur Harris, the wartime chief of Bomber Command
1. Harris, Sir Arthur, 1892–1984   2. Great Britain. Royal Air Force.
Bomber Command   3. Marshals – Great Britain – Biography   4. World War,
1939–1945 – Great Britain
I. Title
940.5'44'941'092

ISBN 1-85367-473-7

Library of Congress Cataloging-in-Publication Data available

Typeset by DP Photosetting, Aylesbury, Bucks
Printed and bound in Great Britain by
CPD (Wales), Ebbw Vale

Contents

List of Illustrations

34. Harris with his Personal Secretary, Flight Officer Peggy Wherry. (*Mrs S. K. Goodman*)
35. With his senior staff officers.
36. With his naval staff. (*Mrs S. K. Goodman*)
37. Harris greets WAAF visitors. (*Mrs S. K. Goodman*)
38. Harris's PA assists him at the Stereopticon.
39. At HQ 4 Group Harris is introduced to members of the staff. (*Mrs. H. Mills*)
40. Bomber Night 1944 at HQ USAAF VIII Bomber Command, High Wycombe.
41. The Commander-in-Chief's residence, Springfield.
42. The family in the garden.
43. 'Dadn' and 'Jacan'.
44. Exhaustion.
45. Harris is invested with the Grand Order of Polonia Restituta, June 1945.
46. Harris represents the United Kingdom at the Oslo Victory Parade.
47. Harris is entertained in Washington by General Arnold, August 1945.
48. Harris and his family land at Eastleigh, Kenya, 1945.
49. Harris is awarded the Freedom of High Wycombe, February 1946.
50. Harris is welcomed in Montreal, April 1947.
51. The first of Harris's ships, SS *Constantia*.
52. With Henry Mercer, September 1949.
53. Dressed for the Coronation, 1953.
54. The Ferry House, Goring-on-Thames.
55. Harris drives the coach *Perseverance* through Oxford.
56. At a dinner in honour of President Eisenhower, 1959.
57. Harris and Winston Churchill (junior) at the RAF Museum, 1981. (*Mr. A. J. Wicks*)
58. Harris and Ira Eaker deep in conversation at Grosvenor House.
59. At the opening of the Bomber Command Museum, April 1983.
60. Harris and Jill with some of the 'old lags'. (*Ray Callow, Danny Boon*)
61. Harris and Jill at home.
62. The Memorial Flight Lancaster pays tribute at Harris's funeral, 1984.

Except where stated, all photographs are taken from the family collections of Jacqueline Assheton and Rosemary Harris. They and the other donors are warmly thanked.

Maps

Maps drawn by John Richards

Charts

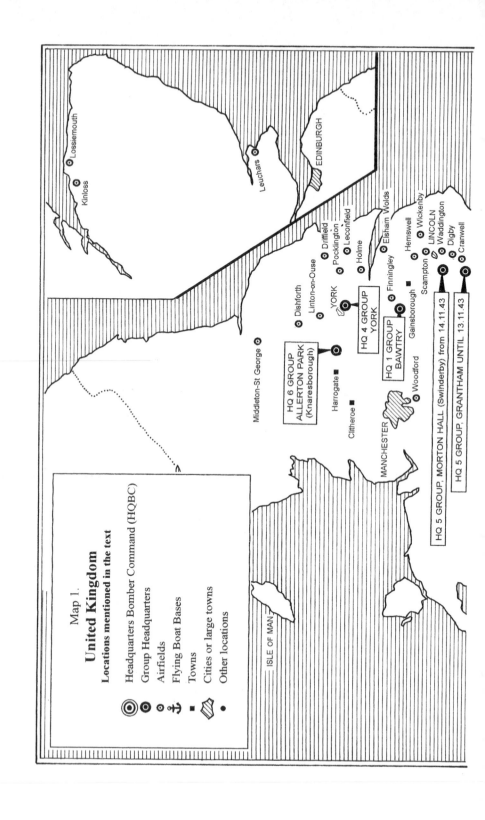

Map 1.
United Kingdom
Locations mentioned in the text

◎ Headquarters Bomber Command (HQBC)
◉ Group Headquarters
⊙ Airfields
⚓ Flying Boat Bases
■ Towns
◈ Cities or large towns
• Other locations

ISLE OF MAN

Lossiemouth
Kinloss
Leuchars
EDINBURGH

Middleton-St George

HQ 6 GROUP
ALLERTON PARK
(Knaresborough)

Harrogate
Clitheroe
MANCHESTER

Dishforth
Linton-on-Ouse
YORK
HQ 4 GROUP
YORK

Driffield
Pockington
Leconfield
Holme

Elsham Wolds
Finningley
HQ 1 GROUP
BAWTRY
Gainsborough
Woodford
Scampton
Hemswell
Wickenby
LINCOLN
Waddington
Digby
Cranwell

HQ 5 GROUP, MORTON HALL (Swinderby) from 14.11.43

HQ 5 GROUP, GRANTHAM UNTIL 13.11.43

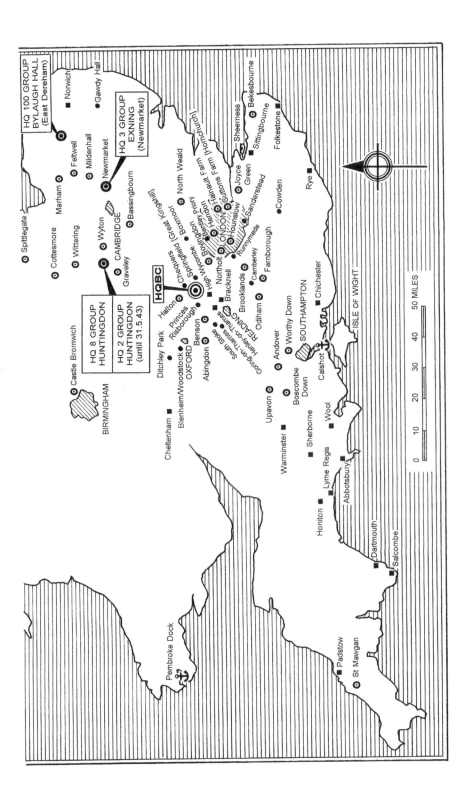

HQ 100 GROUP
BYLAUGH HALL
(East Dereham)

HQ 3 GROUP
EXNING
(Newmarket)

HQ 8 GROUP
HUNTINGDON

HQ 2 GROUP
HUNTINGDON
(until 31.5.43)

HQBC

Spittlegate
Norwich
Gawdy Hall
Castle Bromwich
Cottesmore
Marham
Feltwell
Mildenhall
Wittering
Newmarket
BIRMINGHAM
Wyton
CAMBRIDGE
Bassingbourn
Graveley
Chequers [Great Kinghill]
Boxmoor
North Weald
Spitfield
Hainault Farm [Hornchurch]
High Wycombe
Bovingdon
Bentley Priory
Hendon
Suttons Farm [Hornchurch]
Sheerness
Bekesbourne
Sittingbourne
Folkestone
LONDON
Hounslow
Joyce Green
Halton
Northolt
Runnymede
Sanderstead
Rye
Ditchley Park
Princes Risborough
Benson
Bracknell
Camberley
Farnborough
Cowden
Cheltenham
Blenheim/Woodstock
OXFORD
South Stoke
Goring-on-Thames
Henley-on-Thames
READING
Brooklands
Odiham
Worthy Down
Chichester
Abingdon
Upavon
Andover
SOUTHAMPTON
Calshot
ISLE OF WIGHT
Warminster
Boscombe Down
Sherborne
Wool
Honiton
Lyme Regis
Abbotsbury
Dartmouth
Salcombe
Pembroke Dock
Padstow
St Mawgan

0   10   20   30   40   50 MILES

Glossary

Asst Sec Off	Assistant Section Officer
AA	Anti-Aircraft
ACAS (Ops)	Assistant Chief of Air Staff (Operations)
ACAS (R)	Assistant Chief of Air Staff (Research)
ACM	Air Chief Marshal
ADC	Aide de Camp
ADI (Science)	Assistant Director of Intelligence (Science)
ADGB	Air Defence of Great Britain
AEAF	Allied Expeditionary Air Force
AFV	Armoured Fighting Vehicle
AHB	Air Historical Branch
Air Cdre	Air Commodore
AM	Air Marshal
AMP	Air Member for Personnel
AMSO	Air Member for Supply and Organisation
AOA	Air Officer Administration
AOC	Air Officer Commanding
AOC-in-C	Air Officer Commanding-in-Chief
ASV	Air to Surface Vehicle (radar)
AVM	Air Vice-Marshal
BBSU	British Bombing Survey Unit
C-in-C	Commander-in-Chief
CAS	Chief of Air Staff
CBE	Commander of the Order of the British Empire
CO/OC	Commanding Officer/Officer Commanding
CSTC	Combined Strategic Targets Committee
DB Ops	Director (Directorate) of Bomber Operations
DCAS	Deputy Chief of Air Staff
DD Plans	Deputy Director of Plans
DRC	Defence Requirements Committee
Flt Lt	Flight Lieutenant
Flt Off	Flight Officer
GCB	Knight Grand Cross of the Order of the Bath
GEE	Navigation aid. See p.225
GH	Navigation aid. See p.232
Gp Capt	Group Captain
H2S	Navigation aid. See p.230
JIC	Joint Intelligence Committee

12

JPSC	Joint Planning Sub-Committee
LMF	Lack of Moral Fibre
MAP	Ministry of Aircraft Production
MEW	Ministry of Economic Warfare
MRAF	Marshal of the Royal Air Force
MU	Maintenance Unit
NAAFI	Navy, Army and Air Force Institute
OBOE	Navigation aid. See p.230
OH	Official History of the Strategic Bombing Offensive
ORB	Operations Record Book
ORC	Operational Requirements Committee
OTC	Officer Training Corps
OTU	Operational Training Unit
PA	Personal Assistant
PFF	Pathfinder Force
POW	Prisoner of War
PRO	Public Record Office
PROs	Public Relations Officers
PSO	Personal Staff Officer
PUS	Permanent Under Secretary of State
PWE	Political Warfare Executive
RAAF	Royal Australian Air Force
RAE	Royal Aircraft Establishment
RAFHS	Royal Air Force Historical Society
RCAF	Royal Canadian Air Force
RCM	Radio Counter Measures
RFC	Royal Flying Corps
RNZAF	Royal New Zealand Air Force
R/T	Radio Telephony
SASO	Senior Air Staff Officer
SHAEF	Supreme Headquarters Allied Expeditionary Force
SOE	Special Operations Executive
TRE	Telecommunications Research Establishment
USAAF	United States Army Air Force
VC	Victoria Cross
VCAS	Vice Chief of Air Staff
WAAF	Women's Auxiliary Air Force
WD	War Department
Wg Cdr	Wing Commander
W/T	Wireless Telegraphy

Preface

Given the multitude of books that already exist about Bomber Command in the Second World War and the role of its Commander-in-Chief, Sir Arthur Harris, it may be wondered why there is need for yet another. I myself felt this way when I was appointed to direct the RAF's Air Historical Branch in 1978. Yet I soon discovered that questions about the bomber offensive were taking a substantial amount of my own time and that of my staff, that the controversies and deep differences of view still ran deep, abroad as well as at home, and that central to many of these was Harris himself. He featured large in many of the written accounts, as well as in the press features, the films, and the radio and television programmes, and he attracted verdicts ranging from adulation to hatred. Yet thus far – and understandably, for he was still alive – no biography had been published, and not until after his death in 1984 did Dudley Saward's long-awaited account arrive on the scene.

With many others, I had eagerly awaited its appearance but was frankly disappointed. Saward seemed to concentrate unduly on the wartime story, relying essentially on Harris's personal recollections long after the event and on documents many of which had already been published elsewhere. It seemed not to bring out Harris's personality; there were serious omissions and misunderstandings, and some of the major questions about him were left unanswered. As time went on I came to believe that a further attempt needed to be made, and having failed to persuade anyone else to take it on I decided in retirement to explore the possibilities myself. When I discovered that Harris's own extensive papers resided, hitherto almost unresearched, in the RAF Museum, I realised that here was an historian's goldmine. Then, having discussed the possibilities with fellow historians including Denis Richards, Noble Frankland, John Terraine, Richard Overy and Sebastian Cox, and with Sir Michael Beetham, President of the Bomber Command Association, and Dr Michael Fopp, Director of the RAF Museum, I spoke to Sir Arthur's family. Sir Anthony Harris, Rosemary Harris and Jacqueline and Nicholas Assheton were all immediately enthusiastic, promising full support, and I soon found that their extensive family papers and photographs would also prove invaluable. The stage was set and I started work in 1996.

In so far as I gave myself an objective, it was not to tell the story of Bomber Command's war yet again. While I would have to refer to some of the most important events and issues in order to set the scene it was reasonable to expect readers to turn to other historians for the already oft-repeated details. My task has been firstly to describe Harris's earlier life, both in the RAF and as a family man, as fully as possible. Second I have tried to bring out not just his part in the wartime controversies but the manner in which he conducted his Command's affairs, the intense pressures on him, the way in which he led his men, and his relations with that host of people who were in positions to influence his activities. Third I have related the story of his long life after the war, mostly hitherto untold, and tried to throw light on several issues which, to my mind, have never before been adequately explained. My approach will, I hope, be seen as both critical and sympathetic, and if my final judgement is thought by some to be too kind I hope they will accept that I have tried hard to provide a balanced view.

Inevitably I have been influenced by my own experience. Indeed, one of my reasons for attempting this project was that I felt it should be undertaken by someone who lived through the critical wartime years and was old enough to remember the atmosphere of those days. One of my clearest recollections is of my 14th birthday on 23 December 1940, when I saw the night sky over Manchester, my home city, lit up by the fires in the great warehouses as the Luftwaffe set them alight. I remember the regular air raid warnings over the subsequent years; I saw Whitley, Halifax and Lancaster bombers being turned out in local factories; and I recall the occasions when some school friend, not all that much older than me, was reported missing, all too often in Bomber Command. I heard, too, over the radio, and read in the press, frequent news reports that we were hitting back and – like most others – I used to applaud them with grim satisfaction. Such recollections are, I judge, important to an understanding of the circumstances under which Harris did his job.

Yet not all that long afterwards, in 1950, I found myself serving in Germany, near heavily damaged Cologne, and over the next three years I saw the devastation that had been inflicted on many of Germany's other cities, including Berlin, Hamburg and Munich. I had mixed feelings. Remembering what the Luftwaffe had done in my own country and the overriding importance of winning the war I was disinclined to be apologetic, but I certainly regretted the necessity for the bombing and used to tell Germans whom I met that what mattered now was to work together to ensure that there could never be a third war between us. I have often been back to Germany since and made many friends, including those in Henley's twin town of Leichlingen, and I like to think I understand how they, too, have mixed views about the war – and not least about Harris. Particular friends include the historians Horst Boog and Götz Bergander, both of whom approach these matters with admirable objectivity and have given me invaluable assistance. It was Bergander who took me to Dresden and showed me the Frauenkirche under reconstruction; to my mind that may soon be the most important single symbol of reconciliation between our two countries. Who knows what Harris would have said about it – yet his exchange of letters with Albert Speer in 1976 suggests that he might not entirely have disapproved. At any rate, I hope that my German audience will at least come away with a better understanding of the man whom their forebears came to hate some 60 years ago.

Many of my readers will, I think, appreciate how vast is the amount of material available on so many aspects of this subject. Had I tried even to skim the multitude of books and papers that have been written about it over the years, both in the United Kingdom and in many other parts of the world, I should never have come remotely near completing the task. I have centred my research instead upon Harris's own remarkably comprehensive papers, of which many of the wartime ones are certainly to be found elsewhere but far less conveniently. However, to support these I have consulted a lot of the better known books and have referred readers to these for much of the detail. Among them is Dudley Saward's biography, which remains valuable on many issues and quotes substantially some of the most significant documents. In addition, and most importantly, I have been able to illustrate the story with a variety of anecdotes, drawn both from Harris's own papers and from the memoirs of others, and a good many more from individuals who have kindly sent me their personal recollections. All are named in my acknowledgements.

It remains here to say a special word of thanks to my erstwhile colleague from the Air Historical Branch, Squadron Leader Joe Davies, who volunteered at an early stage to lend me a hand with the research and has since devoted much of his time to delving into official and other records on my behalf. Nothing has been too much trouble for him. The same can be said for Greenhill Books, my publishers, in the persons particularly of Lionel Leventhal and Kate Ryle. Last and most important there is my wife Audrey, who – having enjoyed meeting Sir Arthur and Jill at The Ferry House – not only agreed that I should take the task on but has shared in the 'family research' and, of critical importance, carried out all the computing tasks under the expert guidance of our son-in-law, Andrew Sturla. The finished product is thus very much a joint effort, though responsibility for the accuracy of the book and the views expressed is mine alone.

Acknowledgements

I wish to acknowledge the generous assistance given to me by a great many individuals, including some who are no longer with us. First and foremost are the members of the Harris family who not only gave willing consent to the project but also provided access to their many papers, contributed their personal recollections and views, and read and commented on the manuscript. Sadly Anthony, who was keenly interested, died before I was able to talk to him in depth, and Marigold – in poor health – has only once been able to meet me. Rosemary Harris, however, has been of immense help, particularly in relation to her side of the family, and Jacqueline and Nicholas Assheton have been unstinting in their support and advice. More distant relatives, including Michael Jackson, Peter Prideaux-Brune, Vivienne Lloyd, Dame Diana Collins and Evangeline Elliot, have shown much interest, and Jackie's godfather, Peter Tomlinson, gave me enormous help and encouragement when I visited him in Cape Town not long before his death.

Fellow historians, too, have been generous with their assistance. Denis Richards very kindly read the whole text, offered many invaluable comments and suggestions, and was a source of great inspiration. Other friends such as Dr Noble Frankland, Professor Richard Overy, Dr Vincent Orange and Götz Bergander helped on particular aspects. Sebastian Cox has also been most supportive, not least in placing the archives of the Air Historical Branch at my disposal, and individual members of his staff, including Tony Stephens and Peter Singleton, have been ever ready to lend a hand. The RAF Historical Society – not least Air Marshal Sir Freddie Sowrey and Air Vice-Marshal Nigel Baldwin (past and current chairmen), and Wing Commander Jeff Jefford – has provided much encouragement, as has its President, Marshal of the Royal Air Force Sir Michael Beetham. He has backed me in other capacities too, as President of the Bomber Command Association and as Chairman of the Trustees of the RAF Museum, and to him and both these institutions I am truly grateful. Special mention goes to Tony Iveson and Doug Radcliffe, Chairman and Secretary of the Bomber Command Association, to Dr Michael Fopp, Director of the Museum, and to Peter Elliot, who as Keeper of the Archives has provided the essential access to Sir Arthur's papers. Other invaluable archive sources include the Public Record Office, the Imperial War Museum, the Ministry of Defence Library, Christ Church, Oxford and the Albert Speer collection in Koblenz. I am indebted too to the Aircrew Association (through Danny Boon and Alan Watkins) and the Royal Air Forces Association (Mark Tomkins).

Special thanks also go to the friends who have helped with particular areas of research, including Derek Blooman and Michael Graham-Jones (school-days); Patsy Shand, Micky Townsend, Air Vice-Marshal Alfred Bentley, Group Captain Bill Sykes and Charles Milner (Zimbabwe and South Africa); Professor R.V. Jones, Air Chief Marshal Sir Lewis Hodges, Air Chief Marshal Sir John Allison, Air Vice-Marshal Deryck Stapleton, Wing Commanders Bill McCrea and Bill Newby, Squadron Leader Paul Tomlinson, Mrs Diana Searby, Marjorie Preston and Betty Quihampton (the wartime years); Mrs Ann Lawrence, Mr Winston Churchill and Sir Anthony Montagu-Browne (the Churchill relationship); and Brian Cooke, Ray Callow and James Denny (the closing years).

Many more individuals wrote or telephoned to offer support, among them Donald Allen, Hal Birch, Alan Bramson, John Brown, Evelyn Clarkson, Geoffrey Denis, Margaret Dove, Dickie Dyer, Dr M. Edmond, Dereck French, Anthony Furse, Mrs M.V. Gay, Allen George, Gerry Hobbs, David Irving, Leo Kirby, Linda Lalley, Laddie Lucas, Willie Le Roux, Colonel Van der Poel, John Sands and Gordon Spencer.

To all, and to many other well-wishers, I express my thanks.

Chapter 1

Roots

On Sunday the 19th of September 1982 Marshal of the Royal Air Force Sir Arthur Harris, in his 91st year, returned to Cheltenham, the place of his birth. Accompanied by Lady Harris, he was there at the invitation of the Cheltenham Civic Society and the local branch of the Royal Air Forces Association to unveil the plaque at No 3 Queen's Parade which bears the following inscription:

> 'Marshal of the RAF Sir Arthur Harris, Commander-in-Chief of Bomber Command during the Second World War. Born here 13th April 1892'[1]

What may have been his thoughts on this quiet, low key occasion? Many years had elapsed since he had led the Command in its massive and controversial campaign during the war against Germany. Widely applauded at the time, he had since been the target of much vilification, yet he had come through it, ever determined to defend the reputation of all who had served under him. And now here he was, the last of Britain's great captains of the Second World War, having to his surprise outlived all the rest. Maybe too he thought of what might have been. But for a combination of luck and skill he could so easily not have survived the First World War. Supposing he had decided to return to Rhodesia instead of making his career in the Royal Air Force, what different course would his life have taken? With Jill beside him, did his mind return to his family? Here too it had not always been plain sailing. Perhaps also he was reminded of his own roots; certainly in recent years he had been interesting himself in his fairly complicated family tree and with the help of his sister Maud had traced it back to his great-grandfather, the youngest Captain to have served in the Royal Navy during the Napoleonic Wars.

There seems little doubt that Captain Harris was the son of one Thomas Harris who, after making a small fortune in soap manufacturing, went into partnership with a wine merchant, a distinguished doctor and a playwright to buy the Covent Garden Theatre in 1767. Having eventually found himself the sole survivor of the original four, he owned and managed the theatre until his death in 1820.[2] Altogether he had at least five sons, three of them by his mistress, Jane Lessingham. One of the other two, George, was born in Hastings to his wife, Charlotte, in 1786 and only ten years later

Harris family tree

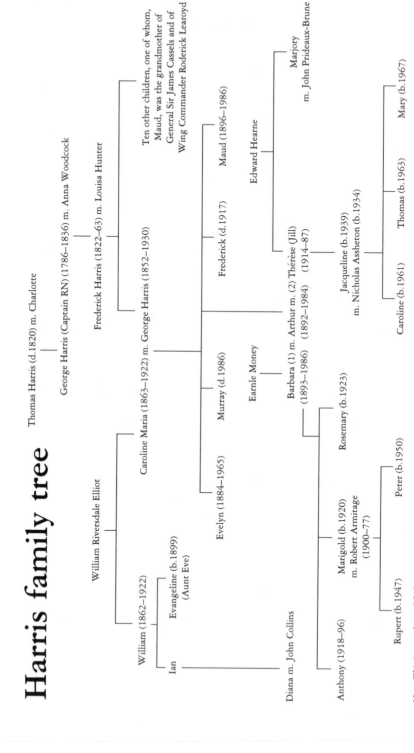

Note: This is a much simplified 'tree', essentially confined to those individuals featured in the book.

entered Portsmouth Academy en route to a career in the Royal Navy. As far as the Navy was concerned he was aged 12; his baptismal certificate appears to have been altered to show his date of birth as 1784 and thus enable him to meet the Navy's minimum age for commissioning. The 'very favourable auspices' under which he entered it at such an early age – whatever they were – may have had something to do with this.[3] So in 1801, actually aged 15, he joined the Navy as a Midshipman, serving aboard HMS *Medusa*; in 1805 he became a Lieutenant; in 1806 he was promoted to Commander; and at the end of 1807 he took command of HMS *Sir Francis Drake*, a frigate operating in the East Indies. Here, according to the writer of his obituary, he gained the reputation of an active, enterprising and intelligent officer. In 1811 'he gained considerable credit for his skill and gallantry in the Straits of Sunda and at the reduction of Java; his conduct at Samanap, where he succeeded in drawing the Sultan of Madura from the French alliance and binding him to British interests, was represented by Rear Admiral Stopford as a master stroke of policy which greatly contributed to the final reduction of the island.' Two years later, commanding HMS *Belle Poule*, in the Gironde estuary, he captured two American warships carrying valuable cargoes to the French in Bordeaux, and in early 1815 this remarkably young and able officer received the CB.[4] Strangely his father seems to have had a hand in this, for on 6 January 1815 he wrote to the Prince Regent, the future King George IV, soliciting such an award for his son.

Captain Harris received his last command, HMS *Hussar*, in 1823, and was soon afterwards court martialled for failing to have his ship ready for sea in order to convey the British Ambassador to Lisbon. Harris was adjudged to have acted throughout with his accustomed zeal and promptitude; the court decided that the blame lay entirely with the Ambassador, who had arrived late. One senses here, reading these brief accounts, that his great grandson may have inherited some of his finest qualities from the gallant Captain. A further comment by his obituarist strikes another familiar chord. Before his early death in 1836, George Harris had turned his attention to various improvements in the manufacture and preservation of rope, particularly by experimenting with New Zealand flax, though with what success remained to be proved. 'In this pursuit, as in all others, he was energetic and indefatigable'.

The Captain had married in 1821. His wife, Anna Maria, was the daughter of John Woodcock of Fern Acres, Buckinghamshire, and their only son Frederick was born the next year. Rather than follow his father into the Navy he decided to embark upon a military career in India, where as a mere 19-year-old he lost no time in getting married. His bride, Louisa Jane Hunter, was the daughter of Captain John Hunter, who had spent his military career in India in the 29th and 16th Native Infantry, and she was even younger than her husband when they married in Cuttack in October 1841. Soon afterwards he was commissioned as a Lieutenant in the 6th Madras Native Infantry; he was promoted to Captain in 1853, later became a Major, and died of a lung disease in Madras in 1863, aged 42.[5] For our purposes his greatest achievement must be reckoned as the fathering of 11 children, the eldest born in 1844, the youngest in 1861, and all but one surviving into adulthood. As a result Arthur Harris was supplied on his father's side with a bevy of aunts and uncles and a whole range of cousins – most having strong connections with India. His links with them, however, were never close, though the extensive family of Aunt Maud, the fourth child, requires brief mention in the Harris story. One of her daughters married a Learoyd and it was their son Roderick who earned Bomber Command's first Victoria Cross when attacking the Dortmund-Ems Canal in August 1940 – while serving in 5 Group under Harris's command. Another daughter married an Army officer, Robert Cassels, who eventually became C-in-C India between the wars, and their son James completed his distinguished career as Chief of the Imperial General Staff in the 1960s. Harris was tickled pink that three top-ranking officers should have been produced in the one family.

The sixth child of Frederick and Louisa was born on 26 April 1852 and subsequently christened George Steel Travers Harris. From very early on he was keen to follow in the family tradition and make his career in the Indian Army, but the severe deafness which he soon developed precluded this. He remained determined, however, to work in the public service in India and therefore concentrated his mind on studying civil engineering and architecture at the Royal Indian Civil Engineering College, Egham (known as Cooper's Hill College), so that he could serve in the Public Works Department of the Indian Civil Service. In 1875, having qualified, he went to work in Burma, where he met Caroline Maria Elliot; they married in Rangoon Cathedral and the bride was given away by the Chief Commissioner of Burma. Caroline, who had been born at Fort St George, Madras, in 1863, was the fourth child of William Riversdale Elliot, a surgeon in the Madras Cavalry and member of another family with long Indian connections. The medical link derived from the distaff side, with descent from the distinguished Dr Lettsom, physician to King George IV; the rhyme attributed to him was often laughingly quoted in the family, not least by Arthur Harris:

> When any sick to me apply,
> I physics, bleeds, and sweats 'em;
> If, after that, they choose to die,
> Why, Verily! I Lettsom.

So the Elliot side of the family also contributed to Harris's stock of aunts, uncles and cousins, and one of the latter – Ian Elliot, the son of his mother's eldest brother – would play a significant part in his life.[6]

George and Caroline returned to India soon after their marriage and – apart from periods of leave – remained there until George's retirement in 1909. From 1894 onwards, as Consulting Architect to the Government of Madras and the Maharajah of Gwalior, he was responsible for designing and erecting a number of fine buildings. Their six children were born between 1884 and 1896. The two girls, Evelyn and Maud, both lived to a ripe old age; of the first three sons the eldest, Murray, went to school at Sherborne, became an accomplished linguist, and worked in banking and a variety of other activities, usually abroad. Charles died aged two, and Frederick, who studied at Eton and Cambridge, joined the Consular Service and was appointed a Vice-Consul in Persia during the First World War. Sent to work among the Bakhtiari tribe, most of whom were anti-British, he died under suspicious circumstances in 1917, a sad end for 'a brilliant young man', as described by his chief, Sir Wolseley Haig.[7]

The youngest son, christened Arthur Travers, was born in 1892, while his parents were on leave from India; Caroline's uncle, General Henry Elliot, was living in retirement in Cheltenham, and his home provided a convenient pied-à-terre. The family returned to Gwalior, where he was baptised, and he remained with his parents in India until the age of five, when they decreed that, like his brothers and sisters, he must return to England to go to school. Adequate though the English schools might be up in the hill stations, they were not thought suitable for the children of the British official classes, so thanks to what Harris called the 'damned snobbery' of those days he spent 12 of the most formative years of his life homeless and separated from his mother and father, who hardly ever came to England and became almost total strangers to him. His mother particularly must have found this split from Arthur and her other children hard to bear for she was a 'motherly, cheerful soul, comfortable to be with', recalled her niece, Evangeline.

Arthur spent his first two years at school at a kindergarten in Cheltenham before moving on in 1899 to a pretentiously described 'preparatory school for Eton' which was also attended by his brothers Murray and Frederick and his cousins Grenfell and Ian Elliot. Owned by a Mr de Selincourt and located first at Upton Park, near Slough, this later moved to Gore Court, a large manor house near Sittingbourne, attractively situated in extensive grounds with a nine-hole golf course and a farm. Whether the young Harris gained much from his prep school is hard to judge – he himself was not impressed by the education it provided – but certainly the school recognised his talent in handling animals, particularly horses and ponies, and it was here that he was given his first opportunity to drive them.[8]

In September 1906 Harris moved on from Gore Court to Allhallows Grammar School, a small public school in Honiton.[9] His two elder brothers having gone to Eton and Sherborne, there was not much money left for number three, so a little known school with a 'Stalky and Co' atmosphere and barely a hundred pupils it had to be. Nevertheless it had a long history stretching back to the foundation of the Allhallows Charity in 1524; called for many years Honiton Grammar School it had eventually reverted to its original designation. It occupied a number of buildings near the centre of the old market town; two of the houses and the headmaster's residence were on the south side of the High Street and most of the others, together with the playground and playing fields, to the north. One of these buildings was the recently restored Chapel, dedicated to the nine Honitonians who had died in the Boer War.[10]

One of Harris's slightly younger contemporaries, E.C. Barton, recorded his recollections of those days. The routine was as one might expect: breakfast at 8.00, chapel at 8.45, followed by work until lunch, more work and sport in the afternoon, tea at 6.00, two and a half hours prep, evening chapel at 9.00, and bed at 10.00. Harris, who achieved no academic distinction at Allhallows, did not think the teaching he received did much for him, but it is hard to believe that the mastery of written English that he demonstrated to such effect in his subsequent career did not owe something to solid, methodical instruction in these formative years. His other main memory of the school regime was of being cold and hungry for much of the time, though he admitted that near-starvation was probably the lot of most schoolboys in those days. Barton did not share this view; he remembered there being plenty of good nutritious food, which was served hot, though there was a hungry gap between midday and tea by which time many felt famished. Barton also commented favourably on the tone of the school and the absence of bullying; there was the occasional fight but things always ended amicably. For Harris, who did see it occasionally, the answer was for a number of boys to get together and 'give the bully a hell of a time' – a sign of the leader and organiser in the making.[11]

There was, of course, more to the Allhallows years than this. While Harris would never achieve great sporting prowess as an adult he did make something of a mark on the playing fields at Honiton, though the standard of competition was hardly the highest. Aged 15 he played as a forward in most School XV matches; 'he is very good at getting the ball at the line-out from touch and is a useful place kick,' recorded the school magazine, which went on to say that he might give a little more attention to training and show a little more energy when playing. Their worst defeat that season – 156–0 by the Royal Naval College Dartmouth – may not have exactly enamoured Harris of the Navy. The following season was better for the team, though Harris playing at three-quarter had little personal success. On the hockey pitch, too, he played regularly for the First XI as an inside forward – 'although rather slow he played a very fair game, dribbling and passing well.' Losing 11–0 to Dartmouth, however, was another unhappy experience. In the summer term, inevitably the game was cricket; playing for the First XI in 1908 he often opened the innings, though rarely with much success, as shown by his average of 9.1 in 16 matches. He had some good strokes, particularly a shot past cover, but was weak on the leg side, and slow in the field. That same year he was runner-up for the Victor Ludorum in the school sports, winning the 100 yards, the high jump and the hurdles, and coming second in the long jump.

The Cadet Corps, too, provided the opportunity for a variety of outdoor activities. In his first year Harris won the junior gymnastic competition and a prize for rifle shooting; in 1908 he was one of the three-man team that won the Gymnastic Cup and was awarded the individual shooting cup; there were expeditions and camps which took him as far afield as Dartmoor and Exmoor; and in February 1909, the year when the Cadet Corps became part of the newly formed Officer Training Corps, he was promoted to Corporal. By this time – fortunately, as it would turn out – he had become 'pretty hot' on the bugle as well.

The school also helped Harris develop his histrionic talents. He was cast in *The New Boy*, the School Dramatic Society's 1907 Christmas Play, as Dr Candy, the Headmaster. 'He did a difficult part with credit,' wrote the reviewer, 'though he might have spoken more loudly.' The following year he played one of the two cousins in *Lucky Miss Dean*; of the two his was the funnier part and 'he had a good reception'. His obituarist at Allhallows summed up these years, and drew attention to another significant aspect.

Already at Allhallows – perhaps because, like so many boys whose parents served overseas, he was frequently boarded out in the holidays – he became increasingly self-reliant, outspoken and mature beyond his years. Speaking in the School Debating Society in 1908 on a proposal that adequate military training should be made compulsory for the physically fit male population of the United Kingdom, Harris pronounced the present system quite inadequate, since if a war broke out and the present reserve troops were called out they would be useless before properly trained troops. In another debate he deplored stag-hunting, saying that a practically tame stag was taken to the meet in a cart and then let loose: that was not sport. An insight perhaps into the true character of the man.[12]

On 21 June 1945 Harris returned to Allhallows to do the honours at the annual prize-giving. In the chair was his old Headmaster, Mr F.J. Middlemist, whose 30 years in office had begun in 1901. Warmly welcoming this very distinguished Old Boy, he said that of the hundreds of boys who had passed through his hands it was natural that he should remember some better than others, but 'although he left school comparatively young and for that reason never became Head Prefect, my memory of the future Chief of Bomber Command is vivid and clear. This shows that even in his schooldays he gave signs of the remarkable personality which he afterwards displayed.' In replying, Harris expressed extreme relief at Mr Middlemist's reticence about the rest of his school career at Allhallows; it was an extraordinary situation to find himself taking a leading spot at a prize-giving. He did, however, win one prize – for drawing – but never since then had he been able to depict the simplest technical object on paper.

Whatever Harris himself may have thought about his days at Honiton – and in purely academic terms he was probably right – they undoubtedly contributed much to his education in the broader sense. One of his school contemporaries, greatly impressed by his return visit, wrote anonymously afterwards to the Editor of the *Allhallows Magazine*:

> He came to the School in 1906, when I had been there four years. I can remember him very well for he soon made his mark. Perhaps it was the shine of his buttons on parade, for he was always a keen cadet; or perhaps it was his prowess on the football field, for he was one of the stalwarts in a team that I captained; or it may have been because we were confederates in many illicit adventures. In all these activities he was a leading spirit, and it was undoubtedly at Allhallows that he began to reveal that quality of leadership that is so eminent in him now.

The fact remains that, whatever others may have thought of him, Harris did not look back on his schooldays with affection and never thought they had done him much good. There was, however, one redeeming feature. With no home to go to during the holidays he usually had to do what many other children of parents working abroad did in those days: stay with well-meaning families, often with church connections, and usually not well fitted to meeting the needs of active adolescents. Only two of those with whom Harris spent his holidays created a positive impression. A vicar and his wife in the Kentish village of Selling did their best, arranging for him to go riding with a young member of one of the brewing families who owned vast hop fields. The family that he really remembered, however, was that of the Reverend C.E. Graham-Jones, Rector of Cowden (between East Grinstead and Tunbridge Wells) and, from January 1908, of Sanderstead. The Rector, born in Liverpool in 1847 and educated at Oxford, was a man of wide interests and great energy who, in addition to his normal church activities, loved the outdoor life. Hiking, cycling, swimming, canoeing, sailing, golf, all appealed to him, as did travelling. Better off financially than many of his ilk, he had spent time on the Continent and as far afield as Egypt and Palestine, and several times a year he would arrange camping expeditions in different parts of England. At home, too, there was always much going on. The Rector and his wife had five children (the eldest son, Jack, was four years older than Harris), the houses were large and rambling, there were servants, gardeners, horses, cows – all adding up to an environment with many attractions for an energetic youngster.

Harris's first recorded visit was for Christmas 1905, one of several he would spend there, two of them in the company of his brother Fred and one of his sister Maud. They were real family occasions marked by all the traditional activities, including charades, amateur dramatics and fancy dress parties, and were described by the Rector in his diaries as 'very jolly' times (and by Harris later as 'all the fun of the fair'). The boy enjoyed his Easter and summer holidays just as much. The Rector would take him and his own sons to help with all sorts of practical jobs connected with their outdoor activities; to his great delight there were carts and coaches to be driven; they went on expeditions, some local, some further afield. The longest of these was in August 1909 when he accompanied the Rector and two others on a week's cruise in a fishing boat in the Solent. On an itinerary which included Lymington, Keyham, Yarmouth, Calshot, Southampton and Cowes, this must have been an eye-opener for the 17-year-old, not least when they sailed past the Fleet off Cowes and spotted some of the great ocean liners steaming to and from Southampton.

Reflecting on these times many years afterwards, Harris felt they had been a revelation to him. The Graham-Jones family gave him the only home he ever had, and he experienced things which previously he never knew existed.[13] His love of children, his delight in entertaining and seeing friends enjoying themselves, and maybe his interest in the wider world too – qualities which he exhibited throughout his life – owed much to what he learnt in the company of the Rector of Cowden and Sanderstead.

Harris did not return to Allhallows, as expected, in September 1909. He had recently met an Old Honitonian, Arthur Chudleigh, who after making his name as an actor was now running the Comedy Theatre and was at the same time extremely supportive of his old school. A regular visitor, he was always popular with the boys and would often provide them with theatre tickets. Harris was given one of these and went to see the play during his summer holidays. It featured a Rhodesian planter who returned to England to marry his snobbish fiancée, fell out with her, married the housemaid – a girl far better suited to be a farmer's wife – and took her back to Rhodesia. This vision of a new country where it mattered not who one was but what one did, fired the imagination and spirit of adventure of a young man who had no solid roots at home, still had no clear idea of what he wanted to do with his life, and was keen to use his already developing practical skills to do something out of the ordinary. So he told his father, who had just returned from India on retirement, that he was not going back to Allhallows and started making enquiries about Rhodesia. His father, who had been hoping his youngest son would make his career in the Army or at least in some other form of government service, was bitterly disappointed but eventually accepted the inevitable and agreed to pay for his second-class ticket to Beira aboard the SS *Inanda*. Little is recorded of what Harris did during his final months in England except that in early January he spent several days with the Graham-Jones family, when he played golf and attended the parish party play, and on 20 February he paid them a farewell visit before making his way to Tilbury, where his father came to see him off. Accepting at last that his son had no intention of changing his mind, George Harris did the decent thing and gave instructions for his son to be upgraded to first class.[14]

The voyage to Beira occasioned Harris's first love affair. The recipient of his affections was Dorothy Blood, a young lady several years older and the niece of the shipping line's owner, who was also aboard with his wife. During the five weeks that they spent together aboard ship, one of the qualities that impressed her was his sense of humour; he used to make up the most droll rhymes about some of the older and very odd females on board, though he was always careful to be polite when meeting them. He would never willingly hurt anyone, she said. He was also kind and considerate; on the overnight rail journey from Beira to Umtali she found herself sharing a compartment with someone she greatly disliked, whereupon he went off to see if he could find her an empty one. The next day, after he had left the train, she discovered that the compartment he claimed to have fixed for her was in fact his own – he had slept in the guard's van. For Harris, waving goodbye as Dorothy's train pulled out on the way to Durban, it seemed like the end of his world. They never met again.[15]

Eighteen-year-olds, however, are resilient, and Rhodesia beckoned. It was a territory twice the size of Great Britain, much of it a fertile plateau 4,000 ft or more above sea level, blessed by a mix of warm sun, cool nights and seasonal rains. True there were the inevitable tropical diseases – malaria, yellow fever, bilharzia, hookworm, and others specific to animals – but provided basic precautions were taken it was a wonderfully healthy place to live. Moreover there was plenty of space. The indigenous population was estimated to be no more than 750,000, and so far there were a mere 23,000 settlers. While most of the early arrivals had been fortune hunters hoping to get rich quickly, the establishment of the British South Africa Company in 1890 had eventually led to a properly considered long-term development policy. In 1907 the Company decided to end the myth of the so-called 'Second Rand' and try to diversify the economy by encouraging European

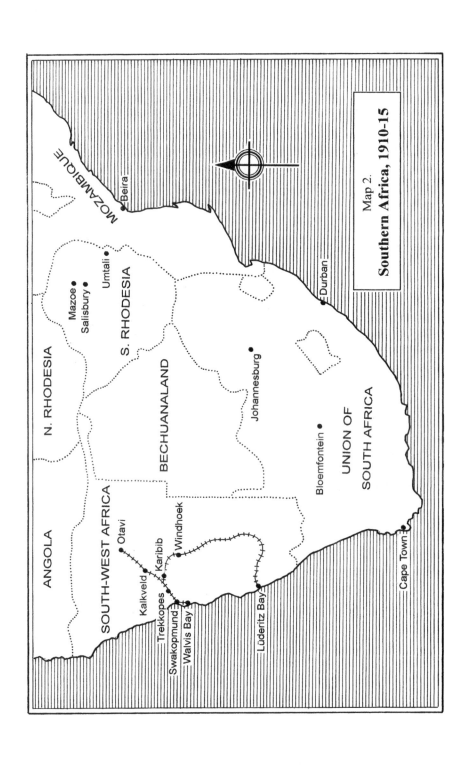

Map 2.
Southern Africa, 1910–15

farming. Before that most settlers had come from or via South Africa, but positive steps were now taken to promote direct European settlement as well, including the opening of an information office in London.

By the time Harris reached Rhodesia in 1910 rapid expansion was in progress. In 1904 there had been a mere 300 European farms; ten years later there would be 2,000, the newer ones concentrating mainly on maize, tobacco and cattle ranching. To help new arrivals accustom themselves to the local scene the Company had established a special 'Rhodes Estate' (something akin to a national park) near Umtali, where for a small fee they would be accommodated, learn a bit of the native language, and receive instruction about the local farming conditions. Harris stayed there for three very useful months and then moved around a variety of farms, turning his hand to whatever needed doing and gaining new skills and experience in the process. There was, for example, much building going on – this was the period when the old pole and daga huts were giving way to simple little homesteads, built of brick, with mosquito-gauzed windows and corrugated iron roofs, and surrounded by broad verandahs that kept the houses cool. It all had to be done, however, on a do-it-yourself basis, and on several farms he found himself not just doing the building, assisted only by native labourers, but also making the bricks, a task in which he eventually became quite skilled.

Harris also became involved in the transport business. Apart from the few railway lines transportation still depended very largely on ox or mule-drawn vehicles following dirt tracks, and here his experience with the Graham-Jones family was invaluable. Horses were rare, for they suffered high mortality owing to the tsetse fly, and coaches were invariably drawn by mules, which were less disease-prone. Like many others, Harris soon realised that the future must lie with mechanical transport. He had a go at driving steam engines, but it was the appearance of the motor car – first the so-called Colonial Models and then the ubiquitous Model T Fords – that was critical. His lasting love of driving, whether in horse-drawn coaches or, more usually, large motor-cars, stemmed from these early days of battling his way around the rough roads of Rhodesia.

The most important of Harris's activities, however, were related to farming, particularly tobacco, the cultivation of which had been catching on since the turn of the century. He especially remembered the big, high barns, where the hands of tobacco were hung on the beams. Wood-fired furnaces outside fed heat into them; he had to get up three times a night in order to attend to the stoking, since the labourers invariably went to sleep. As a commercial crop tobacco had the advantages of being relatively easy to transport, non-perishable when cured, and capable of giving quick returns on capital invested, and the Company was eager to market it. Having tried his hand at ranching and other forms of farming, Harris became persuaded that tobacco planting offered the best prospects, not least because he could see the evidence of its expansion all round him. In 1910 Rhodesian production was 450,000 lbs; in 1914 it would exceed 3,000,000. First, however, he would have to obtain his own farm – still a distant prospect when he mentioned in a letter to Dorothy Blood, who was now living in Ireland, that he was not enamoured of the job he was doing and was looking for another. She responded by suggesting he call on some friends of hers who had a big farm at Mazoe, not far from Salisbury. It was thus in November 1913 that he found his way to Lowdale, a 'magnificent place' as he called it, and met Mr Crofton Townsend, who had emigrated from Castle Townsend, near Cork, and founded it ten years before. He and his family not only took him on but subsequently made him farm manager when they went to England for a year's leave some four months later.

Here at last was real responsibility. The farm grew several crops, including tobacco and maize, it was well equipped, and it employed a substantial labour force. Today's Townsend family, who still own Lowdale, tell stories about Harris. One of his jobs was to deliver the steam-driven maize sheller by ox-cart to another farm, Ballineety, about 30 miles away, see to the shelling, and then bring it back; the round trip took two days, and when Harris returned from his first trip Mr Townsend was horrified to hear that he had charged the owner, Mr Glanfield, for the shelling – something that was simply 'not done' in those days when farmers just borrowed each others' equipment. Harris himself had been equally horrified to find that Glanfield gave their labourers coffee and buns first thing in the morning – this in his view was 'not done'. Then on Christmas morning Mr Townsend knocked on Harris's door to find him still in bed, assuming he could have a short lie-in. 'Get out, get to work, there are fences to be mended!' Eventually, once the Townsends had returned from England, Harris decided to take an option on the allocation of land to which new settlers were entitled – 2,000 acres if one could show that one had the necessary capital to get started on one's own. In four years he had come a long way. He had learnt a whole range of practical skills and could turn his hand to almost anything. He could shoot, improvise, live rough, cook, cope with the unexpected. He was able to organise, to run a small business, and to direct the men and women who worked for him. Above all he had acquired the self-confidence necessary to launch out on his own.[16]

Now, however, circumstances beyond Harris's control were about to take a hand in shaping his future, and before long Rhodesia would be little more than a memory. He was to return there briefly on duty in 1936, and then again in 1945, when, on revisiting Lowdale (chapter 17), he was delighted to find the rusted remains of his old maize sheller, heavily overgrown, in the far corner of a field.[17] In 1959 a letter from Mr Wrightson, an old friend from Umtali days, prompted his recollections of those distant times, when he had helped Wrightson with some mule teams as he was starting up a new farm. Yet such had been the impact of his few years in that wonderful country that for the rest of his life Harris would think of himself primarily as a Rhodesian.[18]

Notes

1. Harris Misc Folder 2. The unveiling followed the Battle of Britain Commemoration Service and took place with the permission of Dr Perrigo, the owner of the property. It was attended by the Mayor, and the Harrises were entertained to lunch afterwards at the Queen's Hotel.

2. For fuller details see the *Biographical Dictionary of Actors, Actresses, Musicians, Dancers, Managers and other Stage Personnel in London 1660–1800*, pp.137–9.

3. Obituary, *Naval and Military Gazette*, 12 November 1836.

4. *Ibid*. A fuller account of Captain Harris's part in these operations is in Marshall's *Royal Naval Biography, Supplement Pt 1*, 1827, pp.285–92.

5. Records of the India Office Library.

6. Most of this information is drawn from family researches undertaken by Anthony and Rosemary Harris, Nicholas and Jacqueline Assheton and Ian Elliot.

7. Letter from Sir Reader Bullard to Sir Arthur Harris, 9 January 1962 – Harris Misc Folder 1.

8. Saward, *Bomber Harris*, pp.3, 4.

9. While Saward puts him at Allhallows from 1904 to 1909 and his RAF record of service says 1905–10, the school archives make it clear he was there for only three years, 1906–9.

10. Despite much improvement work, the school's accommodation became increasingly inadequate; it moved to Rousdon Manor, near Lyme Regis, in 1938 and became known as Allhallows College. It closed 60 years later. Most of the buildings in Honiton survive and have other uses; the Chapel houses the Honiton Museum. The playing fields remain.

11. Lieutenant-Colonel E.C. Barton, *Let the Boy win his Spurs* (provided by Derek Blooman, History Master at Allhallows); Saward, *op.cit.* pp.4, 5.

12. Extract from the obituary written by Derek Blooman.

13. This account draws on Saward's interview with Harris but is largely based on the diaries of the Reverend C.E. Graham-Jones, lent to me by his grandson, Michael Graham-Jones. Harris regretted losing touch with the family in later life, though he did meet the two daughters for lunch in London during the war. Their father had died in 1931.

14. Saward, *op.cit.* pp.5, 6; Allhallows archives; Graham-Jones diaries.

15. Saward (*op.cit.* p.7) visited the lady in question – then Mrs Pollock – when researching his book.

16. On leaving Lowdale he presented Patsy Brooks, the three-year-old daughter of some friends in nearby Salisbury, with a teddy bear. Patsy later married into the Townsend family, and in 1997 she donated her treasured teddy to the Bethnal Green Museum of Childhood.

17. It is still there, with the initials 'ATH' marked in the concrete slab underneath.

18. Saward, *op.cit.* pp.8, 9; Harris-Saward Tape 13; Misc Folder 2; interview with Peter Tomlinson and Air Vice-Marshal Alfred Bentley; information provided by Group Captain Bill Sykes; L.H. Gann, *A History of Southern Rhodesia*, Chatto & Windus, 1965; Robin Palmer, *Land and Racial Domination in Rhodesia*, Heinemann, 1977.

Chapter 2

Fortunes of war

On 4 August 1914, when the United Kingdom declared war on Germany, Arthur Harris knew nothing about it. He happened to be away in the bush and it was only when he returned to Salisbury at the end of the month that he heard the news. Five years previously he had strongly resisted his father's urgings to join the Army and opted instead to seek his fortune in Africa,[1] little thinking that he might thereby find himself in a war zone. Yet now there was no question where his loyalties lay. Like so many other young men throughout the Empire he had to do his bit, and in so doing put an end to what might well have become a lifetime career as a tobacco planter.

For those living in southern Africa there were immediate challenges. The German colony of South-West Africa (today's Namibia) could offer port and communication facilities of great value to the Kaiser's Navy in operations against the Empire's supply routes to and round the Cape. It also provided a base from which to encourage the substantial anti-British sentiment which, in the aftermath of the Boer War, persisted in parts of the newly created Union of South Africa. In September, therefore, the Union forces seized the most dangerous German harbour and wireless station at Lüderitz Bay, destroyed the facilities at Swakopmund by naval bombardment, and deployed forces to the south and east of the German border. So incensed were the anti-Union party that they took up arms, and not until December was their rebellion crushed by General Botha's troops.[2]

In Rhodesia, highly dependent on the Union both politically and economically, few doubted that they must give it full support, and when Harris tried to join the 1st Rhodesian Regiment he was dismayed to hear that it was already fully subscribed. Determined not to take 'no' for an answer, he discovered that two 'specialist' vacancies remained, one for a machine-gunner, the other for a bugler. Having failed to persuade the adjutant that he knew anything about machine-guns he drew on his experience with the bugle in the Officers' Training Corps at Allhallows and landed the job, being attested on 20 October. He and his fellow colonials – 500 of them – were given a most rudimentary training course consisting mainly of drill and were eventually allowed to fire just five rounds apiece from their .303 rifles. Private Harris, already an 'old lag' by virtue of his OTC days, deliberately fired at rocks well away from the targets so that he could see from the spurts of dust how far he was from the point of aim. Now ready for war, the unit left Salisbury on 14 November, spent a few weeks on garrison duties in Bloemfontein while the rebellion was being dealt with, and then moved to Cape Town, where they camped on the foreshore in the shadow of Table Mountain awaiting embarkation. They sailed on 21 December and landed at Walvis Bay on Christmas Day.[3]

South-West Africa, their destination, was one of the territories acquired by Germany during the 'Scramble for Africa' in the late 19th century. Largely coincident with the Kalahari Desert, most of it was a plateau averaging 3,500 ft above sea level; the rainfall was low, temperatures varied widely, and the surface consisted mainly of coarse sand able to sustain only the poorer forms of vegetation. The low-lying 40–100 mile-wide coastal belt was even worse, being absolutely barren and waterless and mainly covered in sand dunes. Throughout, water was obtainable only from wells, there were no roads, and only a few narrow-gauge railways existed. This inhospitable land, over three times the size of the United Kingdom and inhabited by a mere 100,000 people, was defended by some 2,140 regular troops and 7,000 reservists. Although the Union troops would outnumber them by 4:1 the Germans were well organised and supplied and would be fighting in country which favoured the defence.

The South African units taking part in the campaign were divided into four forces, three operating in the south and one from Walvis Bay. It was to this Northern Force, comprising several infantry and mounted brigades, that the 1st Rhodesian Regiment was allocated. The Germans did not dispute their landing or their subsequent occupation of nearby Swakopmund, but they were briefly in action just afterwards. Then in February General Botha arrived to take command and the eastward advance began. Since the Germans were removing the railway track as they retreated, it was necessary to replace it, and the task of Harris's regiment was to protect the engineers who were doing the job. 26 April saw its first battle with the enemy, who attacked the Union forces at Trekkopes in an attempt to cover their retirement from Karibib; while only a minor engagement, this provided Harris with a taste of war. From there the north-easterly march in pursuit of the Germans continued to Karibib, Kalkveld and Otavi, reached on 30 June, and on 9 July 1915 the remaining enemy forces surrendered.

Apart from the fact that for some of the time he wore a German Frau's blouse, such was the shortage of suitable clothing, Harris's principal recollection of his six months as an infantryman was the marching – the exhaustion, the hallucinations, and the 'starvation rations of biscuits which you had to break with your rifle butt, and bully beef which in that climate was almost liquid in the can.' Altogether they must have marched some 500 miles and the South African official history records his brigade covering 230 miles in one sustained advance of 16 days from Karibib to Otavi. Whether this was the greatest marching performance of an infantry brigade in British military history, as he later claimed, may be questioned, but one thing is certain: it made such an impression on him that, as he wrote in 1946, 'to this day I never walk a step if I can get any sort of vehicle to carry me'.[4]

One particular event which also made its impression on Harris was when the one German aircraft in South-West Africa started dropping artillery shells on them. It did them no harm, and the thousands of rounds they fired back at it also achieved nothing, apart from making the CO extremely annoyed at the waste of ammunition.[5] Nevertheless, the incident gave Harris his first experience of aerial bombing – from the receiving end – and he never forgot it. Whether he also observed any of the six steel-built Henri Farmans that were operating with the Northern Force is not recorded, but almost certainly he must have done. They arrived in April to support Botha's advance, the pilots having already flown operationally with the RFC in France, and their reconnaissance work earned the General's warm praise.[6] Many years later, when attending reunion dinners in Cape Town, Harris got to know one of the pilots, the then long retired Major General Van der Spuy; the shared events of 1915 must have provided a fascinating topic of conversation.[7]

With the South-West Africa campaign over the 1st Rhodesian Regiment returned to Walvis Bay, this time in relative comfort along the reopened railway, and thence to Cape Town where they were disbanded. Harris's discharge was confirmed on 31 July; he was allowed 285 days' reckonable service and awarded a conduct and character assessment of 'Good'.[8] Like most of his comrades, he thought to begin with that he had had enough and did not care if the bottom fell out of the Empire, so he went back to Rhodesia and tried to resume his work at Lowdale. Almost immediately, however, he knew this was not the place for him. His local war might be over, but the news from elsewhere was going from bad to worse and the short European war that had been generally predicted was turning into a much longer one. Meeting friends from his old regiment in Salisbury he found them equally concerned about getting back to the job in some way but reluctant to rejoin the Rhodesian Regiment for service in the new campaign to clear the Germans out of East Africa (modern Tanzania). They had had enough of 'bush whacking' and wanted to be in on the real war. Getting to England, however, was another matter, and Harris recalled using the 'old boy net' to help persuade the Union Castle Line to ship 300 or so volunteers to Britain. This resulted in the 5,000-ton freighter *Cluny Castle*, fitted with temporary accommodation in its holds, embarking them at Beira in August and eventually landing them at Plymouth in early October, having charged the Rhodesian government the princely fare of £10 per head.[9] Harris had been away for five and a half years and was returning to a very different England, a nation engaged in a war the like of which nobody alive had ever experienced.

For Harris, who took up residence with his parents in London, there was no time to be lost. Not for him the leisurely homecoming, the ritual visiting of friends and relations, the gradual readjustment to a different, only part-familiar way of life. He had returned (temporarily, as he would constantly remind people) to play his part in the war, and he insisted on only one condition. His experience of marching in South-West Africa had been enough to last him a lifetime; he was, therefore, as he later wrote, 'determined to find some way of going to war in a sitting posture'.[10] Not surprisingly for a man who loved horses his first thoughts turned towards the cavalry, but there were no vacancies – and in any case, he had his doubts about cavalry warfare. The Royal Artillery too were full up, and when it started to look as though he might have no choice but to join the infantry he remembered seeing some pre-war advertisements for the Royal Naval Air Service and the Royal Flying Corps. Not wishing to become a professional sailor he opted for the latter, but quickly found on visiting the War Office that he could be at the end of a very long queue.

It was now that his father came to his aid with a useful lesson for his enthusiastic and determined son on how to beat the system. One of his father's many brothers, Charles, happened to be a colonel on the staff of Lord Kitchener, the Secretary of State for War, so – armed with a suitably worded letter to his uncle – Harris turned up again at the War Office the next day. The response was totally different. He was quickly ushered in to see a doctor who, impressed by his sun-tanned body and his account of his recent feat of endurance with the 1st Rhodesian Regiment, saw no reason not to pass him immediately as fit for flying. That evening he was at Brooklands in a Maurice Farman Longhorn, airborne for the first time. He had been back home little more than a fortnight.

A mere two weeks later, on 6 November, having received a few hours' dual instruction and flown solo for one and a half hours, Harris qualified as a civilian pilot[11] and was appointed a Second Lieutenant in the Special Reserve of the Royal Flying Corps. There was rather less hurry about the remainder of his training, undertaken on the so-called Long Course at Upavon, the home of the Central Flying School. It lasted two months in theory but much less in practice, given the time of year; he recalled flying Bloaters (BE and BE8A) and Martinsydes for no more than ten hours, at the end of which he passed out as a fully qualified RFC pilot on 29 January 1916.[12] Many years afterwards he was delighted to hear from his old friend George Bittles:

> It's just on 41 years since you and I swapped seats on a Martinsyde outside the Bloater hangar at Upavon. I to get out and you to get in – do you remember?

I do, as if it were yesterday. I can see you now holding your Jerry in your hand, your almost ginger-coloured hair blowing in the prop stream and a grin on your face saying (when I could hear) 'Come on dearie, out you get'. We passed out that day and if I remember rightly travelled up to town and spent the weekend together – where we stayed I just can't remember.[13]

In later years such rapid progress through the training system would be unheard of, but it was not unusual in the First World War; nor was it rare for newly qualified pilots to find themselves almost immediately posted to operational squadrons. In Harris's case he quickly found himself at Northolt in one of the training detachments belonging to 19 Reserve Squadron which were spread over various small airfields around London. In the absence of any units specifically charged with air defence these were also being required to try to intercept the German Zeppelins which were attempting to mount their night bombing offensive against south-east England.[14] Small scale and relatively ineffective though it proved to be, this was in fact the first strategic bombing campaign in history, and Harris was about to gain first-hand experience of it.

To start with, as one of his unit's two Anti-Zeppelin Night Pilots (each of whom was on duty on alternate nights), Harris had to learn to fly and navigate his BE2 at night. Without prior training he – and others – were simply sent up to try to find their way around, their only aids being the lights of London (there was no black-out) and the occasional searchlight. Then, if there were reports of an airship, it was a matter of pure chance whether one spotted it. Inevitably much depended on the weather (not to mention, as always, luck), and here Harris was given an immediate object lesson. On a wet and foggy night all duty pilots were ordered into the air, and as he later wrote to his engine fitter, John Kenchington, 'I was waiting in 4112 at the end of the flare path to take off after Captain Penn-Gaskell when he crashed and was killed. Colonel Mitchell, the CO, came and stopped me on the grounds that the weather was unfit for flying, which was indeed true!'[15]

Here was the challenge that brought out one of Harris's great qualities. He knew that if he was to do his job properly he would have to learn from his experience and train himself methodically, and when on 12 April he was sent to command a flight at Sutton's Farm his first move was to institute night flying practice based on the training pattern he had worked out for himself. As Dudley Saward rightly observes:

It was this early experience of being expected to do the most impossible things without any semblance of instruction that set his mind thinking about the value of proper training, a matter that was to become a fetish with him in later life, and to which Bomber Command in World War II was to owe a great deal of its success.[16]

Soon afterwards a new squadron was formed to take over the London area detachments of 19 Reserve Squadron and devote its whole attention to air defence. Initially commanded by Major T.C.R. Higgins, 39 Squadron, with its headquarters at Hounslow and three flights at Sutton's Farm, Hainault Farm and Northolt (later at North Weald), was to do more than any other to counter the Zeppelins,[17] and as OC B Flight at Sutton's Farm (which later became Hornchurch) for the first three months the already relatively experienced Harris played an important role. The new squadron's first engagement was on the night of 25/26 April, when LZ 97, captained by Hauptmann Linnarz, was reported near Chelmsford at about 2230. Eight BE2c aircraft were ordered to take off; hitherto they had been armed with 20 lb HE and 16 lb incendiary bombs for anti-Zeppelin work, but this time some had machine guns fitted and Harris had been issued with the still experimental Brock explosive bullets which eventually proved the decisive counter-weapon against the Zeppelins. He was first away, and on reaching 5,000 ft spotted LZ 97 held by searchlights at an estimated 9,500 ft near Chipping Ongar. Climbing as fast as possible he reached 12,000 ft as the airship turned for home, 2,000 ft directly overhead. He opened fire but his guns jammed after six rounds. Clearing the stoppage, he gained another 500 ft and attacked again from the rear, only to suffer a further stoppage. His chance had gone. One of his colleagues, William Leefe-Robinson, better positioned thanks to a more efficient aircraft, also engaged the enemy, only to suffer similar stoppages, and none of the other aircraft got within range. The failings in terms of aircraft and weapons were obvious, as Harris made clear in his report. Four months later, after Harris had departed but building on the lessons learnt, Leefe-Robinson shot down SL11 at Cuffley and was awarded the Victoria Cross.[18]

By the time he left 39 Squadron in July 1916 Harris had not only established his reputation as an able and thinking pilot, but also as one who understood the importance of his ground crew and the need to get to know them. As Kenchington later wrote to him, 'I remember a foolish flight sergeant was going to crime me because two copper pipes were not highly polished; you arrived at the right moment and said you wanted them painted dull black so as to be non-reflective. You also came round to all our [civilian] billets to see we fellows were behaving properly'. Replying appreciatively, Harris reminded Kenchington of 'Flight Sergeant Church and his invariable demand (which became a flight joke) of "git me an 'ammer" – which he seemed to regard as the cure for every ill of an aeroplane or engine in those days.' He went on, 'it was thanks to people like you that we accounted for the first Zeppelins brought down on English soil.'[19] At the age of 24, without having ever received formal instruction other than as a pilot, the young man was already displaying some of the qualities of the born leader, and his respect for the ground crew who served him – so evident later on – had its roots in his days as a flight commander at Sutton's Farm.

Harris had now been in the RFC for almost ten months, and, incredible as it may seem, was appointed to command a newly formed squadron, No 38. Located at Castle Bromwich, this was to form part of the chain of squadrons being built up north of London to guard against Zeppelins coming in across the East Coast. However, during the summer months relatively little night flying was possible and by the time the squadron was ready to deploy forward to Melton Mowbray in September he was on his way to France – doubtless with mixed feelings, for he had other things on his mind.

Some months previously Harris's elder sister Evelyn had introduced him to an extremely attractive young lady who was staying with her in Kensington. Barbara was the daughter of Lieutenant-Colonel Ernle William Kyrle Money, who had married Alexandra Battye in Canterbury Cathedral in 1890, had served in the 85th Shropshire Light Infantry in India and in the Boer War, and was now working in Military Intelligence. He strongly disapproved of the rapidly developing affair; while he later admitted that he had never seen anyone so much in love, he thought they were far too young (at 24 and 23 respectively). Moreover, as their daughters later reflected, the young couple were totally dissimilar people. Harris, through no fault of his own, had a very limited academic education but a wealth of practical experience of real life; Barbara knew little of the wider world but was well into the London scene with a particular devotion to opera and ballet. In wartime, however, such considerations mattered little. He knew enough about the risks of flying, whether in combat or not, to be able to weigh his own chances of survival, and he and Barbara were not going to allow their love to be denied. So on 30 August 1916 they were married in St Augustine's Church, Queen's Gate – his address shown as Castle Bromwich, hers as 5 Harrington Gardens, Kensington.[20] Evangeline Elliot remembered it as a very happy occasion, graced by the presence of large numbers of young men wearing RFC uniform – the heroes of those days. There was much enjoyment at the reception in Hampstead that followed, with plenty of fashionable people around. The pair had been well launched.

Less than three weeks later Harris was in France with 70 Squadron, based at Fienvillers, west-south-west of Doullens. Equipped with the Sopwith $1\frac{1}{2}$-Strutter, the first RFC aircraft armed with a gun firing through the propeller arc, this squadron had been suffering very heavy casualties in the fight for air superiority against the Fokker monoplane during the Battle of the Somme, and Harris did not last long. On 1 October he crash-landed, was wounded in the left forearm, and quickly found himself on his way back to hospital in England. Early the following year he was allowed to start getting his hand in again at flying with 51 Squadron, based near Norwich on air defence duties, and on 25 April 1917 he was passed fit for general service. Then it was back to France, where he joined 45 Squadron at Ste-Marie-Cappel on 18 June.

The next four months were to be critical to Harris's thinking about war. Little more than 20 miles east of Ste-Marie-Cappel was Ypres and the front line, where on 31 July Haig's armies would launch their attempt to capture the Passchendaele ridge and break through to the coast at Ostend. In the event it took four months, not the planned four days, to take the ridge at a cost of a quarter of a million British, Canadian and ANZAC casualties, nearly a hundred thousand of them dead, and on the German side it was just as dreadful. 'In terms of human casualties, and the appalling conditions in which it was fought, Passchendaele must rank as one of the most gruelling battles in the history of warfare,' writes Philip Warner.[21] It was above this ghastly battleground – or mudbath, as many called it – that Harris and his colleagues in 45 Squadron, part of an RFC force of some 400 aircraft, would be operating.

Their airfield was set amid farmland not far from the small town of Cassel, whose hill provided one of two prominent natural beacons. The other was the Mont des Recollets, and in poor visibility the road from Bailleul to Cassel provided a useful guide. The small field itself was square, bounded by two roads, three ditches, a row of trees, a farm and a poplar-lined paddock; overshooting was all too easy. The aircraft – $1\frac{1}{2}$-Strutters – were housed in Bessonneau hangars, the sleeping quarters were tents, the Mess was built of wood, and its smallness made for close companionship. The squadron had been there since December 1916, its role both offensive and defensive, including line patrols and photo reconnaissance, and it had been taking heavy losses. Norman Macmillan[22] vividly describes the 'feel' of the operations and the scene, the peaceful beauty of so much of the countryside contrasting with the 'great smear, like the trailing slime of a great slug' that lay across it – dirty brown, not the healthy brown of a pleasant land, but the brown mortification of disease, the blight of death.' And overhead were the bursting Archie shells – and the Hun, the Albatros scouts which were exacting such a heavy toll.

To begin with the situation on the ground was relatively quiet, but in the air there was, as always, much to do. Harris, appointed C Flight Commander, quickly hit it off with his CO, one Major Van Ryneveld, a South African whom he would later describe as the 'best squadron commander in the Service.'[23] Pirrie, as he was usually known, had made a very good impression on arrival; forbidden to fly over and beyond the German lines, as were all squadron commanders at that time, he used improvised models to

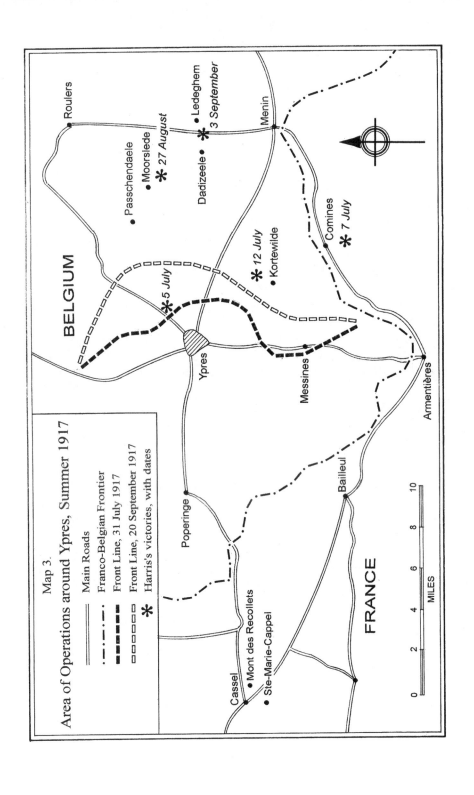

Map 3.
Area of Operations around Ypres, Summer 1917

Main Roads
— ·· — ·· — Franco-Belgian Frontier
━━━━━ Front Line, 31 July 1917
▭▭▭▭▭ Front Line, 20 September 1917
✳ Harris's victories, with dates

BELGIUM

Roulers
Passchendaele
Moorslede
✳ 27 August
Ledeghem
Dadizeele ● 3 September
Menin
Comines
✳ 7 July
✳ 12 July
Kortewilde
✳ 5 July
Ypres
Messines
Armentières
Poperinge
Bailleul
Cassel
Mont des Recollets
Ste-Marie-Cappel

FRANCE

0   2   4   6   8   10
MILES

demonstrate the formations and tactics he wanted used, and personally supervised every mission. Such meticulous methods met entirely with Harris's approval, and he in turn quickly earned the respect of his junior pilots by insisting on flying behind one or other of them until he became familiar with the sector. Macmillan described the new arrival as slim, with fair to ginger hair, very blue eyes,[24] and forthright speech; 'he was an accomplished pilot, with extensive flying experience for that period'. Harris soon demonstrated his skill, destroying one Albatros, with two more 'probables', on 5 July, and when the outclassed $1\frac{1}{2}$-Strutter started to be replaced by the eagerly awaited Camel at the end of the month it was he who was chosen to fly in the second aircraft received. Two weeks later Van Ryneveld was severely wounded when engaging an enemy aircraft over his own airfield, and Harris, who had learnt much from him, took over the squadron. It would be many years before they met again; Van Ryneveld would become Chief of the South African General Staff in 1933, remaining in this post for 16 years, and while their paths rarely crossed they kept in touch until Pirrie's death in 1979.

Harris led the squadron for the next week until Major Vaucour arrived to take over. Then, leading C Flight once again, he resumed his offensive patrols over and beyond the battle area. Macmillan describes one:

> At 1500 an offensive patrol of four Camels led by Harris met about 14 enemy scouts at about 12,000 ft between Ledeghem and Dadizeele, flying in two formations of seven and ably handled. Harris dived at one Albatros who was attacking the rear Camel, fired 150 rounds at close range and saw the machine go down vertically in flames and streaming black smoke. Meanwhile Moore had dived at an Albatros on Harris's tail and fired about 200 rounds at it and it went down out of control. McMaking shot down another ... and Clegg was shot in the knee, broke away, crossed the lines, suddenly nose-dived from 500 ft and was killed. Harris's right Vickers cross-fed a round and jammed, and during violent manoeuvring his seat collapsed under him, leaving him doubly handicapped. Then the pilots resumed their patrol and all reported seeing three machines burning on the ground near Ledeghem.[25]

A few weeks later, having gone down with a bad attack of 'flu, Harris was invalided home.

Macmillan remembers him as a strict disciplinarian. For example, when he first inspected his flight hangar he saw magazine pictures, photographs and cartoons pinned to the internal wood framework – innocent enough anodyne to the unending drudgery of the men's work – and ordered their removal: the interior was to be kept clear in future. This did not endear him to his chaps; in such circumstances he was peremptory and many found his personality disconcerting. On the other hand he was constantly thinking about how to do the job better and using his inventive mind to good effect: for example, he fitted a mechanical digital counter in his Camel to record the number of rounds he had fired. Macmillan himself liked him, and admired him as a good fighter and formation leader. Moreover, in rather less than four months he had scored five victories, which under the accepted conventions of the day placed him in the 'Ace' category.[26]

This episode of Harris's career had, of course, a deeper significance. Although he had not observed the slaughter of Passchendaele on the ground he had witnessed the scene from above and knew enough about it to understand why it made so many members of the British public believe that war must in future be avoided at all costs. For him and other thinking airmen the lesson was different. If another war did occur there must surely be a better way to fight it. The later Field Marshal Lord Birdwood, one of the relatively few generals often to be seen in the forward area,[27] may have had similar thoughts; as 'Father of the British Army', he wrote at least twice to Harris in 1942–3 to congratulate and encourage him and Bomber Command.[28]

The rest of Harris's war was less spectacular. Once he was fit again he spent some weeks on training duties and experimental flying at Joyce Green, and in his eagerness to learn more about aircraft behaviour nearly spun a DH5 into the ground.[29] Then, having been promoted to Major, he took command of a new training squadron, No 191, at Marham, which had been established to teach night flying to pilots designated for the home defence night fighter squadrons and for the night bombing squadrons being formed in France. In June 1918 he was delighted to receive a letter from OC 70 Wing warmly congratulating him on his output of 35 pilots in the previous month; the freedom from accidents showed that this result had been obtained by hard, conscientious work, not by 'more haste less speed' methods.[30] His earlier experience with 39 Squadron was being put to good use, and when he went to Hainault Farm six months later to work up a new Camel squadron, No 44, for the night fighter role, he built it on a nucleus from 39 Squadron. In October he spent a fortnight with Major Quintin Brand, who was already commanding a night fighter squadron on the Western Front, to study the tactics he used, and in off-duty moments to discuss another common interest, southern Africa. Harris, eager to return there after the war, still wore the 'Rhodesia' flash on his uniform, Brand had been born and brought up in South Africa, and both would soon have to decide on their futures.[31]

Notes

1. Harris, *Bomber Offensive*, pp.15, 16.
2. *Union of South Africa and the Great War 1914–18: Official History (General Staff)*, Defence HQ, Pretoria, 1924; pp.1–60 describe the South-West Africa Campaign.
3. Saward, *op.cit.* pp.9, 10.
4. *Official History, op.cit.*; Saward, *op.cit.* pp.10, 11; Harris, *op.cit.* p.16.
5. Interview between Harris and Dewar McCormack (South Africa Broadcasting Corporation, 15 March 1979).
6. Major General Van der Spuy, *Chasing the Wind*. This is an excellent autobiography by one of South Africa's great pioneer airmen.
7. Peter Tomlinson discussion.
8. Misc Folder 1.
9. Saward, *op.cit.* p.11.
10. Harris, *op.cit.* p.16.
11. The Royal Aero Club granted him Aviator's Certificate No 2015, dated 10 November 1915: Misc Folder 2.
12. Saward, *op.cit.* p.13, describes his flying training in more detail.
13. Misc Folder 2.
14. Jones, *The War in the Air*, vol.III, p.162.
15. Letter 7 November 1957, Misc Folder 2. Penn-Gaskell had first arrived in France in August 1914 with 5 Squadron.
16. Saward, *op.cit.* pp.14, 15.
17. Jones, *op.cit.* p.164.
18. Cole and Cheesman, *The Air Defence of Great Britain 1914–18*, pp.130–1. Leefe-Robinson died in June 1919; Harris attended his funeral and the subsequent farewell dinner on 2 July (information from Air Marshal Sir Frederick Sowrey, whose father was present).
19. Kenchington/Harris letters 1957–65, Misc Folder 1; also Folder H76. After the First World War Kenchington emigrated to Australia where he worked as an aircraft engineer. It was Harris who recommended him in 1916 for an all-important course with Rolls-Royce.
20. Family documents; discussions with Marigold Armitage and Rosemary Harris.
21. Philip Warner, *The Story behind the Tragic Victory of 1917*, p.254. For a recent account see John Keegan, *The First World War*, pp.381–95.
22. Wing Commander Norman Macmillan, *Into the Blue*. This is an excellent account of 45 Squadron's history in the First World War, written from personal experience and first published in 1929. Harris was among those consulted in its revision (Misc Folder 20).
23. Letter, Harris to James Brown, 1 May 1980, Misc Folder 2.
24. His family say that his eyes were hazel, not blue.
25. Macmillan, *op.cit.* p.157; see also 45 Squadron Combat Report 3 September 1917.
26. Jefford, *The Flying Camels*, p.473. 45 Squadron's operations in 1917 are described on pp.30–9. See also Shores, Franks and Guest, *Above the Trenches*.
27. Warner, *op.cit.* p.108.
28. Misc Folder 6. Birdwood became C-in-C India, 1925–30. He died in 1951.
29. Saward, *op.cit.* pp.18, 19.
30. Misc Folder 2.
31. Brand later commanded 10 Group during the Battle of Britain.

Chapter 3

Carving a career

For Harris the Armistice declaration on 11 November pre-empted the planned move of 44 Squadron to France and posed him the key question: what next? Should he cut loose from the recently created Royal Air Force to which he now belonged and resume his attempt to carve a career in the country he had come to prefer to all others, Rhodesia? Had he remained single and unattached, the answer would almost certainly have been 'yes'. But now he had both a wife and a baby son, Anthony (born on 18 March), and Barbara had no wish to be uprooted from her family ties. Might it not therefore be better, Harris wondered, to throw in his fortunes with the RAF, in which he had already made such a promising start?

The decision did not have to be made immediately. There were plenty of jobs to be done in the months following the end of the war and Harris was quickly ordered to take command of another night fighter squadron, No 50, based at Bekesbourne, near Canterbury. Getting there just before Christmas he had to face an unfamiliar and unexpected challenge. As he much later reminded his Adjutant, Flight Lieutenant Manby, 'I still recall my arrival there and finding you in the NAAFI quelling with considerable skill one of the demobilisation mutinies which disgraced the conclusion of that particular war'. There was nothing that Harris – and many other COs in similar situations in all three Services – could do about the policy, which had been laid down by the government and had not been well thought out. However, the local demobilisation committee which he set up enabled him to keep the men informed, explain how the priorities were being applied, and hear their views, and he stated that anyone who misbehaved would go to the bottom of the list. This, coupled with practical measures such as removing the magnetos so as to prevent the unauthorised use of motor vehicles, put a stop to the local riots. Harris was not a man to be trifled with. What he could not do, however, was provide his men with worthwhile jobs; indeed, their main task was to receive great numbers of surplus aircraft, tip them up, and burn them. The fact that some were brand new, since the government was keeping production lines open until there was other work for the aircraft factories, only made the task even more depressing.[1]

Harris spent eight months at Bekesbourne, during which time he determined his future. Following the formation of the independent RAF on 1 April 1918 he, in common with many other RFC and RNAS officers, had been asked whether he would consider staying in a permanent air force after the war, and had done the obvious thing by saying yes. Then one morning in early 1919, to his astonishment, his father-in-law woke him with the news that he had been given a permanent commission in the rank of Major.[2] Harris had certainly not expected this, but the Air Force Cross awarded to him on 2 November 1918 had already indicated the high regard in which he was held, and since he felt that his wife would not find life easy on a Rhodesian farm he decided on the next best thing, the flying career that was now in prospect. So Major (soon to be Squadron Leader) Harris quickly found his name on the first Air Force List.

Notwithstanding his decision, Harris was not exactly enamoured of what was going on around him in the swiftly contracting RAF, and when 50 Squadron was disbanded in June 1919 (it would be re-formed in 1937 and would operate in 5 Group under his command in 1939–40), he resolved to stick his neck out by writing to OC 6 Brigade: 'As perhaps the "oldest" home defence night fighter remaining in service I do not wish to give up night flying after four years' experience, and to that end I would desire posting to the Andover School of Navigation for a course of navigation and night flying in heavy machines.' His letter came into the hands of Lieutenant-Colonel C.P.N. Newall, who would end up as Chief of Air Staff from 1937 to 1940. He recommended Harris's request and forwarded it to Colonel E.A. Ludlow-Hewitt, who would head Bomber Command during the same period; he authorised it.[3] Harris had done himself no harm in the eyes of these two influential officers either by applying for the course or by the terms in which he had written.

Nor did Harris fail to do justice to their confidence. The School of Air Pilotage, as it was actually titled, was intended to train up to 50 officer pilots a year in cross-country navigation, but owing to the rapid scaling down of plans for the post-war RAF it actually ran just one ten-week course. Of the 38 students who started, 22 dropped out for various reasons, four failed, and 12 passed, with Harris coming out top having achieved an 88.8% mark despite maths not being his strong point. Years later, as Deputy Director of Plans, he reflected on this and another navigation course he had undergone, urging the need to simplify such training and limit it to what was necessary for the actual job to be done. Hours of explanation of principles of mag-netism and instruction on how to make a compass, for example, were totally unnecessary; all he needed to know about it was the fact that a compass needle pointed in a certain direction.[4] Here was a young officer prepared to think about what he was doing and why, ready to challenge the conventional wisdoms, and determined to be realistic and to concentrate on the essentials.

Despite the pressures of his course at Andover, Harris also found time to apply some different skills. As the Loco Superintendent of the London and

North-Western Railway at Aston recorded, 'Major Harris, RAF, worked a L & NW Railway locomotive during the railway strike in October 1919. In the event of his offering his services in similar circumstances, I shall with confidence accept him.' A later memo told him that £1 18s 0d was being paid to the Air Ministry for crediting to him; it represented $20\frac{1}{4}$ hours' work at the highest rate payable for driving duties. Sadly, Harris's attempts to extract this princely sum from higher authority encountered a denial that the money had ever been received and he eventually gave up the unequal struggle.[5] Such respect as he had for civil servants – and he never had much – was hardly enhanced by this little episode, but he enjoyed being an engine driver and learnt from it how to stoke a fire.

Not long afterwards Harris was again to do battle with bureaucracy. After a few months at Brooklands, where he had done his first flying and which he now had to close down, he went to open up No 3 Flying Training School at Digby in April 1920, and found himself yet again devoting much of his time to disposing of redundant supplies. He remembered vast numbers of two-gallon cans of petrol being brought in; they could be stored only behind barbed wire and on checking them he found thousands of gallons were missing. Having reported this he received a most abusive letter blaming him and requiring him to explain and pay for the shortage. Faced with a possible bill for thousands of pounds he had a brainwave. Two or three petrol companies were asked what evaporation losses they would allow in two-gallon cans stored in the open over a period of, say, a year. Back came the answer: 100%. The resourceful squadron leader duly suggested to the Air Ministry that they owed him a lot of money. He heard no more.[6]

'Serving in the Services in the immediate aftermath of a war is not an exciting or particularly pleasant experience,' said Harris later, and these two years did little to confirm that he had been right to remain in the RAF. He still hankered after Rhodesia, and if that was impossible he wanted to go back to a warm climate where there was actually something to do in terms of flying. So, knowing that there were RAF squadrons in India, and recalling how much of his family history was linked to the sub-continent, he applied to go out East on posting. By this time Barbara was expecting their second child and soon after Marigold was born on 29 November he set sail for India, where he took command of 31 Squadron on 25 January 1921.

Harris was far from enamoured of what he found. His squadron, the first to be based in India, had been there since 1916, was now equipped with the Bristol Fighter, and had moved to Cawnpore in November 1920. It was, however, under Army, not RAF, command, since all British forces in India were answerable to the Viceroy and funded on the Government of India budget. So when Harris immediately protested about his men's living and working conditions it was an officer of the Royal Engineers who told him proudly that the barracks were those which had been defended during the Indian Mutiny. Soon afterwards his station commander, a gunner, accused him of infringing standing orders by letting his airmen work throughout the morning and sometimes also in the afternoon, and doing most of it in the open; in hot weather, the CO explained, the men were not allowed out of barracks between early morning and sunset because of the risk of heatstroke. Harris would have none of this: he had had only one case of heatstroke, whereas the infantry were going down like ninepins, and his men had plenty of essential work maintaining their aircraft to take their minds off the subject. To make matters worse, he later recalled, they had to cope with a dreadful shortage of spares and other essential supplies. On occasion aircraft took off on wheels with bare rims since there were no tyres available, and with axles tied on with locally made rope; and they were still fitted with obsolete single-ignition engines, despite the fact that many dual-ignition engines were being sold off at home as surplus. 'We lacked practically everything which an Air Force squadron anywhere else would regard as essential for maintaining its aircraft.'[7]

Cawnpore was not a happy experience, though a month's detachment to command his unit's hill station did provide a little welcome relief. In mid-1921, however, Harris was told that in November the squadron would be moving to Peshawar, near the North-West Frontier, and he also heard that Barbara would soon be coming out to join him. Heeding his parents' advice she decided to leave the children with them and sister Maud in Folkestone, which was just as well given the appalling conditions on the packed troopship. Arthur eventually met her in Lahore, from where they travelled on by train to Peshawar. Barbara remembered the suffocating heat of that journey, made worse by the steel shutters that had to be closed at night as protection against shots from local tribesmen. On arrival they took up residence in a large, attractive bungalow which they shared with one of Harris's flight commanders, Flight Lieutenant Aubrey Ellwood, and his wife. Domestically this was a happy time. The two families got on well together, which was fortunate because they shared most of their household servants; the wives went riding a lot; there were the usual 'Raj' entertainments, the Peshawar Club, tennis, dances, dinners, racing; there was the occasional sightseeing trip.[8]

For the husbands on duty it was a different story. Just as in Cawnpore, the squadron was being condemned to fly in aircraft that were 'utterly unair-worthy' (Harris's words) over mountain terrain where a forced landing could easily mean being killed outright or suffering an even less pleasant death at the hands of the local tribesmen. Nevertheless they did what they could. Two frontier incidents are worth recording. In one of them Afghan tribes-men had crossed the border and laid siege to a frontier fort; this was held by a company of local militia of doubtful loyalty, and the Indian Political Agent on the spot was sending increasingly urgent messages requesting help. Unfortunately his superior in Peshawar was on leave, so these were simply filed pending his return, whereupon he belatedly rang up Harris who took four aircraft – all he had at that moment – to bomb and shoot up whatever they could see. Harris himself flew as observer to his second flight commander, Flight Lieutenant Alec Coryton, which enabled him to use his Lewis gun, a more enjoyable occupation than just bombing. The RAF accrued some political credit from this small series of raids but according to Harris they did not enhance its popularity with the Army, whose business it was poaching.[9]

The second incident led to a more direct confrontation. It occurred when Harris had taken a flight to an advanced landing ground at Miranshah at the Army's request and was then told the aircraft were unlikely to be needed for several days while the Army got on with the job. Harris replied to the General that he would take them back to Peshawar to keep them in shape in their hangar until they were needed. The General's response was scathing, accusing the air force people of needing always to live in the lap of luxury, of always having to cover up their delicate aircraft, and much else. Eventually calming down a little he conceded that Harris had better get back to Peshawar and his spare parts before he could do any more. 'Yes sir,' replied the infuriated squadron leader, 'it's high time we got back to our ball of string.' The further explosion that followed left him wondering what was likely to happen to his RAF career and reinforced his growing doubts about the wisdom of continuing it. Rhodesia still had its appeal and in May 1922 he went so far as to submit his resignation.[10]

However, Harris had influential friends and there was growing awareness in London that all was not well with the handful of squadrons in India. The Prince of Wales had recently been out on an inspection visit and been outspokenly sympathetic about 31 Squadron's somewhat forlorn condition; it had helped that he recognised Coryton, who had taught his brother (the future King George VI) to fly.[11] Then Lord Montagu had stirred things up in a letter to *The Times* describing the disgraceful conditions under which the RAF was working in India. Sir Hugh Trenchard, Chief of Air Staff, engaged in his long battle to preserve the independent Third Service, felt obliged to intervene. To quote his biographer, 'the RAF was not so well staffed with promising young officers that even one should be sacrificed to the vanity of a general. Too many were inventing reasons for leaving a Service which apparently had little to offer them.' Though not one normally to condone impertinence, Trenchard was more in sympathy with Harris than with his accusers, and the local Air Headquarters was told to take no action against him.[12] At the same time Trenchard despatched one of his most senior commanders, Sir John Salmond, to investigate the RAF's alleged inefficiency. After a thorough and searching enquiry Salmond strongly criticised the poor material support being provided by the Army, stated that the RAF in India was to all intents and purposes non-existent as a fighting force,[13] and recommended far-reaching changes.

Harris's stand had been vindicated. Moreover Salmond had spent a lot of time with him and, impressed not only by his flying and leadership skills but also by the sharpness of his criticisms and his outspokenness, had persuaded him to withdraw his resignation and join him in Iraq, where Salmond was about to become Air Officer Commanding.[14] Suddenly Harris's prospects seemed far brighter. The only fly in the ointment was that Barbara, pregnant for the third time, would not be able to go with him; conditions in Iraq were too unsettled for accompanied tours. So in July 1922, little more than six months after she had arrived, Barbara was on her way back home. They would not meet again for over two years, by which time their second daughter, Rosemary, would be 21 months old.

Harris found an entirely different situation in Basra from the one he had left. In India the Army had totally failed to understand that air power was a new weapon, endowed with flexibility and the ability to strike anywhere within a very wide area at any moment; to his mind, therefore, if this weapon was to be intelligently used it had to be independently controlled.[15] Now, in Iraq, he would be working under RAF command in an unprecedented situation, for at the Cairo Conference in 1921, presided over by Winston Churchill, it had been agreed to back Trenchard's ideas and make the Air Ministry responsible for maintaining law and order in Iraq through a policy of air control. John Salmond was therefore appointed to command not just the RAF squadrons but also the relatively small ground forces that would work with them. To start with Harris joined the personnel staff at the newly formed Air Headquarters – his first, albeit brief, experience of staff work. Then four months later, by remarkable coincidence, he was appointed to command the same squadron with which he had flown over the Western Front in 1917, No 45.

Based at Hinaidi, near Baghdad, the squadron had arrived from Egypt six months previously. It and 70 Squadron were equipped with the Vickers Vernon and being used to provide air transport for the other air and land forces. Harris joined his unit on 20 November and within days was airborne in the Vernon, a very different type of aircraft from those he had hitherto flown. Its speed was only 68 mph, but as the first big enclosed cabin aircraft it could carry up to a dozen passengers or a ton of freight and had seven hours' endurance.[16] Checking him out was one Flight Lieutenant the Hon Ralph Cochrane, who quickly overcame his apprehensions of his new boss's fearsome reputation and found him an excellent CO. Thus began a lasting

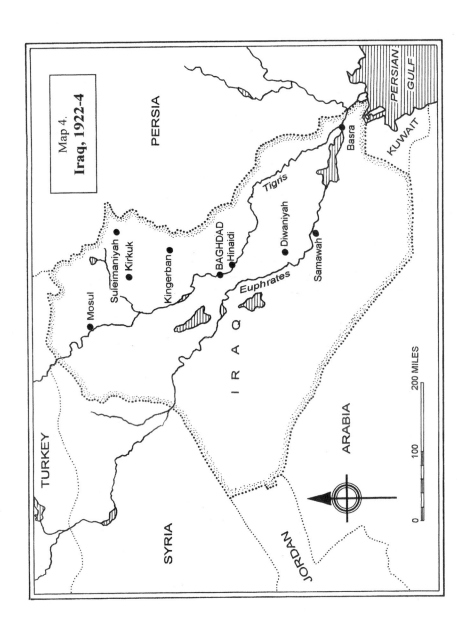

Map 4.
Iraq, 1922–4

and most important friendship, for Cochrane would eventually become Harris's leading Group Commander in Bomber Command. Rapport was equally quickly established with the second flight commander, Flight Lieutenant Robert Saundby, who later served as Harris's right-hand man throughout his wartime years at High Wycombe. Many years afterwards Harris would receive a touching letter from his fitter, J.W. Walker, recalling the great days in Iraq and reminding him not only of Cochrane and Saundby but also of Basil Embry, 'Bones' Ragg and 'Uncle' Lees, all of whose careers benefited from his tutelage in 45 Squadron.[17] Truly he led a fine team.

As Harris subsequently wrote, when he took over the squadron was doing little more than carrying cargo and personnel between bases and opening up part of the air mail route to India. He went on:

> It immediately struck me that here was potentially the most powerful part of the Air Force in Iraq, employed on virtually civil duties and making no serious contribution to our very tenuous military strength in that part of a very disturbed world. I told Sir John Salmond of my feelings and said I could convert the squadron's aircraft into the most useful bombers in the country; he gave me the green light. We had no equipment immediately available and apart from the prospect of at least a year's argument with the Air Ministry over this additional role it would take at least three or four months to get any equipment out by sea. The major requirements were bomb rack 'rails' which were not available locally and were difficult to manufacture out of materials sufficiently strong and light enough not to absorb the total flyable lift of the aircraft. However, with the aid of a brilliant technical warrant officer [Wilkinson] and a WD workshop ... we worried out some roughly finished but serviceable rails from high grade sheet steel. We fitted them up with racks for 20, 50 and 100 lb bombs and incendiary containers, and by sawing an unauthorised hole in the nose of the aircraft we had a magnificent [prone] bomb-aiming position into which we also fitted a home-made trigger release gear operated by a length of shock absorber. With this equipment we could not only bomb far more accurately but were able to make much heavier attacks than the DH9As or Bristols could produce.[18]

While this work was going on Harris was testing bomb sights and organising practice bombing and at the end of January 1923, when Turkish forces were infiltrating across the northern border and threatening Kirkuk, the Vernons (including those of 70 Squadron which had been similarly modified) were sent north to Mosul. On 3 and 5 February Harris himself took part in bombing raids on the Turks and was delighted to be told by Salmond: 'Your satisfactory results are highly commendable to your squadron as the first effort of your unit which has not previously bombed under active service conditions with this type of machine. I realise how much you personally had to do with bringing your squadron to the pitch of efficiency and enthusiasm which it has now reached.'[19]

The squadron still retained its many other roles, of course, as Harris's logbook makes clear. There were support personnel and ground troops to convey, casualties to be evacuated, mail and stores to be delivered, reconnaissances to be carried out, training to be done, and often in conditions which were far from ideal, as exemplified by references to heavy rain, dust storms, and forced landings – the Vernon was very under-powered for use over mountains. At the same time he was constantly trying to find ways of doing things better, such as when he adapted an electric truck to lift the tails of his heavy aeroplanes and push or tow them in and out of the hangars – a device greatly appreciated by his airmen, who had hitherto done the job by hand in shade temperatures exceeding 120°.[20]

Nevertheless, Harris's greatest concern remained to extend the bombing capability of his aircraft. He set great importance on accuracy; the small weight of bombs that could be delivered meant they were useless unless dropped with precision, and in most circumstances the intention was to cause inconvenience, not casualties. Consequently there was much practice bombing, normally from 2–3,000 ft, and Harris – leading from the front as the bomb aimer – achieved an average accuracy of 26 yards in a series of ten such sorties in July 1923. Soon afterwards Salmond approved his suggestion for a Command Bombing Competition, in which the two 45 Squadron Vernons came out easy winners over not only 70 Squadron but all the so-called professional bomber squadrons, some of them using dive bombing. At the same time, drawing on his wartime experience, Harris had begun night flying, and in September he flew the first night bombing experiment. The limitations of instrumentation and the absence of external navigation aids obviously presented great problems but training in night flying continued, a primitive 'marker' bomb was devised and proved very effective on the usually clear nights, and in late 1924 night formation practice bombing was even attempted.[21]

Meanwhile there had been further active operations. At the end of April 1923 Harris commanded a two-squadron airlift of troops to Baghdad following the Turkish withdrawal. Late in the year, soon after providing a fire-power demonstration to the visiting Quetta Staff College (when Harris must have enjoyed showing the Indian Army a thing or two), 45 Squadron helped deal with a tribal rebellion in the area of Diwaniyah and Samawah. He himself flew three of the bombing sorties, and the Vernons' night bombing capability was also used. Then in May 1924 unrest broke out again in the north, at Kirkuk, where Sheikh Mahmud was pursuing his claim for Kurdish independence. Following emergency airlift duties the whole Vernon force, controlled by Harris, was concentrated at Kingerban, from where, after

several warnings had gone unheeded, the Sheikh's headquarters at Sulei-
maniyah was repeatedly bombed. 45 Squadron's records state that this
resulted in the flight of the Sheikh, who lost much of his influence with the
surrounding tribes.[22] One of the better known RAF songs originated from
this incident. Here its first verse must suffice:

> In the year anno domini one-nine-two-four
> 'Twas just outside Suleiman there started a war.
> HQ got excited and sent down to 'Bert'
> To pull operations staff out of the dirt.
> No bombs at all, no bombs at all;
> If our engines cut out we'll have no bombs at all.[23]

Harris had undoubtedly put his squadron on the map and had done it,
as he later wrote, despite 'the appalling climate, the filthy food, and the
ghastly lack of every sort of amenity that our unfortunate men were compelled to put up with in "peace time", for two years at a stretch, away
from their families.' The pressures for economy deprived them of the most
meagre and essential comforts – even adequate bathrooms – and the
Hinaidi swimming pool, so essential to relaxation in such a place, was
economised on to the extent of infecting numbers of men with bilharzia.[24]
Nevertheless, as Basil Embry tells us, Harris did what he could to make
things better: for example, he improved the airmen's food by attention to
detail, he lowered the temperature in barrack rooms with a device that
sprayed water on to matting hung over the windows, and he reorganised
the officers' mess and had it redecorated. Moreover, in the drive for efficiency he tightened discipline, insisting on daily parades and regular physical training – unwelcome measures maybe, but he was not one to court
popularity.

Nor was Harris a CO to be trifled with. Embry recounts a characteristic
incident during the detachment to Mosul in early 1923, not long after
Harris's arrival. The aircrew were living in a very small, cramped mess, only
one room of which – that used by the CO, Saundby and Embry – had a
fireplace. One bitterly cold evening the fire started smoking badly and
Harris found someone had put a wet sack over the chimney pot. Soon
afterwards two revolver cartridges exploded in the fire, showering the room
with bits of burning wood. Harris ignored this for a while, then summoned
one of the young pilots. 'Beardsworth, go to the airfield and see if the
aeroplanes are picketed down securely, because my chimney has been
smoking badly and the wind must have got up.' The airfield was a mile away
and Beardsworth requested transport. 'No,' was the firm reply. Beardsworth
duly reported back that all was well, whereupon another pilot was called for

and sent on a similar errand. And so it continued, with the individual tasks suitably varied; the new CO had delivered his message![25]

The firmness was, of course, matched by a professionalism that commanded everyone's respect. Not only was this evident in the air, it was also apparent in Harris's insistence on ground training in airmanship and technical matters. Indeed, he took personal interest in all the squadron's activities, not least those of its various sports teams. In 1924, as he proudly remembered, 'we won everything in the whole Iraq Command – shooting, bombing, boxing, rugger, soccer, tent pegging, steeplechase!'[26] His influence was pervasive. As Embry recalled, morale soared, esprit de corps rose to a great height, and each member of his unit was proud to say 'I belong to 45 Squadron.'

At the end of September, as his tour of duty in Iraq was drawing to a close, Harris piloted the Secretary-of-State for Air, Lord Thomson, who had been visiting the Command, back from Baghdad to Cairo, and they subsequently exchanged correspondence. 'I often talk about what I call the "Harris landing" as a masterpiece of its kind,' wrote Thomson; they had got on well together.[27] Certainly Harris's time in Iraq had done his reputation no harm. His flying skills (his logbook recorded 455 hours with flights averaging one to two hours), his leadership talents, his inventiveness and ingenuity, his determination to exploit the potentialities of air power: all these had been convincingly demonstrated. Moreover he was acquiring friends in high places. Trenchard had been watching him with approval from afar; Salmond, who would eventually succeed Trenchard, had witnessed his achievements at close quarters; and others, like Ludlow-Hewitt and Newall, had been following his activities with much interest. By taking the RAF's first large transport aircraft and converting it into a bomber, by insisting on operating it at night as well as in daylight, and by stressing the importance of good navigation and accurate bombing, aided by target marking, he had pointed the way for the future. It was little wonder he was about to be chosen to command the first of the RAF's new 'heavy bomber' squadrons in the United Kingdom.

Harris set sail for home aboard the SS *Glengorm* on 14 October 1924 and was soon enjoying some well earned leave with his family over the Christmas period. Now, for the first time, he had the opportunity of getting to know his three young children (aged six, four and almost two) and could reasonably look forward to several years of proper family life before any further separations might occur. Sadly his mother, Caroline, had died in 1922 while he was abroad, so Barbara and the children were now living with her parents in London. 'Granma' and 'Granpa' Money were devoted to their grandchildren, often acting as surrogate parents during the frequent upheavals of a roving Service life, and over the coming years they remained very supportive of Barbara and her husband in bringing up their growing family. Granpa – nicknamed 'Gaffer' – often gave his daughter and son-in-law a helping hand, while a kindly older cousin, Lady Latymer, provided Anthony with his schooling.

Harris's next move was to Worthy Down, near Winchester, which had been opened as an RFC station in 1917 and in 1924 was selected as a base in the Wessex Bombing Area for two squadrons that were soon to be re-equipped with the Vickers Virginia. Having just completed a three months' course at the Army Senior Officers' School at Sheerness, he took over the first of these, No 58, on 25 May 1925. Barbara and Anthony then came to join him, and since the married quarters were unfinished they lived for several months in an old, reputedly haunted house called Drayton Park; Anthony remembered that his father pooh-poohed the ghost stories but was taken aback when a bedroom chair started to creak and move as though someone was sitting in it. When they thankfully moved into quarters, the Nanny, Lilian Chappell, brought Marigold and Rosemary from London to join them. At last the family were united. As was fairly usual in those days, however, the nursery was kept rather separate from the adults and the children saw relatively little of their father. They remembered him as often moody and reluctant to take much notice of them, though there were certainly more relaxed moments, not least when Pa appeared in the nursery for things like pillow fights, at which he was particularly good. Marigold's very first happy memory was of bathtime, when he would soap the end of the bath and slide her up and down to the accompaniment of roars of laughter, and to Nanny's extreme annoyance. He was pleased, too, to see that his elder daughter shared his love of horses, as evidenced by her sneaking rides on the local racecourse, and he obtained equal enjoyment from making a wireless crystal set.[28]

Inevitably, however, it was Harris's work that primarily occupied his attention. The airfield was in fact a poor choice for a bomber station. It sloped considerably and was barely large enough for the heavy aircraft (by the standards of the period) that were to use it, but he had to make the best of it with his Virginia bombers and a few Victoria transport aircraft that his squadron also operated for a while. From the start, at his insistence, there was great emphasis on night flying. His wartime experience convinced him that large, slow, 'heavy' bombers would stand little chance against day fighters and must have the ability to operate at night. Having already worked on this in Iraq he continued to experiment with night flying procedures and equipment, and much of his own flying was done in the dark. His logbook records 536 hours altogether with 58 Squadron, with night-flying practices, flare trials and formation flying featuring regularly; on 4 August 1926 he even carried out a 'raid' on London.

Christopher Clarkson, one of Harris's pilots, later recalled the squadron's tremendous esprit de corps and the very high flying standards he inspired. He had brought from 45 Squadron 'The Rumble Club', a strict set of rules to be obeyed when flying; anyone spotted breaking them was fined and the proceeds were used to buy display items for the Mess. Most people's names appeared from time to time in the Rumble Book, including his own, for everyone else was on the look-out to catch him, whereupon he would produce fantastic arguments as to why he was not guilty. Clarkson was convinced that the Club was a great incentive to good, accurate flying.[29]

True to character Harris also showed constant concern to improve the serviceability and performance of his aircraft, but it was like pushing against a 'cotton wool curtain', and one incident led to direct conflict with 'Boom' Trenchard. Harris had been complaining that a design fault with the voltage regulator was constantly causing flights to be aborted and that it was not his electricians who were to blame as was always alleged by higher authority. Boom gave him a ticking off for his rudeness and when Harris tried to explain the technicalities it was clear that the great man had no idea of what he was talking about. The problem was eventually sorted out, but, as Harris later reflected, Trenchard's inability to understand such matters was typical of the entire upper echelon of the RAF in those days; moreover it was always easier to say no, he observed, for otherwise one had to do something about it. Neither then nor later would Harris ever take that line. For him, as C-in-C just as squadron commander, if there was a genuine problem it had to be properly addressed. Fortunately Trenchard was too big a man to hold such an incident against Harris. Congratulating him on his promotion to Wing Commander in July 1927, Trenchard wrote in his own hand, 'I hope you will go on as in the past.'[30]

Others, too, continued to watch Harris's progress. In 1925 he exchanged correspondence with H.E. Wimperis, Director of Scientific Research in the Air Ministry, about ways of improving bombsights in order to obtain greater accuracy; Harris's practical, inventive mind, as shown in Iraq and now at Worthy Down, was being recognised where it mattered. Sir John Salmond, too, was still very much in the picture, for as AOC-in-C Air Defence of Great Britain he was Harris's operational chief. In October 1925, for example, he congratulated Harris on a non-stop flight he had just completed to Leuchars and back on 3 September. Although Harris had to land his Virginia at Spittlegate on the way back to refuel, he had been airborne for 9 hours 15 minutes, a notable achievement for those days. The following May his squadron was again commended by Salmond, this time for a series of flights carrying MPs, troops, mail, newspapers and so on, during the early days of the General Strike. Harris himself flew to Edinburgh and back on the 5th, and among many other missions several were flown by a newly appointed flight commander, his old friend Bob Saundby.[31]

April 1927 was another landmark, for it saw the arrival of the second Virginia squadron at Worthy Down: No 7, commanded by Wing Commander C.F.A. (Peter) Portal. The next eight months occasioned considerable rivalry between the two squadrons. In 1926, 58 Squadron, led by Harris, had taken part in the Hendon Air Display and won the follow-up seven-hour reliability race, and in July 1927 Portal was determined to beat them. His squadron not only succeeded but went on to win the newly instituted Laurence Minot Bombing Trophy that autumn. Harris's reaction to being upstaged is not recorded, but what really mattered was that he and Portal had established a mutual respect and friendship that would prove of inestimable value in years to come. 'I never met a finer man than Peter Portal,' Harris was to tell Denis Richards many years later.[32]

Reflecting on this period in later life, Harris recalled his station's sporting prowess and in particular – despite its small size – its success in winning the RAF Rugby Football Championship. He remembered, too, allowing the local archaeological society on to the airfield to dig on parts of the site of an ancient Belgic village, traces of which were discernible from the air and on aerial photographs. He was fascinated by their activities and on one occasion, when a fairly modern skeleton was discovered, suggested to the astonished diggers that it might have been a Roman pilot. Less of a 'fun' incident occurred when the Air Ministry (shades of Digby) tried to make him pay for 10,000 gallons of petrol that had disappeared. Eventually the civilian works department was found to blame; when reactivating the station's wartime fuel systems they had left an open pipe and half flooded a nearby area with the best aviation spirit.[33]

By November 1927 Harris had spent almost two and a half years at Worthy Down; indeed, he had now been commanding squadrons for no less than six years. He had become known and respected as a very able pilot, a firm and outspoken leader, a man who was utterly determined to get the best out of his men and machines, and a thinker about the ways in which air power ought to be used. His work had recently been recognised by the award of the OBE. Yet so far he had received little formal training or experience in staff work, nor had he been actively encouraged to broaden his military education. Without doubt the decision that he ought to go to Staff College was strongly influenced by Trenchard and Salmond, but we can only speculate on why he was sent not to Andover, where most of the promising RAF officers went, but to the Army Staff College at Camberley. He had, of course, plenty of experience of the soldiery, and if anyone was likely to be able to represent the RAF on this influential course and argue the case for air power it was Harris, who would stand no nonsense from anybody, regardless of rank or status.

So in January 1928 Harris joined the Junior Division, the first year of the two-year course at Camberley. Apart from one other RAF officer – Squadron Leader C.G. Burge – the remaining 60 students were all soldiers, most of them captains, which meant that Harris, as a wing commander, was not only senior student but also equal in rank to most officers on the directing staff, including the one airman, Wing Commander O.T. Boyd. Harris said little later on about these, for him, relatively relaxed days, with their mix of lectures, discussions, paper exercises, visits, sport and social activities. He seems to have enjoyed himself, not least when challenging the conventional doctrines still being propounded by the more senior Army officers, for most of whom he had little respect. On one occasion he was asked for his opinion about a week's work on tank warfare which they had just finished. He said that having watched the Army mind disposing of the tank as useless because it could not do what the cavalryman and his horse had always done and in the same way, he was sure the Army would never choose a tank to meet all their requirements unless it ate hay and made noises like a horse.[34] Indeed, at one point during this first year he was in danger of being asked to leave. On the other hand he got on well with many of his fellow students, who struck him as first-class officers who deserved better than having their ideas firmly sat upon by the top brass. Not all the directing staff, however, were 'dead-beats', and one of them – Lieutenant-Colonel Bernard Montgomery – struck Harris both as an excellent instructor and a man with advanced ideas on the likely pattern of future warfare. Such thinking was regarded with distaste, even as heretical, among most of his colleagues and seniors, but to Harris it seemed eminently sensible.[35] Ten years later, when they were about to meet again in Palestine (chapter 4), Harris drew on this knowledge of Montgomery and described him to his ADC as 'a very good soldier who will make a damned good general. Incidentally he is the first soldier I have come across who has a proper grasp of the vital role of a tactical air force in land battles. I expect he will be putting it to good purpose before long!'[36]

In 1929 Harris, with most of his contemporaries, moved up to the Senior Division. Here he was the only RAF spokesman, but the Royal Navy was this time represented in the person of Commander John Leach and the two became good friends despite inter-Service arguments that inevitably emerged from time to time. By now Harris was busily engaged in historical reading and research, and while no papers he wrote seem to have been preserved, a lecture that he delivered in 1931 was very largely based upon the work he had done at Camberley. The text is worth a brief summary as the first clear evidence of how Harris's military thinking was developing.

The lecture was given in Cairo to the Army officers attending a major Command Staff Exercise which was intended to study the use of modern weapons and ideas against a backward nation. Having begun by inviting his audience to consider historical precedents, Harris referred them to the tactics of Joshua at the Battle of Ai and pointed out his principles: 'all along he was out to employ new ideas and new weapons, to exploit the element of surprise and consequent enemy confusion. He was out to produce astonishment to such a degree that he did not hesitate in one of his battles to arrange for the sun and the moon to stand still, to the confounding of his enemies.' Moving to the present day, Harris continued: 'The younger generation will always be enthusiastic to use the new weapons science places in their hands. They will always overstate their case – they have to in order to get even half a hearing from the older generation, rooted and stewing in the juice of their pre-conceived ideas.' Urging the importance of thinking about and making proper use of modern weapons and methods, he instanced the Battle of Jutland, where Jellicoe had two carriers with 21 aircraft trained in recon-naissance; properly used they could have told him the exact position and course of the German Fleet, with effects on the whole course of the war. His failure to do so exemplified the 'utter inability of those with "the ingrowing preconceived idea" to grasp the use and appreciate the advantages of new weapons when they lie at hand.' As further examples Harris quoted the 'abuse' of tanks on the Western Front, failure to pay attention to the RFC's early reconnaissance reports at the time of Von Kluck's outflanking move-ment in 1914, and German hesitation over the institution and prosecution of their U-boat campaign. 'With ever increasing rapidity nowadays science places in our hands new and more astonishing, and more effective weapons. You must absorb the methods of using and exploiting these new weapons in the future, quickly, and more quickly every day. You must go on or go under.'

Harris then turned to the theme of the current exercise and urged an unconventional approach, one which would not involve attacking the enemy head-on. 'The very mention of a combined operation always sends cold shivers up and down the spine of the staff. By getting your AFVs through or round by sea, exploiting the troop and supply carrying capacity of your aircraft and your air superiority, you can form a bridgehead anywhere you please.' This brought him, inevitably, to the further role of air power, the one which he had himself already done so much to develop. 'What is air bombing today but a reversion to the principle employed by the first intelligent ape, who gave up man handling and fights on the ground or in the branches because he conceived the more adequate and less risky result to be obtained by pitching a coconut down upon his adversary.' This led him to stress the value of using 'troop carriers' (*ie* bombers) to wreck enemy headquarters and nerve centres, and in conclusion to identify a new principle of war: 'The exploitation of range'. This, in his view, was a far more worthy principle than that blithering word 'security', and he challenged his listeners to recognise the tremendous advantages of the weapons being placed in their hands by modern science and manufacturing. Were they going to make these advantages subservient to their preconceived ideas or were they prepared to exploit them? And finally, 'please do not preface your argument with the old, old tag that is so invariably and so nauseatingly applied to any new idea connected with the exploitation of the air – "and now let's come down to earth".'

How his audience reacted to this pungently delivered, unconventional, forward thinking message is not recorded, but one reader of the script was certainly impressed. Peter Portal, working in the Plans Branch of the Air Ministry, referred to it as 'a real tonic – I would have paid my fare to Cairo to hear it given and to see their faces'.[37]

The Camberley years, very different from Harris's previous career, had certainly been invaluable. Moreover, so impressed were the powers-that-be that they overcame their misgivings to the extent of inviting him to stay on and join the directing staff. Harris would have none of this. While he had managed to keep in flying practice, usually by going back to Worthy Down to fly the Virginia and occasionally fixing himself up with a Wapiti or a Fairey seaplane or a Southampton flying boat, he let it be known that he was determined to get back to the sharp end of the RAF. Consequently at the end of 1929 he was on his way to Egypt.

Camberley had also been a good place for the Harris family. They had rented Durwood, a large house belonging to the Chenevix Trenches, and the three children were of an age to enjoy the semi-rural setting. Their parents were great animal lovers and they acquired quite a menagerie – a small goat called Jenny, rabbits, a borrowed pony named Merrylegs which had some horrible little ways, and a 17-hand bay hunter called Waterford which Harris rode for the College Drag Hunts. Marigold, now old enough to ride herself and strongly encouraged to do so by her father, remembered him as a good 'whip' whose horsemanship proved a great asset among his army colleagues. Then there was Spot, the fox terrier, which belonged to the house and adored Harris, who taught him a brilliant set of tricks. The children recalled their grandparents' visits too; the Moneys came regularly, and grandpa Harris, now extremely deaf, also enjoyed coming – his son called him Popski (not to his face) because he said he looked like the dog owned by Squeak's friend Witskowski in the *Daily Mail* comic strip. There were also car trips. Harris had bought a red Rover with a dicky at Drayton Park and before leaving Worthy Down acquired a yellow Austin 7. He would be into bigger, more powerful cars in due course, for he loved driving. Nor must we ignore the extensive social round of the Staff College, which Barbara greatly enjoyed. These were happy enough years.

1930 was different. Harris went out to Cairo alone, it being intended that the family would follow, but when he wrote to say that the climate was unsuitable for children Barbara decided to travel out to join him, leaving the children to a nomadic existence in the hands of the nanny, a governess, the Money grandparents and Aunt Maud. Then after a year or so in Cairo, Barbara came back home to help look after Anthony, who was seriously ill with tonsillitis. Just when she was about to return she heard from her husband that he was off to Kenya and she should not come, so it was not until he returned to England in mid-1932 that they met again. Meanwhile both in Cairo and Kenya he had made various lady friends, one of them Betty, who later married the young Paddy Bandon (later Air Chief Marshal the Earl of Bandon). His marriage, never an ideal one, was beginning to fall apart.[38]

Harris's tour of duty at Headquarters RAF Middle East in Cairo was not one of the most exciting. He took over, in effect as deputy Senior Air Staff Officer, from Wing Commander Sholto Douglas, who referred to it as 'a rather dull job' before leaving for Khartoum. Nevertheless, to relieve the tedium of the day-to-day staff work there were at least regular opportunities for flying, most of them to visit units in the local area but some taking him in his Fairey IIIF as far as Palestine, Cyprus, the Sudan and Kenya. One flight, on 11 April 1931, was unique. The German airship LZ 127, better known as the *Graf Zeppelin*, had just arrived in Egypt on one of its series of flag-waving missions and the crew had been welcomed with great enthusiasm. They were keen to advertise themselves over Palestine also, to which the British authorities agreed provided they were accompanied by official observers. So while some of the crew (including Dr Eckener, the engineer responsible for much of the development work on the modern German airships) stayed in Cairo for a banquet with German, British and Egyptian officials, Harris went on board and, under the supervision of Captain Lehmann, spent the next ten hours steering the airship all the way to Jerusalem and back. While he later referred to it as a joyride he was impressed by the caution shown by the German officers, who seemed rather nervous in handling their ship. This was hardly surprising; only six months earlier its British equivalent, the *R101*, had crashed in flames at Beauvais.[39]

Later that year the AOC, Air Vice-Marshal Scarlett, was replaced by the influential and highly regarded Cyril Newall, whereupon Harris persuaded him to extend the annual relatively short 'showing the flag' flight to a three-month cruise that would cover much of Kenya, Uganda and Tanganyika, and demonstrate the potential of the aeroplane to many who knew hardly anything about it. The four Fairey IIIFs of 14 Squadron accordingly set out on 11 January 1932. Harris, in command of the expedition, flew aircraft 1704, and the flight was led by Flight Lieutenant Dick Atcherley, one of the already well known Atcherley twins. Eleven weeks and 150 flying hours later they were back. Khartoum, Entebbe, Kampala, Jinja, Kisumu, Nairobi, Mombasa, Dar es Salaam, Zanzibar, Dodoma, Serengeti: these were just some of the many ports-of-call that Harris had entered in his logbook. Moreover, at the request of the local authorities, he had flown over cloud-clad Mount Kilimanjaro, which revealed just enough of itself for a few photographs. Many aerial pictures were taken, often of wildlife, and the Governor of Tanganyika, Sir Stewart Symes, learnt a great deal from his eight-hour flight as a passenger over some of the game areas on 8 February.

Fox Movietone News was another beneficiary when, on 21 March, Harris flew a cameraman with all his equipment over Mount Kenya, where they stayed at 18,500 ft for about an hour, without oxygen, and obtained some magnificent footage. The cameraman, Mr Lieb, was full of praise for Harris's piloting skill and his courteous and useful assistance, and some of the shots were later used in Noel Coward's film *Cavalcade*. Altogether it had been a splendid 'cruise', as evidenced by the extensive album of both aerial and ground photographs which Harris compiled and kept. This brings out, among other things, the type of terrain over which they flew, the hazards the aircraft often faced when taking off and landing, the flying demonstrations they carried out (including supply dropping and bombing), the many people whom they met, and the social round in which they were engaged. It also shows the small menagerie which the flight acquired, including two monkeys, two cheetahs and a lion cub. It would appear that these were brought back to Cairo, and Chaka the lion, which travelled with Atcherley, was eventually presented to Cairo Zoo.[40]

For Harris, this cruise was the highlight of his sojourn in Egypt, and it certainly did a lot for the reputation of the RAF in East Africa. Hardly was he back in Cairo, however, than the Air Ministry told him his next posting was back to Iraq, to command a Vernon squadron. Harris's reaction can be imagined. To repeat a tour of duty he had completed eight years earlier, and again without his family, was simply not acceptable, as he told the AOC in no uncertain terms. Newall was disinclined to argue with the posting but Philip Babington, a good friend who was in charge of personnel matters (and later Air Member for Personnel), unearthed a regulation stating that all postings to and from Iraq must be from and to England, and Harris was off the hook – though he did have to spend two months in Baghdad writing the local defence scheme.[41]

So in August 1932 Harris was home again, and in October he went to Calshot to attend No 16 Flying Boat Pilots' Course. This lasted almost six months, during which he was trained in both the piloting and the navigation of the Southampton flying boat. It was his first, and last, comprehensive flying training course, and he emerged with an 'Above Average' assessment. Reasonably enough his new skills had to be applied, and on 21 March 1933 he arrived at Pembroke Dock, where he took over the base and its resident squadron, No 210, and met among others a most promising young officer named Donald Bennett. Of all his many postings this was the one Harris enjoyed most. He had long wanted to command a 'boat' squadron. He felt this aspect of aviation was encumbered by an unnecessary mystique based on largely spurious nautical lore, and was keen not only to try his hand at it but to prove that flying boats, just like land-based aircraft, could be operated in the dark. As Squadron Leader (later Air Vice-Marshal) Frank Lang, one of his senior pilots, later wrote: 'Bert Harris was a super night pilot – he had night cats' eyes – and he gave us unlimited dual at night in which we later became quite efficient, being the first flying boat squadron to carry out long-distance night flights involving landings and take-offs from distant stations.'[42]

It was not just the different type of flying that Harris enjoyed. There were also ample opportunities for sailing, and the family were together again, this time in a large house in the dockyard area. There seemed every prospect of a happy and satisfying couple of years in West Wales when suddenly word came that on 11 August he was to report for duty in the Air Ministry. The implications of this news were enormous. It meant immediate promotion; it meant that a career which had seemed to be lacking a clear pattern was about to move into an entirely new dimension; it meant that in the critical years that were to follow Adolf Hitler's recent rise to power in Germany Arthur Harris would be able to exercise major influence on RAF policy. There was, however, a downside. It meant that the flying career which he loved was to be cut short, and it meant that he was condemned to the uncongenial pressures and routines of Air Ministry staffwork. It meant, too, the end of his marriage.

Notes

1. Letter to Manby, 29 November 1956, Misc Folder 2; Saward, *op.cit.* pp.20–1.
2. Saward Tapes 12, 13.
3. Harris personal file C3679, letters dated 12 July, 28 July and 7 August 1919, AHB (RAF).
4. Information provided by Wing Commander C.G. Jefford, drawing on a minute from Harris dated 3 November 1936 (AIR 2/2860). See p.75.
5. Misc Folder 2; Harris personal file C3679, letters dated 4 March, 1 April and 23 April 1920.
6. Saward Tape 12.
7. Franks, *First in the Indian Skies*, pp.25–8; Harris, *op.cit.* p.19; Misc Folder 2.
8. Barbara Harris's recollections, recorded by Rosemary Harris. Ellwood completed his RAF career as C-in-C Bomber Command, 1947–50.
9. Harris, *op.cit.* p.20; Franks, *op.cit.* p.29.
10. Saward Tape 10; Franks, *op.cit.* p.30; Saward, *op.cit.* p.25.

11. Franks, *op.cit.* p.30.

12. Boyle, *Trenchard*, pp.356–7. See Misc Folder 2 for Montagu's letter.

13. Slessor, *The Central Blue*, pp.35–6.

14. Saward, *op.cit.* p.27.

15. Harris, *op.cit.* p.21.

16. Embry, *Mission Completed*, p.34.

17. Misc Folder 2. Embry retired as Air Chief Marshal, Ragg as Air Vice-Marshal, and Lees as Air Marshal.

18. Letter to Norman Macmillan 7 August 1958, Misc Folder 2. See also Saward, *op.cit.* pp.29, 30.

19. Letter dated 16 February 1923, Misc Folder 2.

20. Jefford, *op.cit.* p.78; Embry, *op.cit.* p.35; the Air Ministry recognised this invention with a thank-you letter but offered no monetary reward in view of the truck's limited use.

21. Jefford, *op.cit.* pp.79–80, 85; Saward, *op.cit.* p.31.

22. AIR 27/455; Jefford, *op.cit.* pp.83–4.

23. It was at about this time that some naval friends started calling Harris 'Bert', since in the Navy all Harrises were 'Bert'. The name stuck.

24. Harris, *op.cit.* p.23.

25. Embry, *op.cit.* pp.37, 39.

26. Misc Folder 2.

27. *Ibid.*

28. Recollections of Rosemary and Marigold.

29. Extract from Group Captain Clarkson's memoirs, sent by his widow Evelyn. In those days, Clarkson explained, engines were so unreliable that pilots were supposed always to land without using them, thus simulating a forced landing, and using one's engines without good reason under these circumstances, *ie* rumbling, was considered a particularly serious offence.

30. Saward Tape 15; Misc Folder 2.

31. Misc Folder 2; AIR 27/543.

32. Richards, *Portal of Hungerford*, p.94; Harris logbook. Harris in fact flew a Vickers Victoria in the 1927 Display.

33. Letter dated 25 April 1960, Misc Folder 2.

34. Harris, *op.cit.* p.24.

35. *Owl Pie*, the Army Staff College Journal, 1928, pp.3–5; Saward, *op.cit.* pp.35–6.

36. Pelly-Fry, *Heavenly Days*, p.127.

37. Lecture script December 1931; letter from Portal 14 December 1932. Both in Misc Folder 2.

38. Recollections of Anthony, Marigold and Rosemary.

39. Saward Tape 11; Harris logbook; Lehmann, *Zeppelin*, p.285.

40. Saward, *op.cit.* pp.36–9; Harris logbook; Harris photo album 'East African Cruise'.

41. Saward, *op.cit.* p.39.

42. Harris, *op.cit.* p.25; Misc Folder 2.

Chapter 4

Preparing for the inevitable

What, we may ask, caused this totally unexpected change of scene? It can hardly have been the result of long-term planning. Salmond, who knew Harris well and had just handed over as Chief of Air Staff, had steered him into the maritime sphere and must have intended him to stay there for at least a year or two. Yet suddenly he was being summoned to London, to occupy one of the most responsible and influential appointments open to a group captain. The reason probably lies in the rapidly changing circumstances of 1933.

The previous few years had been a frustrating period for Salmond and his staff in the Air Ministry. Amid the economic constraints of the Great Depression they had needed to devote much of their time to countering the pressures for disarmament, with totally unrealistic but strongly argued proposals to abolish bombing leading to interminable discussions in the Geneva Disarmament Conference. Then, in January 1933, Hitler became Chancellor of Germany and two months later won his first election and secured emergency powers. This was the writing on the wall, as Churchill and other government critics were at pains to point out; but theirs were voices crying in the wilderness. The last things the vast majority of the British people wanted to hear were warnings about another war and their views were articulated not only by the Labour and Liberal opposition parties but by many on the government benches too. At this stage there was little that Prime Minister Ramsey Macdonald and his colleagues could do, even had the will been there.

In the Air Ministry, however, there were growing anxieties, not least since they knew something of the covert building-up of a skeleton German air force in the Russian steppes. In the RAF expansion that the growing German military threat would, in the Ministry's view, make inevitable, the development of a strategic bomber force would occupy a crucial place; for some time bombing had been a dirty word, but as the events of 1933 unfolded perspectives changed. So if the bomber was to be put into the situation which Trenchard and his fellows had long foreseen for it, the Air Ministry would need to draw on the best expertise available, which pointed towards Harris. Significantly, too, there was a new Chief of Air Staff, Sir Edward Ellington, who had been appointed in May after serving as Air Member for Personnel. While he himself had no close acquaintance with

AIR MINISTRY 1936

Secretary of State for Air
(Lord Swinton)

Under-Secretary of State for Air
(Captain Harold Balfour)

Chief of Air Staff
(ACM Sir Edward Ellington)

Secretariat (S6)
(Maurice Dean)

The Air Staff

Air Member for Personnel
(AM Sir Frederick Bowhill)

Several Directorates,
including
Director of Training
(Air Cdre A.W. Tedder)

Deputy Chief of Air Staff
(AVM C.L. Courtney)

Director of Staff Duties
(Air Cdre W.S. Douglas)

Director of Signals
(Air Cdre J.B. Bowen)

Deputy Director of Operations
(Air Cdre S.J. Goble)

Deputy Director of Plans
(Gp Capt A.T. Harris)

Air Member for Research
and Development
(AVM W.R. Freeman)

Deputy Director of
Operational Requirements
(Gp Capt R.D. Oxland)

Air Member for Supply
and Organisation
(AM Sir Cyril Newall)

Deputy Director of Intelligence
(Wg Cdr C.E.H. Medhurst)

Harris he was well placed to assess his qualities in relation to those of other candidates for his senior staff. There was also, perhaps even more significantly, a new Deputy Chief of Air Staff, Air Vice-Marshal Ludlow-Hewitt, who knew Harris well and would be keen to have him. Group Captain Peter Portal, too, may have had a say; he had headed the Plans Branch since 1930, had kept in touch with Harris, and was himself due for a move.

So it was that on 11 August 1933, at the age of 41, Harris arrived in Adastral House, at the Aldwych end of Kingsway, to take over from Richard Peirse a group captain appointment in the Directorate of Operations and Intelligence. Five months later he moved across to succeed Portal as Deputy Director of Plans, the post he would fill until May 1937.[1] Contrasted with the Air Ministry of later years this was a small organisation. DCAS, who was the alter ego of CAS, had only the one Directorate responsible to him, and this included not only Operations and Intelligence but also Plans and Operational Requirements; there was no policy branch as such. When Harris arrived, as one of just four group captains, the entire officer complement numbered a mere 22 and as DD Plans he had only three subordinates, one of whom happened to be his old friend Ralph Cochrane. In such a relatively small department the more senior officers could work in close consultation, and on many matters – not least in Plans – often dealt directly with CAS. They worked too with a good many civil servants, and despite Harris's suspicions of them as a breed he came to respect the better ones. He got on particularly well with Ellington's sharp young Private Secretary, Maurice Dean, who thought him very good at his job and was to become a life-long friend.

The pressures were intense. For Harris it was an entirely new, fundamentally uncongenial, situation to be in. While occasionally he managed to get airborne, usually flying a Tiger Moth on a short staff visit, most of the time he was stuck for long hours in his cramped, stuffy, sixth-floor office, or in a conference room, having to turn his mind from one subject to another with bewildering rapidity, and very often irritated by the stupidities of others. The atmosphere of the time did not help. As John Terraine reminds us, the early 1930s were marked by 'a nationwide mood of complete revulsion from the First World War, an event which was almost universally misunderstood and constantly misinterpreted.' Consequently, he goes on, it had to be the war to end wars and hope for the future must depend on the League of Nations and on general disarmament.[2] For Harris and many other thinking military men such views were anathema, and to have to toil in such an unsympathetic, often hostile environment did nothing for his equanimity. In his view, based on his experience of fighting 'the Boche' in 1914–18, there was still 'unfinished business' to be done, and from his recollections of the horrors of trench warfare he was convinced that the bomber offered a better way of doing it. In 1933, however, not many shared his opinion and he had little time for most of the politicians, particularly those of the left wing.

Perhaps not surprisingly, Harris would frequently arrive home in the evening in one of his 'moods', full of the day's troubles, and his wife found these moods increasingly difficult to cope with. When the posting came through he had returned quickly from Pembroke Dock to their previous home at 14 Pelham Street, where Barbara and their two daughters eventually joined him, Anthony being away at school at Oundle. Over the next few months the marriage steadily fell apart and one day in May 1934 Barbara walked out, taking the children with her. Harris then heard that she was instituting divorce proceedings on the grounds of his misconduct with Daphne Leys, a woman whom he had first met in Egypt, and he stated his intention to defend. On 28 June a petition for dissolution was therefore filed, but eventually, in October, after much legal correspondence via their respective solicitors, Miss Leys admitted her misconduct. As a result, a decree nisi was issued on 15 January 1935 and six months later it was made absolute. Meanwhile complex legal discussions had begun about the arrangements for the family's maintenance, and not until May 1936 were these completed. For some time ahead Harris would have substantial financial commitments towards Barbara and their children, who went to live in Harrington Gardens. He himself had moved out soon after the split and for the rest of his time in the Air Ministry shared digs in Ebury Street with Captain Tom Phillips, his Royal Navy opposite number.

Thus ended Harris's first marriage. It had lasted 18 years, but although he and Barbara had been passionately attracted to each other initially, and happy enough at intervals later on, there had not been the meeting of minds and true sharing of interests that would have helped it to endure. Barbara, musically gifted and artistic, was by nature too gentle a character for her forthright and energetic husband, although she had ably supported him during their years together and was equally popular wherever they were stationed. But there had been long periods of separation during which there seems to have been little correspondence between them – none has survived. Other significant friendships had appeared, and not just on his side. When Barbara travelled out to Egypt in 1930 she met a young naval officer named Gerald Boultbee with whom she kept in touch; after the divorce they met again and married. Certainly there had been happier times, such as in India, at Worthy Down, at Camberley, and all too briefly at Pembroke Dock, but even then the home atmosphere had often been strained. Both husband and wife really failed to appreciate one another's qualities and were reluctant to allow the other precedence; it did not help that Granma Money all too often seemed to be around. Nor did Harris's moods, which seemed to invade the whole house, make things easier. In truth, as his daughter Rosemary believes, he probably ought never to have married at all until he was in his 30s, and in any case he and Barbara were basically ill-suited. Nevertheless, at the end of it all, said Barbara in extreme old age, she would never have divorced him over the other women; it was the very rude way in which he spoke to her that finished it.[3]

For much of his time in Adastral House, therefore, Harris had to cope with serious domestic problems, but there is no evidence that his work suffered or that his superiors were caused any anxiety. They knew he was a valuable asset, none was inclined to be censorious, and there was much to do. His tasks as DD Plans were, in essence, to advise CAS (through DCAS) on the development of Air Staff policy, and to work with his Navy and Army opposite numbers on the Joint Planning Sub-Committee (JPSC) which advised the Chiefs of Staff on current and future strategic problems.[4] With such a remit he and his minuscule staff were bound to be involved in just about every major issue relating to the RAF and also in those affecting Britain's defence as a whole, and it is impracticable here to touch on more than a handful of the matters that came his way.

The 'very sombre' (Terraine's words) Annual Report circulated by the Chiefs of Staff in October 1933 must have confirmed the worst fears of the newly arrived Harris about the parlous state of the nation's defences, and Germany's coincident departure from the Disarmament Conference and resignation from the League of Nations merely added to his apprehensions. His work now was to be geared directly or indirectly to the consequences of such events. The government's new Defence Requirements Committee, formed in November, reported in March 1934, with all three Plans branches having contributed to its work, and in July the first of the RAF's new expansion plans (Scheme A) was announced.[5] One of the Air Staff's notes about the approximate size of the air defence force needed to render the United Kingdom reasonably secure against air attack from a rearmed Germany certainly had a Plans input and is worth quoting for its foresight. 'The worst we have to consider is a single-handed war in which Germany is able to operate from Holland and Belgium or both, and in which we are confined to our bases in England.' The enemy could, it went on, concentrate his whole striking force against Britain, ie some 500–600 bombers, able to attack more than once per day; the RAF, on the other hand, would have to fly greater distances and therefore could operate less frequently, so would need a 50% superiority in strength, ie some 400 fighters and 800 bombers.[6]

Over the ensuing months (October 1934–October 1935) the JPSC produced a series of four reports entitled 'Defence Plans for the Event of War against Germany'. In the Air Staff view, strongly represented by Harris in the face of Army and Navy scepticism, an isolated Britain could not be saved from defeat by a defensive fighter force alone; a bomber force would also be needed to counter the expected enemy strategic air offensive by attacking his own bases and economic infrastructure. Harris had no doubt that such a force would need aircraft with long range and able to carry large bomb loads. As he told the newly appointed DCAS, Air Vice-Marshal Courtney, in January 1935, this meant not only that the light bomber was outmoded but that the medium bomber should also be abandoned.[7] In retrospect this single-minded approach seems unjustifiably narrow but Harris was undoubtedly right to urge the importance of developing the heavy bomber if the RAF was ever to be capable of waging a strategic air offensive.

Meanwhile events were marching on. On 1 January 1935 Hitler regained the Saarland and two months later announced the construction of the German Air Force, followed by the introduction of conscription. Then came signs that Mussolini had designs on Abyssinia and in July Harris was asked for advice on the practical problems of countering Italian aggression in the absence of active support from other countries. The pragmatic conclusion he drew, doubtless based on his own experience in Africa and elsewhere, can hardly have impressed the Foreign Office. It suggested that Italy should be given a League mandate in Abyssinia since the latter had shown itself incapable of developing up to 'civilised' standards without a period of mandatory tutelage. He added a possible course of action as a cynical afterthought: 'to connive at Italian conquest by applying sham and ineffective sanctions and letting Italy realise that we are only saving face.'[8] Three months later Italy invaded and Harris's implied prediction was fulfilled.

By this time major political changes were afoot. In June Stanley Baldwin became Prime Minister and appointed a new Secretary of State for Air, Philip Cunliffe-Lister, later to become Lord Swinton, who very soon recognised Harris as a valuable member of the team. Then in November came the General Election, which gave Baldwin the large majority he was hoping for and enabled him to order a proper start on the road to rearmament. Harris, well aware of the situation that confronted the Prime Minister and the nation, never shared the many criticisms later levelled at Baldwin over Britain's lack of preparedness and was convinced that he did most of what he could under the circumstances.[9] Certainly there was a complete change of pace from now on, and while the left-wing critics remained vociferous public opinion as a whole was coming to accept that rearmament was essential. For Harris and his colleagues 1936 would be a busy and less frustrating year.

There was also a new spring in Harris's step, for he had acquired a new girlfriend, Thérèse Hearne. They first met on 4 October 1935 at St Ermine's Hotel, thanks to an introduction arranged by an old school friend of hers whose cousin he had met at Pembroke Dock. After drinks he took the two of them to dinner, but his offer to escort Thérèse home was firmly refused.

Aged only 20 – young enough to be his daughter – she had had a strict and sheltered upbringing. Her mother had died 13 years before, her father Major Edward Patrick Hearne ten years later, and as a Roman Catholic she and her sister Marjory had been educated at Farnborough Hill Convent School. Since then Thérèse had done some secretarial work and a spot of modelling, but as she later put it she was 'very young and innocent'. The mere thought of getting into a taxi with a strange man was quite unacceptable. Yet when Harris rang her up a few days later to invite her to lunch at Rules, the Covent Garden restaurant, she accepted. Almost certainly Maurice Dean and Ann, his fiancée, were there to make up a foursome and this time he did take her home in a taxi. Thus began a courtship which grew over the next couple of years, with 'Bud', as she called him, proposing several times to Thérèse, who for no particular reason he soon addressed as 'Jill'. Thérèse was too pretentious a name, he told her. She, however, was not to be rushed. Much as she liked 'Bud', enjoyed his company and appreciated the protective way in which he treated her, always warning her about things she must be careful of, she wanted to be sure – particularly if she was to go against the strict teachings of her church and marry a divorcee.[10]

Not long after they first met, Harris had to spend several weeks abroad, and was more than happy to go since the destination was his own favourite country, Rhodesia. The defence requirements of British East and Central Africa had been under discussion since March 1934, when Air Vice-Marshal Newall and Brigadier Norman had recommended, inter alia, the establishment of a regular RAF unit, and the matter was discussed at government level when Godfrey Huggins, Prime Minister of Southern Rhodesia (by now separated from Northern Rhodesia), visited London that July and offered to help finance the project. A year later, with the Abyssinian situation worsening, Huggins asked if an RAF officer could be sent to advise on the formation of such a unit. Harris was the obvious choice by virtue of both his RAF rank and experience and also his affinity to the country.

Harris went out in mid-February 1936, having done plenty of homework in respect of recruitment and training of personnel, the provision and maintenance of aircraft, and, of course, costings. His note to CAS explaining how he intended to work was sensible, practical and realistic, showing a proper understanding of the likely attitudes and sensitivities of those on the spot. On arrival in Salisbury he was quickly on good terms with Huggins and his Minister for Justice and Defence, the Hon V.A. Lewis, and found everyone he met highly supportive – apart from the current OC Defence Forces, who was not air-minded and would soon be retiring. It took him barely three weeks to make his recommendations. The eventual goal, he considered, should be a normal air force; the immediate one a self-contained squadron. To this end a staff nucleus would be required; ab initio flying training should be carried out privately by De Havillands, and applied flying training 'in house'; some at least of the technical training should be provided at Halton; and the aircraft should be new, though obsolete, service-type machines provided by the RAF at nominal cost. Many other aspects were touched on, such as repair facilities, airfields, personnel (an exchange scheme was suggested), reserves, and the constitutional position of the future Royal Rhodesian Air Force commander, and the whole scheme was kept within the financial constraints laid down.

Harris's report was speedily considered and accepted, and before leaving he signalled Christopher Bullock, Permanent Under-Secretary in the Air Ministry, urging the allocation of Harts or Hinds. He had been in contact with his old friend Van Ryneveld, who advised strongly against the proposed Atlas aircraft in the local climate and pointed out the practical advantages of the Rhodesians using the same types of aircraft as the South African Air Force. Harris forcibly reiterated this point in his report to CAS in April, saying that his own experience of local flying conditions confirmed it, and pleaded again with Bullock for the Air Ministry to be generous in letting Southern Rhodesia have these aircraft at nominal cost. Referring to the relatively substantial sum of money the Rhodesians were prepared to contribute through this scheme to imperial defence, he stressed that in return for gifting the six aircraft at this stage the RAF would in effect be gaining trained pilots, a training flight, Halton apprentices, and eventually a complete squadron. The scheme went through, with long term consequences that included the establishment of the Royal Rhodesian Air Force and the Rhodesian contribution to the Empire Air Training Scheme.

So well had Harris's initial report been received that he was asked before departing to advise on those points in Southern Rhodesia that were vulnerable to attack. Thanks to the Minister for Mines and de Havillands he was loaned a Hornet Moth, which he used on two long and several short flights to inspect possible targets such as bridges, dams and power supplies. On one or two of these he was accompanied by Polly Brooks – the younger sister of the Patsy to whom he had given a teddy bear (p.32, Note 16), who was one of the most sought after single ladies of the day. Polly, now living in Australia, recalls their flying over Rusape on the way to visit the Henry Birchenough Bridge at Chipinga. Suddenly Arthur said 'I think it would be very nice if you would marry me – will you?' 'It's very nice of you to ask me but I think you are too old,' she replied.[11] Reporting afterwards on the more formal parts of his survey, Harris observed that while air attack was unlikely there was still the outside possibility of Italian 'stunt' operations against any peculiarly vulnerable objectives, especially the Victoria Falls bridge. Here there ought to be anti-aircraft defence, anti-sabotage measures, and arrangements to ensure that rolling stock would always be distributed on both sides. In any future projects of this type, he went on, the design should take account of vulnerability, while in other areas of development, such as electricity generation, the planners should beware of putting all their eggs in one basket. 'As distinct from an air offensive of such weight as to cause an enemy to desist, or at least to revert to a defensive employment of his air forces, the most effective defence is to avoid unnecessary vulnerability,' he concluded.[12] Here was the thinking bomber man at work, advising in accord with the local situation, but in one perceptive sentence happening to point towards Bomber Command's greatest single achievement in the Second World War: the forcing of the Luftwaffe to concentrate on home defence.

By the time Harris returned home in April the international situation had been greatly worsened by Hitler's military reoccupation of the Rhineland, and he was immediately drawn in to the discussions. Already the Chiefs of Staff had set work in hand in case military operations were needed, and on 15–16 April 1936 he joined Courtney at a meeting with French and Belgian representatives to discuss joint air action in the event of German aggression across their frontiers. Only Courtney is formally recorded as speaking but Harris would certainly have had his say. A variety of practical matters were considered, including availability of airfields, operating methods and intelligence, but they had to make it clear that the present condition of the RAF was unsatisfactory for European operations of any magnitude on account of the expansion programme.[13]

Meanwhile the JPSC was being reinforced. With the mounting pressure of work Harris and his Army and Navy counterparts were becoming so preoccupied with the activities of their own departments that they could devote little time to combined planning, so each was given a deputy (Group Captain Hugh Fraser on the RAF side). The three would work together full-time in Whitehall, though remaining answerable to their own departments.[14] Harris was therefore better able to concentrate on purely RAF matters and to exert his influence on such issues as the specifications for new long-range bombers. The responsibility for drawing these up and processing them was not his as DD Plans, as some writers have claimed; it lay with the Deputy Director of Operational Requirements, Group Captain R.D. Oxland. Nevertheless, Harris saw and commented on some of the papers and contributed his ideas at some of the key meetings. He emphasised, for example, the problems of operating in the tropics, where the heat and at times the height above sea level could seriously affect performance; he urged that the range of the new aircraft should at least equal that of foreign aircraft; and, particularly important, he stated that 'owing to the trend towards limitation of the numbers of first-line aircraft, it is essential that our limited total first-line strength should dispose of the maximum possible offensive power for a European war.'[15] The two specifications B12/36 and P13/36, issued in July and September, certainly went along with this principle and led to the creation of the heavy bomber force that Harris would eventually command – though he did not envisage the complementary role of the light bomber, to be so successfully fulfilled by the Mosquito.

Harris was much exercised too by the practicalities of operating the new aircraft. Prompted by a paper written by a young graduate of the Long Navigation Course who was severely critical of the RAF's navigation standards and its wastage of the talents of those who had completed the course, he told Sholto Douglas, now Director of Staff Duties, that Plans had to assume that the bomber crews would be able to reach their objectives, if necessary at extreme range. 'I wish I could believe,' he went on, 'that under the existing conditions in the Service there was any possibility of expecting this essential state of affairs to materialise. I do not believe it.' In blunt language Harris drew on his own experience to endorse the writer's criticisms, to describe the general attitude in the Service towards navigation as deplorable and its standard as lamentable, and to suggest ways of improving matters. In his view, however, the biggest enemy of operational efficiency was 'the personnel policy of attempting to make our pilots masters of all trades so that they never have time to become masters of their own – they are in effect a posting pool for the entire Service. We shall never have an efficient Striking Force . . . until every first-line aircraft is always manned by a complete crew that have worked together through at least one complete squadron training programme.'[16] In effect he was calling for many of the RAF's ground tasks to be undertaken by specialists and for the aircrew to be able to concentrate on learning and practising their collective flying skills.

Such purely RAF matters were bread and butter to Harris at this time, but there were also inter-Service arguments, particularly between him and Tom Phillips. Saward describes the running battle to decide whether a new anti-ship bomb (or mine) should be developed by the Air Ministry or the Admiralty and who should control it operationally.[17] Lord Swinton recalls the debate on the control of maritime aviation. 'These arguments were assembled and deployed with a wealth of practical detail and experience. Two young men on the Air Staff contributed greatly to this work – Group Captains Harris and Slessor. These arguments won the day after long and sustained action. The Navy was given control of the aircraft actually carried on ships; all other aircraft and air activities remained the responsibility of the RAF and the Air Staff.'[18] Lord Ismay refers to the interminable, always inconclusive dispute about the vulnerability of modern warships to air attack. On one occasion Phillips was insisting that if Italy entered the war the Royal Navy would still have free use of the Mediterranean regardless of the strength of the Italian Air Force, whereupon Harris exploded: 'One day, Tom, you will be standing on your bridge and your ship will be smashed to pieces by bombers and torpedo aircraft. As she sinks your last words will be "that was a bloody great mine!"[19] Notwithstanding their professional differences the two were good friends, and none had greater regrets than Harris when the gist of his prophesy was fulfilled and Admiral Tom Phillips and Captain John Leach, his friendly sparring partner from Camberley days, were both killed aboard HMS *Prince of Wales* off Malaya in December 1941.

Usually, of course, the three Directors of Plans worked well together, and never better than in the production of their joint 'Appreciation of the Situation in the Event of War against Germany in 1939'. Circulated under the names of Phillips, Colonel Ronald Adam and Harris on 26 October 1936, this first outlined the probable attitudes and military strengths of the principal nations that were likely to be involved in such a conflict. Thereafter, while not considering the possibility that the war might start in the East, it was on the whole a reasonably accurate forecast of how the war would develop in its earlier stages. The writers rightly drew attention to the advantages of a totalitarian regime over a democracy in making peacetime preparations for war, and thus of the military superiority it would possess at the outset. They also made clear their grave doubts about the ability of France to cope with a German assault, and in considering Germany's strategy thought she might start by trying to seize control of Holland, Belgium and France. Alternatively she might concentrate directly on Great Britain, using her naval and air forces and exploiting Britain's vulnerability to air attack in the attempt to deliver a knock-out blow. Here, as we can now see, the planners went much too far in predicting casualties of up to 150,000 a week, but nobody at that time had any experience of large-scale air war other than the effects of the raids on London in 1916–17, and there were plenty of other people who shared their forebodings.

The appreciation went on briefly to defence measures, and then to ways of using bombers in a counter-offensive during the early critical phase. The first option, namely to try to demoralise the Germans by attacking their cities, was quickly discarded as impracticable and unrealistic. The second, to hit some type of target whose security was vital to Germany during the critical period, was also seen as irrelevant in the expected time scale, and no such critical target could be identified anyway. The only remotely feasible option was to devote most of the effort to attacking the enemy's air striking force and its maintenance organisation in an attempt to reduce the scale of his attack – a counter-force strategy, using the modern jargon. This third option would apply equally if Germany decided on a land offensive.

In the later stages of what they foresaw would be a long war, however, the three planners considered that 'our ability to develop our own industrial output of munitions and to restrict that of Germany might well be the deciding factor', and 'the intervention of Russia would go far towards making the Allied counter-offensive possible'. Here they had succeeded in identifying two of the most crucial factors that were to lead to the defeat of Germany in the Second World War, the others being the protection of the sea lanes (also stressed by the planners) and the intervention of the USA (which they wrongly assumed would not happen). In producing this paper Harris himself felt that he and his colleagues could almost claim to be among the major prophets – apart from their failure to predict the incredibly stupid mistakes Germany was going to make. While we may think his claim a shade exaggerated, their Appreciation and subsequent planning paper of 15 February 1937 did provide the essential framework for the rearmament programme that was now being set in train. Moreover, firmly reflecting Harris's convictions, they spelt out the long-term strategic role envisaged for the recently formed Bomber Command: 'to attack objectives whose destruction will reduce the German war potential'.[20] His views were strongly reflected when a friend to whom Jill had introduced him, the MP Ralph Assheton, spoke in the 1937 debate on the Air Estimates.

In May 1937 Harris departed. He had spent almost four years in the corridors of power. He had contributed much to the development of both RAF and national defence policy over a period of rapidly mounting apprehension about the future. Importantly too, he had made many friends in high places and confirmed his reputation as a man who knew his business, was ever prepared to speak his own mind and make decisions, and would be well able to hold operational command in the war that was almost bound to come. Jim Barnes, an Assistant Secretary with whom he had worked, wrote to him just after the war and expressed the opinion held at the time by himself and many others (though not all!): 'If there was no war you might be out on your ear; if there was a war you would have the highest command.'[21] Lord Swinton, who relinquished office as Secretary of State for Air in May 1938 and is widely regarded as the best of all those who held that position, chose to publish in his memoirs the letter which Harris wrote to him at that time:

Those of us who worked for you, and those also who are experiencing now in the Service the results of your labours, realise the vast debt of gratitude which the country owes to you and will, we feel sure, some day repay. Meanwhile I can only hope that some day in future I shall again be permitted to work under you, and that you yourself are content as indeed you should be, on looking back over what must have been a desperately hard term of office, magnificently completed in a manner which has left the whole Service yours to a man![22]

Now, after a ten-year gap, Harris was selected to return to the bomber force, this time on promotion to Air Commodore as AOC 4 Group, whose headquarters was about to be located at Linton-on-Ouse. He took over five front-line stations, Boscombe Down, Dishforth, Driffield, Finningley and Leconfield, all of which had hitherto been part of 3 Group. Most of the ten squadrons based on them were still equipped with ancient Virginias or elderly Heyfords, but 10 Squadron, at Dishforth, had just received the new Whitley heavy bombers and four more squadrons were soon to get them as well.[23] So for Harris the higher politics were behind him; this was the real world, with its dearth of every kind of equipment and a host of obstacles to be overcome if his growing force of more modern aircraft and their crews was to be prepared to go to war. To take just one example, in order to practise bombing (and Harris insisted on night as well as day training) ranges were needed, and Abbotsbury on the Dorset coast was considered ideal; he got it eventually, but only after long, bitter opposition from the protectors of the nearby swannery, and subsequent experience showed that the swans laid much better when freed from human interference.[24]

When waging such battles Harris was fortunate to have the backing of a C-in-C who he knew well and for whom he had the greatest respect, Sir Edgar Ludlow-Hewitt. Only two months after taking over in September, Ludlow-Hewitt despatched his first stern warning to the Air Ministry about Bomber Command's many shortcomings and the need for urgent action, not least in the sphere of navigational aids, and he and Harris kept in close touch, exchanging views on many practical issues. On one such occasion Harris protested that parachute escape drills were no substitute for proper design of the kind of escape facilities that could actually be used in emergency; few designers were practised pilots and their liaison with the airmen usually came too late to permit the kind of modifications which were really needed.[25] As AOC Harris was determined to give the interests of his crews the highest priority, just as he had done when commanding his squadrons. Moreover he understood how to handle his pilots. One Friday afternoon he was travelling on the *Flying Scotsman* to London when he spotted a Whitley formating at low level on the train. He noted its number, duly signalled 7 Squadron ordering the pilot to report to him for interview, and administered an informal warning. As he commented afterwards, 'anyone who can fly like that is worth keeping'.[26] He was a real pilots' AOC, a man who dealt with them with both firmness and understanding, whom they saw piloting himself around the stations in his own light aircraft and who they knew had done his full share of operational flying in his earlier days. On 18 February 1938 he was reminded of this when he accompanied his C-in-C to Boscombe Down to see his old squadron, No 58, presented with its official badge.[27]

During his year at Linton, Harris persevered in his efforts to persuade Jill to marry him. These were supported by Ralph Assheton and his wife Sylvia, whom they used to visit at their home near Clitheroe and who were eager to reassure her about his suitability as a husband. So at weekends, whenever his duties permitted, he went to London to meet her; if he could not get away he arranged for her to come and stay in York, and early in 1938 his attentions were rewarded and they became engaged. Marriage plans for the summer were quickly laid and when news arrived that he was soon to leave 4 Group and become AOC Palestine and Transjordan, where his new wife would be able to accompany him, the gods seemed to be smiling. Then, out of the blue, his diary was thrown into disarray when Sir Cyril Newall, now Chief of Air Staff, told him he was needed for an urgent and secret mission to North America. He would be going with Sir Henry Self, a senior civil servant, and three other experts[28] to investigate the possibility of ordering aircraft for early delivery to the RAF in order to accelerate the expansion programme. Brief though the trip would be, it was for Harris not just a clear mark of the reputation he had established but a wonderful opportunity to get to know some of the leading American airmen. He did not waste it.

The team embarked for the USA on 20 April and spent a fortnight visiting a variety of factories. Harris was highly impressed with their business efficiency and in particular by the small Lockheed Company, whose Super Electra airliner struck him as ideal for adaptation for reconnaissance work. When he showed interest in a version modified for this purpose and stressed how pressed he was for time they produced overnight an excellent mock-up version. Knowing that in England something similar would take months, he felt certain they would make good all their promises, which they did. The result was the RAF's first aircraft order from the USA, for 200 Hudsons. They, and more of their kind ordered later, proved invaluable for anti-submarine patrols in the early part of the war, and the 400 Harvard training aircraft that were also ordered – the first of some 5,000 – were no less important.[29]

Harris was less impressed by what he saw of the Army Air Corps. Partly at Ludlow-Hewitt's suggestion he had been instructed to stay on for another week after the rest of the team departed, in order to find out what he could about American aviation, including air traffic control, navigational systems, crew policy and airfield facilities. As Ludlow-Hewitt wrote to Newall, 'what we badly want here is first-hand information from an experienced officer who is thoroughly familiar with our difficulties and problems'.[30] The report which Harris wrote was not only thorough, perceptive and critical but also laced with the dry humour and apposite turn of phrase that were becoming widely associated with him and making many of his missives considerable fun to read. To take two light-hearted examples, he described the American War Office as lacking the grandiose entry of Berlin's Air Ministry and the grubby greeting of Adastral. 'In their place a strictly utilitarian and obviously efficient hot-dog stand occupies most of the front hall. I left during the lunch hour, as colonels and messengers elbowed for counter room and access to the communal mustard pot, Hamburger in hand – I would hate to eat the victuals in evidence on the counter.' Later he castigated the internal air conditioning. 'By an ingenious, complicated and very expensive mechanism a pallid populace achieves wholesale and whole time semi-asphyxiation in a damp, tropical and fume-laden atmosphere during even the balmiest temperate spring. They conclude that this is an astonishing achievement in engineering. So do I.'

More seriously Harris commented expertly and in considerable detail on a wide range of flying and equipment matters that he had enquired into during brief visits to several aviation establishments. He was impressed by the civil air traffic control organisation with its 'beam and radio compass' system, its lavish equipment and its ample staffing, but in most other respects including navigation, crew training, fog and night flying landing gear, and ground and ancillary equipment, he felt the RAF had little to learn. He was critical of the B17 'Fortress', shown to him by Colonel Bill Olds; while it had long range and great load-carrying capacity, it could not outspeed a modern fighter and would be practically defenceless against one. Just one subject was closed to him: the Norden bombsight, about which he had been specifically asked to enquire. Nevertheless, with the aid of several high-balls he did elicit some information from officers in one of the Fortress squadrons, and General Andrews told him it was the US Navy which not only refused to allow the release of information on the Norden outside America but also kept the latest improvements secret even from the Army. Harris's conclusions were firm: 'neither in its equipment nor organisation can the American Air Force be counted among the first-class air powers'. America had money, enthusiasm, enormous industrial potential, and a vast reservoir of potentially efficient personnel, and could certainly have a magnificent Air Force if it decided to, but at present it possessed only an elaborate piece of window dressing. These were not views which he kept to himself: he had stated them frankly to the senior officers he had met, including General Arnold, and his honest, no-nonsense approach – based on recognised expertise – had done him no harm. Here was the start of the friendships with senior American airmen that were to be so invaluable in war and would endure for the rest of his life.[31]

Hardly was Harris back home in early June than Newall told him he was no longer going to Palestine but to Fighter Command, as SASO (Senior Air Staff Officer) to Sir Hugh Dowding. Given his background this was a surprising posting and he himself was far from pleased. Dowding had been Air Member for Research and Development when he was in Plans and the two had had lengthy disputes over matters that reflected, in his view, the fact that Dowding was out of touch with flying. Harris told Newall that he could not envisage the two of them working together effectively, but the CAS was not persuaded to relent until his argumentative subordinate added that he was about to get married and his fiancée's trousseau was entirely sub-tropical. The Palestine posting was reinstated and Keith Park went to Fighter Command instead.[32] So when Harris and Jill were married on 17 June 1938 at the St Marylebone Registry Office it was in the knowledge that their honeymoon would be aboard ship, for two days later they boarded the SS *Corfu* for Palestine. The wedding had been a happy occasion, marked by a reception at the Dorchester organised by Adeline Tresfon whose husband, Jean, Harris had first met in his capacity as Managing Director and later Chairman of Boulton-Paul Aircraft Limited. The four of them had become close friends and would remain so.

The Harrises were assured of a warm welcome in Jerusalem. In an exchange of letters with Air Commodore Roderic Hill, the old friend from whom he was to take over as AOC on 13 July, he had been well briefed on such practical matters as dress, the servants whom he and Jill would inherit in the residence,[33] and social commitments; and his financial anxieties – understandable in view of his obligations to his first family – had been allayed. Hill had also mentioned the very good relations that existed with the Army, whose new commander, General Haining, was 'all out for the RAF'.[34] Harris and his wife were not to be disappointed. Their beautifully appointed house, the Villa Haroun al Raschid, was situated on open ground amid olive groves with magnificent views over the city, and they were very soon organised to receive guests. Their visitors' book was opened on the 20th, eight days later they hosted their first party for some 40 guests, and over the next year hardly a day passed without further entries. In addition to visitors from the RAF, the Army, the government and the police, the local business and cultural communities were also frequently represented, a clear indication of how seriously the Harrises understood the importance of knowing and being known, of how much they enjoyed entertaining, and of how well Jill was adjusting to the new way of life so suddenly thrust upon her. Their 21-year difference in age mattered not; they were remarkably well matched.

Intense as was the social round – and there were plenty of official func-tions to attend and less formal hospitality to be received – much work had to be done. The Army and the RAF, co-operating closely together, were charged with helping the civilian authorities in Palestine to preserve law and order in the face of steadily increasing hostility between the Arab majority and the growing Jewish minority. The tension had been growing ever since, in the Balfour Declaration of 1917, Great Britain had promised to establish a

Jewish National Home, and in 1936 the pressure of immigrants from Europe led to the first Arab rebellion. Since then there had been further outbreaks of violence by sizeable rebel bands and the military garrison, including the RAF, had been reinforced. It was two months after Harris's arrival that the rebels suffered their biggest defeat by air action, when 12 aircraft attacked a 400–500 strong gang gathered near Deir Ghassana and, despite heavy ground fire, killed some 130 men. Harris immediately received a personal letter of congratulations from the Governor, Sir Harold Mac-Michael: 'We wanted something of this kind badly and I am delighted.'[35] Since the rebels could not risk a repetition of such great losses they now tended to disperse in smaller groups, often lodging overnight in villages, and this led Harris and his staff to devise an air cordon, or airpin, system. This involved a few aircraft, usually Gladiators, dropping warning leaflets and then trying to prevent anyone leaving a particular village until the ground forces could arrive and search it. Once the Army was convinced of the system's value – and General Haining took little persuading – it rapidly proved its worth, both in Palestine and, in early 1939, in Transjordan.[36]

An Army officer who did need a little persuading was the new divisional commander, Bernard Montgomery, who told the AOC on arriving that the rebellion was a job for policemen, not aircraft. Harris quickly replied that it needed all the available forces; if the General did not need air assistance the other Army commanders would be delighted to have his share. Very soon he was as insistent on air support as anyone else, and Harris took pride in the fact that Monty, who was only too willing to learn anything new and learnt fast, obtained his first real understanding of air co-operation from him.[37]

It is from this period that we gain our first real picture of how Harris was perceived as a personality by someone who worked with him at close quarters. On 24 November 1938 Flying Officer James Pelly-Fry, who had spent three years with 216 Squadron, apprehensively reported to Harris's office on the top floor of the King David Hotel on appointment as his Personal Assistant. He saw sitting behind a large desk a broad-shouldered man with sandy hair and lots of medal ribbons: 'He was wearing half-moon spectacles and when he looked unblinkingly at me over the top of them he gave me a slightly unnerving feeling that I was transparent.' Quickly the tension eased. Having welcomed Pelly-Fry, enquired about his time with 216 Squadron and established that so far he had nowhere to live, Harris invited him to stay for a short time at his residence – a much appreciated gesture towards a young officer who had never before needed to fend for himself in such matters. Then, on their way home to lunch, Harris said he had decided not to use his PA's Christian name but to call him 'Pelly', another informal and pleasing touch. Soon Jill was helping to welcome him with a gin and tonic and as the conversation reverted to 216 Squadron and

Africa he very quickly felt at home. Three days later, his search for lodgings proving fruitless, he was invited to stay on at the villa as one of the family. Nothing could have pleased him more and as time went on he found that in Harris's company a completely new vista was opening up 'because he was so well versed in all manner of subjects outside Service life; he read books avidly and talked in his very stimulating and articulate style.' For Pelly, a breath of spring had arrived, thanks to one man and his wife.[38] On duty it was different:

> Bert Harris was a singularly good example of an energetic commander who wanted to get about and see for himself what was going on. On these occasions two pairs of eyes have a much better chance of putting the visit to maximum advantage although I soon appreciated that his speed of perception and rapid comprehension was exceptional. He not only rapidly grasped the important issues, together with the implications that they raised, he was swift and forthright in his reactions. I have never known any other man who was so quick to appreciate, so accurate in his judgement and so swift to take action. Whenever he spoke about the particular visit afterwards he was pungent in comment and completely articulate. It was a joy to listen to him. Equally, his written word, whatever the subject matter, was succinct and had that certain style about it that was masterful.

Then, the day's work done, it was back home to shed immediately 'that forbidding mien, the silent stare, and when necessary his explosive and withering comment. There was the loving Jill to welcome him and the affection was returned in kind so much that I wanted to vanish like a mirage because I felt I was intruding. The spell would be broken by a gruff voice saying "Pelly, let's have a damned good whisky and soda".'[39]

Pelly noted much else. He welcomed the opportunity to watch his master inspecting his units, to learn what mattered to him and the methods he used. What Harris expected was 'competence from his subordinates and the ability to use their equipment to good purpose rather than a special tidy-up prior to his arrival.' Harris also took keen practical interest in new types of aeroplanes ('he was the first Air Commodore in my experience who was a practising pilot') and when he went to inspect one of the first Lysanders he insisted on test-flying it. The squadron commander must have had his misgivings, for when Pelly asked for a try he was told it was much too precious for PAs to use for joyriding. On another occasion Harris refused to let Pelly fly him to meet Montgomery at Haifa; he would pilot the Gordon himself and take Admiral Sir Dudley Pound as his passenger. If Pelly wanted to come too he could fly his own aircraft. There was the occasional spot of leave, too, most notably in March 1939 when Harris, Jill, Lady Haining, Pelly and an armoured car escort motored to Akaba and back. Pelly describes the trip in detail, the mountain driving, the camping under the stars, the fishing trip, the unforgettable scenery, the visit to Petra, and Harris's insistence, as one of the drivers, on allowing no natural hazards to defeat them.[40]

Not long after this both Jill and Pelly noticed that Harris seemed to be losing his appetite; for a man who not only enjoyed his food but also liked doing his own cooking (and was good at it) this was unusual and disturbing. Since both of them were much younger and inexperienced in such matters they were at a loss to know how to handle the situation, and their attempts to persuade him to consult the RAF doctors met with blunt refusals. Eventually, in June, with his master's health clearly deteriorating, Pelly fixed himself a weekend off at Heliopolis and a discreet interview with the C-in-C, Sir William Mitchell. There he unburdened himself: the AOC was far from well, he and Jill had tried to help and failed, he had not told Jill of his mission, and in his view Harris ought to be got back to England for specialist treatment.[41] Pelly himself never found out whether his intervention had any direct effect, but almost certainly it did. A month later, on 24 July 1939, Harris – now an Air Vice-Marshal – was given a medical board at Sarafand and ordered back to England, where he was seen at the Central Medical Establishment on 12 August, diagnosed as having a duodenal ulcer, and sent initially on a month's sick leave.[42] But for this he would have remained in Palestine until about the end of the year, as Newall had told him to expect,[43] and would have missed at least the initial stages of the European war.

Notes

1. While Harris's record of service shows him becoming DD Plans on 3 April 1934, the Air Force List gives 13 January 1934 as the date when he succeeded Portal. Richards, *op.cit.* pp.100, 104, gives Portal's recollections of his days in that appointment. Since the post was established at Group Captain rank its incumbent was called a Deputy Director and there was no 'Director of Plans'.
2. Terraine, *The Right of the Line*, p.7.
3. Information from Marigold, Rosemary and Peter Tomlinson.
4. Richards, *op.cit.* p.100; Slessor, *The Central Blue*, p.144.
5. Terraine, *op.cit.* pp.25–30 discusses the work of the DRC and Scheme A.
6. AIR 9/69, E88, dated 29 May 1934.
7. Saward, *op.cit.* pp.46, 50.
8. AIR 9/71, E2 (4 July 1935).
9. Saward, *op.cit.* p.44.
10. Based on Saward, pp.47–8; Jill's comments on Saward Tape 10; Tomlinson discussions. Some accounts suggest that they first met at lunch with Maurice and Ann Dean, but Jill made it clear they met at St Ermine's.
11. Letter from Polly Singleton to her sister Patsy. Polly added that she was surprised to hear that he had later proposed to Jill, who was even younger. Polly later married Sandy Singleton, the Worcestershire cricketer.

12. This account is based on AIR 9/66, Saward, *op.cit.* pp.48–50, and information from Group Captain Richard Sykes.
13. AIR 9/74.
14. Lord Ismay, *Memoirs*, p.76.
15. AIR 9/77, minutes of ORC Meetings 27 May 1936, 22 June 1936.
16. DD Plans minute dated 3 November 1936 (see p.46, Note 4), commenting on paper by Flight Lieutenant David Waghorn, who later joined Harris's staff at HQ 4 Group.
17. Saward, *op.cit.* pp.55–7; Folder H62. Harris himself proposed a particular version of this weapon which he entitled the H (Harris) bomb.
18. Swinton, *I Remember*, p.142.
19. Ismay, *op.cit.* p.240.
20. OH IV App.4; Harris, *op.cit.* p.26; Saward, *op.cit.* pp.50–4; Terraine, *op.cit.* p.49; Hyde, *British Air Policy between the Wars*, pp.391–2.
21. Letter from Sir James Barnes, Deputy Under-Secretary of State, 26 June 1965, Misc Folder 11.
22. Swinton, *op.cit.* pp.148–9.
23. The first two Whitley squadrons took part in the fly-past for the German Mission at Mildenhall on 19 October 1937.
24. Harris, *op.cit.* pp.26–7.
25. Ludlow-Hewitt Papers, Folder 11.
26. Peter Tomlinson recollections.
27. AIR 27/543.
28. Namely Mr J.G. Weir, an industrialist, Mr P. Rowarth (AEE) and Squadron Leader C.E. Horrix, a test pilot.
29. Harris, *op.cit.* pp.27–8.
30. Letter dated 7 April 1938, Misc Folder 2.
31. Folder H61; Saward, *op.cit.* pp.59–61; Harris, *op.cit.* pp.27–9.
32. Saward, *op.cit.* p.62; Orange, *A Biography of Sir Keith Park*, p.68.
33. Harris called the cook, Ali, who was not very good at his job, 'the best loafer in the business' – to Ali's delight.
34. Misc Folder 2.
35. Letter dated 16 September 1938, Misc Folder 2.
36. Report of RAF Operations in Palestine, Misc Folder 2. See also Harris, *op.cit.* p.29; Saward, *op.cit.* pp.63–4.
37. Harris, *op.cit.* p.30.
38. Pelly-Fry, *Heavenly Days*, pp.118–20.
39. *Ibid* p.122.
40. *Ibid* pp.124–34.
41. *Ibid* pp.135–7. Mitchell had first met Harris at Northolt in 1916 (p.37).
42. Harris personal file.
43. Newall to Harris 7 July 1939, Misc Folder 2.

Chapter 5

Back to business

So it was that as the summer of 1939 drew on and the war clouds gathered, Harris was both out of a job and lacking even a home of his own. Moreover, Jill was now heavily pregnant. Fortunately their friends Jean and Adeline Tresfon were quick to come to the rescue in their home at Gawdy Hall, in Norfolk, and very soon the quiet, relaxed environment was having its effect on his health. It was here on 3 September that he listened to Chamberlain's fateful statement that Britain was at war once again with Germany. His reaction was predictable and immediate. Regardless of the fact that he was still supposed to be convalescent he could rest no longer.

Knowing that his old friend Peter Portal was now Air Member for Personnel, Harris invoked the 'old boy net' and after some difficulty with congested telephone lines got through to the Air Ministry to ask for a job, preferably in Bomber Command. A few days later, after he had watched the surviving Wellingtons coming home from the first attack on the German Fleet, Portal came back with the news that Ludlow-Hewitt wanted a new AOC for 5 Group and would be delighted for him to take over the job. Having packed their essential belongings into a borrowed Austin, the Harrises promptly took the road to St Vincent's, which housed the Group Headquarters at Grantham.[1] Unfortunately 5 Group had not yet been told it was to receive a new master and Air Commodore R.B. Callaway was shattered when Harris marched into his office on 10 September with the announcement 'I've come to relieve you.' His embarrassed apologies were accepted, a saddened Callaway departed to 18 Group, and Harris assumed command.[2]

Flying Officer Peter Tomlinson, who as the recently appointed PA remembered this incident,[3] had in the previous year been interviewed by Harris for a similar post and wrote later about that first meeting and the impression it had created.

> I approached his desk and stood waiting. He was reading a paper – probably about me – and didn't look up so I had time to study him before he had a look at me. He was a large ginger man, rather pale with a complexion that obviously avoided the sun, with a ginger moustache and hair of a blondish rather than ginger colour. He was wearing black half glasses (obviously only for reading) and when he finally looked up he peered at me over the top of

them which gave him a rather severe look. He had a reputation for being a 'no nonsense' man and I could see why. At the same time he gave off a sort of inner warmth and when I was asked to sit down I had lost a lot of my anxieties. His questions were very much to the point and he seemed to harp on matters relating to night flying – perhaps he already sensed that the inevitable war would be fought by the Air Force at night. I knew at once that I was being talked to by a pilot still interested and active as such; we youngsters were quick to note that anyone above the rank of Wing Commander rarely left his desk to get into an aeroplane in those days. He was gruff and rather frightening but underneath human and considerate.[4]

Tomlinson subsequently observed his master's flying skills for himself.

On 22 September 1939 I collected an Oxford for his personal use. Next day he tried it out. I showed him the controls and did one circuit and landing with him sitting beside me. I was on my mettle – on that day the gods were with me. We came down nicely over the perimeter. A nice height. Steady and gentle. I hardly felt the wheels touch the ground. I had seldom done anything better. Harris glanced at me but never said a word, but I knew I was all right. He then took over and I could tell at once that there were years of experience behind what he was doing. I was wet behind the ears by comparison. But his landing was rougher than mine and I was pleased. After that he did most of the flying himself – fit or not fit.[5]

Thus began a friendship that was to last a lifetime. Very quickly both Harris and Jill were treating Tomlinson like another Pelly, an assistant whose official duties would extend into membership of the family circle, and soon he was accepting an invitation to take up residence with them. Shortly afterwards, on 13 October, their daughter Jacqueline was born and Tomlinson found himself taking on a variety of baby-associated tasks. Then, one day, to his disbelief and delight, Harris took him quietly aside and asked if he would agree to become Jackie's godfather. From now on 'Goffer', as Jackie came to call him, was virtually a full member of the Harris family and would build up an unrivalled knowledge and understanding of his master right up to his dying day.

One of Tomlinson's first tasks was to help the Harrises move into the official residence, a Georgian-style building in the centre of Grantham called Elm House (they moved in November to a larger house, Norman Leys).

His packing cases had arrived, full of things from the East, and I remember how quickly he was able to turn a rather sparsely furnished office of works house into a comfortable and attractive home. He had endless energy. Things were fairly humming at the HQ during the day. One of his first personal jobs

– an indication of the planning mind – was a visit to the local butcher. I clearly remember his name was Fensom, a man of the old school with blue apron and straw hat, and he must have been greatly astonished when a large Humber Pullman bearing an AVM's pennant pulled up outside his old-fashioned shop. They had a brief chat – respect on either side and a complete understanding. I recall the gist: 'I don't care what you do with your grade two meat. I want only the best.' Fensom lived up to it and whatever we were allowed on our ration cards was always the best.[6]

Tomlinson soon realised, however, that while the Harrises wanted to live comfortably and do things in style they were far from well off. Since Jill was not permitted to use the official car her husband decided to spend £25 on a powered bicycle she could use for shopping and asked Peter if he could lend him the money until his next pay cheque arrived. Air Vice-Marshal he might be, but he had no private income and was having to pay maintenance for his first family. Life was not easy.

Nor were things easy on the job. Indeed, Harris admitted later to rarely having been so depressed. He had inherited one of Bomber Command's three so-called 'heavy bomber' groups, whose ten squadrons were based on five well-built airfields in eastern England: Scampton, Waddington, Hemswell, Finningley and Cottesmore. All were equipped with the Handley Page Hampden, whose main virtues in Harris's opinion were its very reliable engines and the fact that it was available in some numbers. On the other hand it failed to meet many requirements of the normal specifications, not least in respect of defensive armament and crew comfort. Yet in due course, as he wrote, 'the crews made the best of it and, being strong and reliable, the aircraft did a sterling job'.[7]

Although Harris did not fly the Hampden himself he saw it as his first major task to familiarise himself with the aircraft and try to remedy its shortcomings under operational conditions. Within days he was writing the first of many letters to Ludlow-Hewitt, telling him about a host of practical issues which were being addressed, such as windscreens and wipers, cockpit heating, armour plating, compasses, bombs and bomb doors, operational speeds, and the need for second pilots.[8] Then on 29 September the destruction of five of his aircraft over the Heligoland Bight taught a salutary lesson about their vulnerability to enemy fighters in daylight.[9] Three days later, having visited Hemswell, Harris provided his C-in-C with a detailed and expert critique of the Hampden's rear armament: the gun itself seemed to be hopeless, the top mounting was 'a rickety, ill-designed, badly made piece of work which would not pass muster as a component of a bit of agricultural machinery', and despite the experience of the First World War – some of it his own – no round counter was fitted. The rear armament provision in the Hampden was in his view 'typical Handley Page junk', and the whole problem needed tackling by people in the armament and aircraft design departments with 'sufficient weight to get things done' (his underlining). Soon afterwards Air Vice-Marshal Tedder, responsible for research and development in the Air Ministry, called in to see Harris, showing himself 'very fully au fait with our armament difficulties and very determined to push on the solution'.[10]

Harris was also pressing for action on the aircraft's other really vulnerable point, the possibility of fire, especially around the outer unarmoured petrol tanks. While he knew of the endless experiments on self-sealing tanks he thought much more could be done to extinguish fires through better tank design and the provision of fire-extinguishing gases. He returned to such matters in discussions with his friend Sir Henry Tizard, telling him in November that he could not understand why the RAF still had no self-sealing tanks while everybody else did. 'Presumably Farnborough are still trying to make our self-sealing tanks play "God save the King", and meanwhile our people will die for lack of them, while our enemies live.' Eventually Harris was relieved to hear from Air Vice-Marshal Linnell, AOA (Air Officer Administration) at Bomber Command, that not only was armour plating on order for the Hampden outer tanks but delivery of self-sealing tanks would begin in February.

Meanwhile much else had been done to improve the aircraft, as Harris told Ludlow-Hewitt on 10 November, but many concerns remained. For example, more protective armour was needed, especially for the rear gunners; he was convinced that the normal 25 yard ranges were far too short for proper training in air gunnery; and, remembering the discomfort of his own long-distance winter flying at Worthy Down, he urged the importance of warmth, which meant among other things that flying clothing must be kept absolutely dry. Throughout the winter months of 1939–40, when fortunately his Group's operations were largely limited to North Sea patrols and security sweeps, many such practical flying matters engaged his attention; he was determined to give his crews the best conditions he could for the more serious operations that he knew must lie ahead.

Harris was much exercised too about the bombs his aircraft carried and how they could best be delivered. Tizard's November visit coincided with some successful low-level bombing trials, and the two men spent much time discussing, among other things, the problems of simplifying navigation to an objective, and the development of a gyro-stabilised bombsight. Harris followed this up with a strongly worded note to Ludlow-Hewitt, pleading the urgency of such a bombsight and recommending further pressure on the Americans to allow the purchase of the Norden sight. 'Alternatively, Americans being about as venal as most people, are our Secret Service really unable to get hold of a Norden sight or working drawings?' These were forlorn hopes, as Harris doubtless recognised, and in practice he and the rest of Bomber Command would have to rely on the mercies of the RAE (Royal Aircraft Establishment) at Farnborough, of which he was not greatly enamoured. After a bombsight meeting he attended in December he wrote to Ludlow-Hewitt:

> The fellow who sat at the top of the table and introduced all the negative and destructive scientific data and reasoning seemed to me to be an absolute menace. Very useful as a calculator or a designer to order, he seemed to be entirely divorced from any knowledge of practical requirements or from any apparent intention of fulfilling them if he could. On the other hand the fellow at the back who piped up with his very practical and sensible ideas for the solution of our troubles seemed to be exactly the type to be encouraged – scientifically capable both of appreciating and meeting practical require-ments. I got the impression that the rest of the Farnborough professional scientific wolf pack were in full cry after him ... I doubt whether he has survived to get on with the job ... but I hope he has ... and will get every assistance and encouragement.

This was not the first time Farnborough had been the target of Harris's trenchant criticisms. A week earlier he had written to an old friend at Harrogate, Air Commodore Andrews, about the RAE's attitude regarding the urgent need for body armour for air gunners, and concluded:

> Half the essential equipment which we so urgently require is not at our disposal merely for the reasons that most of our authorities, and Farnborough in particular, cannot get it into their heads that half a loaf is better than no bread, that they will invariably make the best the enemy of the good, and that hopeless delays are always occasioned while they try to put final and usually unessential finishing touches to some already reasonably serviceable article.

Harris's realistic, down-to-earth approach was equally illustrated in his attitude to the RAF supply system. Having requested the establishment of a depot for Hampden spares in 5 Group he was upset to hear that a new MU (Maintenance Unit) was already being set up for this purpose near Man-chester, and leapt into action: 'It is fundamentally wrong, even stupid, to make a triangle out of a line of supply when a direct line is all that is necessary.' Observing that 5 Group was the sole user of Hampdens for war purposes he urged that spares supply should be organised direct from the manufacturer: 'Minutes, let alone hours, days or weeks, will count when the war really starts.'

If the aircraft were important so were the men who flew them, and many of the ideas, criticisms and complaints which Harris fired at all and sundry originated from the friendly, informal crew-room discussions in which he regularly engaged. With only a handful of stations in his Group it was not difficult to visit them all frequently, and since several of his station commanders had previously served with him and knew him moderately well there was an atmosphere of co-operation and understanding. He would usually arrive in his Oxford, chat with the CO, and then go to the crew rooms, where his evident knowledge and experience of flying made him instantly acceptable. Since there were no operational training units in the early stages of the war the pilots received no formal training in fighting tactics and the AOC lost no opportunity to add his advice to that being delivered by the more senior squadron leaders. Tomlinson recalled one such incident. A pilot who had flown a daylight mission in a formation of three said: 'The enemy fighters simply and at their leisure came across us at right angles and blew the hell out of us.' Harris replied, 'You must turn away at once and get your rear gunners in a position to fire directly back at them.' Guy Gibson, who was one of Harris's pilots in 5 Group and whose book *'Enemy Coast Ahead'* excellently describes the operations and the atmosphere of those days, records his AOC joining in the merriment when Gibson was trying to explain in the Mess at Scampton why he had mistakenly found himself over Copenhagen.[11]

Afterwards it would be back to the office, where Harris would often sit quietly, smoking his Camels, stroking his moustache, just thinking. He kept a tidy desk, dealing with things as they came in and summoning his male civilian shorthand typist to take his dictation; his drafts were often cleared without amendments. In the mornings he could be irritable and liverish, and his PA usually advised favoured visitors to come in the afternoon; nevertheless he gave little indication that his ulcer was worrying him and steadfastly refused to diet or go anywhere near a doctor. He would normally lunch at home and only if unavoidable did he stay away overnight; his domestic life was highly important, but he and Jill understood the value of being able to entertain influential visitors at home and refused to allow the increasing difficulties of wartime to deter them unduly.

Their entertainment was not limited to the great and the good. Tomlinson recalled that his master was a great practical joker, a source of huge embarrassment to junior officers:

At weekends during the early part of the war young officers from the dominions and colonies with no homes to go to were invited to stay from a Friday to Monday at his official residence. Many came reluctantly 'on orders' in fear and trepidation. One of my duties was to set in front of some South

African or New Zealander a glass of phoney beer or some other. Some didn't notice and the joke went off hugely and the ice was broken but others immediately spotted the deception and dragged out the agony by ignoring the beer to the bitter end, suffering agonies throughout the meal until, on prompting, they had no option but to carry out the dumb charade to the best of their ability. Another toy was one of those things that you put under a cushion and when one sat down it made a rude noise. This was the agony of all agonies but it did break the ice and with the good food and good cheer they soon felt at home.

Given his Rhodesian background it is not surprising that Harris felt an affinity towards the men from the Dominions who had come to England as volunteers for pilot training. So when in November 1939 he found a lot of them being employed on basic aircraftman duties on his stations instead of being given preliminary training until flying school vacancies were available he lost no time in voicing his displeasure directly to Portal. In fact Harris had somewhat overstated the problem and Portal was able to allay his anxieties, but the AOC had made an important point. Nor was he slow to highlight other personnel matters, as in October when he expressed grave concern about his aircrews' lack of leisure amenities and the difficulties of travel at a time when the war had not yet hotted up and their morale needed to be maintained for the tests to come. Rather curiously his worries on this score did not extend to the ground personnel, who seemed to him to be living comfortably and out of danger and whose lot in wartime was 'cushy' indeed. If there was an element of truth in this in 1939 it would not long endure and he would soon change his tune.

On other matters too Harris was responsive to his aircrews' needs. He was appalled to be told, for example, that officers ordered to disperse to a scatter aerodrome could not proceed because they had literally no money to pay for their food: surely a suitable allowance could be devised? It was. There were promotion grievances, as he told Portal. Many career officers who could normally have expected substantive promotion were, under wartime rules, being granted only temporary promotion, doubtless at the instance of the Treasury, whereas the Navy was increasing considerably the number of substantive regular promotions. In October 1940 the doctors were criticised for being over-cautious in their medical assessments of fitness to fly; they needed telling that there was a war on, that top-class pilots were all needed, and that they should not be denied for specious reasons the opportunity to use their skills. Nor were the findings of courts of inquiry sacrosanct, even when supported by the C-in-C. A young pilot who had crashed his Hampden and been badly injured while practising a flarepath landing had been blamed for it by a poorly qualified court because he had not set his altimeter, but Harris, while not condoning the omission, disagreed that it had caused the accident; having carefully studied the evidence in the light of his own long experience, he was convinced that the pilot had made an error of judgement, no more. The AOC was not a man to tolerate injustice, as he had earlier shown when Ludlow-Hewitt criticised an experienced pilot from Cottesmore who had been killed when his aircraft crashed into a hill in bad weather. 'I am at a loss to see how accidents of this description can be avoided unless we restrict ourselves to fine weather flying,' replied Harris.

When firmness was required it was another matter. As Tomlinson said, 'if a dressing down was needed it would come with the most deadly force; many an officer would prefer fire and water than be up on the mat in front of him. He was always most decisive, knew exactly what he wanted and never suffered fools gladly. He never put up with nonsense from anyone.' Harris knew, too, that 'lack of moral fibre', as it soon became known, had to be firmly dealt with, and insisted on his COs applying the rules as laid down by the Air Ministry in April 1940. In 5 Group the man would be referred by his CO to the medical officer who, if he considered the individual was trying it on, would send him to the AOC. Tomlinson never knew what he said or the tactics he used, but often the man was talked round. As one said quite simply to Tomlinson afterwards: 'I'm going to go back and give it another go.'

Here then was the leader at work, blending firmness and discipline with encouragement, sympathy and understanding. But there was much more to it. By the end of 1939 it was clear to Harris that one of the greatest weaknesses of his Group lay in the absence of proper operational training. 'There is not so much a gulf as an abyss between the product of the training side and the article required, ready for use, by the operational side,' he wrote to Ludlow-Hewitt early in 1940. 'I assume that we are going to continue to get nothing but half-baked fledglings from the training organisation, and I make a still more confident assumption that our squadrons cannot operate now with efficiency for lack of trained personnel and training time, and will fail under the stress of real war casualties to produce even the present standard of accomplishment.' He therefore announced that he was starting his own elementary training organisation at Finningley. Suitably equipped, this would enable newly arrived crews to be taught and practise their operating procedures under realistic conditions on the ground, stop valuable aircraft being used merely as classrooms, reduce accidents, and free experienced aircrew for more important purposes. The unit would be partly staffed by full-time permanent schoolmaster-type instructors who possessed proper teaching skills and would cost much less than aircrew, who usually could not teach anyway. He returned repeatedly to this theme in the search for what he called 'bloodless training', pleading not only for an end to the 'incoherent bosh and balderdash which comprises the average Air Force instructional lecture' but also for proper accommodation and facilities, and for the provision of newer techniques such as cinema films. It was, however, one thing to press his case in strongly worded letters and quite another to persuade higher authority to act, and act quickly. So in practice Harris and Group Captain R.B. Maycock, Finningley's enthusiastic station commander, had to set up their school by self-help, without any extra establishment, and had to fight a steady battle to prevent the key personnel being posted. That they nevertheless managed to do well is shown in a letter Ludlow-Hewitt wrote to Richard Peirse, now DCAS, after a visit: 'A tour round the classrooms and a glance at the syllabus would be an education to anybody who had not had practical experience with the operation of large bombers.'[12]

There were many other frustrations on which Harris vented his feelings. In November 1939 he contrasted the alleged shortage of men for urgently needed building work on his stations with the BBC's announcement that national unemployment was increasing, mostly in the building trades. In December the continued presence of auditors on operational stations was an 'astounding unreality', a fantastic distraction of staffs hard-pressed to cope with the stark realities of war. In January 1940 he complained about the Treasury's attitude to the costs of running official residences and providing duty entertainment:

> I am already at my wits' end, let alone at my banker's wits' end, to keep my enormous establishment going without resorting to such palliatives as sacking most of the servants ... my car has already gone ... one will just be forced into that course in view of the wholesale inroads and depredations that the Treasury is making on one's meagre income from every conceivable direction. Personally I like blacking my own boots and cooking my own breakfast but I doubt if it would go with a swing officially in an AOC's residence.

Soon afterwards he was urging the Air Ministry to stop classifying everything Secret and forcibly telling Ludlow-Hewitt that the supply and organisation departments seemed not to realise that there was a war on.

> One gets the impression that the automatic reaction to every request is negative ... I have long ago adopted in my own Headquarters the principle that in any matters of everyday routine no-one has the power to say "no" to a unit. If they think it ought to be said they have to come to me. Yet all our urgent operational requirements seem to go meandering through a maze of offices and, no matter how urgent, to be subjected to endless scrutiny, delay, obstruction, idle chatter and superfluous minuting by whole legions of departmental subordinates, some of whom quite obviously haven't the vaguest idea what it is all about.

Ludlow-Hewitt 'got quite a kick out of this' but foresaw no improvement except as a result of a devastating German bombing raid. Then in February Harris asked, in the interests of security, for all civilian workers in messes on operational stations to be replaced by airmen or airwomen.

Unrealistic though some of Harris's ideas and protestations might be and irritating as they were to some of their recipients, they showed nonetheless an intensively active and fertile mind, eager to leave no stone unturned in the effort to prepare his Group for the concentrated operations that lay ahead. In the event these began in April 1940 when the Germans attacked Denmark and Norway, and they coincided with the departure from Bomber Command of the man whom Harris described as 'the most brilliant officer I have ever met in any of the three services': Sir Edgar Ludlow-Hewitt.[13] For Harris this seemed a disaster at the time and the two exchanged warm letters, with Ludlow-Hewitt saying how he had followed with great interest Harris's successful efforts to increase the strength of the Hampdens. 'The new and enterprising scheme which you have started at Finningley will, I am sure, do for the crews what you have already done for the aircraft.' A confidential note which he wrote for Portal, his successor, read:

I have had considerable experience of Air Vice-Marshal Harris's work and am very impressed with the rare qualities of personality which arise from an exceptionally active and stimulating mentality. He has an exceptionally alert, creative and enterprising mind balanced by long practical experience together with energy and force of character to give his ideas practical shape and realisation. He has rendered great service in respect of improvements in the technical equipment of the aircraft in his command, and also in the creation and organisation of novel methods of dealing with the extremely difficult problems of crew training. His particular talents lie mainly along practical lines, but his ideas are inspired by an unusually well developed imagination, and it is this combination which makes him a very valuable officer in any task where creative ideas and the energy to put them into effect are required. As a commander his exceptional air experience gives him a sympathetic insight into the attitude of mind of the crews, which is well understood and appreciated by them.

Peter Tomlinson, shown this note in 1996, commented: 'this is dead right'.[14]

Upset though Harris was at Ludlow-Hewitt's departure, he was certainly not inclined to complain about the choice of Portal to succeed him. The two of them had kept in touch ever since their days at Worthy Down and as convinced 'bomber men' had great respect for each other's abilities. It was just as well. Five days after Portal's arrival at Bomber Command the Germans launched their attack on Denmark and Norway and three days later,

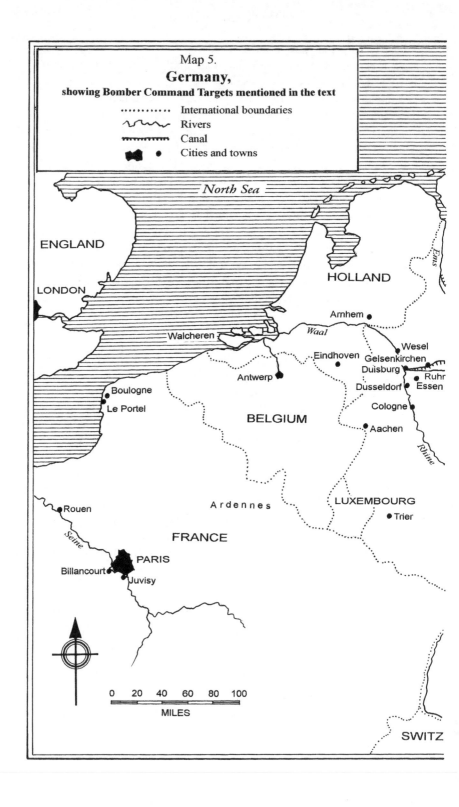

on 12 April, six of a force of 12 Hampdens were lost when the squadron
commander exceeded his orders by trying to attack a German warship in
Kristiansand harbour. Harris spent some hours that night at Waddington
discussing this episode with the survivors and had to tell Portal that, despite
what 'he thought he had previously and adequately expressed in all
squadrons', the leader had not adopted the proper tactical formation. Harris
received an understanding but firm reply. Meanwhile Portal had already told
all his AOCs that it was now Cabinet policy to conserve the bomber force,
which implied the avoidance of unprofitable operations.[15]

In practice, for the heavy bombers – including the Hampdens – this
meant that they would no longer be used by day, and during the Battle of
France their support for the Army was largely restricted to raids on factories
and oil targets far behind the enemy lines. On 19 June, however, came the
first of several precision attacks on the Dortmund-Ems Canal, which Harris
recognised in a signal warmly commending all concerned at Hemswell and
Scampton for the crews' outstanding skill and resolution. The best known of
these attacks came on 12/13 August, when Flight Lieutenant Learoyd,
piloting the last of a force of five Hampdens, broke the critical aqueduct and
was awarded the Victoria Cross. Harris was equally enthusiastic when
Bomber Command's second VC of the war went to another 5 Group airman,
Sergeant John Hannah, for his heroism over Antwerp on 15 September.
'This is one of the clearest examples of most conspicuous bravery and
extreme devotion to duty in the presence of the enemy under the most
harassing conditions that I have come across,' he wrote. These were but the
highlights of the Group's intensive operations against German invasion
barges, airfields, communications, and even Berlin, during the critical
months of the Battle of Britain. This was a team effort, as Harris and his men
understood. Concluding a brief letter about Luftwaffe casualties, Harris told
Sir Hugh Dowding at Fighter Command on 7 September:

'All my fellows are full of admiration for the magnificent efforts of the
fighters, and are almost getting to the stage where they are beginning to
hope that you will leave a few for us.'

Replying a few days later, Dowding wrote:

'I assure you that we shall not grudge you any Germans which you can
blow up on the other side. There are still plenty left! Thank you for your
appreciation of the fighter pilots; they are indeed magnificent.'[16]

These two strongly contrasting personalities might have had their differences in the past, but now there was mutual respect, with Dowding
certainly not averse to Bomber Command taking the war directly to the
enemy. Harris, one of those who believed that Dowding was unjustly treated
after the Battle of Britain, later called him 'the only commander who won
one of the decisive battles of history and got sacked for his pains.'[17]

Yet while that battle was being fought under the full glare of 1940-style publicity (shared to some extent by Bomber Command), the Hampdens were embarking upon a new silent war, one which neither then nor subsequently received the recognition it deserved but did, in fact, contribute much to the eventual defeat of Germany. Having interested himself in 'bomb-mines' when Deputy Director of Plans, and having learnt in late 1939 that the Germans were already laying magnetic mines, Harris pressed for them to be developed by the British and used for aerial minelaying. It then transpired that the Hampdens were the only aircraft suitable to lay them, and by April 1940 they were conducting their first such operations in enemy waters. Almost immediately there were criticisms from on high – though not from Portal – especially after three aircraft were lost on one night and nine more returned still carrying their mines (or 'vegetables' as they were normally referred to). Harris decided to set out his stall for the benefit of the Air Ministry. If the mines were brought back, he explained to Portal, it was because the Admiralty rightly insisted that they be laid accurately or not at all. The weather, therefore, was all-important but all too often very hard if not impossible to predict. What he went on to say was to apply just as much throughout his years as C-in-C Bomber Command as it did when he wrote it on 17 April 1940; it may all seem obvious now, but at the time he believed it had to be said. It is essential to an understanding of Harris's approach to operational decision-making:

As you so well know, the problem of deciding whether to send the aircraft out or not has to be decided in the light of the most inexact science of all, and even then on an amount of information not comparable to that available in peacetime. One might describe it as being one-third a scientist's job, one-third a bookmaker's job, and the remaining third as pure hunch. It is 25 years since I was first faced with guessing the weather for night flying. Touching wood ... my guesses so far have been as good as most people's. From time to time the luck will be with us and we shall get away with it more than the factors would appear to justify. From time to time we shall guess wrong and meet, perhaps, with terrible disaster. Such occurrences, as you well know, are inseparable from the occasion, but they will not be avoided by the Air Ministry sending on semi-official instructions unrelatable to hard realities. My method is to allow station commanders to decide, and I only overrule them when I think it is necessary ... I am the only person close enough in touch with all the factors relating to my own aircraft and crews, and the weather and the job, and in a position to give adequate weight to them all when the moment arrives to decide. The first requirement is to remain as unflustered as possible, an attitude made no easier to achieve by the receipt of advice, however well meant, from people in Whitehall who know nothing about my aircraft, or my crews, or the details of the weather, or the minutiae of the technical aspects of the job in hand.[18]

So from now on minelaying was a permanent task for the Hampdens, one which Harris, as Slessor later wrote, took to with 'far-sighted enthusiasm', and which Harris himself called 'the one really bright spot in 5 Group's operations.'[19] In these early days, however, it was hard to know what was actually being achieved, and he kept up a barrage of complaint to both Bomber Command and the Air Ministry about the failure of the Intelligence staffs to collate, assess and circulate the available information about his minelaying activities. Consequently not only were his crews disheartened and resentful at receiving no indication of the significance of their work but other Air Force commanders and staff knew nothing about it either. 'It is obvious to me,' he wrote to Louis Greig in October, 'that the Air Ministry's Intelligence Organisation for forwarding such information is futile. We have long abandoned any hope of getting any sense or any reasonably complete information out of them. We seriously contemplate employing a press-cutting agency to keep us informed.' Nor did he exempt the Admiralty from blame. He was sure they could do much more to provide information and could not help feeling that one reason for not doing so was 'their notorious jealousy of giving credit to anyone not a sailor for any successful work at sea.'[20] On the other hand he was unstinting in his praise for the contribution of his own Naval Liaison Officer to the planning and briefing of the minelaying operations, and he kept the lines open to Admiral Tom Phillips in the Admiralty, congratulating him on 3 May on the matelots' recent efforts and asking for his help in persuading the production people to step up the supply of 'vegetables'. The last was another of Harris's constant criticisms, as when he told Norman Bottomley, now SASO (Senior Air Staff Officer) at Bomber Command, about 'the grossly inefficient system, or entire lack of system, under which the mines are supplied to stations' and described 'the atmosphere of casualness, chaos and apparent lack of appreciation, outside Bomber Command, of these vast efforts being made.'

Linked with this were the charges Harris levelled at the public relations organisation. Convinced that the Germans would know by now that mines were being laid by aircraft he went so far as to send Portal a draft communiqué for issue to the press about these operations, and there ensued substantial dialogue with Air Commodore Harald Peake, Air Ministry Director of Public Relations, who paid him a visit. Gradually, in this as in other matters, the situation improved, with Squadron Leader W.A.J. Lawrence, now the Press Officer at Command HQ, exercising considerable influence, but Harris remained far from satisfied. Indeed in a letter to Portal's successor, Sir Richard Peirse, in October, he urged fuller press publicity for Bomber Command's overall achievements in recent months. He saw no reason, for example, not to release some of the damage reports quoted in a recent Intelligence Summary;[21] but while one can applaud his desire to secure fuller recognition of the bombers' activities he seems to have been accepting too readily the accuracy of information and assessments which supported his own convictions. The strange world of intelligence was not one of which he, in common with many other senior officers at that time, had all that much understanding.

Harris's rather subjective approach to such matters was reflected too in his ready acceptance of the claims made by crews to have found their way to their targets. Reporting on 5 Group's operations against precision targets in Germany in May 1940 he spoke of their standard of navigation having improved considerably, with most crews expected to be able to arrive within a few miles of their objectives by dead reckoning and W/T.[22] This is not to say that he was complacent – he was pressing hard for a navigator-operated radio compass to be provided for use by Hampdens in bad weather and, as he told Bottomley in November, felt utterly frustrated at the attitude of the signals staff: 'They are always promising us something better than that which we know to be thoroughly satisfactory from outside sources and are always signally failing to produce anything at all worth having.' The promised TR1335 equipment (later known as GEE) about which Bottomley had just informed him typified this approach, he said, and the whole business left him in a state of complete despair.[23] One can sympathise. Throughout his career he had railed against the 'experts' for their failure to produce what was actually needed by his squadrons and now, under pressure of war, his men were still not getting what they required. What he was not appreciating were the changes now being made possible by rapidly advancing technology, a technology with which he was unfamiliar. He would learn soon enough the advantages of GEE and the subsequent radar aids to navigation, but his initial reaction to its development indicated a degree of mindset that would continue to hinder some of his relations with the scientists.

Yet always at the back of his mind was a very real concern for his crews. As Tomlinson said, he never showed emotion over losses but deep down he certainly felt them and anything he could do to minimise them took high priority. In December 1939 he reported in detail on the shooting down of two Hampdens by RAF fighters and on the urgent need for modifications to the dinghies, and went on to criticise the teaching of aircraft recognition: 'Many fighter pilots and AA gunners regard the entire onus of recognition as resting on the bomber, and consider themselves perfectly justified in opening fire without any attempt whatsoever at recognising the type of aircraft at which they are firing,' he said to Ludlow Hewitt. He later extended his castigations to the Royal Navy with its policy of 'shoot on sight' and to the ever increasing number of barrage balloons being flown 'under conditions more dangerous to us than to the enemy'. He even had a go at a local factory which, encouraged by the Ministry of Aircraft Production, had raised its own private army to defend itself against any aircraft approaching without navigation lights. 'Will you please have this pirate gang apprehended and, if thought fit, properly incorporated in the defence system of the country?' he asked Air Vice-Marshal Richard Peck, Assistant Chief of Air Staff (General) in the Air Ministry. He was determined, too, to make his crews parachute-minded. Writing to Ralph Cochrane, with whom he kept up regular contact on many important matters and who was now at HQ 7 Group, concerned with operational training, he stressed: 'It cannot be too strongly impressed upon all pilots that it is an unforgivable stupidity to kill crews by attempting to pull off landings in bad weather, under circumstances where those crews could have easily and safely parachuted over this country,' the trained pilots being of far more value than the aircraft.[24]

One other safety issue greatly concerned him; indeed, Tomlinson recalled the deaths of a crew whom Harris knew and who had ditched in the North Sea in April 1940 as the only occasion when he actually showed emotion. They were spotted from the air in their dinghy but the rescue launch despatched by 18 Group failed to find them. Harris, following these events, eventually spoke direct to the master of the launch, obtained highly unsatisfactory replies to his questions, and lodged a strongly worded complaint both about the officer's conduct and competence and about Coastal Command's failure in this and a previous incident. Two months later he found that Air Vice-Marshal J.E.A. Baldwin, AOC 3 Group, shared his concerns, and in August Harris took up the cudgels with Portal. Since he could not envisage the Air Ministry acting with the necessary urgency he proposed that the Command should act on its own; he therefore asked for authority to co-opt a private firm to build a prototype airborne dinghy capable of being dropped by a Hampden, and for the allocation of a flying boat and an amphibian for additional rescue purposes. Portal gave him immediate backing and within days an MAP (Ministry of Aircraft Production) representative appeared at Grantham to discuss the detailed specification for the dinghy. Thus began the Air-Sea Rescue service which did so much to help Bomber Command crews for the remainder of the war.

Harris realised too the importance of developing leadership skills at station and squadron levels and of keeping the better men within the system. Writing to his station commanders in December 1939 he sharply criticised many of the aircraft captains he had met, men who did not know about basic matters relating to their aircraft and their crews, and often did not even seem to care. 'I expect every captain of aircraft to be able to give me an exact and explicit account of the abilities of his own crew, etc etc', he went on, and station and squadron commanders must take more serious notice of sins of omission. 'I look to station commanders to be ruthless in ferreting out "duds".' A month later he gave Ludlow-Hewitt the names of no less than four squadron and three flight commanders who had been posted from his operational squadrons in less than five months, adding that the Air Ministry had now ordered him not to query any future postings.

Then in April he returned to the attack on official postings policy in one of his best missives, this time to Portal. He explained that he was anxious about morale in a situation where his crews had to fight off their own doormats amidst the otherwise undisturbed luxuries of peace, and had to rely considerably upon civilians for support. The station commanders were nice enough chaps but were usually dug-outs passed over for promotion, the wing commanders appointed to lead the squadrons rarely had the necessary up-to-date operational experience, and the youngsters with that experience could see little chance of advancement. The solution, Harris proposed, was to make the station commanders simply 'housekeepers in the German fashion', install the wing commanders as administrative and operational supervisors, divide each current squadron into two smaller ones, and allow the young and lusty and war-experienced squadron leaders – now the flight commanders – 'to command and lead their squadrons' (Harris's underlining). In May, following on signs that the Air Ministry was beginning to think along similar lines, he returned to his theme, firmly suggesting that there be three wing commanders on each station, one employed on operational duties, one in charge of aircraft maintenance, and the third on administration. In other words, he was proposing the three-prong structure that eventually became almost universal. The prospect of important organisational changes did nothing, however, to improve the general posting situation, and in September he reiterated to Portal his worries about the Air Ministry's constant attempts to deprive him of operational personnel: 'Our priceless operational crews, ever dwindling as they are, cannot be regarded as a posting pool for half of the odd jobs in the Service.' In November, however, such was the need for more operational pilots to be made available as instructors to feed the RAF's expansion that Peirse and Bottomley were compelled to override his fiercely argued refusals to contribute. Hard though he might fight, he was not always going to get his own way.

Nevertheless he often did, as on the classic occasion when he and the technically-minded CO of Hemswell, Group Captain E.A.B. Rice, bent the rules and went searching for an engineering firm which could be persuaded to design and build a new gun mounting to replace the inadequate one fitted to the Hampden. The family firm of Rose Bros, in Gainsborough, fitted the bill, and within weeks was starting to meet an order for 2,000, enabling the Hampden to double its effective fire-power. With Linnell's quiet support at

High Wycombe, the account was duly settled and Rose Bros' valuable association with Bomber Command continued for the rest of the war.[25]

By this time Harris was becoming reasonably happy with the Hampden. In May 1940 Portal sought his views on whether fewer refinements and somewhat lower standards could be accepted in some of the RAF's aircraft so as to allow for greater production, and while Harris regarded the Hampden as a 'simplified production type' he already thought it could continue to be a good night bomber, if given automatic controls, for the rest of the war. He went on to suggest that it could be a mistake to cease its production in preference to 'the over-complicated, under-defended Halifax', and later thought it had considerable potential for increased range and bomb-load. Not surprisingly he was also becoming less caustic about its manufacturer, Handley Page, and when a trophy arrived at 5 Group, made by the company's craftsmen, he acknowledged it in generous terms. 'Many owe their lives to the rugged design and honest workmanship which so often brings Hampdens home with structural damage which by all normal criteria should have proved fatal.' By now, however, Handley Page were concentrating their efforts on the four-engined Halifax and there was no question of altering the Air Ministry's already well-advanced plans for the production of this and the other two heavy bombers. So in September Harris went to Boscombe Down to see one of the prototypes of the Avro Manchester, about which he immediately wrote to Linnell, sharply criticising numerous points of design which would have to be dealt with before operational aircraft went into production. Soon afterwards he was in touch with Tedder about the Manchester's planned armament, which needed rethinking, and he later suggested that if the aircraft was to be used only at night an experimental model should be produced without turrets but with guns firing through openings in the fuselage, thus saving weight and greatly increasing its bomb-carrying capacity.[26]

So there emerges the picture of an operational commander with great driving force, constantly engaging his mind on how to rectify problems and do things better, and possessing deep knowledge of his business. Nor was Harris averse to offering ideas affecting other people's business. He sought, for example, to persuade the Air Ministry to allow WAAF officers holding civil pilots' licences to fly RAF communications aircraft; he protested repeatedly during the Battle of Britain that flying training schools did not appear to be working hard enough; he slated a BBC broadcast which gave the impression that fighter pilots required greater skill than bomber pilots; and he drew on his own experience to advise against letting the Army take over responsibility for airfield defence, and to argue for the RAF to have its own defence formations.

Harris also wrote to personal friends who happened to be in senior positions. In September 1939 he wrote to Major Archie Boyle, in the Directorate of Intelligence, recommending his elder brother Murray for some kind of war work that would utilise his language skills and his diplomatic and business experience in the Middle East; Murray duly received a temporary commission and served on the RAF staff in Cairo, though not on duties that took proper advantage of his abilities. Harris later returned to his brother's cause, and in October 1941 Murray went to Washington as a squadron leader for intelligence duties. He resigned his commission in May 1942. In February 1940 Harris reminded Newall, as CAS, of his work in Air Plans on air/sea warfare and urged – as he had previously suggested to Air Marshal Wilfrid Freeman, Air Member for Development and Production – the provision of cheap, light, expendable fighters to be carried in convoys and launched by catapult to counter enemy long-range aircraft.[27] In May he mentioned to Slessor, still Director of Plans, the great use the Germans had made of seaplanes in Norway, and suggested they might do something similar on some of the large stretches of inland water in the United Kingdom. In July he wrote a chatty letter to General Haining, back from Palestine and now in the War Office, comparing the new situation on the continent with that of 1808 as analysed at the time by Wellington. Soon afterwards, in another letter to Haining, he suggested experiments in dropping light containers of petrol in quantity in order to present a barrier to an enemy seaborne invasion; this letter was passed on to Lord Hankey, Chancellor of the Duchy of Lancaster and in charge of anti-invasion measures, who not only found it interesting but also made clear his very high opinion of Harris, with whom he had worked when Secretary to the Committee of Imperial Defence in the mid 1930s.

The Harrises also recognised the importance of entertaining, but found it much more difficult in wartime Britain than it had been in Palestine. As he wrote in October 1940, 'as the occupant of an official residence I have a large number of official visitors, most of whom I am only too glad to see, some of whom I hate the sight of, all of whom I have to feed.' On average he was providing 100–200 meals a month without any extra supply of rationed articles, which he considered grossly unfair, particularly to his own family and staff. Nevertheless hospitality was provided, and often to influential guests. Trenchard came twice; after the first occasion Ludlow-Hewitt referred to its great success and how much the great man had enjoyed himself. Several leading scientists were welcomed, including Sir Henry Tizard and Professor Blackett, who came to talk to Harris in detail about bomb sights. There were many senior officers, ranging from Ludlow-Hewitt, Portal, Peirse, Brooke-Popham, Gossage, Tedder and Cochrane to his own commanders. The aviation journalist C.G. Grey not only exchanged letters but came to stay, as did Squadron Leader Learoyd VC, his distant relative.

Maurice Dean came several times, keeping open Harris's private links with the Air Ministry, and there were frequent visits from other family friends, including the Tresfons, Jill's relatives the Prideaux-Brunes from Padstow, the Asshetons, and the Tomlinson family, including Peter's brother Paul, who would later become Harris's PA at Bomber Command. One visitor who left a sour taste was the portrait painter Eric Kennington. At Portal's request Harris had agreed to sit for Kennington in September 1940, but as he later wrote to Harald Peake, he was horrified by the result and refused to allow copies to be made for publicity purposes. 'If I had the money to waste I would buy the original and burn it. I regard it as a libellous caricature.'[28]

By this time Harris, who had recently received the CB, knew that he was on his way. Portal, who handed over the Command to Peirse in October before taking over as Chief of Air Staff, told Harris on the 3rd that he was likely to be joining him in the Air Ministry fairly soon, and two days later he wrote to thank 'Bert' in words that encapsulated the first 15 months of Harris's war:

> On leaving here I feel I must send you a hasty line of thanks for all the wonderful work you have done during my six months. Owing to the paper shortage it would be madness for me to start cataloguing your virtues, but I will say that without you and your personal support, to say nothing of the amazing spirit of your Group, I should often have felt discouraged. Don't bother to answer – I just wanted to let you know a fraction of what I feel about you and what you have done for this Command. Au revoir.[29]

These words of such fulsome praise show beyond doubt not just Portal's respect and admiration for his subordinate's ability as an operational commander but his conviction that here was one of the key players he would need alongside him in the hard years that lay ahead. They had long been friends. Now there was a bond between them strong enough to survive whatever differences might arise.

The formation of another bond, equally important, was also to begin before Harris left Grantham. On 26 October the Station Commander at Waddington, Group Captain C.T. Anderson, applied for a redress of grievance over an adverse confidential report raised on him by Harris. Anderson thought Harris had it in for him because he (Anderson) was a friend of the Prime Minister and therefore a potential danger and source of irritation, and during the subsequent interview he allegedly told Harris he had already ruined several officers, including Tedder. The wires to the Air Ministry were quickly humming, for Anderson had in fact been one of Churchill's sources of secret information about the RAF during the later 1930s,[30] and on 11 November Harris found himself lunching among other distinguished guests with the Prime Minister at Ditchley Park. Churchill duly raised the subject, as Harris reported to Air Marshal Gossage, the Air Member for Personnel, next day, in an atmosphere of understanding and complete good feeling. The Prime Minister was patently annoyed and distressed at realising Anderson's presumptuous habit of using his name, or of implying that it was behind him. Churchill also indicated how glad he was that Harris had been able to deal with the 'threat' incident without going to extremes, and Harris told Gossage he would not press for any further action.[31] For Anderson it was a sad business; for Harris this meeting started a relationship with the Prime Minister that would prove a critical factor in the conduct of Bomber Command's affairs, and a friendship that would continue throughout Churchill's declining years.

Notes

1. Saward, *op.cit.* p.68.
2. According to the Group ORB (AIR 25/109) he took over on 14 September.
3. Discussions with the author.
4. Tomlinson, unpublished manuscript, 'Bomber Harris, the man as I knew him'.
5. *Ibid.* Harris was in fact passed fit again for solo flying in February 1940. Folder H114, E82.
6. *Ibid.*
7. Harris, *op.cit.* p.33.
8. Except where otherwise stated, the material for the rest of this chapter is derived from Folders H107–H114 and in particular H108, together with the Tomlinson discussions.
9. W.J. Lawrence, *No 5 Bomber Group RAF*, p.24.
10. For details of the Hampden's armament see Harry Moyle *The Hampden*, p.13, and Thetford, *Aircraft of the RAF since 1918*, p.313.
11. Gibson, *'Enemy Coast Ahead'*, p.60.
12. Ludlow-Hewitt Papers, Folder 12, letter 23 February 1940, together with Folders H107, H113, H114.
13. Harris, *op.cit.* pp.35–6.
14. Ludlow-Hewitt Papers, Folder 11.
15. Richards and Saunders, *The Royal Air Force 1939–45*, p.84; Folder H107.
16. Folder H110, letters 7 and 11 September 1940.
17. Probert, *High Commanders of the RAF*, p.19. Whenever the subject of the Battle of Britain arose in his later years, Harris would stress that the Hurricanes deserved the main credit for the victory.
18. Folder H107 E53A.
19. Harris, *op.cit.* p.39; Slessor, *op.cit.* p.380.
20. Folder H110. Wing Commander Sir Louis Greig was Sinclair's Personal Air Secretary.
21. OH vol.I, p.242; AIR 14/1941; Folder H110.
22. OH vol.I, p.157.
23. Folder H111, dated 14 November 1940. This runs counter to Saward, *op.cit.* p.95.
24. Saward, *op.cit.* pp.84–5; Folders H108; H110; H113.
25. Harris, *op.cit.* pp.39–40.

26. See Saward, *op.cit.* pp.81–3, for fuller details about the Manchester; Folders H109–113.
27. AIR 2/7187.
28. Visitors' Book; Folders H110; H111.
29. Misc Folder 9.
30. Anderson, previously Harris's Senior Personnel Staff Officer at 5 Group, had started feeding information to Churchill from his training post in the Air Ministry in 1936. Martin Gilbert's *The Coming of War*, p.742, documents the story.
31. *Ibid*; Harris Tape 15. See Gilbert, *The Finest Hour*, p.900, for details of the Ditchley gathering. The other guests included Bracken, Eden and Lindemann. Harris is not specifically mentioned.

Chapter 6

Action behind the scenes

On 24 November 1940 Harris re-entered the doors of the Air Ministry, this time to take over from Sholto Douglas as Deputy Chief of Air Staff, responsible to Portal and Freeman, his recently appointed Vice-Chief, for the day-to-day conduct of the RAF's operations. The prospect of working again amid the fearsome bureaucracy horrified him. Moreover he was returning to a London frequently under heavy air attack, and would often need to work from 8.30 in the morning until late into the evening, so clearly it made no sense to bring the family into the city. They were therefore lodged instead with Jill's aunt, Dorothy Hett, and her husband in their home at Aldwickbury, near Harpenden, where Harris could join them occasionally at weekends. The rest of the time Harris shared Ralph Assheton's flat in Westminster Gardens. Ralph was now Parliamentary Secretary to Ernest Bevin, the Minister of Labour, and when civilian labour problems arose, not least in connection with airfield construction, the two of them would put their heads together and try to influence their respective departments.[1]

Harris was not enamoured of the wartime Air Ministry he found. Its staffs were 'fantastically bloated', he wrote, with exaggerated ideas of their own importance. He immediately stopped his own subordinates writing 'directed' letters to commanders-in-chief, who he insisted must be treated as responsible people.[2] He then followed up his predecessor's moves to reduce the size of the Air Staff by insisting on 'an enormous and very suitable clear-out', but could do nothing about the number of civil servants.[3] He also let his irritations be known. Jargon, for example, was anathema to him: 'I cannot think that the very apparent tendency, especially in the Air Ministry, to slip into schoolboy code language consisting mainly of initials, comic names and cryptic phraseology is in any way necessary'; it merely impeded understanding. In a protest to Portal about a note from Professor Lindemann to Churchill concerning air defence measures he wrote: 'our work is made no easier by the continual necessity of leaving it in order to answer the naive queries of outside busybodies who peddle second-hand information in the guise of esoteric knowledge until it finally boomerangs back to us in the guise of a bogey or a new discovery.' The welfare of his staff concerned him too, and particularly that of the airwomen who worked at night on war room and cypher duties and had to subsist on sandwich meals. The WAAF Director was offered his support in improving their facilities and he later returned to the fray with a detailed minute stipulating precisely what needed to be done.

A particularly important area that worried him was the security arrangements for transmitting highly classified documents, and even the influential Dr R.V. Jones was criticised for endangering security by distributing one of his reports too widely. Sadly this was not their only disagreement. In a minute to ACAS(R) on 1 February 1941, Harris was sceptical about the value of the Luftwaffe's beams as aids to target finding. 'We use no beams ourselves,' he wrote, 'but we bomb just as effectively as the Germans bomb, deep into Germany.' In fact by providing advance information of enemy intentions the beams were of more use to the RAF than the enemy, he contended, and there was little point in trying to bomb the transmitting stations. 'Long may the Boche beam upon us!' he concluded. This was certainly not one of Harris's better missives and it did nothing to persuade Jones that its writer had sufficient understanding of the more advanced technologies that were going to be so important in the future. In fairness Harris subsequently admitted that he did not then have the high regard for the ability of the scientists that he later acquired.[4]

Not surprisingly the policy for the bomber force was one of Harris's main preoccupations as DCAS. Hardly had he taken over than he was telling Freeman that the bomber was the only weapon with which to win the war, that it would have to operate by night, and that it would need every means of protection. Next he reorganised his own department. Hitherto the Directorate of Home Operations had dealt with both defensive and offensive operations and was giving more weight to the former; if the policy and operations of the bomber force were to be adequately directed and controlled a separate Directorate was needed, he told Freeman. His proposal went through and Air Commodore Baker was appointed the first Director of Bomber Operations.[5] It was the right move, though in due course the Directorate Harris had created would cause him a deal of trouble.

Not long afterwards, on Sunday evening, 29 December 1940, Harris was still at work when the Luftwaffe launched its great incendiary attack on the City of London. Climbing to the Air Ministry roof to see what was happening he saw the Dome of St Paul's Cathedral standing out amid a sea of flame and called Portal to witness 'a sight that shouldn't be missed'. As they turned away from the scene Harris spoke quietly: 'They are sowing the wind.' That was the only occasion, he wrote after the war, when he ever felt vengeful,[6] and quickly he was back to business as usual, informally advising Peirse – in advance of a new directive – to concentrate his immediate planning on the offensive against German synthetic oil plants.[7] Continuing to keep a watchful eye on Bomber Command's operations, he also opposed any attempts by the Air Ministry to breathe down the neck of the C-in-C.

After relatively heavy losses had been sustained on 11 February 1941, for example, he minuted Sir Archibald Sinclair, Secretary of State for Air, deprecating any tendency to demand special and urgent reports, 'as if they were something utterly unexpected and extraordinary'. Meteorology was an inexact science, Harris went on; unless the Command was to be over-cautious to the extent of vastly reducing its efforts it was bound at times to be badly caught out.[8]

By March 1941 there were growing signs that Hitler might turn his attention to the Balkans and the prospect of a German attack on Yugoslavia prompted Harris to propose that Bomber Command should give the Yugoslavs moral support by a series of concentrated attacks on Berlin or possibly Hanover or Cologne. The object would be to cause the maximum damage to populated areas 'as a demonstration of that ruthless force which we shall have to employ against Germany sooner or later if we are to get the full moral effects out of our air offensive.' Portal agreed and forwarded the idea to the Prime Minister, but the pace of events precluded further action. In any case, Bomber Command lacked the power that would have been needed, but his thinking was clear. Fourteen months later his concept would be converted to reality over Cologne.[9]

Harris was also supporting Bomber Command in the face of criticism being levelled at its achievements by the MEW (Ministry of Economic Warfare). Seizing on a MEW report admitting that the Gelsenkirchen oil plants had been seriously damaged in a raid on 14/15 March, he slated its previous assessments which had gone out of their way 'to stress the futility of our bombing and belittle its effects' and accused it of ignoring entirely the tactical factors which made Gelsenkirchen so hard to find and hit. Fair such comments might be, but Harris unfortunately went on to read across from the MEW's admission and 'confidently claim to have *entirely* destroyed' a number of the other plants which had been attacked and to have seriously damaged the remainder. 'What the writer has still to learn is that far more damage always exists than will or can appear in a photograph.'[10] Harris was not helping his cause in the corridors of power by exaggerating his claims, and the MEW, which he considered was usurping the Air Ministry's functions, would remain an arch enemy.

By this time, however, oil was no longer Bomber Command's prime target, for in March Churchill had issued his Battle of the Atlantic directive under which the bombers' main effort was to be devoted to the maritime war. Ever since taking over as DCAS Harris had been involved in naval matters; indeed, his working relationship with Tom Phillips, now Vice Chief of Naval Staff, was re-established in November 1940 when he offered his thoughts on convoy defence against U-boats and long-range aircraft and again urged the adoption of the expendable catapult fighter. Soon afterwards he was advising Portal along similar lines and also suggesting ways of improving the air defence of coastal shipping.[11] There were questions too about how far the bombers of Coastal Command should be allowed to attack objectives not directly connected with the naval war, and – even more fundamental – about who should own it. Prompted by Lord Beaverbrook, Minister of Aircraft Production, there had been intensive top-level argument in November about the merits of transferring Coastal Command to the Admiralty, leading to the Defence Committee's decision in December that operational control, but not command, would rest with the Navy. There remained staff work to do in order to spell out the procedures, and in February Harris and Phillips jointly headed a small sub-committee to devise these. Harris was able to ensure that 'operational control' did not become a euphemism for 'command' and could not lead to a repetition of Inskip's pre-war decision to transfer the Fleet Air Arm to the Navy. The resultant agreement formed the basis for the remarkable co-operation that was to exist between Coastal Command and the Royal Navy for the rest of the war.[12]

There were other important maritime-air matters too in these early months of 1941, when the nation still stood virtually alone, and Harris disagreed strongly with a Joint Intelligence Committee assessment of the likelihood of German invasion. In his view the more serious threat was that of blockade, accompanied by bombing, and he had no doubt about the critical importance of the U-boat war – however much he might disagree with the Navy about the roles of air power in fighting it.[13] He accepted that the essential minimum of reconnaissance and striking effort should be put into the convoy areas to help keep the submarines down and make them less resolute in their attacks, he saw the advantages that ASV radar would bring, and, as he told Professor Blackett (Personal Scientific Adviser to C-in-C Coastal Command), he believed the B24 Liberator would prove the best aircraft for the job. On the other hand, he made clear his view to both Portal and Phillips that the correct use for the bomber force was to attack the German and French ports and factories where the kernel of the problem was to be found – not over the wide ocean spaces, spending thousands of hours on largely wasted flying.

He identified the broad strategic issue a few days later, telling the Director of Intelligence that there were two obvious ways of losing the war: one was on the shipping routes, the other was by giving Germany almost complete immunity from air attack. 'A balance has to be struck between these requirements, and it would be as vital a mistake to over-insure ... on trade protection and freeing Germany thereby from all the effects of air action as it would be to under-insure on trade protection and lose the war in consequence.'[14] Certainly Harris was not going to lose sight of the need to take the war to the German homeland. Indeed, as he minuted Sinclair on 29

April about the possible resumption of the oil offensive: 'Bombing oil plants does not kill Boche ... we know that the Berlin attacks have badly shaken the Boche and he would sooner we attacked anything else anywhere else first. The Luftwaffe will be the last to go short of oil and petrol – and want but little.' Like Churchill, like Portal, like his own Director of Bomber Operations, he was becoming convinced that Bomber Command would need to target industrial areas as a whole in order to inflict serious damage on the enemy.[15] But he knew too that much remained to be done to make the force effective.

As early as December 1940 Harris had protested to Freeman about the 2:1 ratio between fighter and bomber production, and about the 8:1 ratio in planned purchases from the USA. He next tackled Portal, first questioning the need to run two fighter forces, one for day and another for night defence, now that the Luftwaffe had been forced to switch to night bombing. He went on to detail various 'diversions' that were affecting Bomber Command and taking away so many of its trained crews – minelaying (of which he was surprisingly critical), the Mediterranean war, Coastal Command duties, the war against the beams, the increasing demands of Hugh Dalton's Special Operations Executive,[16] and so on. 'One very sure way of losing the war is to reach a condition of stalemate whereby the whole populace becomes fed up with going on with it. If we continue to postpone the development of our bomber potential by such means ... we may well find ourselves on the road to this particular method of ruin.' His desire to see the main bomber force built up quickly for its central role was understandable, as was his frustration about the diversions, and these would be recurrent themes – though whether as DCAS, as opposed to C-in-C Bomber Command, he should have taken quite such an uncompromising line is another matter. Nevertheless his representations bore fruit. The Prime Minister authorised the expansion of Bomber Command in January, the formation of new squadrons was set in train, including a second one of Manchesters, and Harris insisted to those concerned that the build-up must take priority over all else. In April, however, he had to give Portal the reasons for the Command's comparatively small front-line effort and explain that almost all the Stirlings, Halifaxes and Manchesters were grounded owing to technical problems. Neither man could be under any illusions that a long, difficult road lay ahead.[17]

The build-up entailed not just aircraft but aircrews. Hardly had Harris left 5 Group than he was urging again, this time to Freeman, that the dissipation of experienced bomber crews from the 'bomber circle' must stop. Very rarely indeed were such men essential in posts further back in the training organisation than the Operational Training Units. After their first 200-hour tour, he suggested, pilots could rotate either to the OTUs or to night fighters (which many were keen to do) and back for a second tour of 100–

200 hours before eventually moving to staff or wider training appointments. Hopefully an embargo could be placed on those who completed two tours – unlike their Luftwaffe opposite numbers they would have done their whack. The OTUs themselves came in for criticism. Concerned about the wastefulness of using large numbers of operational aircraft as flying classrooms instead of putting them in the front line, he returned to another 5 Group theme in recommending much greater use of synthetic ground training. At present, he observed, Bomber Command had 594 heavy bombers in the front line and 410 in the OTUs – a hopeless imbalance. Another key issue arose when Peirse asked for senior officers from outside the Command to be posted in to fill some of his squadron and flight commander appointments, and Harris felt compelled to voice his profound disagreement with the C-in-C. Again reflecting on his time at 5 Group – and also during the First World War – he considered it was asking too much of the average individual to compete with those who had been brought up in the immediate school of war. Occasionally there might be an outstanding man who could cope, but the best COs were to be found among 'the youngsters who themselves had done the job'. This was a rare difference of opinion between the two men and Harris was at pains to write carefully and politely to explain his views.[18]

The weapons available to the bomber force were another matter of concern, for evidence was now available that the Luftwaffe's lighter-cased blast bombs were proving more effective in disrupting essential services than the RAF's heavy-cased fragmentation bombs. Soon, therefore, he was pressing for the introduction of the former, with their bigger explosive charges, and in December 1940 he strongly supported the efforts of his old friend, John Salmond, now working in the Ministry of Aircraft Production, to arrange the manufacture of 2,000 lb and 4,000 lb blast bombs: soon these were coming into use.[19] Where Harris was less perceptive was in his assessment of bomb failure rates. Advising Portal how to respond to Churchill's enquiry on this subject in February 1941 he referred to the 10% of 'duds' occurring in German bombing, to various RAF tests, and to the absence of reports of failures in the previous two months. 'I am satisfied that the "dud" bomb era is now past and that the results we are obtaining are of a far higher order than those obtained by our enemies,' he concluded. Given the impossibility of acquiring accurate information this was an unwarranted assumption – he was certainly not immune to the feelings of optimism about the RAF's performance that affected the judgements of many senior officers in those relatively early days of the war.[20]

Important to Harris as were the affairs of Bomber Command and the waging of the Atlantic war there was much more to his work as DCAS. Concerned though he was about the ratio between fighter and bomber production, in December 1940 he firmly reminded Sinclair that Fighter

Command might have to cope with a renewed daylight assault by the Luftwaffe. At the same time he was ordering a search for experienced pilots capable of reinforcing the night defences. Shortly afterwards he was following up his own initiative at 5 Group by organising a full air/sea rescue service, to be placed under Coastal Command, and searching for the right man to run it; three months later he could report not only on its formation but its already remarkable success under its Director, Air Commodore Croke. In January 1941 he was pressing on Freeman one of his repeated themes, namely that there were many military jobs which could be performed just as well, if not better, by women. Flying balloons, wiggling searchlights, operating anti-aircraft guns were but examples – 'After all,' he wrote, ' they ferry out aircraft – and in the face of the enemy!' Ferrying was coming up in another context too. A better Transatlantic organisation was needed, making use of pilots trained in OTUs in North America and under RAF command, a task for which Harris considered 'the most efficient pilot he had ever had under him in the RAF', Donald Bennett, entirely suitable.[21]

Sometimes his mind would turn to general reflection, as in April 1941 when he addressed a curious minute to VCAS. In this he presented a bluntly-worded, jaundiced view of the Army and its failure to move beyond its horse-bound traditions and prepare adequately for modern war. Although less scathing about the Navy he concluded that the war would have to be won by the Air Force: 'We either get on fast enough with tank-destroying aircraft to save the war, and with heavy bombers eventually to win it, or we perish.' Freeman doubtless kept this effusion to himself. It would have done nothing for the cause of inter-Service relations, and if meant seriously – as Harris said it was – reflected a distressingly partisan attitude, one much influenced by his earlier experiences with the Army. In truth he was probably trying to make his point, as he often did, by exaggerating it, and we must remember that he had a good many Army friends, among them Montgomery and Haining. The latter was, in fact, now in the War Office and they were exchanging helpful letters on such matters as the air defence of the Malta airfields, the reinforcement of Iceland, and anti-tank weapons. Whatever Harris may have thought in private he knew that in practice co-operation was essential.[22]

Even so, he was not averse to tendering some of his views about the other Services in high places. Advising Portal apropos Churchill's interest in the proportion of personnel to serviceable aircraft in the Middle East, he contrasted the 56 soldiers required to maintain one field gun with the 77 airmen needed to keep one aircraft operational and asserted that the latter were 'incomparably more hardly worked'. The Mediterranean war was a continuing preoccupation, not least in connection with the policy for despatching reinforcements and the practicalities of increasing the use of the

Takoradi route to the Middle East.[23] Then in April 1941 Harris was greatly irritated by a long list of complaints about the RAF received from the C-in-C Mediterranean, Admiral Cunningham, and wrote at length to Phillips seeking to explain that the Air Ministry was not shirking its responsibilities to the Navy in relation to the many operations on which the Admiral was engaged. Dealing with these various issues in some detail Harris made it clear that ultimately it all came down to total resources and the need to set priorities: 'I am sure your C-in-C will see things in better proportions when the present intolerable load of his anxieties is lessened.' This letter shows Harris at his best – firm but sympathetic, balanced and fair, in full command of his subject and demonstrating wide perspective. It turned out to be the last he would write to Tom Phillips, and Harris's closing words indicate the respect these two seasoned warriors had for each other. 'Do not think I write in any bitterness, because, as you are well aware, for the many years in which we have been (not unprofitably I hope) associated we have always mutually adopted the practice of speaking our minds. Here is mine.'[24]

Their paths now diverged. Phillips would soon sail East towards disaster (pp.75–6); Harris was about to head West to the USA. Ever since his visit to Washington in 1938 he had followed the growth of the RAF's purchasing programme and observed the various American reactions to the war, ranging from the strong isolationist sentiment of much of the public to the generous covert assistance being provided by those who understood what was at stake. Then as DCAS he had met General Arnold again, this time in the Air Ministry, and heard him comment as they walked along the passage to meet Portal: 'It's extraordinary, Bert. Nobody seems to be moving. Everyone's working away happily in their offices. Don't you people realise you've lost the war?' 'Good God no,' replied Harris, 'we haven't started the ruddy war yet.'[25] There was still much to be done, Harris realised, if the Americans were to be brought on side, and for the moment there was little he personally could do beyond helping American air officials in the United Kingdom – not least by authorising them to carry RAF markings on their communications aircraft so that they could fly around the country. Meanwhile, however, there had been extensive staff conversations in Washington in which Slessor represented the RAF, leading to a secret agreement to exchange military missions, and Portal asked Harris if he would go to America to lead the RAF Delegation.[26] Somewhat reluctantly, for he had set his heart on an operational command appointment, he accepted.

Harris had been DCAS for a mere six months. He had not enjoyed it; staff work did not enthuse him, and the Air Ministry atmosphere and routine depressed him. Nor had he been in the best of health. His ulcer was nagging him and on one occasion Portal ordered him away from the office for five days and told him not to return without a report from his doctor. Moreover he had often found himself under criticism from the much senior Wilfrid Freeman, Portal's alter ego. Yet that distinguished officer recognised afterwards that Harris's decisiveness and capacity for work was far greater than that of Bottomley, who succeeded him. Writing to his wife in July 1941, Freeman referred to the heavy additional load imposed on him in the absence of Portal and Bottomley: 'Portal will only go away if I am here, and yet Bottomley must get away as he is not strong. I miss Harris tremendously ... he was a much better man.'[27]

The month of May was devoted to handing over his Air Ministry post, to staff discussions about the composition and terms of reference of the Delegation, to a fight with a parsimonious Treasury about the scale of allowances, and to family preparations. Jill and Jackie were being permitted to accompany him and the Navy had offered them passage aboard the battleship HMS *Rodney*, together with the Heads of the Navy and Army Delegations. The Harrises were excellently accommodated in the 'Admiral's Flat' but the incessant vibration and rolling of the ship made for an uncomfortable voyage, especially for Jill, who was a bad sailor. So Harris had to act as nursemaid for the 20-month old Jackie, solving the attendant problem of nappy disposal by discreetly discarding them through the porthole, contrary to naval regulations forbidding any rubbish to be thrown overboard in wartime, as Captain Dalrymple-Hamilton light-heartedly informed him later on. 'A U-Boat captain would hardly expect to find a battleship at the end of a line of nappies,' replied Harris. Slightly less humorous was his reaction when the ship opened fire on an instantly recognisable Whitley which had emerged from low clouds. The journey ended at Boston on 12 June, Harris went on directly to Washington, where he was soon joined by Jill and Jackie, and they took up residence in a suite at the Shoreham Hotel, in Connecticut Avenue.[28] By a strange coincidence his cousin Ian Elliot, who was a member of the British Purchasing Commission, was also spending much of his time at the Shoreham: Ian already had many friends in the American business world and was to provide Harris with invaluable counsel and contacts.[29]

The task Harris faced was highly unusual, calling for special skills of tact and diplomacy. He and his staff, most of whom had arrived at the beginning of June, were housed in offices at 1424, 16th Street, New York, a building owned by the American Trucking Association and bearing no external evidence of RAF use. Their postal address was the civilian-run British Air Commission (BAC), which was the purchasing agency for American aircraft and represented the Ministry of Aircraft Production. The presence of an RAF staff was not something to be advertised in a country still largely determined to steer clear of active involvement in the war, and when, in August, Harris was formally appointed CAS's representative on the British Joint Staff

Mission the memorandum was classified secret. His work lay behind the
scenes. Moreover he could not command; he could only request or suggest.
His duty, as summarised in the History of the Delegation, was 'to try to
guide the young, inexperienced, self-conscious and rapidly expanding Service
of a foreign nation and, simultaneously, to draw off a proportion of the
aircraft, supplies and equipment which that nation needed for itself.'[30]

Harris, now promoted Air Marshal, wasted no time getting down to
business. His Director of Administration and Finance, Mr W.C.G. Cribbett
– a senior civil servant whom he quickly came to admire – wrote to the
Permanent Under-Secretary in the Air Ministry, Sir Arthur Street, at the end
of June: 'Harris has been very energetic since his arrival – but is suffering a
little disillusionment from the discovery that promises in high quarters do
not always materialise.' Already he had renewed old contacts with American
airmen and manufacturers and established new ones, and after the news
broke of the German invasion of the Soviet Union on 22 June he and his
Navy and Army opposite numbers, Admiral Little and General Wemyss,
found themselves accompanying the Ambassador, Lord Halifax, to the
White House to discuss the situation with President Roosevelt. The *New
York Times* quickly got wind of this, publishing a photograph and referring to
the three officers as 'members of the British Ministry of Defence Supply'.
Already their presence was known; it could be only a matter of time before
their real status and roles leaked out.

This major extension of the war was to give Harris one of his main
concerns. Following the passage of the Lend-Lease Act through Congress in
March, Slessor had negotiated a formal agreement setting out the basis for
allocation of American aircraft to the RAF;[31] this was in force when Harris
arrived. Then came the invasion of the USSR, the decision of Britain and the
USA to send them all possible supplies, and the despatch of the Beaver-
brook/Harriman mission to Moscow in September. At the same time the
Americans were accelerating their own rearmament and, anxious about
Japan, stepping up supplies to China. So as Harris and his staff went about
their business they became aware of growing pressures to reduce the aircraft
allocations that Slessor had agreed and by October he was sufficiently
worried to raise the matter with the Ambassador. His note stressed how the
RAF training and works programmes were oriented to make the fullest use
of these aircraft, referred to repeated assurances that the Slessor formula
would not be unilaterally denounced, and pointed out that Harriman's
proposals arising out of his visit to Moscow were completely at variance with
this; the cuts in bomber allocations in particular would be 'catastrophic'.
Soon afterwards he wrote to General Arnold requesting the full American
release programme over the coming months, only to be told that the
situation was constantly changing and that only relatively small numbers of

aircraft, especially the heavy bomber category, were now planned for allocation up to mid-1942. Thoroughly though Harris had argued his case the Slessor Agreement was effectively dead.[32]

Harris was more successful in other ways, including helping to organise the supply of spares for those aircraft which were still being sent to the RAF. American aircraft manufacturers and military services seemed to have little comprehension of the practicalities of carrying out military operations worldwide and of the quantities of spares required, and an RAF equipment staff was set up in late 1941 to liaise with them and provide experienced advice; as a result the USAAF formed a number of Defence Aid Depots to handle such supplies.[33] He also had a hand in the Takoradi Agreement of August 1941, which enabled the Americans to deliver aircraft directly to the Middle East via West Africa.

Even more important was Harris's work in setting up the Arnold-Towers flying training scheme. In April Arnold had offered the RAF a third of the USAAF's capacity for primary, basic and advanced pilot training, and in May Admiral Towers had offered similar USN facilities at Pensacola. The first batch of 550 pupils arrived in June and further batches followed at five- to six-week intervals. The completion of the complicated details of these schemes, together with their administration, was a major task for the Delegation and Harris, who kept in close touch with Air Vice-Marshal Garrod, the Director of Training in the Air Ministry, devoted much time to it. He went on well-publicised visits to some of the training bases at Dallas and in Florida and Alabama,[34] and the training got under way without arousing adverse political comment. One problem at the United Kingdom end, however, did arouse Harris's ire and led him to request Freeman's personal intervention. For the third time, he wrote in September, a training course had arrived very late. 'Whatever the reason it is totally unacceptable to the US Air Forces and I can find no answer or apology adequately to justify these occurrences to increasingly infuriated US Departments. Any repetition will inevitably result in loss of training facilities. I cannot help feeling that the US might be right in assuming that these matters are being dealt with by junior staff officers in unimaginative, offhand or irresponsible manner. They are furious.'[35]

This was but one item in Harris's copious correspondence with the Air Ministry. Maurice Dean remembered his long reports, written with insight, always interesting and full of amusing anecdotes; greatly looked forward to in the Air Ministry, they were usually widely circulated – but not always. On 15 September he sent Freeman an honest, and highly critical, reflection on the American scene as he and his staff saw it:

It is a mistake to imagine that contact and discussion with individuals such as Arnold, Lovett, Stimson and even Hopkins and the President is the path to accomplishment here . . . their promises often peter out to nothing in practice through material lack or departmental opposition . . . the arrogant American assumption of superiority and infallibility makes it hard indeed to get them to accept even our ideas – still less our help or our material demands . . . we have been living in a fool's paradise where expectations of quality and quantity in American production and releases are concerned . . . however if the war goes on long enough the sheer weight of production made possible by their unlimited resources and manpower should make up for it in smothering effect. As to production generally, up to date they have had a damn fine war on British dollars . . . they are firmly convinced they are taking a major and direct part in the war . . . they are convinced of their own superiority and super efficiency and of our mental, physical and moral decrepitude . . . there has been no inkling of any interference with their own high standards of living. The best of them, however, now appreciate that we are getting not only nothing like enough American production for our vital minimum requirements, but not even our money's worth by any standards of business honesty. Meanwhile the most impressive, not to say oppressive, factor in the atmosphere today is our wishful thinking . . . about the probability of US entry into the war. They will come in when they think we have won it . . . but if they come in in any other circumstances, short of being kicked in, I'll stand you a dinner and eat, as my share, a pink elephant, trunk, tail and toenails – and raw at that. I am not out to depress you, but I note such a vast divorce between things as they are out here and the wishful thinking evident at home (but not by you!) that it seems appropriate to state our view of the US as it appears to us.[36]

Certainly this was not a document to be extensively distributed. As a blunt commentary on the USA in late 1941, as seen through the eyes of a senior commander and his staff who had recently left a sorely pressed, beleaguered Britain, it was, however, a reasonable enough appraisal, designed to dispel illusions and paint an honest picture.

An incident recorded by Ian Elliot on the basis of what Harris told him provides an example of what he had to put up with. Attending a meeting of Service Chiefs and Heads of Missions with General Marshall in the chair, he had to listen to Colonel Elliott Roosevelt (the President's son) reporting on a visit to the Middle East and criticising the unloading arrangements at Takoradi. The Colonel went on to criticise the RAF for its failures at Dunkirk, in Greece and Crete, and so on, whereupon Harris interrupted him: 'It is possible, General, that the Royal Air Force is the worst trained, worst organised, worst disciplined force in the world, as Colonel Roosevelt appears to suggest, but it is still good enough to kick hell out of the combined air forces of Germany and Italy.' 'Good morning,' he concluded, and walked out.[37] The reaction was understandable and could do his reputation no harm whatever in some quarters – though not, of course, in all.

With the President himself Harris's relationship was totally different. As he later recalled, Roosevelt and his close adviser, Harry Hopkins, 'leant over backwards to help us – indeed once or twice Roosevelt was on the verge of being impeached for helping the British. He told the Service Chiefs not to be stand-offish and was always sending for us and asking if there was anything more the Americans could do – within the limitations.' On one occasion Harris asked the President if he could help by providing civilian ferry pilots and he promised to ring up Arnold. As a result there arrived in Harris's office a 'blonde bombshell', Jacqueline Cochran, the holder of several flying records, who offered to fly anything and asked how many more women pilots were wanted. Thus started another aspect of Anglo-American co-operation and a lasting friendship.[38]

At the social level, too, Harris got on well, ably supported by Jill, whose rapid acceptance was marked when she was featured as 'Beauty of the Week' in the *Times Herald* of 27 October:

Transplanted from England to the United States, she made a perilous trip with her young baby aboard a battleship. She's to be here indefinitely with her husband, who holds the rank of air marshal and is head of the British Air Mission in this country. Her beauty contributes much to the Washington scene, but taking care of her baby and doing war work leave her little time for frivolities. She's typically English, with her skin like a garden rose and shining dark hair. Wears her clothes with a real flair, but like most women of her country leans towards the conservative.

They were a good pair, accepting and returning the extensive hospitality that was on offer and recognising its value in supporting Harris's official duties. Nor were their activities limited to Washington. Keen to widen their knowledge of the USA, they visited tourist attractions such as Williamsburg and travelled as far as Miami, where they were entertained to a fishing weekend by Henry Mercer, a shipping magnate to whom they had been introduced by Ian Elliot.[39] Here were business contacts, as distinct from military ones, that would prove invaluable when the war was over. For the present, however, Harris and his wife, like all around them, were subject to the march of events and the consequences of the Japanese attack on Pearl Harbor on Sunday 7 December 1941.

Harris vividly remembered the panic-stricken atmosphere that day in the War Department, where he was immediately pressed by Stimson, Secretary of State for War, to cancel as many as possible of the supplies that had been ordered. He then met Lovett, the Assistant Secretary for Air and a good friend, who told him in horrified terms that the whole Pacific Fleet had been destroyed. His reply 'so what?' was similar to his response a few days later when Lovett told him the *Prince of Wales* and *Repulse* had been sunk. 'This is where we start,' he observed, anxious to try to bring some calm into the situation. Now, of course, they were all allies, and the British officers switched from plain clothes to uniform as indicated when the three Heads of Mission were featured in the *New York Times* studying a map of the Far East. Behind the scenes, however, Harris was soon confronting a temporary freeze on all movements of aircraft and spares and trying to persuade the Americans to view the war in its proper perspective so as to release to the RAF the bare essentials it needed. Cribbett, reporting on 29 December to the Air Ministry, spoke of Harris's 'conspicuous skill' in these negotiations, which among other things had secured the release of nearly all the Kittyhawk requirements.[40]

Meanwhile the Heads of Mission had been preparing for the arrival of Churchill, Beaverbrook and the Chiefs of Staff on 22 December, and on the 23rd the Harrises, together with Portal, were present in the Gallery to listen to the Prime Minister's momentous address to Congress. There followed the first Washington Conference about Allied strategy, some of whose sessions Harris attended, and in the course of which it was decided to set up the Combined Chiefs of Staff Committee. This was to prove the crucial instrument in determining Anglo-American strategy for the rest of the war, and since it would normally meet in Washington it was agreed that the three Heads of Mission should represent their Chiefs on day-to-day matters. Initially the RAF role would fall to Harris, but already he knew it would not be for long.

Early in January Portal had taken him aside to tell him that he wanted him to take over as C-in-C Bomber Command and would be speaking to the Prime Minister about it. Churchill agreed, as Portal told Harris the next day. Elliot, who soon heard the news, later reflected on it. 'Harris had always regarded World War I as unfinished business and had dedicated himself, through his career, to the vital necessity of striking at Germany in her homeland, where it would really hurt.' Now he would have the opportunity. Wing Commander Wilf Oulton, a member of his staff, was with him on the night he was told. 'He was a solid character, very steady, unemotional; he had a young wife and baby daughter, all of which had psychological effects, I'm sure. I found him firm, strong, reasonable. My impression was that he had been told to do this job – a horrible one – and was going to do it with all his might and main.'[41]

Harris had, in fact, been under consideration for Bomber Command for some time, Peirse having been under marked criticism for the Command's poor performance. So when a new Air C-in-C was required for the Far East in the wake of the Japanese attack Sinclair consulted Portal and on 10 December suggested to Churchill that Peirse should take the job and be replaced by Harris.[42] Certainly in some quarters there were concerns about the way Harris had been getting on in the USA. Lord Halifax in particular thought him a failure, telling Freeman that his downright speech and personality were considered unpleasant and domineering; the Americans disliked his superiority complex.[43] Essentially, however, his move to Bomber Command was for positive, not negative reasons, and in any case the critics took insufficient account of all his dedicated work in fighting the RAF's corner and the many influential friendships he had been able to establish. Roosevelt, Hopkins, Harriman, Lovett and Marshall were important allies, as were the senior American airmen. As Pete Copp summarises it, the impression he left behind in the War Department was of 'an independent-minded, outspoken bomber advocate – articulate, forceful, sure of the correctness of his views, and wickedly critical of those high or low who differed with him.'[44] 'Hap' Arnold's farewell letter of 4 February was in the warmest terms, speaking on behalf of the USAAF of his 'splendid co-operation and ever present spirit of helpfulness. Your presence here aided materially in bringing our airplanes up to combat standard and in changing our organisation from one of peacetime training to one of preparation for war.'[45] Ira Eaker, who had been appointed to lead the Eighth Air Force, was also on net. At a dinner for Portal on 18 January he and his wife, Ruth, quickly established rapport with Bert and Jill, notwithstanding Bert's immediate attempt to persuade Ira to join him in the night bomber offensive rather than employ his bombers by day: 'God knows, I hope you can do it, but I don't think you can.'[46] The foundations of the great alliance between the two bomber forces had been laid.

The Harrises sailed for home aboard the armed merchant cruiser *Alcantara* on 10 February 1942, leaving behind them a great fund of goodwill, and not just among the high and mighty. Ian Elliot, who saw them off from the station in Washington, walked back along the platform with Ennals, his driver, who was obviously devoted to Harris: 'Mr Elliot, I hate like hell to see him go.' 'So do I,' replied Elliot, 'but he's going to a far more important job. What are you going to do now – back to the FBI?' Ennals' face fell: 'Do you think he knew?' 'Of course he did,' said Elliot, 'he wasn't born yesterday.'[47]

Notes

1. Family recollections; Harris, *op.cit.* p.9. The post of VCAS had been established earlier that year and was first filled by Sir Richard Peirse.
2. 'Directed' letters, starting with the format 'I am directed to inform/request/instruct [etc]', were widely used by Air Ministry staff officers writing formally to Cs-in-C and other high-ranking RAF commanders, thus implying that they were speaking on the express authority of their superiors. Harris disliked this practice.
3. *Ibid* pp.9–11.

4. Folder H116; discussion with Professor Jones; Harris, *op.cit.* p.52.

5. Folder H116, dated 24 November and 10 December 1940.

6. Harris, *op.cit.* pp.51–2; Tape 11.

7. Folder H112, dated 2 January 1941; AIR 20/8144; OH vol.IV, p.132.

8. Folder H116, dated 11 February 1941. Of 79 bombers attacking Bremen, 22 had crashed on return to England because of fog.

9. AIR 20/8144, dated 1 April 1941.

10. Folder H115, dated 9 April 1941.

11. OH vol.IV, p.133–5; Folders H112, dated 28 November 1940; H116, dated 4 December 1940.

12. AIR 15/227; Folder H116, dated 1 February 1941. Terraine, *op.cit.* pp.240–4, describes the whole debate.

13. Folder H116, dated 2 February 1941; Saward, *op.cit.* p.88.

14. Folders H115, dated 19 March 1941; H112, dated 21 March 1941; H115, dated 25 March 1941.

15. AIR 20/8144.

16. Harris accepted this obligation but insisted to Hugh Dalton (as Minister of Economic Warfare he had been placed in charge of SOE) and others that they must not try to dictate to the RAF how such operations were to be carried out. AIR 20/2759, dated 27 February 1941.

17. Folders H116, dated 8 and 23 December 1940 and 4 and 18 February 1941; H115, dated 26 April 1941; Saward, *op.cit.* pp.89–90.

18. Folder H116, dated 25 November 1940 and 26 January 1941; AIR 20/2759; H112, dated 26 January 1941; H115, dated 3 April 1941; Saward, *op.cit.* p.91.

19. Folder H116, dated 28 November and 19 December 1940; Saward, *op.cit.* pp.91–4, covers this subject in detail.

20. Folder H116, dated 23 February 1941.

21. Folders H116, dated 7, 8 and 30 December 1940, 13 and 28 January 1941; H115, dated 3 April 1941.

22. Folder H115, dated 17 April 1941; Saward, *op.cit.* pp.96–8, quotes at length from the minute to Freeman and from a subsequent letter to Professor Lindemann about anti-tank weapons.

23. Folder H116, dated 30 November 1940 and 30 January 1941; AIR 20/2759. For details of this route see Humphrey Wynn's *Forged in War*, pp.9–11.

24. Folder H112, dated 25 April 1941.

25. Harris Tape 9; Saward, *op.cit.* p.96.

26. Slessor, *op.cit.* p.351.

27. Furse, *Biography of Wilfrid Freeman*, p.164.

28. Harris, *op.cit.* pp.60–2; Saward, *op.cit.* pp.99–100.

29. Elliot had made his career in iron and steel, first with GKN and then the British Iron and Steel Corporation. In 1940 he went to New York to help organise the purchase of steel from the USA.

30. *History of the RAF Delegation, Washington*, AIR 45/2, on which most of this account is based.

31. See Slessor, *op.cit.* pp.327, 358, for details.

32. AIR 45/2, Section II. See Gwyer, *Grand Strategy*, vol.III part 1, chapter 6, for full discussion of the impact of Soviet needs on the supply of American equipment to the UK at

this time. Gwyer makes it clear that the cuts would heavily reduce Bomber Command's strength during precisely the period when the bombing of Germany was likely to be most important.

33. AIR 45/2, Section III.

34. Harris was provided with two aircraft for his personal use, one Army and one Navy, neither of whom was prepared to stand down for the privilege; Ian Elliot, unpublished memoir, p.132.

35. AIR 45/2, Section IV. See also Saward, *op.cit.* p.103, where the civilian flying training schools are also mentioned.

36. Folder H98, together with other letters to Freeman and Sir Henry Self, Head of the British Air Commission.

37. Elliot memoir, pp.126–7.

38. Harris Tape 9; Saward, *op.cit.* pp.102–3. In 1955 Harris wrote the Foreword to Cochran's autobiography, *The Stars at Noon* (Misc Folder 22).

39. Family albums.

40. Harris Tape 9; Folder H98, dated 8 December 1941; Saward, *op.cit.* pp.103–4; Harris, *op.cit.* pp.65–6; AIR 45/2.

41. Saward, *op.cit.* p.105; Elliot memoir, p.132; Air Vice-Marshal W.E. Oulton in RAFHS, *Reaping the Whirlwind.*

42. Probert, *The Forgotten Air Force*, p.106.

43. Portal Papers, Box C File 5 E1, memo Freeman to Portal. Freeman told Halifax that the RAF had only released Harris unwillingly and he could fill any number of jobs with distinction if he came back home. Since Furse, *op.cit.* pp.200–1, does not identify Halifax as the critic, he unfairly implies that these views were generally held.

44. Copp, *Forged in Fire*, pp.222–3; he also describes Harris's close dealings with Roosevelt and Hopkins.

45. Misc Folder 7.

46. Parton, *Air Force Spoken Here*, pp.130–1; Copp, *op.cit.* pp.226–7.

47. Elliot memoir, p.132.

Chapter 7

The year of experiment

Harris was appointed Commander-in-Chief Bomber Command on 22 February 1942. He had arrived at his Headquarters near High Wycombe (30 miles West of Central London) a few days earlier to take over from Air Vice-Marshal Baldwin, who as AOC 3 Group had been holding the fort since Sir Richard Peirse's departure for the Far East on 6 January. Unfortunately Springfield, his official residence at Great Kingshill, five miles from the Headquarters, was not yet available; as he had been told by signal in mid-Atlantic the Secretary of State had agreed that Lady Peirse, for reasons of ill health, could remain there probably until May. Harris was not best pleased about this and when he subsequently discovered that Lady Peirse appeared far from unwell his annoyance turned to fury. 'My residence is my operational accommodation in the field,' he wrote to the helpful Air Chief Marshal Courtney, Air Member for Supply and Organisation, on 10 March, and he wanted it without further delay.[1] Thankfully the offending lady departed a fortnight later, enabling the Harris family – and General Eaker, their first living-in guest – to move in. It had been an annoying episode, only partly alleviated by the generous hospitality afforded by his Air Officer Administration, Air Vice-Marshal Ronnie Graham, in his own official residence on the Bradenham estate, Queen's Gap.

Already, during the first month, Harris had gripped his new Command. He had been sent there at the critical moment when its whole future was at stake. For one thing the strategic bombing offensive thus far was being revealed as much less effective than the claims made for it had suggested. Back in August 1941 a report prepared at the insistence of Lord Cherwell by Mr D.M. Butt, of the War Cabinet Secretariat, had concluded that of all the bombers recorded as having attacked their targets in June and July only one in three had got within five miles, and in the case of the Ruhr, whose targets were the most difficult to find, the proportion was a mere one in ten. These findings, though viewed sceptically by Peirse and his colleagues in Bomber Command, set alarm bells ringing not just in the Air Ministry but in Downing Street too; unless night navigation could be radically improved the assault on Germany would contribute little to winning the war.[2] Then on 7/8 November an attempted major night for Bomber Command had turned into disaster, when 37 of 400 bombers sent to a variety of targets, including Berlin, failed to return – an unacceptable loss rate of 9.25%. Peirse himself was partly blamed for this, having failed to make proper allowances for an adverse weather forecast, and it was an important factor in the decisions to replace him by Harris and to conserve the bomber force over the winter months in order to prepare it for larger scale operations in the spring.[3]

Not that there was all that large a force to conserve. The front line that Harris inherited, spread in five Groups across eastern England between East Anglia and Yorkshire, consisted of a mere 44 medium and heavy bomber squadrons, six of them not yet operational, 2 Group's handful of light bomber squadrons, and 17 Operational Training Units. For practical purposes this represented a strategic striking force of less than 400 serviceable aircraft and an average availability of about 300. Of the 44 squadrons 20 were flying Wellingtons, sturdy and reliable aircraft but lacking the range and bomb-load necessary for the longer term. Nine more were still operating Hampdens and Whitleys, soon to be phased out. This left only 15 squadrons of 'heavies', mostly equipped with the recently introduced Stirlings, Halifaxes and Manchesters, all of which were undergoing teething problems – and worse in the case of the Manchester. So far just two squadrons had received the Manchester's four-engined derivative, the Lancaster, and neither was operational when Harris took over.[4] Clearly there would be much to do, and his task would be made no easier by the loss of previously promised supplies of American aircraft, a subject on which he required no briefing.

Thanks to his recent experience in the USA Harris also had a good feel for the pressures that would now affect the determination of Anglo-American strategy. He applauded the decision of the Washington Conference on 23 December to give the defeat of Germany priority over that of Japan, but he knew there were many influential Americans whose enthusiasm for engaging in another European war was outweighed by their desire to deal with the Japanese, the perpetrators of Pearl Harbor. It was important, therefore, that nothing be said or done to discourage the American airmen from bringing over their bombers to join the RAF in a combined offensive against Germany. So when Sir Stafford Cripps, Lord Privy Seal, spoke most ill-advisedly in the House of Commons on 25 February about a review of the policy of bombing Germany this caused consternation not just in the Air Ministry and at Bomber Command – where Harris had just arrived – but also in Washington. As the Delegation immediately signalled the Air Ministry, this public statement implying that the British government might be losing confidence in the strategic bombing offensive could well strengthen the hands of the 'Japan first' lobby and might adversely affect the American production programme for heavy bombers.[5] So as Harris bent to his task he knew that his Command faced a crisis of confidence, not only behind the closed doors of Whitehall but also in public, both at home and abroad. Action more spectacular and effective than hitherto was essential, and

AIR MINISTRY 1941–5

Secretary of State for Air and
President of the Air Council
(Sir Archibald Sinclair)

Parliamentary Under-Secretary
of State for Air
(Captain Harold Balfour)

Chief of Air Staff
(ACM Sir Charles Portal)

Air Member for Personnel
(AM Sir Philip Babington;
AM Sir Bertine Sutton, 17 August 1942;
AM Sir John Slessor, from 5 April 1945)

Air Member for Training
(AM Sir Guy Garrod;
AM R.M. [later Sir Peter] Drummond,
27 April 1943–27 March 1945)

Assistant Chief of Air Staff
(General)
(AM Sir Richard Peck)

Assistant Chief of Air Staff
(Operational Requirements
and Tactics)
(AVM R.S. Sorley)

Note: This chart is greatly simplified, being merely intended to show where the officers referred to in the text fitted into the overall structure.

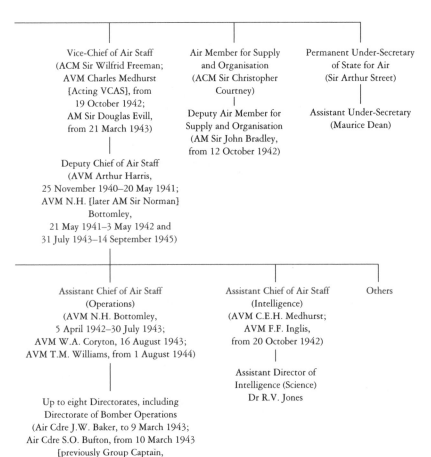

Vice-Chief of Air Staff
(ACM Sir Wilfrid Freeman;
AVM Charles Medhurst
[Acting VCAS], from
19 October 1942;
AM Sir Douglas Evill,
from 21 March 1943)

Deputy Chief of Air Staff
(AVM Arthur Harris,
25 November 1940–20 May 1941;
AVM N.H. [later AM Sir Norman]
Bottomley,
21 May 1941–3 May 1942 and
31 July 1943–14 September 1945)

Air Member for Supply
and Organisation
(ACM Sir Christopher
Courtney)

Deputy Air Member for
Supply and Organisation
(AM Sir John Bradley,
from 12 October 1942)

Permanent Under-Secretary
of State for Air
(Sir Arthur Street)

Assistant Under-Secretary
(Maurice Dean)

Assistant Chief of Air Staff
(Operations)
(AVM N.H. Bottomley,
5 April 1942–30 July 1943;
AVM W.A. Coryton, 16 August 1943;
AVM T.M. Williams, from 1 August 1944)

Up to eight Directorates, including
Directorate of Bomber Operations
(Air Cdre J.W. Baker, to 9 March 1943;
Air Cdre S.O. Bufton, from 10 March 1943
[previously Group Captain,
DD Bomber Ops,
from 14 November 1941])

Assistant Chief of Air Staff
(Intelligence)
(AVM C.E.H. Medhurst;
AVM F.F. Inglis,
from 20 October 1942)

Assistant Director of
Intelligence (Science)
Dr R.V. Jones

Others

Senior Air Staff Officer
(AVM Robert Saundby;
AVM R.D. Oxland, from 24 February 1943;
AVM H.S.P. Walmsley, from 8 February 1944)

Operations Staff
(including Operational Research,
Army and Navy Liaison Staff, Public Relations)

HQ No 1 Group, Bawtry
(AVM R.D. Oxland;
AVM E.A.B. Rice, 24 February 1943;
AVM R.S. Blucke, 12 February 1945)

HQ No 3 Group, Exning (Newmarket)
(AVM J.E.A. Baldwin;
AVM The Hon R.A. Cochrane,
14 September 1942;
AVM R. Harrison, 27 February 1943)

HQ No 2 Group,
Huntingdon until 31 May 1943
(AVM A. Lees; AVM J.H. D'Albiac,
24 December 1942)

HQ No 4 Group, York
(AVM C.R. Carr;
AVM R.D. Whitley,
12 February 1945)

BOMBER COMMAND 1942–5

Air Officer Commanding-in-Chief
(AM Sir [later ACM] Arthur Harris)

Personal Staff Officer (Gp Capt T.D. Weldon; Wg Cdr W.A.J. Lawrence,
18 July 1945)

Personal Secretary (Asst Sec Off [later Flt Off] M.E.K. Wherry)

Personal Assistant (Flt Lt Paul Tomlinson, 26 February 1942;
Flt Lt Etienne Maze, 28 September 1943;
Flt Lt Walter Pretyman, 15 September 1944;
Flt Lt Peter Tomlinson, 11 June 1945)

Deputy AOC-in-C
(AM [later Sir] Robert Saundby,
from 24 February 1943)

Air Officer i/c Administration
(AVM R. Graham;
AVM R.D. Saunders,
from 1 January 1943)

Air Officer Training
(AVM A.J. Capel)

Staffs of the Services

Equipment	Navigation	Intelligence
Engineer	Signals	Armament
Meteorological	Accountant	Medical
Dental	Photography	Education
Works	RAF Regiment	Miscellaneous Appointments
Physical Training	WAAF Staff Officers	Aeronautical Inspection
Financial Adviser to AOC-in-C		

HQ No 5 Group,
Grantham until 13 November 1943,
Morton Hall (Swinderby)
from 14 November 1943
(AVM J.C. Slessor;
AVM W.A. Coryton,
25 April 1942;
AVM The Hon R.A. Cochrane,
28 February 1943;
AVM H.A. Constantine,
16 January 1945)

HQ No 8 Group (PFF),
Huntingdon
(AVM D.C.T. Bennett,
13 January 1943)

Several non-operational
Groups, mostly
concerned with
operational training

HQ No 100 Group,
Bylaugh Hall (East Dereham)
(AVM E.B. Addison,
8 November 1943)

HQ No 6 Group (RCAF),
Allerton Park (Knaresborough)
(AVM G.E. Brookes, 25 October 1942;
AVM C.M. McEwen, 29 February 1944)

quickly, if Bomber Command was to receive the resources of every kind that it needed, and if the American determination to join in was to be sustained.

So what were Harris and Bomber Command being called on to do? Soon after his departure to the States the Air Ministry had sent his predecessor an important new directive. Dated 9 July 1941, this at last recognised that it was not practicable to find and hit precise targets in Germany by night and that the most cost-effective way of using the bomber force was to concentrate on 'area' targets, *ie* large towns and cities which by their nature would contain many installations of military and economic significance. Moreover such attacks would hit at enemy morale, increasingly seen as a worthwhile objective. The directive therefore stipulated that the main effort of the bomber force should be devoted to dislocating the German transportation system and destroying the morale of the civilian population as a whole and of the industrial workers in particular. Then on 14 February 1942 the instruction to conserve the force was cancelled, the value of the offensive in supporting the Russians was stressed, and its primary objective was stated simply as civilian morale, particularly that of the industrial workers. Attached was a list of 'area targets' for attack. This was the directive that Harris found on arriving at High Wycombe a week later.[6]

Let it be clearly stated: the policy of area bombing was not conceived by Harris, as all too many critics have alleged. It was determined by the Air Ministry under Portal's direction, with the support of the other Chiefs of Staff and of the War Cabinet. Certainly Harris espoused it, as one would expect, for it needed a man of his convictions and temperament to carry it out. Certainly he interpreted the policy too single-mindedly for some, particularly towards the end. The ultimate responsibility for what was done, however, lay not with him but with those who undertook the higher direction of the war and decided that an area bombing campaign had an essential place in British strategy.

Chief among these was the Prime Minister himself, who had written on 8 July 1940:

> When I look round to see how we can win the war I see that there is only one sure path. We have no continental army which can defeat the German military power. The blockade is broken and Hitler has Asia and probably Africa to draw from. Should he be repulsed here or not try invasion, he will recoil eastward, and we have nothing to stop him. But there is one thing that will bring him back and bring him down, and that is an absolutely devastating, exterminating attack by very heavy bombers from this country upon the Nazi homeland.[7]

By 1942 Churchill was taking a less absolute view, telling Sinclair on 13 March that bombing Germany, while not decisive, was better than doing nothing, and indeed was 'a formidable method of injuring the enemy'. He went on to remind the Secretary of State how widely the existing policy was being challenged by opinion: for instance, the Archbishop of Canterbury had recently spoken to him for half an hour on the failure of the high-level bombing.[8]

On that very day Harris wrote his first minute direct to Churchill, answering a request for a comparison between the opening GEE attacks on Essen, carried out on 8–10 March, and the German raid on Coventry. Harris, originally sceptical (p.101), was now well persuaded of the significance of GEE as a navigational aid and the Prime Minister was keen to know how effective the new equipment was proving. In a frank reply Harris admitted that the attacks had achieved less concentration than had been hoped for but the crews were enthusiastic and the lessons learnt were being applied.[9] Then on the 22nd Harris was invited to spend the evening with Churchill at Chequers, only a few minutes' drive from Springfield; the immediate purpose was to discuss the plans for a heavy bomber attack on the battleship *Tirpitz* in Trondheim Fjord. Writing to Churchill immediately afterwards, Harris said: 'I appreciate very much your thoughtfulness in proposing to send a message to the crews. I was going to ask you to give them this encouragement. It is hard to think ahead of you.'[10] That the Prime Minister was already impressed by Harris is clear from his private comment to Roosevelt on 29 March: 'Harris is doing so well.'[11]

Thus began Harris's visits to Chequers, which took place frequently during 1942 and 1943, though only occasionally thereafter. Sometimes he would be there of an evening, sometimes over a weekend, and usually in the company of others. Occasionally Jill would be with him, but normally he went alone, and thanks to the Prime Minister's unbelievable social and working routine would not be home until three or four in the morning – not that Harris minded. His reflections on the way they discussed their business are worth quotation:

> The worse the state of the war was, the greater was the support, enthusiasm, encouragement and constructive criticism that one got from this extraordinary man; it was all done with the utmost kindness, though not without a mischievous dig now and again just for the fun of it. He did not mind your expressing views contrary to his own, but he was difficult to argue with for the simple reason that he seldom seemed to listen long to sides of the question other than his own ... I found it more satisfactory to listen than to argue, only sticking in a word here and there with the intention of steering the conversation round to the subject ... on which I wanted his opinion and guidance. If I wanted to get anything across or give any complicated explanation I found it much better to send him a paper ... if it ran to no more

than two or three pages – and everything was put tersely and crystallised into snappy sentences so that he could get the meaning quickly – then I always found him very willing to investigate one's point of view and do all that he could to help ... He never failed in encouragement, just as he never failed to apply the spur. When a week or two of bad weather prevented us from doing anything much to get on with the offensive he would express his disappointment but conclude by saying 'I am not pressing you to fight the weather as well as the Germans: never forget that.'[12]

Without doubt Harris drew much of his inspiration from these nocturnal têtes-à-tête, and it is hard to think of other top RAF commanders who could have established the same degree of rapport with this greatest of wartime Prime Ministers. They shared a sense of history; while Harris was no author he was an avid reader of military history and could appreciate Churchill's insights and perspectives. Each had his vivid recollections of the First World War and its lessons. Neither had subsequently had any doubts about the dangers of a resurgent Germany; for both there was 'unfinished business' to be done. Above all there was, in both men, an overriding conviction that one wins wars only by taking them to the enemy. The offensive spirit, the single-minded tenacity, the outspokenness that Churchill observed in Harris were qualities that matched his own; here was the kind of high commander he needed in those dark days, a man who shared his convictions about the nature of the war they were fighting and the hard things that had to be done to win it.

It was of course a highly unusual relationship, cutting across all the conventional lines of command and responsibility. Churchill was always keen to be in on the action and therefore wanted to know his operational commanders, but the position Harris found himself in was considerably closer than usual and could so easily have presented the Air Ministry with much embarrassment. As the biographer of Sinclair, the Secretary of State for Air, comments: 'Like Beaverbrook, Harris had a peculiar influence over Churchill which he used to great effect. Obstacles to the expansion of the bomber campaign miraculously dissolved after his arrival. Although he never got all he asked for, his ability to influence Churchill meant that the Prime Minister essentially allowed Harris to wage a private war.'[13] This oft-repeated allegation about a 'private war' goes too far, for Sinclair was in general strongly supportive of the bombing campaign, as was Portal, who recognised not only that the liaison between Prime Minister and Commander-in-Chief must be accepted but could also be turned to advantage. If the strategic offensive was to be prosecuted effectively it would be well worth having the ear of the Prime Minister in a way that would never be possible within the normal processes of government. In practice it worked well; Harris kept Portal and his colleagues informed about their discussions and learnt to be careful what he said on matters strictly outside his own competence.

Their very first meeting on 22 March had provided an object lesson. In discussing Bomber Command's forthcoming operation against the *Tirpitz* from airfields in northern Scotland, Harris had warned Churchill that it might be prejudiced by lack of hard runways at Kinloss and Lossiemouth, whereupon the Prime Minister expressed surprise and invited his guest's views. Harris, as was his wont, did not mince words: 'Apart from labour troubles, our engineers and contractors have a vast amount to learn in regard to the use of labour-saving heavy machinery on such jobs as runway laying.' The Americans, by comparison, had tremendous machines which needed few men and could build roads and runways far more quickly. For Churchill these were thought-provoking ideas and Harris was instructed to send him, through Lord Cherwell, a minute about the subject. This Harris did, and wisely wrote also to Courtney, whose concern these matters were in the Air Ministry, to forewarn him. Courtney's reply was a firm put-down, telling Harris that his criticisms of the RAF's airfield construction programme were far from justified and he ought to do his homework first. Harris quickly came back, reminding Courtney that he had found himself being pressed by 'a past master in the art of disembowelling witnesses, however reluctant', and refusing to accept that his views about American superiority were incorrect. Courtney's response was more emollient, recognising the situation in which Harris had been placed but also observing that the runways in question had not been built earlier because Bomber Command had not asked for them earlier.[14] Harris would be a shade more cautious in similar situations from now on.

For normal purposes the chain of command took Harris either to Portal or Freeman, or to Air Vice-Marshal Norman Bottomley, who had succeeded him as DCAS. It was Bottomley who sent him his day-to-day instructions and suggestions, often drafted by Air Commodore John Baker or Group Captain Sidney Bufton of the Directorate of Bomber Operations. All three were bomber men; Bottomley had led 5 Group in 1941, Baker had flown light bombers between the wars in India and the Middle East, and Bufton had extensive wartime operational experience, having commanded Whitley and Halifax squadrons. Sadly, however, the constructive and helpful working relationship which one would have hoped for between them and the Commander-in-Chief failed to develop. For Harris, the way he organised and ran his Command and directed its operations was his business; the Air Staff were there to provide policy guidance and to help him when necessary, but not – as 'junior officers' – to tell him how to do his job. The Bomber Operations staff, on the other hand, held their own carefully analysed views on how operations should be conducted and the bomber force developed, and in presenting them often aroused the ire of the C-in-C, as we shall see. Personality differences did not help. None of the three would have been acceptable to Harris in Bomber Command – he actually turned down Baker as a group commander – and some of the other officers on the Air Staff had considerable sympathy with Harris in his confrontations with them.[15] 'The three Bs', as Harris and his wife jokingly called them, were among his pet aversions.[16]

Often enough, however, business was done on a friendly basis and particularly with Bottomley. One of their earlier exchanges was on 9 April, when Bottomley referred to Harris a Foreign Office proposal to broadcast a list of 20 German towns to be dealt with progressively. Harris spelt out his objections in no uncertain terms. The weather factor precluded dealing 'progressively' with anything; the force was far too small to do such a job; the inevitable failure would be fully exploited by Goebbels, and the strengthened enemy defences would increase the losses. 'With the present size of the force,' he went on, 'if we can knock out pretty seriously two or three really worthwhile towns in the most vital parts in Germany, and at the same time by our other attacks in France and elsewhere in Germany and our minelaying efforts make the maximum possible contribution to the war as a whole we shall be doing well indeed.' Here, as observed by Webster and Frankland, the authors of the official history of the strategic bomber offensive, was the attitude of stark realism, amounting at times almost to pessimism, that Harris would always adopt towards the question of operational feasibility, and which would colour his reactions to many of the ideas thrown at him from the Air Ministry and innumerable other directions.[17]

Already he was beginning the limited campaign he had just outlined. The first of his 'commercial traveller's samples', as he called his early bombing attacks,[18] was delivered on 3 March 1942 against the almost undefended Renault factory at Billancourt, near Paris. Highly successful, this showed the value of concentration in time and space but taught nothing about finding and destroying heavily protected targets deep in Germany. The next one did. On 28 March Harris chose Lübeck, one of the cities specified in his directive, as a target for testing the effect of heavy incendiary attack, and in operational terms it met with great success. The third such attack – in fact a series of four raids starting on 23 April – was directed at Rostock, which, like Lübeck, was outside GEE range but relatively easy to identify, and achieved similarly encouraging results at very modest cost. Well publicised, these carefully planned raids showed what forces of aircraft usually less than 200 strong – and mainly consisting of medium bombers – could actually achieve, though the various attempts to exploit GEE against Essen during this period met with little success.[19]

One very different raid carried out on 17 April deserves special mention for it shows that Harris, despite his commitment to the night bombing of large urban areas, had not closed his eyes to the possibilities of daylight precision attacks. Quickly seized of the potential of the Lancaster bombers that were now reaching the Command, he decided to despatch 12 of them to Augsburg in an attempt to destroy the U-boat engine production plant. Flying at extreme low level along a carefully chosen evasive route, eight aircraft got there just before dusk and hit the target. Ultimately only five returned, a prohibitive loss rate which demonstrated that such missions were not feasible operations for Lancasters in 1942. Nevertheless the raid caught the public imagination, excited Churchill's admiration and earned its leader, Squadron Leader J.D. Nettleton, the Victoria Cross. John Searby recalled its effect on the crews and squadrons of the Command – pride in their achievement and the realisation that a new era had dawned tempered the loss of seven crews. It was like a shot in the arm.[20]

There was, however, a sequel. On 27 April Lord Selborne, Minister of Economic Warfare, protested to the Prime Minister about the choice of target, which, instead of ignoring the priorities laid down by his Ministry, ought to have been made in consultation. Portal immediately leapt to Harris's defence, telling Churchill of the tactical considerations affecting this experimental raid, of Harris's desire to assist in the Battle of the Atlantic, and of the critical importance of preserving security. On 2 May Harris followed up a conversation with Churchill with an excellent minute of his own, spelling out in detail the operational factors that had limited the choice to Munich, Nuremberg and Augsburg, and ruled out Schweinfurt and Stuttgart, which the MEW would have recommended. On security he was uncompromising: 'I could not in any circumstances agree to discuss projected attacks outside my Headquarters with other Departments. I do not even tell my crews, to whom security is a matter of life and death, where they are going until the last moment before briefing.' Churchill called this explanation 'careful and admirable'; it completely satisfied him, and at his suggestion Harris and Selborne subsequently lunched together. The rapprochement Churchill was hoping for did not, however, materialise; while the MEW gained growing influence in the Directorate of Bomber Operations, Harris remained far from convinced of the value of its assessments and became increasingly suspicious of its advice.[21]

Nor was he impressed by a proposal from Freeman on 26 May to continue the daylight bombing experiment with 12 specially armoured Lancasters, soon to be followed by a further 100. Reasonably enough Harris saw himself, as the official historians explain it, 'being invited to sacrifice a significant proportion of the best element in his night striking force to the interests of an experiment which would be highly expensive and totally ineffective.' His firm reply was answered in uncompromising terms. 'I thought that over a period of $1\frac{1}{2}$ years,' wrote the exasperated Freeman, 'I had got accustomed to your truculent style, loose expression and flamboyant hyperbole, but I am not used to being told – as you imply – that I am deliberately proposing to risk human lives in order to test out an idea of my own which in your opinion is wrong. I should be glad if you would carry out the order given to you.' Harris took great delight in telling Freeman that nearly all the offending letter had been worded by his staff and thus reflected their views as well: 'If this armoured Lancaster proposal is to stand I must ask for an official directive to which I can register an official protest,' he concluded. In the event the scheme never materialised, but the dispute provided a good example of the kind of pressures to which the C-in-C was already being frequently subjected from on high.[22]

Coincident with this exchange Harris's mind had been much engaged on weightier matters. Thus far his successful attacks had shown what forces of 200–300 aircraft could achieve against relatively small targets, but to have a real chance of convincing the critics of what an expanded and modernised Bomber Command might eventually be able to achieve he decided upon a 'coup de théatre' – a concentrated attack at maximum strength on a major industrial city. Then, as he and his SASO, Robert Saundby, thought this through they realised that the magic figure of a thousand aircraft might be achievable if they could augment his normal 400-strong front-line with bombers from the Operational Training Units and from other commands, particularly Coastal. In cold logic it was an outrageous scheme and Harris did not underplay the dangers when he floated it with Portal and then, backed by his full encouragement, with Churchill at Chequers. The Prime Minister took little persuading – it was a proposal that accorded with his deepest instincts of how the war should be taken to the enemy – and as Harris drove back to Springfield on the night of 17 May he found himself humming the tune associated with Winston's greatest ancestor: *Malbrouck s'en va t'en guerre.*[23]

The stakes were enormous – indeed, they were too high for the Admiralty, which back-tracked on the First Sea Lord's initial undertakings and refused to endorse Air Marshal Sir Philip Joubert's agreement to allow Coastal Command's 250 bombers to take part. Understandably, given the critical importance of the Battle of the Atlantic, the Navy could not accept the risk of losing large numbers of maritime aircraft and their experienced crews, but to Harris this was a serious setback. Yet undaunted he and his staff pressed on, scouring their own training units even further and ending up with a force of 1,046 aircraft, many flown by trainees or by experienced instructors who would be very hard to replace. At risk if the weather or other things went wrong were not only Bomber Command's front line but its seed corn as well. Yet as Harris told his AOCs, if sufficient skill and resolution were shown the large concentration of aircraft over the target area would render the enemy defences comparatively impotent. In launching 'the first really great independent bomber attack in history' he was taking a carefully calculated risk, and if the Thousand Plan was successful the course of the entire war might be altered: 'the whole basis of future strategy will crystallise on the lessons of the results achieved.'[24]

This is not the place to retell the dramatic story of Operation Millennium, the attack on Cologne on the night of 30/31 May 1942.[25] Suffice to say that at what would eventually come to be recognised as the maximum acceptable cost – 4% of the attacking force – it achieved what Harris had hoped for. It had inflicted heavy damage to a major target, given Bomber Command itself an enormous boost, caught the nation's imagination and raised its morale, and hugely impressed Britain's allies. Churchill, warmly congratulating Harris and his Command, saw this proof of the growing power of the British Bomber Force as 'the herald of what Germany will receive, city by city, from now on'. General Arnold described the attack as 'bold in conception and superlative in execution' and looked forward to his own air forces joining in 'these decisive blows against the common enemy'. And from Harris's opposite number in the Red Army came a warm tribute to the precision and effectiveness of this immense operation and the valour and skill of the air-men.[26] In Germany the initial reactions were of utter disbelief, though the actual casualties and damage – albeit considerable – eventually turned out to be much less than had been claimed. The deeper purpose, however, had been achieved. Millennium was the strongest declaration of intent that Harris could have possibly devised, and John Terraine, hard-pressed to think of many examples of Allied leaders in the Second World War being called upon to accept such risks and decide matters of such moment, judges that 'Harris's calm, deliberate decision to stake his whole force and its future on that night showed the true quality of command.'[27]

Greatly encouraged by his success against Cologne, Harris immediately took advantage of the force he had gathered together to mount a second 'thousand' attack on 1/2 June, this time on the particularly important target of Essen and its Krupp factories. Unfortunately Essen again proved difficult to find and despite lower losses (3.2%) the bombing was widely dispersed and relatively ineffective. Even so, Harris was beginning to think that such heavy raids, maybe twice a month, might become the norm for Bomber Command's operations, an idea which he floated with Portal,[28] and meanwhile he pressed on with plans for a third raid, this time against a city with obvious importance for the Battle of the Atlantic. Newly knighted and armed again with Churchill's support thanks to another evening at Chequers, he secured Portal's help in obtaining a 100-strong contingent from Coastal Command[29] and launched some 900 aircraft (not quite the magic figure this time) against Bremen on 25/26 June. At 5% the losses were higher but considerable damage was done – and significantly despite much of the bombing having to be done blind with the aid of GEE. Taken together the three great attacks had not only put Bomber Command on the map but taught 'incomparably valuable lessons about the administrative control and tactical handling' of large bomber forces and demonstrated what concentrated bombing could actually achieve.[30] Yet as Harris was coming to realise, it was just not practicable to go on regularly milking the OTUs; for this and many other reasons his work for a long time to come would have to be done by substantially smaller attacking forces.

Certainly there were many great questions to be addressed during these summer months of 1942, with the Germans driving the Red Army eastward once again, Rommel advancing towards the Nile Delta, the Atlantic battle finely poised, and Japan at the peak of her conquests. Small wonder, then, that despite Bomber Command's recent successes there remained many doubts about its role, and these tended to be reflected by the opinion of Mr Justice Singleton on the likely results of continued bombing of Germany in later 1942 and 1943. Reporting on 20 May he was, hardly surprisingly, unable to provide the firm conclusion hoped for. He could go no further than state that bombing should not be regarded as of itself sufficient to win the war; if, however, Russia could hold Germany on land, continued, intensified and increased bombing would affect 'her war production, her power of resistance, her industries and her will to resist'.[31] This sort of thing was far too vague for Harris and when he was at Chequers in June he seized his opportunity. As he wrote to Portal immediately afterwards:

> The Prime Minister showed me a paper of his on continental intervention. I expressed my horror at the idea until, as previously agreed, Germany had been softened up by bombing and by exhaustion on other fronts. He twitted me on 'the cobbler's opinion on the value of leather' – I replied, as everyone else seemed to have opportunity to state opinions in the use of bombers otherwise than on bombing, I as the cobbler would like to give him mine. Hence the attached paper – purely personal opinion – I should perhaps have sent it to you first, but time was very short and I was sick of a 'quinsy'.[32]

Harris's paper of 17 June was a forcible expression of his conviction that the war could be won by proper application of strategic bombing. 'Victory, speedy and complete, awaits the side which first employs air power as it should be employed,' he wrote, and it would be totally wrong to use it as a subsidiary to land and sea campaigns. A continental land campaign – except to mop up – would play into enemy hands, and as for Coastal Command, its work was entirely defensive and it was 'merely an obstacle to victory'; the best contribution air power could make to the anti-submarine war was to attack U-boat production directly.[33] One can understand the motives behind Harris's argument. Tasked to build up Bomber Command and use it to take the war to the German homeland he was already frustrated at the failure to give him the priorities he needed, and in his resolve to make his case preferred to overstate it rather than let it go by default. On the other hand he was exaggerating what bombing had so far achieved, virtually ruling out the likelihood of an invasion in the West, and denying the critical importance of naval/air co-operation in securing the Atlantic sea lanes on which the rest of the war effort, including his own offensive, depended. This was Harris at very far from his best, but Churchill knew his man well enough to take it with a large pinch of salt. What mattered to the Prime Minister was not that some of the C-in-C's views on wider policy were ill-judged, but that he was never afraid to speak his mind and was doing the job he had been given: revitalising his Command and imbuing it with his own fighting spirit.

Ten days later Harris sent Churchill a further note detailing Bomber Command's limited front-line strength and what it was actually achieving. Fully half its effort was being employed against the enemy's sea-power through minelaying and attacks on surface vessels, naval bases and pro-duction facilities, and its attacks on German towns and cities were seriously damaging industry and transportation. In consequence the enemy was having to devote increasing effort to minesweeping, anti-aircraft and night fighter defences, and damage repair. Here was a realistic appraisal – if somewhat exaggerated at this stage in the war – and it was rounded off with a sensible enough conclusion: 'Bomber Command provides the only means of bringing assistance to Russia in time, the only means of physically weakening and nervously exhausting Germany to an extent which will make subsequent invasion a possible proposition, and is therefore the only force which can in fact hurt our enemy in the present and in the future secure our victory.'[34] This was not in fact the 'unrepentant reiteration' of Harris's previous paper that Saward calls it.[35] It certainly presented the case for the bomber offensive but was better based on facts and avoided the more ten-dentious assertions. Moreover – and reflecting maybe Churchill's influence – it admitted the possibility of a land invasion. Both papers were subsequently circulated to the Cabinet on Churchill's direction; Harris had set out his stall and from now on nobody at the top would be in any doubt about his convictions.

So much for long-term policy. More immediately, notwithstanding his recent successes, Harris had pressing anxieties, not least (as he told Portal on 7 July) the constant reduction of his Command through the constant dribbling away of many of his squadrons, leaving him with no more than about 30 able to operate at night. He understood that the pressure to increase Coastal and Army Co-operation Commands was at times irresistible but felt they could do more to provide for their own needs. On the 18th he made similar points to Churchill in answer to criticism that the offensive was 'tailing off', and having explained some of the practical constraints concluded in ringing tones:

> The Army fights half-a dozen battles a year. The Navy half-a-dozen a war. But poor Bomber Command! Every night that the weather gives us a breather, even though our monthly sortie ration is always attained, every night that for such reasons we fail to stage and win a major battle, the critics rise in wrath and accuse us of doing nothing yet again!

Keeping up the pressure, Harris tackled ACAS (Ops) on 7 August, formally requesting no further transfers of squadrons to the Middle East, India or Coastal Command, no further drafting of aircrew or maintenance personnel to the Middle East, and the return from there of all operationally expired OTU-trained aircrew; he was pulling no punches. On the 22nd his efforts were rewarded with a letter from Portal: 'I am preparing to start, on the Prime Minister's return [from Moscow] a drive for building up Bomber Command in all possible ways', and a month later Churchill told Sinclair that Bomber Command's 32 operational squadrons must be increased to 50 by the end of the year.[36] Though far from persuaded that the Command could win the war on its own Churchill was convinced it must play a major part and for its build-up Harris was assured of his support.

It was not, however, going to be plain sailing. On 4 September, for example, he had told the Prime Minister that he could not possibly accept responsibility for training and transporting the airborne divisions that the Army was proposing to raise. Already he had set forth his views to the Air Ministry, observing that Bomber Command could either continue its offensive role or turn itself into a 'training and transport command for carrying a few thousand airborne troops to some undetermined destination for some vague purpose'; it could not conceivably do both, he argued with a wealth of practical reasons. This was one of the most preposterous proposals Harris was ever asked to consider and he rightly dismissed it without ceremony.[37] At about the same time, on 3 September, he returned to the realms of grand strategy in another lengthy paper to Churchill and Portal in which he urged the immediate concentration of all the heavy and medium bombers available to the United Nations in order to raze to the ground 30–40 of the principal German cities; this, he contended, would fatally affect German morale and production, provide decisive assistance to Russia, and end the war within a year. Churchill reacted calmly to these totally far-fetched ideas, warning Harris not to spoil a good case by overstating it; air bombing was not going to win the war on its own, and in no way could the war be brought to an end in 1943.[38] Portal, on the other hand, was becoming increasingly irritated by all this and when Harris wrote complaining about Headquarters Middle East holding on to too many of its Bomber OTU-trained pilots and suggesting it did not need bombers anyway, he reacted strongly.

> I do not regard your letter as either a credit to your intelligence or a contribution to the winning of the war. It is wrong in both tone and substance and calculated to promote unnecessary and useless friction ... I am sure that great benefit would be gained if you could manage to take a rather broader view of the problems and difficulties confronting the Air Ministry and the other Commands...[39]

Portal's annoyance was clear. Satisfied though he was with Harris's work at Bomber Command, he could well do without the aggravation his subordinate was causing elsewhere.

Nor was the Navy exempt from Harris's attentions. Back in March 1942 he had exchanged friendly letters with Dudley Pound, now First Sea Lord, about his intention to increase Bomber Command's minelaying operations in support of the maritime war and his need for more Naval Liaison Officers to help direct them.[40] The extra assistance was quickly forthcoming and despite occasional difficulties over the supply of mines and the lack of proper publicity for the work and achievements of his crews Harris felt able to write after the war that 'relations with the Naval mining authorities were always excellent'.[41] This silent campaign, steadfastly pursued throughout the war, was a fine piece of bi-Service co-operation, favoured by Harris not least because the work could usually be done in weather conditions that precluded major bombing operations. On other matters, however, he did not always see eye to eye with his Naval counterparts. Indeed, Pound's postscript to his letter about minelaying should have sounded a warning note: 'Shall hope to have a yarn with you and show you a paper we have just put in to the effect that unless we get at least as great an effort from the air over the sea as do our enemies then there will be grave danger of our losing the war at sea and then amongst other things there will be no petrol for your bombers.'

This prophetic remark seems not to have greatly impressed Harris, who was never persuaded that bombers patrolling over the ocean wastes were as gainfully employed as they would be delivering bombs to the submarine yards and their supportive industries; hence his subsequent strictures on Coastal Command and on the Navy's refusal to allow its use against Cologne. Indeed later that year, in a paper entitled 'The Strategic Control of our Anti-Submarine Campaign', he went so far as to argue that the anti-U-boat war should be won primarily by offensive air action and therefore ought to be the responsibility of the RAF. Here again Harris was demonstrating his conviction that strategic bombing offered the one quick route to victory. As Charles Messenger comments, Saundby – on whom Harris first tried his paper – realised that this suggestion would lose his C-in-C what little credit he still had with the Admiralty and fortunately persuaded him that it should go no further.[42]

Influencing Harris in these views was a major practical issue arising out of the Atlantic Battle. On 21 October, writing to Portal about the increasingly frequent dispersion of the bomber effort, he had referred to plans being mooted to bomb the concrete U-boat pens on the French Atlantic Coast – a futile operation which would serve only to delay the direct offensive against Germany. A month later, having received a specific instruction, he returned to the charge. Referring to the ineffectiveness of the American bombing that was already under way and the high civilian casualties that were likely to result, he urged the case for concentrating instead on mining the harbour approaches and bombing the building yards; the Admiralty, he thought, might be open to persuasion. This was a fight he did not win. Despite Portal's support the wider anxieties about the U-boat war were judged by Churchill and the Admiralty to demand direct action, and after further debate Harris was firmly tasked on 14 January 1943 to devastate several ports, including Lorient and St Nazaire. His response was unequivocal: the desired result was unobtainable by the means indicated, the concrete shelters housing the submarines were impenetrable, and even the destruction of entire towns would only impede but not prevent their maintenance, while at the same time causing bitter resentment among the Bretons – some of Britain's best and stoutest friends.[43] But orders were orders, and over the next two months much of Harris's effort was devoted to this campaign, thus delaying the start of the main offensive against the Ruhr for which he had been preparing. Its outcome was exactly as he had forecast, and his coincident attacks on the construction yards – much more to his liking – also achieved little in relation to the critical Atlantic battle.

Various 'panacea targets', as Harris described them, worried him too – as he had also told Portal on 21 October. One of these was synthetic oil production, whose destruction the 'oily boys' had long been urging; now they were identifying Pölitz and Leuna as critical targets, and given the wildness of their earlier forecasts he simply refused to believe them. Another was Schweinfurt and its ball-bearing factories. Back in April Baker had suggested giving it 'the Lübeck treatment' and Harris, though doubting if the Germans would have left themselves with such a dangerous bottleneck, said he was keeping an open mind on it: 'Given the right conditions I might decide to burn the town and blast its factories.'[44] Now, in October, he confirmed to Portal that he still had some faith in this particular panacea but did not share the enthusiasm of 'the Schweinfurt fans', by whom he presumably meant the MEW and DB Ops. In 1943 he would be more strongly opposed, but at this point he was not as 'completely sceptical' as the official historians suggest.[45] What comes across unmistakably, however, from these and the many other pressures on him in the second half of 1942, is the immense frustration they caused him in his efforts to build on his initial successes and to develop the striking power of his Command. Indeed, his front-line strength at the end of the year was no greater than when he had taken over, though the much larger proportion of heavy to medium bombers was making it considerably more effective.

During this time the Command had been spreading its attentions across a wide area of Germany. Rarely did a raiding force exceed 500 aircraft; usually they numbered only 200–300, and their degrees of success varied greatly, as did their losses, which occasionally reached as high as a totally unacceptable 13%. In part these reflected the growing strength of the enemy's defences, and while this was a bad thing for Bomber Command Harris recognised the long-term strategic advantages of compelling the Germans to devote more of their resources away from the land fronts. So there was experience to be gained in trying to evade and counter these defences, as well as in using the newly arriving navigational aids and target finding techniques (see chapter 11). Indeed, all the attacks were now being carefully analysed and Harris himself was constantly keeping an eye on the lessons and trying to apply them. To take just one example, in response to a request to attack the Gelsenkirchen oil plants, he wrote to Bottomley:

> This would be a waste of time and effort. They are very small and difficult to find in the smoky and hazy atmosphere of the Ruhr, I do not believe we have ever succeeded in damaging them and thousands of sorties have been wasted in the attempt ... if we have learnt anything it is that only under very exceptional conditions can the very best crews find these small individual factories in the Ruhr, and then only if luck attends their efforts.[46]

Here was an honest, realistic view – a far cry from some of the claims he and others had made about the bombers' achievements in earlier days.[47]

A further diversion from the assault on Germany occurred towards the end of 1942, when Harris was instructed to give priority to targets in Northern Italy in support of the Allied invasion of North Africa. In the event some 15 sizeable raids, mainly on Genoa and Turin, took place in November and December, and on 13 November, at the request of Churchill and Portal, he submitted an appreciation on the further use of Bomber Command in the attempt to force Italy out of the war. This included consideration of the practicalities of either basing some of its squadrons in North Africa or using airfields there for shuttle bombing, concepts which he and his staff advised against both for practical reasons and because they wished the force kept intact for its prime purposes. In their judgement the Command could adequately take on the cities of Northern Italy from its normal bases. As Harris told Portal: 'I hope nothing will be done to switch the offensive off Germany and I am sure you agree with this. I am at present attacking the Italian targets under conditions where it is either impossible to attack Germany, or advisable to keep out of too much moonlight.'[48] Again, here was the realist at work.

It was this same ability to assess the operational practicalities that led Harris to resist the early pressures to go for the one target which he might have been expected to prefer above all others: Berlin. True, the German capital had been targeted several times by his predecessors, Portal and Peirse, but at heavy cost and never with much success other than in terms of injuring German pride. So when Portal told Harris on 28 August 1942 that Churchill was keen to have it attacked Harris spelt out the facts. Berlin was well defended, only a force of at least 500 bombers would be able to inflict serious and impressive damage on a city of such size, and the attacks would need to be sustained – one isolated attack would merely play into the hands of enemy propaganda. With the present size of his force it would be hard to put together more than 300 suitable aircraft and on recent raids of this size losses had been about 10%. Keen as he was to bomb Berlin, he was not prepared to do so unless he could make a good job of it.[49] Portal was certainly not minded to override him. Five months later, however, on 16/17 January 1943, with political pressures building up and more Lancasters in service, Harris – still somewhat against his better judgement – despatched 200 Lancasters and Halifaxes in Operation Tannenberg, his first raid on 'the big city'.[50] Surprised and encouraged at the loss of only one aircraft, Harris repeated the raid the following night and lost 22 (11.8%). The next attack, on 1/2 March, cost 5.6% – still too high to be acceptable – and after two more raids in late March he kept away from Berlin until the end of August 1943.[51]

Unquestionably the impetus behind these early operations against the German capital stemmed from the desire to be seen to be assisting the Soviet Union. It was when Churchill had first met Stalin in Moscow, in August 1942, that he came to appreciate just how strongly the Russians felt about the inability of the Western Allies to do more to assist them, and in particular to open a 'Second Front'. Hard as Churchill tried to show understanding of their desperate plight and to explain the limitations on what the West could do in the short term he seemed to be getting nowhere until the subject of bombing Germany came up; this, as he later wrote, 'gave general satisfaction'.[52] According to the minutes of the meeting, Stalin told Churchill that 'some military experts were inclined to underrate the importance of the bombing but he did not. It was not only German industry that should be bombed, but the population too. This was the only way of breaking German morale.' Churchill, agreeing that morale was a military target, went on to speak of plans to shatter 20 or more German cities and – if need be, as the war went on – to shatter almost every dwelling in almost every German city, words which had a very stimulating effect on the meeting, whose atmosphere became progressively more cordial.[53] Churchill told Sinclair and Portal five days later that Stalin attached particular importance to the bombing of Berlin and this prompted Portal's request to Harris on 28 August 1942.[54]

Soon afterwards Harris provided Churchill with a book of bombing photographs to send to Stalin,[55] and on 19 January 1943, after the Prime Minister had told him about Bomber Command's continuing operations, including the renewed attacks on Berlin, Stalin replied: 'I wish the British Air Force further successes, most particularly in bombing Berlin.' He telegraphed again on 15 March, 'I would welcome the British aviation striking hard against German industrial centres', and in similar terms on the 27th. On 7 April, responding to a report from Churchill, Stalin went even further: 'Every blow delivered by your air force to the vital German centres evokes a most lively echo in the hearts of many millions throughout the width and breadth of our country.'[56]

By this time the Western Allies had achieved some marked successes, most notably at the Battle of El Alamein and in North Africa, but it was on the Eastern Front that the great mass of the German Army was still being engaged – and would continue to be. For the Russians the Mediterranean war was a sideshow; what they wanted was direct assistance in actually fighting Germany in Europe, and so far only Bomber Command was providing it. For Churchill, who realised this only too well and understood the importance of the Russian campaign for the eventual winning of the war, the strategic bomber offensive was an essential political as well as military tool, and as long as Harris continued to deliver the goods he would have the Prime Minister's strongest support. In 1943, as we shall see, these goods were going to be despatched in far fuller measure.

First, however, we need to consider the way Harris and his Command were being perceived in the outside world, the way he was leading the multitude of men and women who worked – and often died – under his orders, the many changes he was bringing about, the Allies who were coming to operate so closely alongside him, and, to begin with, his Headquarters and the home which to all intents and purposes was a part of it.

Notes

1. Folder H88, E4.
2. OH vol.I, pp.178–80. Lord Cherwell, formerly Professor Lindemann, was Churchill's Scientific Adviser.
3. Terraine, *op.cit.* pp.459–60.
4. AHB Narrative vol.III Appendix A4; Harris, *op.cit.* p.73.
5. OH vol.I, pp.328–9; Saward, *op.cit.* pp.116–17.
6. OH vol.IV, pp.135–7, 143–5.
7. Gilbert, *Finest Hour*, pp.655–6. In 1982 Harris commented on this minute to Gilbert: 'It was the origin of the idea of bombing the enemy out of the war. I should have been proud of it. But it originated with Winston.'
8. Portal Papers, Folder 3.
9. AIR 14/3507. The attack on Cologne on 13/14 March is generally considered as the first successful GEE-led raid. See chapter 11 for a brief explanation.
10. Messenger, *op.cit.* p.68; Folder H65, E3. The message was sent and the attack took place on 27 March, though with only limited success.
11. AIR 8/424.
12. Harris, *op.cit.* pp.151–5. When Harris wrote (pp.153–4) of talking to Churchill about whether to hold on to Tobruk, his memory must have failed him, for the decision to do so was made in April 1941.
13. De Groot, *Liberal Crusader*, p.186.
14. Folder H88, letters dated 23 March–7 April 1942.
15. Conversation with Air Vice-Marshal Deryck Stapleton, who as PSO to VCAS in 1943–4 was one who sympathised.
16. Author's conversation with the Harrises, 1979.
17. OH vol.I, pp.384–5; Folder H47; AIR 8/424.
18. Harris, *op.cit.* p.104.
19. Details of these attacks – and other later ones – are contained in the OH and many other books about the bomber offensive.
20. OH vol.I, pp.440–2; Air Commodore John Searby, *The Everlasting Arms*, p.42.
21. OH vol.I, pp.463–4; vol.IV, pp.220–7; Folders H53; H65; AIR 14/3507. See Terraine, *op.cit.* p.493, for further discussion.
22. OH vol.I, pp.451–4; Folder H16; Furse, *op.cit.* pp.205–6.
23. Harris, *op.cit.* p.10.
24. AIR 14/2026. The figure of 1,046 aircraft is taken from OH vol.I, p.406.
25. For this see Ralph Barker's *The Thousand Plan* and the various histories of Bomber Command.
26. Saward, *op.cit.* pp.145–6.
27. Terraine, *op.cit.* p.485.
28. Portal Papers, Folder 9 dated 20 June 1942.
29. Portal Papers, Folder 3; Harris Folder 81, E70–73. Harris had hoped for 200 aircraft from Coastal Command.
30. OH vol.I, pp.411–17.
31. OH vol.I, pp.336–40; OH vol.IV, pp.231–8.
32. Portal Papers, Box C File 2 E2, 18 June 1942.
33. AIR 14/3507; OH vol.IV, Appendix 18; Folder H65. See also Saward, *op.cit.* pp.160–2, for a substantial summary.

34. Folder H65, E27A, reproduced in full in OH vol.IV, pp.239–44.

35. Saward, *op.cit.* p.163. Saward implies that only the second paper – an amended version of the first – was circulated. In fact there were two quite separate papers – Folder H65, E26, 27.

36. Folders H81, E93, 112; H65, E28; H66, E15; Portal Folder 9, E50, 51; OH vol.I, pp.342–4.

37. Folders H66, E21, 24; H65, E30; Portal Folder 3, E32; Carrington, *Soldier at Bomber Command*, p.108.

38. AIR 8/424; Portal Papers, Folder 9, E54; Folder H63. See Saward, *op.cit.* pp.168–70, for a summary of this paper. See also chapter 8.

39. Folder H81, E139, dated 5 October 1942; Portal Folder 9, E63. This was not the first complaint Harris had lodged about the Middle East – see Terraine, *op.cit.* p.369, note 2, for one in March 1942, also referred to by Tedder in *With Prejudice*, pp.253–4.

40. Folder H101, dated 7 and 8 March 1942.

41. Harris, *op.cit.* p.139.

42. AIR 14/1454, dated 19 December 1942; Folder H64; Messenger, *op.cit.* p.103.

43. Folders H81, E146, 164; H67, dated 27 January 1943; AIR 8/424.

44. Folder H53, E7.

45. OH vol.I, p.466; OH vol.IV, pp.249–52.

46. Folder H47, dated 10 September 1942.

47. Equally realistic had been his reply to Churchill's enquiry in June about a possible 'raid in retribution for the German destruction of the Czech village of Lidice'; it could be done but 100 bombers attacking at low level would be required to eradicate a small target (AIR 14/3507). No such attack was made.

48. Saward, *op.cit.* pp.180–1; Folder H81, E160; author's article in *Italy and the Second World War*.

49. Folder H81, dated 29 August 1942; Saward, *op.cit.* pp.165–6.

50. Churchill, told beforehand that only 150 Lancasters were to be used, had expressed surprise at the small size of the force and Harris met him to explain his plan. Portal Folder 4, dated 6 January 1943; Folder H82, dated 7 January 1943.

51. Richards, *The Hardest Victory*, pp.164–5, 203–4; Harris, *op.cit.* pp.135–6.

52. Churchill, vol.4, p.432.

53. Gilbert, *Road to Victory*, p.179; see also Harriman, *Special Envoy*, p.153.

54. OH vol.I, p.351.

55. Folder H65, E33.

56. Gilbert, *op.cit.* pp.302, 364, 370, 378. Harris circulated this last message throughout the Command. See also Bergander, *Dresden im Luftkrieg*, pp.289–93, and Overy, *Why the Allies Won*, p.102.

Chapter 8

Headquarters and home

The buildings that housed Harris's Headquarters had been constructed in the late 1930s amid the Chiltern beechwoods between High Wycombe and Princes Risborough, and by the time he arrived they had been occupied for nearly two years. He therefore inherited a fully functioning organisation set up by Ludlow-Hewitt and Portal and developed by Peirse, working in purpose-built accommodation and centred upon a modern underground Operations Room. His own office on the ground floor of the well-designed Air Staff block was not more than a stone's throw from the entrance. Here at Southdown, the code-name for his Headquarters, he was to preside for three and a half years.

Most of Harris's staff had awaited his arrival with trepidation; he was reputed to be difficult, intolerant and opinionated. His WAAF personal secretary, Assistant Section Officer (later Flight Officer) Peggy Wherry, hardly thought he would want her and doubted if she could work with such a character. The reality proved entirely different. She found him kind and considerate, a particularly just man who would listen carefully to all sides of any question, and having made up his mind would act decisively. He was, too, a very compassionate man, and she saw nothing of his reputed fierce temper. She stayed with him to the end of the war.[1] Peggy herself was something of a martinet – not unusual for WAAF officers in those days – and the young WAAF typists had to be wary of her. Occasionally Harris himself would defuse some little incident; one of them recalled him walking in when she was on her knees having been told to clean some mud off the carpet before the arrival of a VIP. 'Playing bears?' he asked with a slight grin. They remembered him as a quietly-spoken, 'teddy bear' sort of person with a great sense of fun, though he never engaged in casual chat or met his junior staff socially. Nor was he given to offering direct praise or saying thank you; those who worked for him just sensed from his demeanour whether their work was satisfactory, and anyone he disliked was quietly posted.[2]

His first PA, Paul Tomlinson, who knew him at home as well as in the office, felt much the same. Paul, a Cranwell cadet and a brother of Peter, had met the Harris family at Grantham and when Harris asked him to come to High Wycombe he was delighted to accept. Like Peter, he was quickly absorbed into the family circle and found himself amazed at the consideration with which Harris always treated him, notwithstanding the immense burden his master was carrying. 'Only once,' said Paul, 'did he ever show any sign of irritability in my presence ... he shouted at me one morning when I was trying to ascertain his plans for London and this was simply due to the appalling losses of the night before, about which I did not know at the time.' Those who remember Harris are unanimous: almost never did he raise his voice in anger – he did not need to. As Peter Tomlinson commented when watching John Thaw's portrayal of him in the film *Bomber Harris*, 'his remarks were in character but the delivery would have been quieter, more restrained and almost certainly more effective. He would never have shouted.'[3] Another subordinate who also lived in at Springfield was Group Captain Harry Weldon, a Fellow and Tutor of Magdalen College, Oxford, whom Harris had got to know in Washington and then invited to become his Personal Staff Officer. They became good friends, with Weldon participating in many of the formal and less formal meetings and frequently bringing his own literary skills to the assistance of his master.[4]

One of the few members of Harris's senior staff who ever published their recollections of High Wycombe was the Army Liaison Officer, Colonel Charles Carrington, who served there twice, in 1942 and 1944. He had no doubts about 'the strong, silent man' who had taken over the Command. Harris was 'the most dominating personality I became acquainted with in World War Two'. He never played for popularity, never wasted words or time on mere civilities, but instantly made his presence felt. 'Bomber Command knew it had a master', and the whole machine tautened up, seemed to move into higher gear. As Carrington later commented:

With his power of concentration on the aim, while excluding the irrelevant, he retained a rugged common-sense which was displayed in flat statements about unpalatable facts; he enjoyed shocking the pedants. He was not uncooperative, not hostile to the interests I represented, and when committed to a combined operation with the Army or Navy, even if he had opposed its inception, he gave full support.

Yet sometimes, Carrington also commented, Harris's manner seemed almost a calculated rudeness. Invariably his working day began with the Operations Room conference at which he appeared, sat at his little table without word or smile, and expected and got the punctual attendance of those he wanted to consult. There was trouble if the right man was not there or not ready to reply. Then as soon as the conference was over he left the room without another word or smile; it was rare to see him again, except by appointment. By 1944, when Carrington returned, this morning ritual (or 'High Mass', as the less reverent called it) had become more formal and ceremonious than ever.[5] The distinguished Pathfinder commander, Group Captain John

Searby, who was at this time on Harris's staff, described the nine o'clock routine that was performed down 'the Hole' and what happened subsequently.

> A small desk placed in the centre of the Ops Room awaited the arrival of Sir Arthur who was punctual to the minute, and the senior members of his staff stood around in a half circle; the Deputy Commander-in-Chief stood next to the C-in-C with the Senior Air Staff Officer, Air Commodore Ops, the Senior Intelligence Officer and we lesser fry tailing off around the circle. At his right hand stood Doctor Spence the Chief Meteorological Officer with his synoptic charts at the ready; the Senior Engineer Staff Officer and Armament Officer attended and occasionally the Air Officer in charge of Administration. It was a small drama enacted every morning with unfailing regularity; we heard his quick step as he descended the stairs and braced ourselves for the encounter. There was always an air of mild nervousness; his personality was powerful and there was a hushed silence as he entered the Ops Room. He removed his hat, reached into his left-hand breast pocket and took out his packet of American cigarettes, lit up and asked the first question, one which seldom varied. 'Did the Hun do anything last night?' This was answered by the Intelligence Officer who then handed to Sir Arthur the list of priority targets. He studied the list, sometimes conferring with the Deputy, and selected the targets for the night: then it was the turn of Doctor Spence who dilated on the forecast weather conditions – both for the target area and the home bases. Spence's task was no simple exercise for the C-in-C probed thoroughly; he had a feeling for weather and rarely accepted the forecast without putting Dr Spence through the hoop. He would not be put off with simple statements and occasionally endeavoured to nudge the forecast in the direction he wanted but Spence stood firm and Harris would smile faintly and give up. I think he enjoyed this kind of delving but he never overruled his Chief Met Officer. Then, always provided he was satisfied, it was a matter of how many aircraft, the appropriate bomb loads and a time on target commensurate with the weather forecast. The details of routes, wave timing, diversionary attacks and similar matters were left to the Deputy C-in-C and Senior Air Staff Officers. The first planning conference lasted not more than a few minutes and Sir Arthur left for his own office.
>
> Then the work of putting together the attacking forces began, usually with the Deputy picking up the green telephone and talking to the Pathfinder Group as to the method of marking and possible diversionary raids using Bennett's Mosquitoes. A second meeting with the C-in-C took place later, when all the ends had been tied, attended only by the Deputy and Senior Air Staff Officer. The final Met conference took place at midday but in the meantime the orders had gone forth to the Bomber Groups in the shape of a detailed operation order and the work of preparing the aircraft was put in hand. Once these orders had been dispatched all decisions were taken by the

Deputy and Sir Arthur was not approached further. He took the full responsibility for launching up to a thousand heavy bombers over enemy territory and for recovering them on the return. If Sir Arthur's judgement was at fault, chaos could ensue on the return, with aircraft unable to get into their own airfields and possibly being scattered all over England, with the likelihood of not being recovered for days. In effect, Sir Arthur fought a set-piece battle most nights in the week and the strain must, at times, have been enormous.[6]

Not always did the conference go smoothly. One night when a large attack had been ordered on the Ruhr the Duty Group Captain, Denis Barnett, became worried about possible fog on the way back. The Deputy C-in-C was away, the SASO could not be located, and he was reluctant to bring the C-in-C into it, so he did what was unheard of for a mere Group Captain and cancelled the operation. In the event the weather was only borderline and all concerned awaited with trepidation Harris's arrival next morning. Told of the cancellation he asked who did it. 'I did, Sir,' answered Barnett. 'Why?' 'I was not satisfied we could land them back at base, Sir – the visibility was deteriorating rapidly.' There was a deathly hush, then just two words: 'Quite right.' As Searby comments, the C-in-C had backed up Barnett without asking questions, knowing that – whether right or wrong – he had taken action which in his judgement was correct.[7] Lesser mortals might well have started an inquest. Not Harris.

The morning meeting over and the immediate decisions taken, it was usually back to the office where the routines of telephoning, meeting senior staff and visitors, studying reports and dealing with a vast amount of correspondence kept him totally engaged. His shorthand typists remember the long dictating sessions. His desk would be covered in papers when one went in, there would be no pleasantries, and he started almost before one sat down. He spoke clearly and without notes, his material coming straight from his head, and never changed his mind. Then back came the drafts which he usually cleared with only slight amendments. They remember too his inveterate smoking, his immense capacity for work, his concern for security, and the implicit trust he placed in them to keep their mouths shut; if the phone rang they simply stayed put.[8] The afternoon was much the same. He was not one to be out and about in his headquarters and so was rarely seen other than by his personal staff, his senior subordinates, and those called on to brief him personally.

Nor did Harris socialise in the Mess, though he was certainly not averse to others doing so. Here was one of the roles which he was happy for Bob (or 'Sandy') Saundby, his SASO and later his Deputy, to play on his behalf. Charles Carrington, always an astute observer, described how Saundby helped to oil the wheels. 'A tall, broad, stout man with a jolly red face and a twinkle in his eye, interested in everything and everybody, he never imposed his authority, never condescended.' He was usually to be seen in the centre of a group, senior or junior, 'always the life and soul of the party with everybody laughing'. He might be back from the Air Ministry with 'a new load of calculated indiscretions about how absurd they were', or passing on inside information to a junior, or welcoming a new face in the Mess, yet 'he had natural dignity and no-one took liberties with him.'

Friends since their days together in Iraq, the two men made an excellent partnership.[9] To begin with Harris intended that Saundby should, in due course, become his leading group commander and eventually be in line for C-in-C, but as time went on and the Command grew in size and complexity he resisted various attempts to move his SASO and persuaded the Air Ministry to promote him and allow him to remain at the Headquarters as his Deputy, an invitation which Saundby was more than happy to accept.[10] So the pair remained teamed up for the rest of the war, with Saundby living in at Springfield and thus able to keep his master constantly in touch with what was going on down the line. Certainly Harris had every confidence in him but unfortunately, as Sam Elworthy later observed, Saundby did not stand up to his master as much as he should have done when the C-in-C needed to be told he had got something wrong. In mid-1944, for example, Elworthy, then one of Harris's most trusted group captains, remembered him one day specifying the routing for an attack on targets near Falaise, whereupon the staff studied the operation in detail and became convinced that the attack would be safer and more effective if the bombers approached from the opposite direction. Saundby, requested to advise Harris accordingly, refused to try to persuade him to change his mind and under continued staff pressure eventually departed, not feeling very well! Elworthy himself then went to the C-in-C who immediately agreed: 'Of course you're right – change them round.'[11]

The great majority of people at the Headquarters, therefore, never set eyes on their master, except when he was being driven (or, more usually, driving himself with his driver, Maddox, in the back seat) in his black Bentley or his American Buick at a furious pace between the office and Springfield. Since he nearly always went home for lunch he did the return journey twice a day and when not in too much of a hurry was often observed giving lifts to local children on their way to or from school. He also took the opportunity to maintain his driving skills on some of his regular journeys to the Air Ministry. His former PA, Pelly-Fry, who visited him on occasion, recounts the classic story of his being stopped by two police motor-cyclists when speeding home one night along Western Avenue. 'Sir, you are travelling much too fast; you might kill someone.' 'I am on important business,' replied Harris, adding 'Now that you mention it, it's my business to kill people: Germans.' 'Are you Air Marshal 'Arris, Sir?' Harris nodded. 'That's different, Sir. Sorry I stopped you. Please follow us.' As Harris told Pelly afterwards, 'It was the quickest trip I ever made – they must have liked me.'[12]

The atmosphere of the Headquarters has often been criticised, with the implication that Harris's own remoteness and style of leadership were at least partly to blame. One of the denigrators was Group Captain (later Air Commodore) Bufton, who had constant dealings with Harris and his staff from his position in DB Ops. While accepting that the C-in-C ran his Headquarters efficiently, Bufton felt he ruled it with an iron rod which effectively deterred anyone from producing ideas that ran counter to his own.[13] Another particularly sharp critic was Freeman Dyson, a young civilian scientist working in the Headquarters on Operational Research. He, like Bufton, had no time for a system in which the C-in-C was told only the things he wished to hear. In his view secrecy pervaded the hierarchy from top to bottom, the C-in-C accepted no criticism either from above or below, and never admitted his mistakes.[14] Nor was Dyson impressed by his staff officers, who seemed to him more like Oxford dons. Another widely quoted witness was John Collins, the RAF padre who arrived at the Headquarters in July 1944 and described it afterwards as soul-destroying and depressing. 'There the civil and, according to some whose views can scarcely be ignored, militarily unsatisfactory policy of the carpet bombing of German cities was planned, and its execution controlled.' Most of the personnel were simply clerks in uniform, he went on, the rest were officers taken off operational duties or deadbeats, and there were the few who made up the close entourage of Harris and were directly responsible for the work in the underground operations room.[15]

There were elements of truth in such observations. The Headquarters certainly was a large and not particularly cheerful place. There was much specialised work to be done, a lot of which could be efficiently undertaken by people without front-line experience, and much as Harris would have liked to bring in more practised 'operators' the demand for such staff elsewhere in the Command – not to mention in other parts of the Air Force – was insatiable. Nevertheless it was not fair to say, as Bufton did, that Harris, Saundby and all their cronies were 'non-operational' and never flew the aeroplanes they commanded, with the implication that they were all out of touch. Harris himself wished he could have kept up with his flying, but his medical category precluded it, and – like Saundby – he had done his full share in his earlier career. As for his senior staff, those whom he inherited included a number who did possess recent operational experience – men like Elworthy and Barnett – and as time went on he brought in many more.

What Harris would not do, as some think he should have done, was allow the really senior ones to fly on operations, and for one particular reason above all others: they knew too much and he dared not risk their falling into enemy hands.

One feels too that he ought to have communicated more with his extensive staff. Like many others whose status makes one think they ought at least to have met him occasionally, Bob Hodges, who served as a Wing Commander Ops in mid-1944, never did. For him Harris was the aloof figure that he observed only at the morning briefing and whose phone calls to the Operations Room by night as well as day were awaited with trepidation. Yet somehow the C-in-C conveyed confidence and it all seemed to work.[16] As Charles Carrington wrote about this same period, when he returned for his second tour: 'A fortnight at Bomber Command revives my impression of the efficiency of this smooth-running organisation.'[17] It may indeed be that Harris's unique style of command was in fact essential in this unique situation, and if we are to try to understand why he adopted it we need to recall the pressures under which he had to work.

First and foremost, his was the responsibility. Never a day could pass without the need to decide whether to commit part or all of the bomber force and if so against which targets, and these decisions – with their implications for the lives of his men – were inescapably his and not for delegation. So for almost three and a half years Harris took no leave; Paul Tomlinson recalls him spending just one night away at Padstow, attempting to recover from 'flu.[18] He therefore had to pace his daily routine. At lunch time it was better to relax for a short while at home (provided that guests were not being entertained) than to socialise in the Mess; in any event he would probably not have thought it seemly to do so having just ordered his men into action. In the evenings there were often visitors and he would keep in touch with events by telephone. Though usually in bed by 10.30 he seldom slept until he knew 'the boys' were home. It did not help that he continued to suffer from the duodenal ulcer that had troubled him since his Palestine days, but he never went near a doctor. If these strains are set alongside the overall direction of his Command and the incessant pressures to which he was subjected from all quarters, from the Prime Minister and the Air Ministry downwards, it is small wonder that he was ill-disposed towards many of the new ideas that he was asked to consider and often gave short shrift to those emanating from within his own headquarters. We may find it hard to believe today that he could have driven his Command and himself the way he did, and that higher authority allowed him to do so. There were, however, no ground rules for how one should lead an unparalleled campaign in an unprecedented war of national survival, and Harris was utterly determined to spare no effort to do the job with which he had been entrusted to the very best of his ability. Critics there inevitably were, but many more who had dealings with him matched such doubts as they had with understanding.

Sam Elworthy was one. As Wing Commander Ops 1b, within days of Harris's arrival he was summoned to brief him on a plan prepared in consultation with DB Ops to test the relative merits of bombing with incendiaries and high explosive. The plan entailed bombing Lübeck with an 80:20 ratio of these weapons instead of the usual 20:80, and as Elworthy was explaining it Harris interrupted him: 'Why did you choose Lübeck?' Elworthy described the nature of the city and how it would burn. 'What are the houses built of?' 'They are old brick houses.' 'Bricks don't burn.' From then on the briefing got steadily worse until Harris said: 'I don't think you are any use to me. You're fired. Get out.' Several days later Elworthy reported to the SPSO, wondering what he was now supposed to be doing, and was summoned back to the C-in-C. 'I don't think I was altogether fair,' said Harris, 'I lost patience with you because I wasn't in sympathy with what you were telling me. It wasn't your fault – you were telling me what you were told to. If you're prepared to stay I'd like you to do so. If in the light of what I said to you the other day you want to leave I shall quite understand.' Here was a mistake generously admitted. Elworthy stayed on and, as he said, from that day never looked back with Bert Harris.[19]

Dr R.V. Jones was another. From his standpoint as Assistant Director of Intelligence (Science) in the Air Ministry he had long wished to be allowed more contact with front-line bomber units than Harris would permit, and in 1944, so concerned was he about the need for accurate bombing of certain of the German V1 sites, he decided to beard the C-in-C in his den. Somewhat to his surprise he was well received. Harris spoke with great common-sense, and Jones went off to brief the crews personally. As Jones later commented: 'I was dismayed that Harris was appointed C-in-C – he had been so critical of electronic warfare – but who else could have stood up to what he had to do?'[20]

And what of Padre John Collins, often portrayed as one of Harris's arch enemies? The truth is rather different. It so happened that Collins' wife, Diana, was the daughter of Ian Elliot, Harris's cousin, and not only was she invited to stay at Springfield from time to time but John came too if his duties permitted. Diana records the oft-quoted occasion in late 1944 when John invited Sir Stafford Cripps to lecture at Bomber Command and he raised the sensitive subject of the supremacy or otherwise of the individual conscience, whereupon Harry Weldon was asked to deliver a counter-lecture. She also describes how the two men got on in private, notwithstanding John's views about Bomber Command itself:

He and John differed in their politics and in their outlook on life but they had similarities: both held strong views and were prepared to stand up, speak out and do battle for the things in which they believed. The media labelled them both with public images that were absurdly far from the truth, and which produced regular supplies of 'hate mail'. They developed a sincere mutual respect, and John really liked Arthur.[21]

It was those, like Collins, who visited Harris at Springfield who came to appreciate that off duty – or at least away from the office or the Operations Room – he presented a totally contrasting personality. Pelly-Fry had found this in Palestine and Peter Tomlinson at Grantham; now Paul Tomlinson recognised it and so did Charles Carrington: 'Bert Harris at home was a different man from the autocrat of the Ops Room – he sent for me occasionally to report on this or that, and then talked about matters far removed from bombing.' Group Captain Peter Johnson writes[22] in similar terms about visiting Harris in May 1945 before taking command of his initial survey group in Germany (see chapter 16). In the office 'he showed little of the aggressive, not to say bullying, technique for which he was well known'. Afterwards Harris drove him home – one of his more alarming experiences – and luncheon, with the C-in-C's wife as an excellent hostess and no-one else present, was an unmitigated pleasure. 'Harris emerged as a thoroughly civilised, if very opinionated, man and I really enjoyed more than an hour's conversation on many subjects outside bombing.'

Diana Collins was another perceptive observer. 'Arthur, when not too exhausted or weighed down by his responsibilities, was very good company. With his wife, Jill, he enjoyed entertaining, and was a humorous, somewhat cynical observer of the human comedy, witty and amusing, and never pompous or self-admiring.' His daughter Rosemary, who came to visit fairly frequently, describes the house as a constant hive of comings and goings; her father – a great raconteur and mimic – always seemed to thrive in non-stop company, regardless of the anxieties and responsibilities of war. Not always, of course, was he relaxed; certainly there were times when, as he confided to his son, Anthony, he was weighed down by 'the beastly business' of war, and this and his illness could make him silent and moody, or impatient. Yet, as Rosemary adds, Jill was very good at restoring his spirits.[23]

The pair of them made an excellent team, as many of their visitors observed, and with the ubiquitous and much loved Jackie – or Jacan, as she was nicknamed – often bouncing around there was a general atmosphere of fun and relaxation. The young family of Dr Alan Johns, the next-door neighbours, were also very much part of the scene; some say it was Johns who gave Jackie the train set which her father himself used to play with, but others attribute it to Ira Eaker. Then there were the livers-in from the staff – Sandy Saundby, Paul Tomlinson and his successors, and Harry Weldon, the PSO – and occasional long-staying guests, most notably Ira Eaker. It was a busy place. Set amid an attractive, well-maintained, good-sized garden, part of a 27-acre property, the house itself was extremely comfortable.[24] Much of it, including the stable block, had been built in the late 18th century, and the interior – something of a rabbit warren – was large enough for the entertainment and accommodation of numerous visitors. Thanks to the excellence of Simmonds, the RAF cook, aided from time to time by Harris himself, a high standard of cuisine was maintained. In wartime England this was not easy, though fresh fruit and vegetables from the extensive kitchen garden helped, and the overall costs of looking after the many official guests who poured in were way beyond his £25 monthly entertainment allowance. Writing to AMP (Air Marshal Sir Bertine Sutton) in August 1942, he stated that he was still receiving no more than he had as AOC 4 Group in 1937; a month later he protested that the allowance had just been cut to £20 – and he was still trying to cope with over 100 official guests a month. Continuing the battle with a somewhat unsympathetic AMP and totally unhelpful Treasury he next took AMP's advice and asked the Chief Inspector of Taxes for an income tax reduction, only to be referred back to the Air Ministry. As he then pointed out to AMP, he was the only C-in-C to be involved in such 'missionary work' and it was ruining him financially. 'It goes against the grain when I have to fill the bellies of many people I loathe, most of whom are sent to me by the Air Ministry, so that we can carry on propaganda in the good cause.' He never really won this long-running battle, yet somehow they coped, and not just with those who came on business of some sort or other – 5,000 or so, Harris estimated, by the end of the war – but also with a regular stream of relations and friends.[25]

Foremost among the relations were Harris's older children, whom he was delighted to see. Anthony, commissioned in the Wiltshire Regiment, came in 1942 when stationed nearby; Marigold, who served in the First Aid Nursing Yeomanry and later as a despatch rider for the London Fire Service, visited several times in 1943 and 1944; and Rosemary, working in London for the Red Cross and later in the canteen of the Forces Français Libres, came often for the weekend or even longer. She would usually be picked up at the station either by her father – the most skilful driver she ever knew – or by her step-mother in a pony and trap; under no circumstances would Harris allow wives, including his own, to be driven around in staff cars. Other relatives who appeared included his brother Murray, now home from the USA, his cousin Ian Elliot, also back in London working in the Ministry of Production, and Jill's sister and brother-in-law, John and Marjory Prideaux-Brune from Padstow. Their names, together with those of many old RAF and other friends and present colleagues, appeared regularly in the visitors' book, though one significant signature was missing. Jackie's godfather, Peter Tomlinson, who had been posted in 1941 to photo-reconnaissance duties, had soon afterwards crash-landed near Utrecht following engine-failure and been taken prisoner, so for the rest of the war all that the Harrises knew about him was gleaned from POW postagrams addressed to a Mrs Harris at a private address. His connections with 'Bomber Harris' were never revealed to his captors.

Of the 'official names' that came to Southdown during the war, most of whom crossed the threshold at Springfield, it is possible to mention only a few, but enough to indicate the levels at which Harris often had to work and the immense range of influence that his visitors could exert. Significantly one of his very earliest visitors was Lord Trenchard, who had followed his career with deep interest and saw him as a man after his own heart. Of all Harris's supporters it was Trenchard who gave him the most unqualified backing, and Harris not only met him from time to time but sent him copies of some of his more controversial papers. Trenchard in turn helped with introductions to key people, as when he invited Harris to dine 'behind closed doors' with the Air Parliamentary Committee at the Dorchester on 10 June 1942. Soon after this came Harris's first top-level 'political' contact (apart from Churchill himself), when Stafford Cripps, Lord Privy Seal and Leader of the House of Commons, came to Springfield at the end of August. Harris had already described Cripps to Trenchard as 'the really important man, intelligent enough to size up arguments if the opportunity to argue with him was presented', and when they met he felt he succeeded in opening his visitor's eyes to various key aspects of the war as a whole. In the process he showed Cripps a new strategy paper he had just drafted, whereupon his guest observed that several members of the Cabinet did not like the style he used in his reports: 'I think you would make your points better and achieve more if you were more careful about your form of expression.' The unrepentant Harris replied that he felt it his duty 'to tell home truths in plain language regardless of susceptibilities. I am not a diplomat, God forbid – look where the diplomats have got us.' Cripps promptly offered to borrow the draft and return it with suggestions the following day. 'One would be a fool not to accept such an offer from such a brilliant advocate,' commented Harris afterwards. Cripps was as good as his word. The expertly revised draft appeared, went into Harris's files as 'the 3,000 Guinea Brief', and was sent together with a further amended version to Portal and the Prime Minister (see p.141).[26] Cripps' visit had paid off; while he would never be the greatest champion of Bomber Command (Harris would occasionally refer to him irreverently as 'Stifford Crapps'), neither was he going to be an arch enemy.

Many other senior politicians appeared at Springfield from time to time, some for specific purposes but mostly to find out for themselves what the bomber offensive was all about. Usually their host would take them into his 'conversion chamber', a room specially set aside for the stereoscopic

Right: George and Caroline, Arthur Harris's parents, 1911.

Below: George Harris and his sons, Arthur (left) and Frederick, 1908/9.

Above: Allhallows School hockey team, 1909, with Harris in the centre.

Left: Harris at Sanderstead, 1910.

Below: With Dorothy Blood, aboard SS *Inanda* en route for Rhodesia, 1910.

Top left: The Rondavel in which Harris lived at Lowdale.

Above: Riding 'Soda' in Rhodesia.

Left: Before the Battle of Trekkopes, SW Africa, 1915.

Left: Harris 'flat out' after the battle.

Left: 2nd Lieutenant Arthur Harris, Royal Flying Corps, 1916.

Above: Harris's BE2c, No. 4412 – his 'first personal aircraft' – 1916.

Below: Harris's Sopwith Camel at Ste-Marie-Cappel, 1917.

Top left: Harris (left) with some of his mates in France, 1917.

Left: Part of the battlefield at Passchendaele, 1917. Photograph from Harris's own album.

Above: With Barbara and Anthony at RAF Digby, 1920.

Right: With Barbara in India, 1921/2.

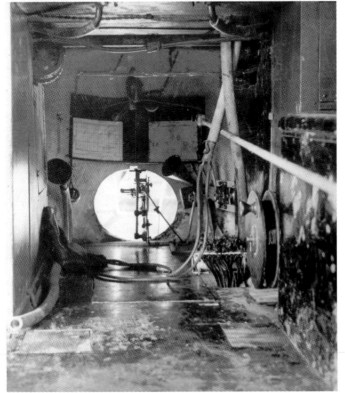

Top: Harris's Vickers Vernons, 45 Squadron, Iraq, 1923.

Above: 45 Squadron's pilots, including Bob Saundby, 1924.

Left: The prone bomb-aiming position devised by Harris in his Vernon.

Opposite page: Harris's first family (clockwise from top left): Barbara, Anthony, Rosemary and Marigold.

Top left: Harris's Vickers Virginia, 58 Squadron, RAF Worthy Down, 1927, in which he introduced the first nose and tail turrets.

Left: Harris flies the German airship *Graf Zeppelin* between Cairo and Jerusalem, 1931.

Above: Accompanied by Dick Atcherley, Harris takes part in a lion shoot while visiting Kenya, 1931.

Below: Preparing to take a Movietone cameraman over Mount Kenya.

Above: The Harris family at Bexhill, 1933.

Below: Harris with 210 Squadron colleagues at Pembroke Dock, 1933.

Opposite page: Harris's second family: the wedding, 1938 (Maurice Dean on the right); Jill; Harris and baby Jackie, 1939.

Left: Villa Haroun al Rashid, Jerusalem, 1938.

Left: Harris with a colleague in Palestine, 1938/9.

Left: Harris and Jill relaxing in the Dead Sea.

Right: Jill with Jackie's godfather, Peter Tomlinson, 1940.

Below: Harris visits the Flying Training School at Arcadia, USA, 1941.

Starting work at HQ Bomber Command.

examination of bomb damage photographs. One of his earliest visitors was the Home Secretary, Herbert Morrison, accompanied by his Parliamentary Secretary Ellen Wilkinson; Morrison used to spend occasional weekends at a cottage in the vicinity and throughout the war would call in from time to time to keep himself up to date. On one such visit during the German V1 offensive, Harris took pains to explain that the consequences for London were likely to be far less serious than the Home Secretary seemed to think. Another early caller was the Foreign Secretary, Anthony Eden, who took little persuading of the importance of what Bomber Command was doing; the two men found that they shared recollections of Passchendaele, whereupon Harris brought out his own aerial photographs and sent Eden copies. Others who came in Harris's first 18 months or so included Clement Attlee, Deputy Prime Minister; Ernest Bevin, Minister of Labour; Archibald Sinclair, Secretary of State for Air; Brendan Bracken, Minister of Information and a close confidant of the Prime Minister; and Oliver Lyttelton, Minister of Production. Some such guests came alone; others used their days out to help influence visitors of their own. Lyttelton, to quote just one example, headed a party of nine, mainly American and Canadian production chiefs, in October 1943, and expressed his gratitude for the excellent lunch and all the trouble Harris had taken to entertain them.[27]

Many of the visitors, of course, were from the RAF itself: members of his own senior staff, Group and other commanders, and men from the Ministry – though not, it appears, Portal, whom Harris met regularly in London. Far fewer in number, but particularly important in his view, were representatives of the other Services and he lost no opportunity to encourage them to call in. Admiral Godfrey, Head of Naval Intelligence, was one. In April 1942 Harris had protested to him about the failure of one of his reports to give the bombers due credit for the damage caused to the *Scharnhorst* and *Gneisenau* during and after the Channel Dash by minelaying and by the bombing at Kiel. Godfrey, in a conciliatory reply, asked to pay him a visit, to which Harris readily agreed. Admiral Stark, Commander of the United States Naval Forces in Europe, was another. After he and his deputy, Admiral Blake, had visited High Wycombe in August 1942 Blake was warm in his praise of the hospitality 'which must have almost denuded your larder and your cellar', and for the impression created. 'When we arrived we expected to meet the Wicked Uncle,' he wrote, 'but in a short time were made to realise that he was completely misrepresented and was in reality a Fairy Godmother exclusively occupied in caring for the requirements, needs and demands of the Navy.' If there was a spot of tongue-in-cheek about this the general tone of the letter tells us something of the charm and persuasiveness that Harris was well able to turn on on such occasions – and of the importance he attached to them. Later guests included Captain Cowie, Director of Minelaying, and Admirals Boyd (5th Sea Lord) and Brind, who came to Springfield following an exchange of letters suggesting that Harris thought the Naval Staff were antagonistic towards Bomber Command. Whatever disagreements might arise, Harris was going to let nobody in his Headquarters think the Navy did not appreciate its efforts.[28] They were in the war together.

He was equally concerned about relations with the Army. In August 1942, shortly before he heard of the proposal to form an airborne division (p.142), Harris was asked informally by an old Army friend General Paget, now commanding GHQ Home Forces, if 350 aircraft could possibly be provided for an autumn exercise in airborne operations. In a polite but frank reply Harris turned down the idea and invited Paget to visit him; as always, if requests for help were to be turned down he wanted the chance to explain his reasons and ensure they were understood. Others who came included General Wavell, back for a while from the Far East where he had not always appreciated the dictates of the bomber offensive, and General Morgan, appointed to direct the planning for the eventual invasion of France. Then on 10 January 1944 arrived his most important Army visitor, General Montgomery, who had just returned from the Mediterranean to command 21 Army Group. He wrote afterwards to Portal: 'Thank you very much for suggesting I go and see Bert Harris. I stayed Sunday night with him; we discussed many things and reached complete agreement about how he can best help the land battle. I like him very much.'[29] To Harris he wrote: 'It was a great thing to be able to discuss the problem with you, and a greater thing to know that we think alike on the whole business of making war.' Thus, with some assistance from their earlier dealings at Camberley and in Palestine, were laid the foundations for Bomber Command's support to the soldiers during Operation Overlord.

Perhaps even more important was the steady stream of American visitors. The first to arrive was the Commander of the Eighth Air Force, General Ira Eaker, whom Harris insisted should live at Springfield until his own residence was ready. He stayed until July, when he wrote 'Jillie' the warmest of thank-you letters. He recalled the comfort and charm of Springfield, the lump in the throat when he departed, the grand dinners they had enjoyed with 'the lion-hearted old sage calling you an old trout and your fitting reply: you are a cad. Perhaps after dinner you'd kneel by the fire and brew us a cup of coffee. There'd be Sandy standing legs apart glass in hand, expounding on the foibles of misguided people who prefer to fight on the land or the sea.' He would never be able to repay Jill and 'Buddy' for their many kindnesses. Thus began a lifetime friendship between the two families – the two men even shared birthdays – and a degree of understanding between the commanders of the two bomber forces that proved critical to their build-up and their operations.

Then, on 12 April 1942, came General Marshall, the Chief of Staff of the United States Army, keen to learn about the strategic air offensive in which his airmen would eventually take part. There followed in due course several of the USAAF's most senior airmen, including Carl ('Tooey') Spaatz, Hayward ('Possum') Hansell, George Stratemeyer and Hap Arnold. Also in evidence were some of the top American politicians, most of whom, like the airmen, Harris and Jill already knew from their time in Washington. William Bullitt and John Winant were among the first, followed in April 1943 by Averell Harriman – who discussed at length the 'politics' of the USAAF strategic bombing campaign (see chapter 12) – and in May by Bob Lovett, with whom Harris kept in regular touch.[30]

The Russians came as well, with Mr Maisky, the Soviet Ambassador, leading the way on 19 July 1942 at the suggestion of Sinclair, who felt that one of Harris's 'inoculations' would demonstrate to him that a Second Front was already being opened. That this visit paid off was shown by the appearance of another Soviet diplomat a month later, and Harris's appreciation of the value of the link was shown in a note he wrote to Trenchard in March 1943: 'In regard to getting the American bomber force over here, you might be able to do a lot of good through Maisky, taking along the Essen photographs and rubbing into him what it means in repercussion on all fronts.' At least two further groups of Russians – and one of Chinese – appeared at Springfield later on, more than happy to receive Harris's 'treatment'.[31]

There were many more dignitaries too. On 23 June 1942 Eden asked through Portal if Harris could show General de Gaulle (who was being 'very difficult' at this time) round the Headquarters, only to discover that the General had in fact been there on the 19th and greatly enjoyed himself. Easier visitors to entertain included Jan Smuts and 'Pirrie' Van Ryneveld from South Africa, Godfrey Huggins from Southern Rhodesia, and Vincent Massey from Canada. On 16 June 1944 came William Temple, Archbishop of Canterbury, who looked out of the window at one point and murmured, 'the precipitation may congeal,' to which Harris responded, 'you mean it will bloody well snow.' Most important also were members of the Royal Family. The Duke of Kent was one of Harris's very first guests on 31 March 1942, the Duchess of Gloucester came on 26 October 1943, and 7 February 1944 witnessed the highlight, when King George VI and Queen Elizabeth paid a much appreciated official visit. Pelly-Fry, who as Extra Air Equerry to the King helped organise it, describes how absorbed His Majesty was in all he saw, how the Queen demonstrated her immense charm and special style of communicating with people, and how Harris subsequently arranged for the King to have his own Blue Book and for Saundby regularly to visit the Palace to update it.[32]

The importance that Harris attached to the highly demanding task of coping with so many guests, and the value of their visits, are impossible to over-estimate. He himself summed it up in a note to Portal on 11 December 1942 complaining at the failure of the Intelligence Branch and Ministry of Economic Warfare to provide the people who mattered with a complete and convincing picture of the bombing and its effects:

> I say this because, in the last three months, I have had nearly 500 people to my house of the type who should have been educated along these lines by the Air Ministry; almost without exception they have exhibited complete ignorance of almost everything that has been done in the bomber offensive, and utter astonishment when faced with the photographic proofs and such other evidence as I placed before them. For instance, Eden has been convinced by Continental sources and by me – not by the Air Ministry.[33]

And so it went on. For all his urgings far too little was ever done elsewhere, in his view, to spread the word about his Command's achievements around officialdom, either at home or abroad, and he saw no choice but to be his own propagandist – helped, of course, by his public relations staff under the trusted John Lawrence.

There were wider implications of this role as well. It was not enough to be trying to convince the decision makers. It also mattered that the media – in those days confined to the newspapers, the cinema, and the radio service of the BBC – should be aware of the rationale and achievements of the bombing offensive, and Harris had no qualms about including influential pressmen and broadcasters, and not just British, on his visiting list. One of the first to come, on 8 May 1942, was R.M. Barrington-Ward, Editor of *The Times*, whom Harris found to be quite pleasant but bone stupid; his paper was 'entirely in the hands of servile reactionaries' whose thoughts ranged little beyond the arquebus and the culverin. Asked eight months later by the supportive Richard Peck to try to persuade Barrington-Ward to take a more understanding line, Harris refused: 'I will do a lot for my country but am damned if I will have him in my house again – he is a waste of good whisky.' In June 1942 Harris fared better with Lord Camrose, owner of the *Daily Telegraph*, and their talk – according to Richard Peck, who organised it – was a 'magnificent success'. Harris himself later commented on the value of his subsequent support and that of his newspaper. Soon afterwards Peck pointed Mr Bondarenko, the very co-operative Russian who represented the TASS News Agency, in Harris's direction. Then came a more difficult but profitable discussion with a journalist, Commander Stephen King-Hall, who had been writing somewhat critically about the bomber offensive, and a useful talk with Mr Sulzburger, of the *New York Times*, who acknowledged the hospitality most appreciatively and promised to give full support. Another who was firmly convinced was Lord Kemsley, owner of the *Sunday Times* and various other British newspapers, who came in July 1943 at the instigation of Harold Balfour, the Parliamentary Under-Secretary for Air and another regular visitor to Springfield. Portal, too, had a hand in some of the visits, such as that by James Reston, London correspondent of the *New York Times*, in November 1943, and a New York industrialist, Mr Isaac Harter, Vice-Chairman of Babcock and Wilcox, in May 1944. The letter written to Portal after this visit typifies how so many of the Harris guests felt: 'We stayed at Springfield and enjoyed our visit immensely. We saw the "big books" [of photographs] – the results are stupendous – Harter will return to the US very terribly aware of Bomber Command's hitting power. Harris was kindness itself, as was Lady Harris, and we really had a delightful and most happy evening.'[34]

It was a strange mix. For much of the time Harris was the remote, hard man who drove his Command with a rod of iron, and few who worked for him ever really got to know him. At home, on the other hand, he was the charming, relaxed, considerate host, a role which he combined with talking business whenever it was called for. How he coped with all the pressures nobody will ever really know – and among those pressures was the knowledge that he and his Command were subject to constant public scrutiny, praise and criticism. We need to turn now, therefore, to how he – and through him the force he led – was presented to and portrayed by the world at large.

Notes

1. Diana Collins, *Partners in Protest*, p.133.
2. Interview with Marjorie Preston and Betty Quihampton, 1997.
3. Conversation with the author as we watched the film together in 1997.
4. Dean, *The RAF and Two World Wars*, p.311.
5. Carrington, *op.cit.* pp.75, 85, 131, 139.
6. Searby, *op.cit.* p.184. See also Hastings, *Bomber Command*, p.248. Others present at the morning conference included the Naval and Army Liaison Officers and an Eighth Air Force representative.
7. Searby, *op.cit.* p.181. Denis Barnett later reached the rank of Air Chief Marshal.
8. Discussion with Preston and Quihampton.
9. Carrington, *op.cit.* pp.19–20.
10. Folders H72, dated 4 March 1942; H82, dated 14 June 1943; Portal Papers, Box C, File 5, 5 July 1942.
11. Interview between Group Captain Haslam, Head of AHB, and Marshal of the Royal Air Force The Lord Elworthy, 1975.
12. Pelly-Fry, *op.cit.* p.255.
13. Furse-Bufton interview.

14. Freeman Dyson, *Disturbing the Universe*, chapter 3.
15. Canon John Collins, *Faith under Fire*, p.69. After the war Collins played a major role in the Campaign for Nuclear Disarmament.
16. Author's discussion with Air Chief Marshal Sir Lewis Hodges, 1997.
17. Carrington, *op.cit.* p.136.
18. There may have been a few more brief visits to Devon to stay with an old friend from RFC days, Wing Commander Bill Hooper (information from Squadron Leader J. Sands).
19. Haslam/Elworthy interview.
20. Author's discussion with Professor Jones, 1997.
21. Diana Collins, *op.cit.* p.133. For the Cripps incident see p.135; John Collins, *op.cit.* p.89; Hastings, *op.cit.* p.250; Essay by Dr David Hall on the contrasting views of Weldon and Collins, published in 1997 in the *Journal of Canadian Military History*.
22. Johnson, *The Withered Garland*, pp.264–5.
23. Carrington, *op.cit.* p.117; Diana Collins, *op.cit.* p.133; note from Rosemary Harris.
24. Springfield, later renamed 'Springfields' or 'Springfields Lodge', remained until 2000 the residence of the Cs-in-C at Bomber and then Strike Command. Air Chief Marshal Sir John Allison kindly showed me round in 1998.
25. Rosemary Harris note; Folders H72, E70, 97; H74, E174.
26. AIR 8/424; Folder H50, E13,17; Portal Folder 9, E54; Ian Elliot memoir, p.161. Elliot was present during this discussion.
27. Visitors' book; Ian Elliot memoir; Folders H34; H36.
28. Folders H105; Misc 7.
29. Folders H25; H104; Portal Papers, Box A, File 5, E1.
30. Visitors' book; Folders H65, E43; Misc 7.
31. Visitors' book; Folders H50; H51; Rosemary Harris.
32. Visitors' book; Folder H81; Pelly-Fry, *op.cit.* pp.245–6. Harris's Blue Book contained photographs of Bomber Command's main targets in Germany. Churchill and Roosevelt had copies.
33. Folder H81, E181.
34. Folders H51; H27; H28; Portal Papers Box A, File 3, E40; Harris, *op.cit.* p.156.

Chapter 9

The public image

When Harris took over in February 1942 Bomber Command was not receiving a particularly good press. Certainly the most had been made of its limited-scale operations in 1941, and the film *Target for Tonight* had vividly portrayed the nature of its work, but the growing doubts in Whitehall about its future were now being reflected both in Parliament (see p.127) and by the war correspondents. So if Harris, hitherto a virtually unknown figure outside the Armed Services, was to put his Command on the map he knew that he must persuade not just officialdom but public opinion too. Moreover, if this meant that he himself would have to take the stage – albeit reluctantly – so be it.

The importance Harris attached to this task was demonstrated in one of his first letters to Portal, on 5 March: 'I must bring to your urgent and earnest attention the deplorable effect on morale of the spate of largely ignorant and uninstructed chatter against our bombing policy and against the general efficiency and co-operativeness of the Air Force.' Dirty linen should be washed in private, not in public by interested parties in the other Services, by certain MPs and other people of high standing, and by the gutter press. During the Battle of Britain, Harris went on, Churchill's immortal words had done more for RAF morale than any other sign of approval; now, in contrast, the airmen were having it repeatedly impressed upon them that what they were doing was not only badly done but, in relation to bombing policy, of no avail anyway. Under such circumstances, 'it is not within the compass of human endurance to maintain indefinitely resolution and a smiling countenance in the face of the appalling risks with which they are normally confronted.' Concluding this *cri-de-coeur* he asserted, 'there is only one person vitally and urgently seized of the necessity to discount the bombing policy or to break up the RAF – Adolf Hitler. Those who in this country serve that purpose – wittingly or unwittingly – serve the enemy. They should be told in no uncertain terms.' Soon afterwards Harris wrote to Trenchard, who was equally anxious about the Command's image in Parliament and the press, enclosing a draft retort to a critical article by the air correspondent of the *Evening Standard* and making it clear that the most serious aspect of the unjustified belittling of the bombing efforts was its inevitable impact on the morale of the crews. For Harris this was understandably an issue of major importance.[1]

There were, however, practical difficulties in actually presenting the news, as Freeman indicated in a sharp note to Harris about one of his Command's daily communiqués. 'This account is grossly and dangerously exaggerated,' he wrote. 'It reminds me of the worst statements produced in the October 1940–June 1941 period. Bombast is entirely contrary to our policy. Please ensure that in future your communiqués bear a closer resemblance to the facts.' The example chosen by Freeman hardly justified such forthright strictures but Harris's reaction was restrained except that he called Freeman's final remark unkind and asked him to quote other examples of ill-worded communiqués so that 'if my lack of precision in expressing myself on paper has again betrayed me – as it so often does – I can take additional care to keep on the rails.' That said, he lodged a counter complaint. While bombastic claims were certainly futile and dangerous, far too little was being done to put across what his Command was actually achieving in attacks on industrial targets. Part of the problem, Harris argued, was that the press was only interested in 'hot' news, whereas confirmations of the effects of damage, which could take weeks to obtain, lacked the immediacy and headline appeal which the press demanded. The answer might be to write up periodically the results of the offensive say two or three months back on the basis of all the evidence available, but 'subject to the old difficulty – the most serious of all – of not compromising the source.' That Harris was thinking hard about this important question was clear, as Freeman indicated in his sympathetic reply, and Harris's subsequent efforts to educate and influence the press, ably supported by Richard Peck in the Air Ministry, need to be seen in the light of such constraints.[2]

Already, therefore, Harris was appreciating that the process of assessing the consequences of bombing economic objectives was bound to take time, but neither he nor most if any of his contemporaries can have appreciated how long and hard the task of appraisal would eventually prove. If we are inclined to criticise him and his colleagues for not being more cautious in their conclusions we need to remember not just the near impossibility of obtaining accurate information in wartime about what was actually happening in the enemy camp but also the great difficulties experienced even after the war by research teams and historians alike. Today, at last, we seem to be better placed, but Harris and his colleagues, the men charged with doing the job, could do no more than make their own judgements based on very limited information, and these were bound to colour their dealings with the media whose support they needed.

The newspapers themselves had given Harris the conventional welcome accorded to newly appointed commanders-in-chief, but he was not best pleased to find himself referred to as 'Ginger'. Fortunately this alleged nickname did not stick. His formal audience with the King was reported on

18 March 1942 and a message he sent to munitions workers urging them to help him keep up the export trade to Germany appeared on 8 April. Not until May, however, did the verbal portrait-painting really begin, when the *Daily Express* depicted him as 'a shrewd dynamo of air strategy', a man of decisiveness and with the same cast of thought as his bomber crews, 'a first-class commander in a good English tradition, downright like Fisher, abrupt like Wellington'. A few days later the *Express* printed his first public statement of intent: 'If I could send 1,000 bombers to Germany every night, it would end the war by the autumn. We are going to bomb Germany incessantly ... the day is coming when the USA and ourselves will put over such a force that the Germans will scream for mercy.' Harsh words, yes, but in May 1942 they were what the mass of the British people wanted to hear. The Americans, too, were getting the message, with the *New York Sun* presenting Harris as one of the RAF's toughest and most experienced officers, dynamic, direct and impatient. His audacity in mounting the Augsburg raid was particularly seized upon (inaccurately) and he was well summed up: 'He is 50. He hates red tape and likes men who know their jobs. He has always carried a punch, but never before has it been so spectacularly in evidence.'

It was, without question, the attack on Cologne on 30/31 May that imprinted the name of Harris on the nation's consciousness – and that of the wider world. Initially reported to have been carried out by 1,250 aircraft, it was variously headlined as, for example, 'The World's Biggest Air Raid', 'The Greatest Air Raid in History', and 'One Bomber every Six Seconds', and Harris's personal message to the crews at their briefing was reproduced in full:

> The force of which you form a part tonight is at least twice the size and has more than four times the carrying capacity of the largest air force ever before concentrated on one objective. You have an opportunity, therefore, to strike a blow at the enemy which will resound not only throughout Germany, but throughout the world. In your hands lie the means of destroying a major part of the resources by which the enemy's war effort is maintained. It depends, however, on each individual crew whether full concentration is achieved. Press home your attack to your precise objective with the utmost determination and resolution in the foreknowledge that, if you individually succeed, the most shattering and devastating blow will have been delivered against the very vitals of the enemy. Let him have it – right on the chin.

Reinforcing Harris's stirring words came the warm congratulations of Churchill, coupled with a stern warning to the enemy: 'This proof of the growing power of the British bomber force is also the herald of what Germany will receive, city by city, from now on.' The vivid descriptions of the attack that took pride of place in most newspapers strengthened the impact of these and other messages, as did the optimistic reports of the second 'thousand' attack on 1/2 June, and these were quickly followed by several new articles featuring the man of the moment, some of them written by correspondents who had been to see him. Now his RAF nickname 'Bert' came into more general use and many details of his earlier career began to emerge, though not always accurately. One particular false statement, oft repeated, was that when flying he would never allow anyone else to take the controls. Also featured was the way in which he ran his Headquarters and directed his Command's operations. To Godfrey Winn, of the *Sunday Express*, one of the best interviewers, he took the opportunity to stress that the public must not expect such large raids every week: 'I do hope the people will be patient and not expect miracles.' Then in a film interview, reported in the *New York Post* on 9 June and next day in the *Daily Telegraph*, he reminded his audience of the German bombing campaign, referred to the RAF's still limited but steadily mounting strategic offensive and the massive power of the USA that would be joining it in due course, and concluded:

> It may take a year; it may take two; but for the herrenvolk the writing is on the wall. Let them look out for themselves. The cure is in their own hands. A lot of people (generally those with no qualifications to speak, if to think) are in the habit of iterating the silly phrase 'bombing can never win a war'. Well, we shall see. It hasn't been tried yet, and Germany, more and more desperately clinging to her widespread conquests, and still foolishly enough striving for more, will make a most interesting subject for the initial experiment.

This was strong stuff and from hindsight looks highly exaggerated. Yet at the time his sentiments were widely applauded – as was the knighthood awarded to him on the 11th – and nobody was being left in any doubt about his conviction that bombing, properly applied, could prove a war winner. He had nailed his colours to the mast.

All this publicity was bound to raise misgivings in some minds, and on 18 June Commander Bower asked in the House of Commons whether it was government policy to allow Commanders-in-Chief in the other Services similar freedom to express their opinions. Attlee, replying on behalf of the Prime Minister, refused to be drawn, merely suggesting that the publicity accorded to Harris's views was directly connected with the exceptional operations recently carried out and rejecting the suggestion that such pronouncements might deceive the public into thinking they reflected official policy. A different kind of question was posed by Major Oliver Stewart of the

Evening Standard on 8 July. He accepted the brilliant way in which the recent heavy raids had been planned and executed and their heartening effect, but pointed out that the amount of damage done to enemy industry was not known with any certainty; casualty estimates, too, varied widely. Experience in Britain showed how well it was possible to recover from the effects of bombing, so if large-scale area bombing was to help win the war regular follow-up raids would be required, together with land or sea action to consolidate them. Three weeks later Stewart returned to the subject. Though in his view Harris was overstating his case,

> my admiration for him is not diminished by his excessive enthusiasm – on the contrary it is enhanced one hundredfold. We want men who believe in the weapons they have to hand and who believe fanatically and furiously . . . he is determined to make the bomb work for the United Nations as it has never worked for any country before. We can only stand aside in admiration and respect, and wish him good luck.

Stewart had caught the national mood at that moment, and it was a mood largely created by Harris and his men.

Strangely Stewart's second article was occasioned by bureaucratic muddle. On 20 July Peck had sent Harris the draft of a pamphlet being prepared by the Political Warfare Executive for dropping over Germany, and two days later Harris returned his amended version. Although he had never been enthusiastic about the value of dropping supplies of 'lavatory paper', *ie* propaganda leaflets, to the Germans he agreed to allow his name to be used. The next he heard of it was when, to his astonishment, the text was transmitted by the BBC and the following morning the newspapers proclaimed that he had just broadcast a message to the Germans. The *Daily Telegraph*, under the banner headline 'RAF to scourge Reich from end to end', went so far as to state that he had spoken in German (a language of which he knew not a word). He was even more irritated by the fact that the published 'speech' differed considerably from the version he had originally agreed; it omitted, for example, his comment 'we know that you Germans are brave people; we know that you fight well, if stupidly.' The central message, nevertheless, was the same. Germany was being bombed, not out of revenge, but to make it impossible for her to continue the war. While the preferred targets were factories, shipyards and railways, those who worked in these plants lived nearby and were also going to be hit – regrettable but necessary. Moreover, although the German defences were inflicting losses they were averaging less than 5% and soon, as the huge American effort built up, the Third Reich would be scourged (Harris had written 'flattened') from end

to end if the Germans made it necessary. It was up to them to end the
war and the bombing by overthrowing the Nazis and making peace.[3]

So Harris, instead of distributing a load of leaflets over Germany, ended
up being credited – in North America as well as Great Britain – with a
belligerent speech which he had not made but could not publicly disclaim
and which would be widely quoted from then on both by his supporters and
by his detractors. On 4 August the 'broadcast' was debated in the House of
Lords, with the Labour Peer Lord Addison and other critics of the bombing
campaign contending that it was wrong for government policy to be
expounded by an officer who was not a responsible minister and could not
therefore defend it in Parliament. While they were careful not to criticise
Harris personally they were far from happy with the bombastic language
which they implied had been put into his mouth. The next day Harris wrote
to Brendan Bracken, the Minister of Information, who had been told
nothing about the message beforehand. 'I had hoped that means would have
been found to get newspaper editors and such people as Addison to "lay off"
the subject – not that I care a twopenny damn myself – because the sort of
stuff that has come out in the papers today about the incident is thoroughly
bad for the morale of the youngsters in the Command.' In Germany,
however, the broadcast did not arouse the attention for which the Political
Warfare Executive must have hoped. Afterwards it seemed to the PWE that
Goebbels' Propaganda Ministry had decided to suppress all mention of the
message through fear of its possible effect on the German population, and
only in overseas propaganda was Harris referred to by name.[4] His vilification
would come later.

Fortunately, and for Harris thankfully, there was now to be a period when
the spotlight would increasingly be diverted elsewhere. In part this resulted
from the absence of further Bomber Command 'spectaculars' and the limited
scale of effort that it remained possible to deploy: at the same time it
reflected the switch of media attention to other events, notably the victory at
El Alamein, the North Africa invasion and, above all, the campaign on the
Eastern Front which culminated in the Battle of Stalingrad. This is not to say
that the bomber offensive was to be ignored. Far from it. There would,
however, be rather less emotive publicity and rather more considered discussion. An article by J.C. Johnstone in the *Daily Telegraph* of 26 August
1942 particularly caught Harris's eye, for without mentioning him by name
it drew on some of the ideas that he had put to Lord Camrose[5] and proved
remarkably prophetic. The writer's theme was that the 'second front' should
be regarded as comprising two interdependent phases: the first would be
exclusively delivered from the air to knock out at least half the enemy's
punch, *ie* his productive apparatus, communications and public morale; the
second would be delivered mainly by land. He did not open up the possi-

bility that a successful phase one might render phase two nugatory, as Harris might have wished, but he was certainly putting the bomber offensive into the key place in Western strategy where Harris wanted it to be.

There were other ways too of spreading the message. In September 1942 Harris arranged with Harold Balfour for Squadron Leader Morris, a highly regarded photographic officer, to run an exhibition of photographs in the House of Commons, and Balfour's thank-you letter referred not just to the splendid organisation but to its success in engendering political goodwill for the RAF in general and Bomber Command in particular.[6] One consequence of this was the despatch of Morris to mount a similar exhibition in Washington and Ottawa early in 1943. Harris, who had keenly supported a publicity visit to the States by Squadron Leader Nettleton and had since been urging Bracken to step up the RAF's propaganda in America, was delighted to hear how well Morris had done. Nor did the potential of the cine-film escape Harris, as when he agreed to provide a specially equipped Mosquito to take photographs of a night attack and later asked Bracken to consider distributing a 35 mm version of Movietone's excellent bomb damage film to the nation's cinemas. He was not blind either to the publicity value of the occasional stunt, such as in January 1943 when several Mosquitos arrived over the Reichstag in Berlin just as Goering was about to speak.[7]

At the opposite end of the scale Harris made time to support local RAF occasions. On 17 April 1943, for example, he and Jill attended 'RAF Night' at the Oxford New Theatre. As reported in the *Oxford Mail*, three hours of wonderful entertainment by well-known show-business personalities were rounded off when Harris took the stage. 'One could see why he is so popular with the Service when, after remarking that he had never seen such a large gathering of airmen before, except on pay parades, he wanted them to show their appreciation of the artists in the traditional way,' and then added: 'But, as we are a new Service, I suggest a new form of acclamation' – and instead of three cheers he gave three 'Hi-de-hi's', to which the audience roared in response 'Ho-de-ho!' On 29 May, accompanied by General Eaker, he took the salute at the Town Hall in High Wycombe when a huge parade of the local military and civil defence services marched past at the start of Wings for Victory Week, whose target was £400,000, the cost of 20 Mosquitos. Afterwards, at the inaugural ceremony on the Rye, the Mayor introduced him as 'Bomber Harris', the name by which history would surely remember him, and Harris responded by reflecting on the story of the war thus far and stating that Bomber Command had just completed delivery of its first 100,000 tons of bombs; the next 100,000 would be better bombs, better aimed and much quicker arriving. Another similar local week soon followed, this time in Reading with the aim of funding a squadron of heavy bombers, and for this he authorised a special fly-past.[8]

Meanwhile the BBC and the national press had been enthusiastically covering the mounting offensive, particularly against the Ruhr. Bomber Command now had its own resident BBC correspondent, Richard Dimbleby, who was called to Harris's office on arrival, told how welcome he was (not least because he would be flying on operations), and heard the C-in-C tell his PA: 'Mr Dimbleby can talk to anyone he likes, go where he likes, and see anything he likes, and be directly responsible to me.'[9] From then on all doors were indeed opened to him, and on 18 May he found himself reporting the greatest 'spectacular' of all Bomber Command's operations, the breaching of the Möhne and Eder Dams (see chapter 13). The entire media took up the story. Harris himself was stated to have been at Scampton, following the progress of the operation and greeting returning crews, and his message to them was quoted: 'Your skill and determination in pressing home the attack will for ever be an inspiration to the RAF. In this memorable operation you have won a major victory in the Battle of the Ruhr, the effects of which will last until the Boche is swept away in the flood of final disaster.' The sense of thrill that swept across the nation as the news of this event was heard, read about and digested brought Bomber Command and its Commander right back to the high point of a year before, and the succession of major city attacks that followed gave the press ample opportunity to continue to exploit the Command's achievements and return the spotlight to Harris himself.

The articles about him were now more accurate and perceptive than in earlier days. On 23 May a 'Special Air Correspondent' in the *Sunday Express*, for example, discussed his working routine, his concentration on the job, his ways of choosing his staff, his constant efforts to be receptive to new ideas, and his attitude towards his aircrew. One of his former 5 Group squadron commanders was quoted as saying 'We all love him; he's so bloody inhuman.' On 10 July Colston Shepherd, Editor of *The Aeroplane*, wrote him up in *Picture Post* as 'The man who picks the target for tonight'. Persistence was one of his key qualities; he would never 'let-up', and nobody could take liberties with him. His was not a brilliant mind but an uncommonly lively one, provided it was well fed. By ordinary standards he was not a popular commander but was respected for his untiring enthusiasm and devotion, his thrusting persistence, his forthrightness. 'His was a long-term job from the start; he recognised the paradoxical essence of the task – that it could only be a success over a long period if it never got stale. So far it never has,' concluded Shepherd, 'and therein lies his true greatness.' Already in 1943, those who knew him well were weighing him up and appreciating his qualities in a way that few would argue with today.

Not everyone, of course, supported Harris or grasped the right message about him and his Command. In March 1943 he wrote to Portal about a pamphlet issued by the Bombing Restriction Committee entitled 'Stop Bombing Civilians', suggesting it might be subversive, but Portal and Sinclair decided to ignore it rather than give it gratuitous publicity. On a lighter note a Londoner, Mr Henry How, wrote just after the Dams Raid protesting about the way people's sleep was constantly being interrupted by German aircraft and urging him to attack their airfields. Mr How may not have enjoyed Harris's reply:

> Over 13% of the very few German aircraft that reach our coasts are brought down. The results achieved by the remainder are ludicrous in extent, even if occasionally tragic to a few individuals. My bomber crews seldom get 'reasonable rest' at night. I am therefore delighted to hear that yours is also occasionally disturbed. We have more important things to do than to ensure 100% safe snoring for the infinitesimal few with views and ideas like yours. Your personal chances of getting hurt by the present scale of German attack are one in ten million. If that fearful risk keeps you awake at night, ask a friend, if you have one, to explain why. Probably your best friend wouldn't tell you.[10]

On the continent, too, there were different points of view, and Harris may have obtained some amusement from the translation of an article about him published in Switzerland in 1942. It was remarkably imaginative in some respects. He had, for example, led the air defence against the Zeppelins and gone down in the annals of the First World War as the St George of the air who had conquered the flying dragons. He was also one of the most senior and experienced military pilots in England, could fly all types of aircraft, and had already piloted bombers on flights over Germany. Nevertheless, it was not unfavourable towards him, quoting Hannen Swaffer of the *Daily Herald* as calling him a bomb that had fallen in the centre of the Air Ministry – a bomb that had a moustache peppered with grey, made a quite appalling noise, and had the effect of a tornado. He had bound together the straggling twigs of his Command, and from the same rods which the enemy wielded only weakly and often enough broke in doing so had fashioned a birch of truly formidable power. He would soon be attacking Germany every night with a thousand aircraft.[11]

In Germany, as the bombing increased, the picture became very different. Prompted by the Dams Raid the *Westdeutscher Beobachter* wrote on 23 May 1943 of the Air Marshal with his cold, brutal features and grey hair who had the task assigned to him by Churchill of bringing the fiery air terror to bear against the fortress of Europe:

> How eagerly he launches his bombs against German women and children to an accompaniment of most unmilitary speeches and articles in which he

expresses his grim satisfaction in the doing of it. He is the right man to fight against those who have no defence ... they have small and miserable minds who plan and carry out such undertakings ... Harris may be a savage, he may be the best man for his job, but in him one sees the means to which England, so old and once so proud, is reduced in this fight for existence.

On the same day Goebbels' paper *Das Reich* contemptuously described his background:

His parents had no social standing, he lacked any trace of culture or respect for the cultural achievements of other countries, and his Air Force career, though it had provided wide experience, had been undistinguished. Then, when England chose to intensify the bombing offensive in preference to fairer and more open methods of war, the unscrupulousness of his methods and his harsh treatment of those beneath him were naturally a recommendation.

His personality, the article continued, was marked by an overwhelming and alarming manner of dealing with visitors and colleagues, an attachment to an unpleasant and deliberate habit of swearing, his use of 'common expressions', and above all his 'savage methods of waging war, which civilised human beings believed to have become part of the distant past.'

Then in August, following on the series of massive attacks on Hamburg (chapter 13), the German radio turned directly on Harris in words widely reported in the British press. As the *Daily Mail* summarised them: 'Brutality, cold cynicism and an undiluted lust for murder are his chief characteristics. You have only to look into his eyes to know what to expect from such a man. He has the icy-cold eyes of a born murderer. He has accepted a task which many others would have declined – the total war against the Huns, as they call us.' The British commentators recognised that Harris could hardly be a popular hero in the heavily bombed areas of Germany and pointed out that in picking on him Goebbels was giving Bomber Command's victims a figure whom they could curse and blame. Harris himself was totally unmoved. For him such personalised assaults served merely to indicate that he was well on the way to achieving his objectives – a reaction well appreciated by the British newspapers as they contrasted the man they knew with the caricature being presented to the Germans.

So from now on Harris had to live with the knowledge that in Germany he had become the most hated member of the British military establishment – more hated even than Churchill. The enemy press also began to present him as the inventor of a new doctrine: 'Pacification by Bombing'. They harked back to the time when he had flown bombers in France in the First

World War and then been stationed near the Khyber Pass, where his bombers razed to the ground the insurgents' villages and left their survivors to spread through their horror tales new respect for England's power; it was around this time that Churchill discovered him and made him his protégé. Now Sir Arthur, with his single-track mind – which was completely devoid of imagination and was the normal mind of the English civil servant born in India – made no difference between an Arab village and, say, Nuremberg or Naples. He was indifferent to what happened to the victims and no longer saw bombing as part of the prelude to military invasion but as a complete substitute for it.[12] Most of this was inaccurate and far-fetched – though the final point had elements of truth in it – and Harris treated it with the contempt it deserved. He was not going to let himself worry about anything the Germans might say about him and if he reacted at all would usually do so only with humour. In January 1944, when told of a German broadcast reporting that many members of the British military staff were moving out of London for fear of German reprisals over the bombing of Berlin, he heard that he himself had just paid £8,000 for a house in Blackpool! 'I never had 8,000 shillings in those days,' he commented later.

It needs to be said here that in attracting the hatred of the enemy on himself Harris was to an extent paying the price of the failure of his superiors to admit the true nature of the bombing campaign. He himself thought that Sinclair in particular should have been more forthright in the House of Commons; it was asking for trouble not to describe the kind of bombing being carried out. 'There was nothing to be ashamed of, except in the sense that everybody might be ashamed of the sort of thing that has to be done in every war, as of war itself.'[13] Max Hastings, a stern critic of Harris on some matters, considers that he deserved credit for wanting to tell the British public what he was seeking to do to the Germans, whereas ministers constantly prevaricated in response to repeated questions from Peers and MPs. The contrast was well brought out in a letter to Sinclair from Lord Salisbury on 26 November 1943, in which the writer quoted Harris's statement that the attacks on Berlin were to go on until the heart of Nazi Germany ceased to beat. This ran counter, he suggested, to repeated government declarations that only military and industrial targets were being attacked and that casualties to women and children were merely incidental.[14] As usual, for political reasons, Sinclair hedged. Harris was being left, in effect, to carry the can both at home and abroad, and not least in Germany.

Harris was also making his views abundantly clear on paper. Writing formally to the Air Ministry on 25 October he complained about the kind of statements being made by authoritative speakers implying that Bomber Command's offensive was essentially concerned with attacking specific installations and that, unlike the Americans, the British were not doing this very well. What his operations were in fact designed to do, he pointed out, was to wreck enemy cities and turn them from assets to liabilities: the RAF ought to be making this plain and stressing how much it was facilitating the highly publicised Russian advances in the East. He felt strongly that unless the public properly appreciated the value of Bomber Command's offensive before Germany collapsed nobody would recognise its efforts afterwards. In response Sir Arthur Street, on behalf of the Air Council, told him that the guiding principle in all official pronouncements was that the widespread devastation being caused was not an end in itself but 'the inevitable accompaniment of an all-out attack on the enemy's means and capacity to make war', and that it was desirable to present the offensive in a way that would provoke the minimum of public controversy. Far from happy with this, Harris reiterated his wish for officialdom to give the bombers proper credit for their contribution to the achievements of the Allied ground forces, and to make it clear that the cities of Germany – including their working population, houses and public utilities – were literally the heart of the 'war potential' that he was being required to attack. What he wanted, and what his crews needed to hear, was an authoritative, unequivocal statement that the devastation was being deliberately produced. Street's reply on 2 March 1944 gave him no satisfaction: the Council was insistent that the objective was not the destruction of cities *as such* but was limited to those which contained 'military installations or any war production or organisational potential' – a policy distinction which could and must be clearly maintained. What this meant was that the government, generally content to support Harris behind closed doors, was not prepared to be honest to the world at large about what he was actually trying to do.[15] Norman Longmate, who covers this whole subject at some length, calls it a sordid story, from which only one man emerged with credit: Sir Arthur Harris.[16]

Much of the British press, nevertheless, remained supportive as the offensive mounted – coupled with that of the Eighth Air Force – in the later months of 1943, and as the targeting moved increasingly to Berlin. Among Harris's backers was Major Oliver Stewart of the *Evening Standard*, who judged that he recognised that bombing's span of full effectiveness as a weapon of war might be short. If so, argued Stewart, this was the critical time to exploit its full potential and the priority allotted to heavy bomber production should be fixed accordingly. Lieutenant General H.G. Martin, Military Correspondent of the *Daily Telegraph*, stressed the need to bring the war to an end as quickly as possible on account not just of the strains of fighting it but also of the huge economic problems that would surely follow. To ensure that speed, and prevent a stalemate, Germany's vitals must be hit by air power so as to knock the fight out of the whole evil organism and enable the grand assault to go in from all sides and win quickly and cheaply.

Martin differed from Harris in stating that bombing alone would not win the war but he had no doubts about its critical importance in preparing the way. Brigadier J.G. Smyth echoed this theme in the *Daily Dispatch*, seeing Harris's great attack on Berlin, together with the Russian offensive, as giving the highest hopes of finishing the war in the shortest possible time. Harris had once been described to him, Smyth wrote, as a man with a one-track mind: 'If that is so I wish we had more men with minds and determination like his.'[17]

In early 1944, as Harris's massive winter offensive ground on remorselessly, the media had even more to report, and on 30 January they exploited to the full 'the biggest blitz ever' of the previous day. Altogether some 2,000 aircraft, 800 of them American, had attacked Berlin and Frankfurt, and alongside the story was the picture of ' "Bomber Harris" – the man who is razing Hitler's Reich with brilliant air strategy'. 'Germany is indeed reaping the whirlwind,' wrote Oliver Stewart. The Americans too were applauding: *Illustrated*, for example, wrote that his Command had been called (by a neutral correspondent) the 'Hammer of the Reich' because, for the first time since the days of Frederick the Great, the Germans had been made to feel the wounds of war inside their own country – and it was Bomber Command of the RAF which had done it.[18]

Throughout this central period of the bomber war the personal portraiture too had continued. The correspondents came to High Wycombe to see Harris at work and report back on the way the battle was being conducted. 'He lives, talks and works to the tempo of a machine gun,' wrote one; his first question, as always, was 'How many did we lose last night?' and his constant interest in the well-being of his crews provided the human side to his character. 'He loathes unnecessary delay because he seriously believes that bombing attacks will shorten the war and therefore in the end save lives,' wrote another. Lady Harris, too, had her share of being interviewed and lent a hand in presenting her husband's point of view:

> He is a realist who knows you cannot make war without hurting your enemies, but he doesn't want the war to go on a day longer than it need. One reason is that he remembers the land battles of the last war and the enormous slaughter they caused; he knows that bombing will save innumerable lives, and I should say that is what he sees most clearly with what the Germans call his 'icy-cold eyes'.

On occasion there were lighter touches, such as C.P. Thompson included in a particularly perceptive appraisal: 'He cares so little for pomp that when the merry-go-round broke down at a War Weapons Week in a local village and the showman couldn't get it re-started, he took off his coat, went to work, and fixed it, steam organ and all.'[19]

There were other activities which also caught the attention of the public, and show that Harris did get out and about at least occasionally. On 26 August 1943, for example, he was at a Buckingham Palace Garden Party, where *Stars and Stripes* featured him talking to wounded airmen of the Eighth Air Force. On 3 September he and Jill attended the *Daily Express* 'Path to Victory' exhibition at Burlington House, where the displays included a model of blitzed Essen, stereoscopic viewing of bomb damage, and an electrically operated bomber turret. There were events with the Americans, helping to cement relations between the two Air Forces (see chapter 12). Important too was the Soviet dimension: on 8 June 1943 he and Jill lunched with the Soviet Ambassador and Mrs Maisky; in February 1944 the Order of Suvorov – their highest military order – was presented to him at the Soviet Embassy; and in March the Harrises were numbered among 1,100 top-level military and political guests at a major reception held by the new Soviet Ambassador, Mr Gusev, to mark the anniversary of the Red Army. Willi Frischauer, who wrote of this spectacular gathering in *Illustrated*, spotted Madame Gusev entertaining her special friends, including the Harrises, at a little table. As he raised his glass he gave a one-word toast: 'Victory.' 'It is when diplomatist hosts like the Soviet Ambassador and his wife go out of their way to honour a guest that there is a political significance in the social encounter,' Frischauer went on. 'That handshake with "Bomber" Harris, in different language, meant: "Russia appreciates the work of your bombers over Berlin".'[20]

Amid all the publicity being accorded to the bombing of Germany it was all too easy to ignore the fact that Bomber Command had other tasks, not least the minelaying by which Harris had always set great store, and in March 1944 he wrote to Mr Dingle Foot, at the Ministry of Economic Warfare, protesting at a speech in which the Minister had allegedly given the entire credit for this to Coastal Command in conjunction with the Navy. Foot's reply made it clear that he had been misreported by the press and had in fact mentioned Bomber Command's contribution; in future he would certainly lay proper emphasis on it. Probably as a result of this incident Macdonald Hastings, War Correspondent of *Picture Post*, was soon afterwards allowed to fly aboard a Stirling on a minelaying operation. His subsequent article gave an excellent feel for the nature of the mission and the importance of such work in the offensive against enemy shipping, and an accompanying photograph of Harris with Captain de Mowbray, the senior naval officer on his staff, was a reminder of the importance he personally attached to helping the Navy in this unspectacular but highly effective role.[21]

Harris was less convinced about another role being envisaged for Bomber Command, namely direct support for the Allied invasion of France, and in

January 1944 the press began to speculate about where he would be fitting into the new command structure being set up under General Eisenhower. As the *Daily Mail* pointed out, there were many who believed that, given sufficient facilities, the Anglo-American heavy bombers could now virtually finish the war on their own; on the other hand the invasion would obviously require their participation and some formula would have to be found to give Harris a role commensurate with his tremendous achievements of the last two years.[22] So much for the present on how Harris was perceived by the world at large and indeed, as Richard Overy suggests, was contributing to the leadership of the nation as a whole.[23] We must turn now to the way he was regarded by the men and women under his command and how he led them and fought their cause.

Notes

1. Folders H81, E9; H50, E2.
2. Folder H16, E16–18, dated 1–6 April 1942. The communiqué in question described 21 individual sorties as 'widespread attacks on objectives in the Ruhr and elsewhere in Germany'.
3. See Folders H51, E36 and H106, E4, for Harris's draft. The actual 'speech' is in Harris, *op.cit.* pp.116–18.
4. Hansard; Folders H87, E9, 10; Misc 22.
5. Harris, *op.cit.* p.156.
6. Folder 27, E4; Carrington, *op.cit.* p.108. Carrington gave Morris a hand.
7. Folders H51, E9, 80; H87, E16, 17.
8. *Oxford Mail* 19 April 1943; *Bucks Free Press* 4 June 1943; *Sunday Times* 30 May 1943; Folder H82, E310.
9. Dimbleby, writing in *Home Chat*, 13 December 1958.
10. Folder H82, dated 29 March and 9 April 1943; Harris scrapbook 1942–3.
11. Article in *Die Weltwoche*, Zurich, dated 18 September 1942.
12. Article in the *Frankfurter Zeitung*, dated 30 August 1943.
13. Harris, *op.cit.* p.58. See, for example, Sinclair's replies to Richard Stokes (Hansard 1 December 1943), when he refused to be drawn on bombing policy beyond stating it to be directed at 'vitally important military objectives'. See also De Groot, *op.cit.* pp.192–3.
14. Hastings, *op.cit.* pp.170–3. On p.177 Hastings quotes another of the strongest opponents of area bombing, the Bishop of Chichester, who argued (Hansard 9 February 1944) that 'wholesale destruction of cities was going too far' and criticised Harris personally over some of his public statements. In fairness, on this occasion Lord Cranborne (Dominions Secretary) mounted a strong defence.
15. Folder H98, dated 25 October, 15 December and 23 December 1943, and 2 March 1944.
16. Norman Longmate, *The Bombers*, pp.369–77.
17. Articles dated 1 September, 29 November and 30 November 1943.
18. *Sunday Graphic* 30 January 1944; *Evening Standard* 3 February 1944; *Illustrated* 25 March 1944.

19. *Daily Mail* 29 July 1943; *Daily Sketch* 13 August 1943; Evelyn Irons in *Evening Standard* 21 August 1943; *Sunday Graphic* 14 November 1943 (a similar article appeared in *This Week* in the USA on 12 December 1943).
20. *Illustrated* 11 March 1944.
21. Folder H36, letters dated 10, 16 and 30 March 1944; *Picture Post* 8 April 1944. The author was the father of Max Hastings.
22. Colin Bednall in the *Daily Mail* 19 January 1944.
23. Overy, *Why the Allies Won*, p.20.

Chapter 10

The leader and his men

Very few of even his severest critics have ever adjudged Harris as other than a great military leader. Yet most have always been puzzled about how he managed to get his personality across to his men, to win and hold their trust, loyalty and respect, when he gave hardly any of them the chance even to see him, let alone talk to him. His remoteness and virtual isolation at High Wycombe flew in face of the conventional wisdom about one of the great requirements of military leadership: that one must meet and be known by as many as possible of those one commands. Slessor, one of the best qualified of his contemporaries to comment, was among the many who never resolved the paradox. Writing to Professor R.V. Jones in 1973 he recalled his own frequent visits to units as C-in-C Coastal Command, but went on: 'Bert virtually never did. Yet on the whole I think no one would say he was anything but a good C-in-C Bomber. I've often wondered how he did succeed in "getting it across" to men who were suffering terrible casualties – in earlier years with very little to show for it – and went on doing so until Bomber Command at last made its decisive contribution to victory.'[1]

It is not strictly true to say that Harris never got out and about. In October 1942, for example, he went to Wyton to make his mark with the recently established Pathfinder Force and was warmly thanked by Donald Bennett for a visit which was 'an inspiration and a stimulant of the greatest value ... the personnel of the PFF are all most impressed by the interest you are showing in their work and in their results. This is a tremendous incentive to them.' On 11 May 1943 he was at Pocklington, the home of 102 Squadron, where he met, among others, three of the survivors from a Halifax which had ditched in the North Sea and been picked up by a rescue launch. Soon afterwards came his visit to Scampton on the occasion of 617 Squadron's Dams Raid, and he also took this opportunity to address the pilots of 57 Squadron, who were based there as well, together with other pilots from nearby stations, including some Poles. Bill McCrea remembers the event. The C-in-C spoke in the Briefing Room for some ten minutes, telling the men how proud they should feel to be the only fighting men who were able to hit back at the Hun. He knew it was rough, and it would get a lot rougher. He finished by saying, 'I want you to look at the man on either side of you. In six months' time only one in three will be left, but if you are the lucky one I promise you this. You will be two ranks higher.' As he strode towards the door there was strumming on the table tops, the Poles started to cheer and soon everyone was joining in; there seemed to be genuine affection for the man who had just told them he would send them over Germany again and again until, finally, only one in three remained. Reaching the door he waved the other members of his party on and turned to face the pilots. 'Suddenly silence returned to the room. Butch half opened his mouth but no sound came. Instead he took a short step forward, lifted his arm in a smart salute, turned on his heel, and was gone.'[2]

On 15 September, as Max Hastings records, Harris called on 76 Squadron at Holme, whose 'early return' and 'lack of moral fibre' statistics were indicating a serious slump in morale. Here he reminded the crews of their duty 'in the most forceful terms' and many questions were asked and answered.[3] The next day he was at Elsham Wolds, the home of 103 Squadron, where he spoke to the aircrew in the station cinema. Norman Ashton, a flight engineer, recalls the terrific cheer that greeted him, the way he dispensed with formalities, and his invitation to the audience to offer suggestions, criticisms and opinions – nothing barred – on anything that might improve the aircraft, squadron or command. Ashton describes the impression he made:

> He looked older and kinder than I had imagined, but there was no doubt that he had a cool, calculating brain, and his whole bearing suggested that he would be utterly ruthless when occasion demanded. It was obvious that he was proud of his men and aircraft, and he promised us an extremely busy time in the coming months. The man-to-man talking revealed the fact that he was no mere figurehead, content to sit at HQ and pull strings, but that he knew most of the answers and could slug it out with the boys in a manner which proved he valued an honest opinion, be it expressed by Group Captain or Sergeant. I felt that his one ambition was to batter the enemy into an early submission and that he believed Bomber Command, given a free hand, was powerful enough to do it.[4]

A different sort of event occurred in late 1944, when Harris flew in his Miles Messenger to Graveley to present 692 Squadron (Mosquitos) with its Badge; knowing how rare were his visits, the men 'felt ten feet tall' as they marched past and their C-in-C took the salute. Sometimes, too, he would be seen at the Group Headquarters. Hugh Constantine was SASO at 1 Group in 1943 when Harris arrived, driving his Bentley at speed through the entrance at Bawtry Hall and damaging the sump on the metal gate catch in the centre of the road. 'Get that bloody thing removed before I leave or you have had it,' he ordered the young Air Commodore. Action was taken and the story went the rounds.[5]

The fact remains that such occasions were rare and the vast majority of his men – and of the many airwomen who also served in his Command – never encountered their master. Much as he would have liked to see far more than he did of his aircrews he felt it was out of the question for him, as C-in-C, to get round to most of the stations. For one thing, as he much later told Denis Richards, he would have found it difficult to be suitably light-hearted with men he could be ordering to their deaths. Nor could he ever have covered them all and could therefore have been accused of favouring some at the expense of others. So with his time and energies at a premium he judged it right to concentrate very largely on the crucial decision-making and the influencing of policy at High Wycombe and in London. Visible leadership in the generally accepted sense was simply not practicable in a Command of such size and complexity. Other ways had to be found.

One of these we have already discussed. If the image of and stories about Harris were being presented to the nation through the press they were certainly reaching the domestic readership of the RAF itself, and in a world which lacked television it was the newspapers (not least the *Daily Mirror*), together with the radio and the newsreels, which were telling the men and women of Bomber Command about their own more notable achievements and the significance of what their C-in-C was himself doing. The influence of the media was a major factor in establishing Harris's reputation as the leader of Bomber Command.

Another was the bush telegraph. Group Captain Hamish Mahaddie, a key figure in the Pathfinder Force, one of Bomber Command's great characters and a man with an acute sense of its history, understood the importance of the down-to-earth stories that came percolating through the system and showed Harris poking fun at the establishment. Irritating and exasperating though his pointed comments might be to those in authority, they were just the kind of remarks that appealed to ordinary mortals, themselves critical of top brass, in wartime. In his later book, Mahaddie remembers their impact:

Harris seldom left his HQ, unless it was to welcome home his Dambusters. But we knew where he was and what he was doing. And there was this warming, compulsive feeling that something was stirring, something was happening. Slowly delightful little stories began to spread ... as DCAS he had maintained a running battle with one of the more senior civil servants ... if they met in the corridor what would pass for a growl at the Battersea Dogs' Home implied 'Good Morning' ... on one occasion the Chief encountered this rather uncivil servant head on. In place of his customary growl he offered a question. 'And what aspect of the war effort are you retarding today?' he inquired. True or false, it was heady stuff.[6]

Not all the stories came from on high. An airframe fitter who used to work on Harris's Anson remembered helping himself to the occasional dram of whisky from the bar on board the aircraft. One day Harris took him aside: 'Young man, it's bad enough you sampling my whisky, but please don't top the bottle up with water!'[7] The tales were legion and they did Harris no harm where they were recounted – in the crew rooms, the hangars and workshops, the billets, the messes. He was recognised deep down as 'one of their own'.

Harris's frequent official messages of exhortation and congratulation did him no harm either. We have already seen two of these (pp.185 and 190); John Searby quotes another, despatched in March 1943 after a particularly successful attack on the Krupp factories:

> The attack on Essen has now inflicted such vast damage that it will in due course take precedence as the greatest victory achieved on any Front. You have set a fire in the belly of Germany which will burn the black heart out of Nazidom and wither its grasping limbs at the very roots. Such attacks, which will continue in crescendo, will progressively make it more and more impossible for the enemy to further his aggressions or to hold where he now stands. The great skill and high courage with which you press home to your objectives has already impressed the inevitability of disaster on the whole of Germany and, within the next few months, the hopelessness of their situation will be borne in upon them in a manner which will destroy their capacity for resistance and break their hearts.

As Searby comments, the old hands rejoiced over the contents whilst the new men were impressed. 'The message went home and we bent to the task with fresh energies ... we felt he was never far away and, though commonly referred to as "the Butcher", this was more a term of affection than anything else.' Searby knew men who volunteered for additional sorties after their prescribed tour of duty had ended – they wanted to do 'a few more for the Butcher'.[8]

Mahaddie, who was never quite sure whether the Chief really sensed the warmth and feeling that the whole Command had for him, or the degree of understanding there was of his incredible task, was another who appreciated the value of Harris's 'Churchillian' signals, always addressed to the squadron commanders. Such messages came directly to the crews with the stamp of the C-in-C, and as the squadron commanders read them out at briefings they became something personal for each of them.[9] If today we are tempted to regard such sentiments as brutal, callous and lacking in human values, we must always remember that this was – unlike more recent conflicts – total war. As the American historian Richard Hallion puts it, Harris was pursuing it in a way that was peculiarly Anglo-American: 'We are slow to anger, but once we get into a war we strive to achieve decisive and overwhelming effect. Harris should not be faulted for his part in that.'[10] Somehow, to quote Charles Messenger, he was able to go on making his crews believe that, provided they kept at it, Germany would eventually crumble,[11] and his pungent messages played their part in convincing them.

Alastair Revie puts his finger on another of the ways in which Harris kept in touch, namely his tireless personal questioning of individuals and crews about what was going wrong or what deficiencies needed remedying.[12] He was not prepared to rely solely on information that had been acquired and processed through the normal staff channels, important though these were. As a long practised professional aviator he wanted to know what the airmen who were actually doing the job thought about it themselves, and he would find out not through time-wasting and stage-managed formal visits to stations but by one-to-one contact either in person or over the telephone.

A New Zealander, Allen George, then a Pilot Officer, recalls what happened to him on 17 July 1942. He had just been posted to Bassingbourn as an OTU instructor after completing an operational tour on Wellingtons with 115 Squadron at Marham when he was ordered into a staff car, driven to High Wycombe and conducted to the C-in-C's office. He was warmly greeted, quickly put at his ease, and questioned in detail about his flying experience with 115 Squadron, with particular emphasis on the aircraft's new de-icing equipment. Harris then invited him to talk frankly about any other operational flying matters, and he seized the opportunity to air his views on the unreliability of the photo-flashes and the consequent frequent failures to obtain target photographs. Harris listened intently before turning to Saundby and telling him: 'Fix it.' After further discussion George was thanked, sent off to the Mess for a beer and lunch on the C-in-C's account, and driven back to Bassingbourn. Soon afterwards he heard that a better, more reliable photo-flash was being issued to the squadrons. A further such visit (most went unrecorded) occurred on 13 November 1944, when Wing Commander K.H. Burns, a recently repatriated prisoner-of-war who had been wounded when his 97 Squadron Lancaster was shot down over Berlin in September 1943, came to see him at Bennett's suggestion.[13]

Harris was keen too to recognise achievement. Andrew Boyle records what Leonard Cheshire remembered of his summons:

For the whole half-hour he spent in Harris's presence, Cheshire's brain was in a whirl. A hard and belligerently practical man, the C-in-C had a 'soft spot' for pilots who did not realise when they had done more than their stint of operations. The gruff gentleness of his welcome was the first shock; the second was his statement, still in those velvety tones, that he wanted to

congratulate him before anyone else on winning a Victoria Cross. Cheshire
was reduced to a stunned silence. The VC of all things! He had never thought
of Harris as a 'fatherly man' with feelings and a heart. The interview was like
a fantasy with wish-fulfilment, a triumph of hope over experience. Harris did
not seem to notice his bewilderment. He was used to the spectacle. 'On every
occasion when I informed anyone that they had been awarded a very high
honour, they have invariably been overcome with astonishment and given the
impression that it was the last thing they expected or deserved,' he told me. 'I
have never known any recipient of the VC not to be astonished at the news of
the award – but I have sometimes met others astonished that they have not
been awarded the VC.'[14]

Cheshire's latest biographer records another version of his recollections of
this meeting: 'He sent for me ... I thought I'd done something wrong ...
and he was very nice, and very fatherly and very friendly and I liked him very
much.'[15]

Nor must Harris's personal letters be forgotten, such as the one he wrote
in December 1942 to the father of Pilot Officer Middleton, an RAAF airman
who had just been awarded a posthumous VC for his role in an attack on
Turin. Harris could think of no more gallant episode than this in the annals
of the RAF; Middleton, he wrote, had laid down his life deliberately to save
some of his crew, and if possible his Stirling aircraft.[16]

One further personal story is well worth recounting, notwithstanding that
Bill Newby, the sergeant in question, was not serving in Bomber Command.
Harris had repeatedly attempted to have part of the Photographic Reconnaissance Unit, located at Benson, placed under his authority, but without
success, so he had to rely on Coastal Command for the photographs and
other reconnaissance information that were so essential for his operations. In
practice there were, of course, close ties between the PRU and his own staff,
and Newby vividly recalls the moment early in 1944 when he was summoned to the Briefing Room soon after returning from a morning Mosquito
sortie over Berlin. He was placed in a sound-proof booth with a scrambler
phone and told by an ADC that the AOC-in-C Bomber Command wished to
speak to him. Harris quietly identified himself, checked Newby's credentials,
and asked whether he thought he, the navigator, would have had a better
view of the Berlin scene than the pilot. There followed a whole series of
questions – all well controlled and totally pertinent – about the weather
conditions over the target and en route, the effects of the heat of the fires on
the clouds above, the extent of the observable damage, the intensity of the
anti-aircraft fire and where it was coming from, enemy fighter activity, and
so on. They talked for some 20 minutes, leaving Newby in no doubt that
Harris was genuinely interested and on top of the operational realities, before

the phone was put down and he was told to say nothing to anybody. He didn't – though eventually, by putting two and two together, he realised that his was not an unusual experience for men in his business. Indeed, he and Harris spoke again in early July after a sortie over the area of Dresden and Chemnitz; this time the C-in-C was particularly keen to know about railway movements.[17]

Here then was another element in Harris's leadership – not one that yielded him wide publicity (and sometimes none at all) but one that demonstrated to ordinary mortals that their master was not only concerned about what they were doing but was also conversant with it and keen to ensure that his decisions took account of what they could tell him. Some might say that he would have done better to spend more time getting to know and listening to his own staff and relied more on delegation in order to find out what people were thinking out in the sticks. Yet surely it cannot have been wrong to try to retain his personal 'feel' for what was actually happening at the sharp end, which was where the young men he led were being required to put their lives on the line.

For most purposes, however, Harris depended on his subordinate commanders, the AOCs of the front-line Groups, to maintain the contacts with the stations, squadrons and crews and keep him informed. Of those already in post when he became C-in-C, the particularly able Slessor (5 Group) and Baldwin (3 Group) were soon to move on to higher things and be replaced by officers with whom Harris had flown in earlier days and in whom he had great confidence: Coryton and Cochrane. The other two 'heavy' groups, Nos 1 and 4, were also commanded by men whom he knew well: R.D. Oxland and C.R. Carr. Lees, who led the light bomber squadrons of 2 Group, was another good friend from the Iraq days. The top team was further strengthened when Bennett took over the Pathfinders, and in early 1943 (at which point 2 Group was moved elsewhere) Harris contrived further changes to produce the team which ran the Command for the next two critical years. At 1 Group Oxland was replaced by Rice, whom Harris remembered as a first-class CO and a very good operational commander in 1939–40. To 3 Group, succeeding Cochrane, went Harrison (hitherto Harris's Deputy SASO), whom Harris described to Portal as 'the first AOC in this war with personal operational experience, and that of itself has many attractions'. Carr, a thoroughly practical and very energetic commander, in Harris's words, remained at 4 Group, and Cochrane moved in at 5 Group to relieve Coryton. Bennett at the recently named 8 Group, and Brookes of the RCAF, at the newly constituted 6 Group, completed the picture.[18]

To allege, as some critics – including Sidney Bufton – have done, that Harris almost entirely appointed 'non-operational' people as his AOCs, men who were unable to bridge the gulf between the realities in the sky and the routines of the Headquarters, is unfair both on him and on the men he helped to choose.[19] For one thing the sort of men he wanted were usually in heavy demand elsewhere and Portal and his Air Member for Personnel were not always open to persuasion. Hugh Lloyd, back from distinguished service in the defence of Malta, was a case in point; Harris pressed hard for him and he would have been ideal, but Portal had other ideas. Not until 1945 did Harris get him, when Lloyd was appointed to command Tiger Force. Surely, too, it was not essential for the AOCs to have seen operational experience during the war itself; certainly such men would have suited Harris, as he said in relation to Harrison and later in the war when getting Hugh Constantine to take over 5 Group, but to exclude slightly older men of talent just because they had not flown on wartime operations would have made little sense. For Harris what mattered in this regard was that they should have had extensive practical flying experience and know what they were talking about.[20]

Another vexed question was whether the AOCs should be allowed to fly on operations. Some certainly wanted to. They were keen to find out for themselves what it was like and to be seen to be leading by example; moreover, as the Eighth Air Force began its offensive they observed its senior commanders going to war with their men. Baldwin had in fact gone on the big Cologne attack, but when Harris heard about this he decreed that in future no AOC was to fly on operations without his permission. He fully understood their reasons for wanting to do so but as he later told Bennett, who was keen to take part in an attack on Berlin in April 1943, he would not permit it. Bennett tried again in August, pleading to be allowed to act as 'raid commentator' for the forthcoming operation against Peenemunde: the need for accurate bombing against this important target, the absence of strong defences, and the value to him personally of having up-to-date operational knowledge were sufficient to justify making an exception on this occasion. Harris would have none of it. 'You must give up the idea of going on operations for an indefinite period,' he told Bennett. 'We depend very largely on your personal knowledge for the exploitation of Pathfinder methods during the next critical few months . . . and you know too much. If you are taken prisoner the Germans have their own means and methods of extracting information involuntarily, and I have no intention of allowing them to operate these methods on key personnel.' There was no answer to this, though Bennett still did not entirely give up (see p.232).

On the other hand there was a line to be drawn and it was only AOCs and Base Commanders, who possessed knowledge of technical, tactical and strategic matters, together with awareness of new methods and future specialised equipment, that Harris placed under embargo. Station Commanders and other senior officers on the Group staffs were free to go occasionally. This firm line brought the C-in-C under criticism in some quarters, in public as well as in private, but under all the circumstances it is hard to fault.[21] He was not, however, entirely inflexible, as he showed in May 1944 when defending AOC 1 Group for allowing a newly appointed Base Commander to fly in a raid on France. The aircraft had been shot down and Air Commodore Ivelaw-Chapman taken prisoner. Since he had recently held an Air Ministry policy appointment, VCAS felt he should have been refused permission. Harris quickly pointed out that the Command had not known the nature of his work, was keen not to be too restrictive, and needed to be properly briefed if mistakes were to be avoided.

Harris also took a strong line regarding one of his AOCs, Alec Coryton. The two of them were in growing disagreement about certain types of operation and, as Searby recalls, matters came to a head in early 1943 when Harris ordered the despatch of a small Lancaster force to the Ruhr on a night of bad weather; they were to bomb on skymarkers dropped by the Pathfinders with the primary object of keeping the Germans awake. Coryton, reluctant to send his crews over Germany in such doubtful conditions, saw no point in operations like this, or – to take another example as quoted by Harris – small-scale 'political' attacks on clear nights against Berlin. Increasingly concerned about the differing operational judgements which lay behind such arguments, and by the fact that Coryton seemed to be soft-hearted and unable to bear the thought of casualties to his crews, Harris decided to recommend his move to a different appointment and on 23 February wrote to his subordinate to explain why. It was a hard letter to write. They had known each other since serving together in India and Harris not only recalled their long friendship but paid glowing tribute to 5 Group's many achievements under Coryton's leadership, to his own vast contribution to these, to his outstanding personal efficiency, and to his exceptionally high sense of duty. What Harris could not accept were the perpetual and persistent disputes which had characterised their relationship, and the constant prognostications of disaster which met operational instructions. 'I have repeatedly reminded you that it is for me to say what shall be done and when, and broadly how; and for you to accomplish it. The responsibility for the outcome is mine and mine alone ... where you fail is through your inability to divest yourself of a moral responsibility which is not yours.'[22]

Harris had done what he believed he had to. His top team could not work if one of its members was out of step – even though, as Harris told Coryton, he might be right. The job was done with firmness, with frankness, and with sympathy. Harris made clear there was no question of an adverse report and was sure that there would be plenty of applicants for his services. There were. Portal found good jobs for Coryton first in the Air Ministry and then the Far East, and he ended up an Air Chief Marshal. It was a matter of horses for courses and Harris judged that leadership in the bomber war was not a task for unduly sensitive minds.

This brings us to one of the greatest questions about Harris's own leadership. By the end of the war, of the 125,000 aircrew who had served in Bomber Command 55,000 had been killed, a quarter of those who lost their lives in the whole of the British Armed Services. It was he who made the operational decisions that led to the deaths of the majority, and to many of the 18,000 further casualties listed as wounded or taken prisoner.[23] How did he cope with the likely and actual consequences of his decisions? Did he even actually care? Some have accused him of not thinking about them, of closing his mind, of concentrating so exclusively on hitting Germany that his own casualties were incidental. Certainly there were some of his crews who would have echoed the words of a later historian, Alexander McKee, who said that many nicknamed him 'the Butcher' not so much because he cared nothing for the lives of German civilians but because they believed that he cared nothing for their own either.[24] Other historians have compared Air Marshals such as Harris with the First World War generals who stayed well behind the lines and sent their men to die in morasses which they, the generals, did not know of and refused to admit existed.[25] Harris has been at times portrayed as a latter-day Haig, with implications that are unfair to them both. Sidney Bufton, who did much good work in the Air Ministry on behalf of the bomber offensive but was unable to hit it off with Harris, also slated him on this critical issue. Accusing him of not 'leading' his men, *ie* of never leading them on an operation over Germany or even of qualifying as a captain of any of the aircraft they flew, Bufton alleged that Harris always thought of losses in terms of aircraft, not of human lives – lives such as that of Bufton's own brother, John,[26] who had been killed piloting a Hampden in October 1940.

It is true that many who had dealings with Harris in the normal course of business never really knew how he felt about the losses from the human standpoint. Nobody doubted the importance he attached to minimising them for all the obvious practical reasons, but what he actually thought about the many thousands of his men who failed to return was never revealed. Searby, one of the most perceptive observers, said that it was only long after the war that he came to appreciate how deeply his master felt about them. Harris knew that the nature of his operations made substantial casualties inevitable, and always in his mind, as he told Dewar McCormack,[27] was the thought of the million British soldiers who had been mown down amid the carnage of the First World War. His determination to try to win the war by bombing was fuelled by the conviction that such battlefield slaughter must never be allowed to happen again and that it was the task of his men to prevent this. As he wrote of them afterwards in his most moving tribute:

There are no words with which I can do justice to the aircrew who fought under my command. There is no parallel in warfare to such courage and determination in the face of danger over so prolonged a period, of danger which at times was so great that scarcely one man in three could expect to survive his tour of operations.[28]

Yet had he at the time allowed those under his command to think that he was weighed down by doubts about having to send so many men to their deaths he could probably never have done his job as it had to be done, and almost certainly this was one of his reasons for keeping his distance from most of those he led. Just occasionally his defences slipped a little, as in his letter to Coryton when he wrote 'you cannot bear the thought of casualties,' and went on 'but you have no monopoly in this. I only hope you may never have on your heart and conscience the load which lies on mine.'

Nevertheless, some of those closest to him did know. As Peter Tomlinson said, and his brother Paul echoed, he never showed emotion over losses, but deep down inside he felt them. Pelly-Fry, who visited Springfield in 1942, heard him speak of the 'very nasty, tough, uncomfortable and frightening game' of being a bomber airman. His cousin Ian Elliot understood, too, as did Ian's daughter, Diana Collins, who commented that what she herself saw of him confirmed that 'his concern for his men's welfare and his distress at casualties went very deep'. Jill, too, had no doubts about his feelings, as we have already seen. One of the many historians who goes along with this verdict, Alastair Revie, quotes Harris asking, 'Do you honestly think that I would have risked aircrew unnecessarily when I admired and valued them as much as I did?' Let Max Hastings have the final word on this: 'Those who seek to present him simply as a latter-day "Donkey", indifferent to casualties, do him an injustice. He was passionately concerned to give every man in his Command the best possible chance of survival.'[29]

In his determination to minimise losses while at the same time operating effectively, Harris fully understood the importance of high morale and spared no effort to try to ensure that the conditions under which his men served were fair and reasonable. One critical aspect was the length of the operational tour of duty each airman should be expected to complete. The original requirement was for 200 hours of operational flying, but by August 1942 Harris was convinced that this rule was allowing some of the poorer, less determined crews to avoid pressing home their attacks and was also unfair on the better crews. He therefore floated with his Group Commanders the idea that the full operational tour should in future consist of 30 sorties, each to be validated by the squadron commander on the basis of photographic evidence. At an Air Ministry meeting on 4 February 1943 Harris obtained formal agreement to this scheme, accompanied by provision for a second tour not exceeding 20 sorties. To quote John Terraine, 'with its definite promise of relief this was a sheet anchor of morale in Bomber Command.'[30] It was not, of course, perfect – and never could have been. Harris himself saw the dangers of trying to define the term 'operational sortie' as though it formed part of some trade union contract and firmly defended the prerogative of the squadron commander to judge whether a sortie was satisfactory or not.[31] Then in March 1944 he nearly came unstuck when his Command was required to devote much of its effort to short-range, relatively 'soft' targets in France. Realising that these frequent operations were quickly going to absorb the effort of many of his experienced crews he consulted the Air Staff and decreed that such sorties would count only as one-third of an operation. The reasoning was sound, the effect on morale less so, and in May he had to compromise.[32]

Another important factor affecting morale, in Harris's judgement, was crew leadership. This was one of the earliest matters which he raised with Portal, when he pointed out the dissatisfaction among heavy bomber captains that many of their posts were still ranked only for sergeants and asked for all to be established for flight lieutenants, warrant officers or flight sergeants. By the turn of the year, with seven- or eight-man crews now the norm rather than the exception, he was concluding that all captains ought to be flight lieutenants, a view strongly endorsed by his AOCs, by the Inspector General (Ludlow-Hewitt), and – he believed – by Portal from his own experience when C-in-C. Urging the case upon Air Marshal Bertie Sutton, AMP, he stated that no NCO, even a warrant officer, appeared capable of exercising command in the operational sense over his brother NCOs. Consequently 'decisions in NCO-manned crews are normally the subject of a mothers' meeting, and as in all councils of war whatever decision is made is inevitably one to disengage from the enemy'. Harris was utterly convinced that the responsibilities entailed in captaining heavy bombers required officer rank; NCOs with the necessary initiative and ability should therefore be commissioned, and those not deemed fit to be officers were not fit to be captains. The reasoning was impeccable, the reactions of the Air Ministry and the Treasury predictable. A year later, in March 1944, having battled long and unproductively, Harris wrote despairingly to Harold Balfour, who had shown interest in the subject, and outlined the background. 'My own conviction . . . is that until the Air Ministry resolves to approach the question in a new spirit with the intention of getting something done instead of obstructing all attempts at improvement it is completely futile to discuss the matter further. Inertia and obstruction are the only reactions I raise.'[33]

Harris got nowhere either when venting his spleen about pay. Sutton was again on the receiving end in March 1943 when Harris warned that the Services should consider overriding the Treasury's obstructionism to all proposals for fair and reasonable rates of pay. Morale would not hold up indefinitely while the men and their families were subjected to intense financial worries and put nowhere in competition with the overpaid so-called 'workers'. 'I am quite frankly astounded at your attempt to justify(?) the existing state of affairs by comparing the rate of pay of a 21 year old idle scruffy mechanic in an aircraft factory or motor works, probably with no responsibility, with that of a flight lieutenant. The three Services,' he went on, 'have got to get together without interference from the financial Dutch auctioneers, those vipers which we nourish in our bosoms, and demand fair treatment for junior service personnel . . . I implore you to treat this question as a matter vitally and closely connected with the morale of the Services now.' Whatever we may think of his language, his logic and his tactics, Harris's convictions about the needs of his men were clear. Moreover he was not averse, as he told Sutton, to bending the ear of his friend Ralph Assheton, just appointed Financial Secretary to the Treasury, on these matters.[34]

A further long-running financial issue that greatly worried Harris and which also he never satisfactorily resolved arose from a matter of operational principle. At a meeting with CAS and the other Cs-in-C on 7 April 1942 he pleaded for the issue of an Air Ministry Order requiring all operational crews, including married personnel, to live on their stations; the growing intensity of his operations and the impracticability of deciding on their timing other than at very short notice made it essential for all crews to be quickly available. The other Cs-in-C, who were not subject to similar pressures, disagreed, whereupon Harris stated his intention of enforcing such an order unilaterally and asked for the married men to continue receiving their full marriage allowance. He duly issued his edict and was promptly instructed by the Air Ministry Finance Branch to discontinue it; he was also told – to his considerable annoyance – that no special allowance could be authorised for married officers required to live in the mess. He had already taken issue with Sutton about these allowances, being unwilling to accept the argument that his aircrews could not be treated differently from many other officers (and not just RAF) who were required to live in. As far as Harris was concerned his was a one-off case justified by urgent operational requirements; it was intended to offset the additional expenses unavoidably incurred by the men involved, and the Air Ministry was so far not prepared to fight it. 'They lack the moral courage to order my men to live in, and leave me holding the baby,' he told Sutton. 'You would not allow this matter to drop if you were in my position, and I will not . . . the absence of an equitable allowance is definitely detrimental to my operational efforts and, therefore, anybody who obstructs this decision is obstructing our operational effort.' Harris followed up by formally telling the Air Ministry that he would not cancel his existing orders and requesting urgent solution of his personnel's financial difficulties. Thereafter the allowances debate became bogged down in the bureaucracy, notwithstanding attempts by Balfour and Assheton to exercise their influence, and we are left yet again with a picture of the C-in-C forcefully deploying his verbal armoury on behalf of those who were doing the fighting but unable to shift officialdom from its overriding determination to control the budget and steer clear of creating awkward precedents.[35]

So in these and many other ways, such as pressing the importance of gallantry awards, Harris constantly worked on behalf of his crews, yet he knew all too well that the maintenance of high morale also required a full measure of discipline. At 5 Group he had himself had experience of applying the 'lack of moral fibre' (LMF) regulations (see p.93) and now, as C-in-C, he was determined to ensure the firm handling of those suffering from combat stress – those, to quote one of his best station medical officers, Squadron Leader Stafford-Clark, who 'allowed their fears and sense of self-preservation to outweigh their sense of duty and obligation to their comrades'. Harris had little sympathy with the 'weaklings and waverers' who were liable to 'contaminate' others in their crews and his views were shared by all in Bomber Command and elsewhere who realised the implications.[36] On the other hand, recognising the enormous investment represented in the training of his men he was concerned not just for them as individuals but also to try to ensure that they gave a proper return, and a letter he wrote to AMP in May 1942 about the value of squadron medical officers provides a most useful perspective:

> It is possible for a good doctor to anticipate the onset of stress and to encourage and assist some individuals through a passing phase of slight loss of confidence ... he can also advise the CO whether an individual is a genuine case of stress ... or should be dealt with by disciplinary means under Air Ministry procedure. This I consider most important. Firm but just handling of cases may prevent and will certainly limit the incidence of failure from either medical or moral fibre causes.[37]

The message here is of firmness rather than the harshness that some critics of Bomber Command's handling of LMF have alleged, though inevitably some individuals were treated with undue severity. Overall the best estimate is that only 0.4% of bomber airmen engaged on operations and in OTUs were actually classified LMF, a figure which John Terraine and Mark Wells regard as remarkably small under all the circumstances.[38] Noble Frankland agrees: 'Although he was supposed to be rather brutal about such matters, Harris was actually a very sensitive man, and his leadership was the primary reason why the LMF figures were so low.'[39] When he wrote after the war that 'morale was never a problem' Harris almost certainly meant that it was never allowed to develop into one, which is a remarkable reflection on him and his men.

We must bear in mind in these discussions the international nature of the force that Harris led. As his Despatch tells us, no less than 37% of his pilots in January 1943 were Canadians, Australians or New Zealanders, and two years later the percentage had risen to 45%.[40] While many served in RAF units an increasing proportion were in specific RCAF, RAAF and RNZAF squadrons, reflecting the Dominions' desires to have their contributions properly recognised. It needs to be said that not all Dominion airmen were enthusiastic about having separate squadrons; they realised the operational value of integrated units within which their men could profit from the wider experience of their RAF colleagues and advance to command positions on individual merit, and this became a subject of continuing controversy – particularly in Canada, which provided well over half the Dominion pilots in Bomber Command. In 1943, however, Air Vice-Marshal Edwards, Air Officer-in-Chief RCAF Overseas, was under firm remit from Ottawa to push forward the 'Canadianisation' policy under which all RCAF squadrons, hitherto mixed-manned, were eventually to become entirely Canadian, and to arrange for a separate Canadian Bomber Group to be formed.[41]

Given the major and growing Dominion contributions to his force these were matters of considerable importance to Harris, who shared the doubts of the Canadian critics and of men such as Carr, 4 Group's New Zealand AOC, about the wisdom of forming separate squadrons.[42] On this matter he bowed to the inevitable, but in August 1942 he raised with Freeman a wider issue arising from a decision that Bomber Command's immediate expansion should be based almost completely on new Canadian squadrons. 'Canadians make good crews,' he wrote, 'but I for one should be most perturbed to see almost the entire expansion going into Canadians for the rest of the year. We are always being accused, as a nation, of fighting with the bodies of Colonial and Dominion personnel in preference to British – so far unjustly. But why lend colour to it?' The consequence, he went on, would be a Canadian Group out of all proportion to the others, and with other 'national' squadrons being added Bomber Command could end up with most of its operational squadrons being manned by what he called 'coloured troops'. This was a plea for more balanced expansion, but while Freeman readily took Harris's point he could hold out little hope of altering the situation.[43]

A few days later Harris told Portal that Edwards and his staff were going round some of his bomber stations in connection with plans for the future Canadian Group without having made any attempt to seek his authority, and were also upsetting some of the existing Canadian crews. They had never met, Harris said (though he had heard Trenchard describe Edwards as an appalling fellow quite unsuited for any sort of command), and hopefully Portal could do something to put matters right.[44] They did in fact meet soon afterwards, when Edwards accompanied Power, the Canadian Air Minister, to High Wycombe. Power, warned to expect the worst, found his host most co-operative and expressing willingness to help in every way; 'Of all the senior officers we have met overseas on our two trips,' he wrote in his diary, 'Harris has put himself out more than anyone else, thus belying the reputation that has been built up for him both by our people and by the UK authorities.'[45] He had turned on the charm, presented himself as one of the RCAF's greatest supporters – which indeed he was – and come to terms with the fact that the Canadians were going to be allotted their own Group and must be given every assistance.

It would not, however, always be plain sailing. Harris remained unenamoured of Edwards, as indicated when he wrote again to Portal complaining of the Canadian's 'ignorant and voluble chatter' in asserting that 'no crew stands a hope of completing a second tour'; this false assertion was gaining widespread currency, was having serious effects on morale, and reflected badly on Edwards' discretion. Nor was Harris impressed by Brookes, who became 6 Group's first AOC on 1 January 1943: according to the Canadian official historians he was alarmed at the prospects of 6 Group under Brookes' command.[46] Both officers were replaced a year later, the latter by a man who very quickly won Harris's confidence, Air Vice-Marshal C.M. McEwen. Another serious matter was the poor type of commanding officer that the Dominions seemed to produce – 'mostly hangovers from a prehistoric past; at best completely inexperienced, at worst awful,' he told Portal on 10 January 1943. 'I heard a comment the other day that the Canadian fighting crews were venting strong objections to being commanded by officers whose experience was limited to six months' flying training and 25 years' political intrigue.' His worries were not limited to the Canadians, he went on. Of his 63 squadrons, 20 were already foreign or Dominion; two more were in the offing (Dutch and Free French), and the Royal Australian Air Force was already talking about collecting all its crews together into a group-type organisation. If these processes were to continue it could become more and more difficult to maintain proper control of the bomber force, and there would be repercussions with the Americans who would be able to claim to be the preponderant national air force in the United Kingdom.[47]

There were practical problems too. Hardly had 6 Group been formed than Harris had to draw attention to the need for Canadians (and others) to accept the same obligations as the RAF to undertake first and second tours of operations split by a period of instructional duties. In October 1943 his anxieties on this score were confirmed when the RCAF decided to grant special home leave to its aircrew after their first tour of operations and he lodged the strongest protest. There had been no consultation and the implications for his Command's operations and training had been totally ignored. He reacted just as forcibly when the RAAF announced – also without consultation – that its aircrews would be repatriated after one operational and one instructional tour. The strong domestic pressures in both countries were understandable, but Harris, just embarking on his great winter offensive, found these decisions hard to take.[48] Commissioning was another aspect of personnel policy that caused difficulties, with the Canadians in particular urging that all aircrew should hold officer rank, but here Harris was sympathetic. Moreover, whatever the problems occasioned by the Dominions air forces, he had no doubts about the overall value of their contributions and specifically acknowledged the fact that Canada met the whole cost of 6 Group and of all the RCAF's operational squadrons.[49]

Notwithstanding his constant concern about the interests of his aircrew, Harris never lost sight of the needs of that far greater number of personnel on whom their operations depended. In August 1942 he sought to convince AMP of the importance of bringing his maintenance personnel up to establishment. The current shortages, which he described as criminal, together with the scandalous position in the domestic trades, were reducing efficiency and increasing unserviceability and accident rates: 'We shall not win this war by building more aircraft for units to crash,' he wrote. Yet three months later, having been asked, in common with other Cs-in-C, to offer his ideas on manpower economies, he was quick to ventilate his ideas and show that he still understood the realities of station and squadron life. The crux of the problem, he suggested, was to raise the standards of skill and organisation; the duties on heavy bomber stations were becoming so complicated that more training was needed than could possibly be provided on the spot, and external courses – one of Harris's career-long themes – were essential. A second requirement was better working conditions. On many stations, especially in winter, output was far less than it would be in well-lit, adequately heated, and properly equipped hangars and workshops; and where aircraft maintenance had to be done in the open the airmen – and shortly airwomen – ought to be suitably clad and equipped. Thirdly, much time and therefore staff would be saved by reducing dispersal distances between domestic and working sites, and by a variety of RAF-wide administrative measures, including the merging of the administrative structures of the WAAF and RAF.[50]

Though not all that much positive action resulted from such ideas, Harris continued the pressure. In August 1943, for example, he stressed to VCAS the serious undermanning in many trades, the inadequacy of some of the manpower establishments especially in the electrical trades, the shortage of unskilled aircrafthands (which meant that basic tasks had to be done by specialists), and the ever-increasing substitution of WAAF for RAF personnel. He fully recognised that women's aptitudes and skills were well suited to many types of work; he particularly admired the thoroughness of their office work and the way they could be depended upon to keep their mouths shut.[51] On the other hand they were seldom capable of the same degree of physical effort as the men, or of handling heavy equipment with a comparable economy in numbers. Soon afterwards he returned to the appalling amount of time being wasted by skilled men having to walk the long distances from point to point on his modern dispersed stations. While the large-scale issue of bicycles had been agreed it seemed likely to be another year before his requirements were met. 'I need 40,000 now and it is no exaggeration to say that failure to meet this need is gravely prejudicing the efficiency of the command,' he told AMSO's deputy.

It was in such ways – and there were many more[52] – that Harris showed his understanding of the demands being made on the men and women who served under him, on the ground as well as in the air. He appreciated too that the dangers were not confined to aircrew: as he reminded Portal in 1945, many lives were also lost in explosions, accidents and test flights. Summarising the debt owed to the multitude of airmen and airwomen who laboured to support his operations he wrote: 'It is apparent to me that few people appreciate the terrible miseries and discomfort and the tremendous hours of work under which the ground personnel of Bomber Command on the airfields have laboured for nearly six years.'[53] He, their leader, had no doubt, and though he was never able to improve their lot to the extent he wished it was not for want of trying. Let none question Harris's deep concern for all in Bomber Command. It was one of his greatest qualities of leadership.

Notes

1. Slessor to Jones 22 June 1973, copied by Jones to the author 8 May 1997.
2. Recollections of Wing Commander W.E. McCrea DFC, given to the author in 1999. Neither the Scampton nor 51 Squadron ORBs (Operations Record Books) mention this visit.
3. Folder H57, dated 10 October 1942; 102 Squadron ORB; Hastings, *op.cit.* p.218; and AIR 27/651.
4. AIR 28/255; Ashton, *Only Birds and Fools*, pp.30–1 (the text was drafted in 1945 and eventually published posthumously).
5. John Archbold recollections and AIR 27/2216; RAFHS vol.6.
6. Extract from Mahaddie's *The Bombing Years*, quoted in Lucas, *Wings of War*, pp.224–5.
7. Related by Robert Paton.
8. Searby, *op.cit.* p.96; Revie, *op.cit.* p.202, makes similar points. See Folder H49 for some of his other messages.
9. Lucas, *op.cit.* p.225.

10. RAFHS, *Reaping the Whirlwind*, pp.59–60.

11. Messenger, *op.cit.* p.205.

12. Revie, *op.cit.* p.176.

13. Letter to the author from Squadron Leader Allen George DFC DFM, dated 16 April 1997; Folder H57.

14. Boyle, *No Passing Glory* (based on letter from Harris, 13 January 1955, Misc Folder 19/2).

15. Morris, *Cheshire*, pp.180–1.

16. Herington, *The Air War Against Germany and Italy 1939–43*, pp.463–4.

17. Author's discussions with Wing Commander G.W.E. Newby DFC in 1998. Newby was shot down and taken prisoner in August 1944.

18. Folder H74, E160A; Saward, *op.cit.* pp.156–7, 192.

19. Furse-Bufton interview. See also Hastings, *op.cit.* p.351.

20. Harris interview with Group Captain (now Air Vice-Marshal) Tony Mason, RAF Staff College, 1982.

21. Messenger, *op.cit.* p.202; Folder 57, dated 5 and 10 August 1943; AIR 14/1451; Folder H15, dated 16 May 1944. Bennett implied in *Pathfinder* that he did fly occasionally on operations, presumably unbeknown to Harris.

22. Folder H59, dated 23 February 1943; Searby, *op.cit.* p.185.

23. Middlebrook, *The Bomber Command War Diaries*, p.708.

24. Most of his men abbreviated 'Butcher' into the more affectionate 'Butch'.

25. Quoted in Messenger, *op.cit.* p.200.

26. Bufton-Furse interview

27. Interview, 15 March 1979.

28. Harris, *op.cit.* p.267

29. Pelly-Fry, *op.cit.* p.186; Diana Collins, *op.cit.* p.134; Revie, *op.cit.* p.254; Hastings, *op.cit.* p.244

30. Terraine, *op.cit.* pp.523–7; Folder H49, E18.

31. Folder H67, dated 2 February 1943; AIR 20/2860.

32. Article by Oliver Clutton-Brock, Bomber Command Association Newsletter, September 1996; Folder H68, dated 8 March 1944.

33. Folders H81, dated 7 March 1942; H74, dated 28 January and 19 February 1943; H27, dated 27 March 1944. See AIR 1008 for the full discussion.

34. Folder H74, dated 17 March 1943.

35. Folders H66, dated 10 and 30 October 1942; H72, dated 23 September 1942; H27, dated 9 February and 1 April 1943.

36. Mark Wells, *Courage and Air Warfare*, pp.186–206, an excellent discussion on LMF and Bomber Command. On 28 December 1942, for example, Harris showed his concern in a letter recommending a further LMF category – 'probably lacking in moral fibre'. AIR 2/4935.

37. Folder H72, dated 4 May 1942.

38. Terraine, *op.cit.* pp.528–35; Wells, *op.cit.* p.206; Neillands, *The Bomber War*, pp.93–4.

39. As reported in RAFHS, *Reaping the Whirlwind*, p.62. See also p.63 for comments by Professor Brandon.

40. Harris Despatch, p.16.

41. Greenhous et al, *The Crucible of War*; chapter 2 covers this subject in depth. Herington, *op.cit.* pp.45–6, discusses it from an Australian point of view, indicating that those serving in Bomber Command on the whole preferred integration with the RAF.

42. *Ibid* pp.65, 570.
43. *Ibid* pp.599, 600; AIR 20/2978; Folder H16, dated 29 July 1942.
44. Folder H81, dated 12 August 1942.
45. Greenhous, *op.cit.* p.78.
46. *Ibid* p.636.
47. Folders H82, dated 10 January 1943; H67, dated 19 January 1943.
48. Folder H67, dated 19 January and 8 October 1943.
49. Harris, *op.cit.* p.134.
50. Folders H72, dated 2 and 9 August 1942; H66, dated 18 November 1942.
51. Comment to Eaker, Copp, *op.cit.* p.253.
52. He waged a long campaign, for example, to secure commissioned status for the civilian meteorologists whose work was so critical to his operations (Folders H71, 74). Among the beneficiaries was his own 'met man', Dr Spence, who became a Group Captain in 1944.
53. Richards, *op.cit.* p.325.

Chapter 11

Tools and techniques

If Harris's men were important to him so were the tools of their trade and the way they were used: the aircraft, the bombs, the equipment and techniques needed to help them reach, identify and hit their targets, the means of defending themselves and minimising their losses, and much more. Thanks to his long experience as pilot, squadron commander and AOC he took no persuading of their significance and was always quick to draw upon the many lessons he had learnt over the years. On the other hand he did not find it easy to keep up with the increasingly rapid pace of technological change occasioned by the pressures of war, and where disagreements and controversies arose they were often linked with new inventions and ideas which could be difficult to understand and appraise. Nevertheless, as a man with great practical skills he had an excellent feel for many of the key questions that affected the performance of his bomber force, and even though he did not fly his front-line aircraft himself he had an almost instinctive grasp of their virtues and their weaknesses.

To begin with, as we have seen, Harris had to make do very largely with the types of aircraft he had inherited, of which the Wellington still equipped much of the force, but for the future he knew he would have to rely on the four-engined bombers that were coming into service and by August 1942 his mind was made up. The Handley Page Halifax, one of the two supposedly good long-term prospects, was, he told Portal, causing serious anxieties. No 4 Group, which was operating the aircraft, had recently had to be briefly withdrawn from operations to allow it time to recover not just from the loss of 32 aircraft to the Middle East but also from heavy casualties on operations over Germany, and Harris and his staff were concluding that the Halifax's vulnerability was mainly due to the poor performance of an overloaded aircraft. Soon afterwards he followed this up to Freeman. Describing the Halifax as a 'virtual failure' he suggested various structural modifications but predicted that within a year, even with these, it would not be fit for European operations. As much production as possible should therefore be switched to the Lancaster – but if necessary also to the Stirling – and the Halifax converted to troop and cargo-carrying. 'I am sure you will agree that whatever we do to the Halifax we can never make it a patch on the Lancaster although basically it is the same aircraft to the same specification and with the same engine,' he concluded.[1] Thus Harris identified early on what he would eventually describe as 'without exception the finest bomber of the war', and he always remembered the debt owing to its designer, Roy Chadwick. As he wrote to Chadwick's daughter in 1976: 'Your father never received a tithe of the honours and recognition due from the Nation for his services.'[2]

Despite Harris's preference for Chadwick's bomber – and the strong support of the Air Staff – it was never possible for the Ministry of Aircraft Production to switch resources to it as much as he hoped. In November 1942 he argued against the use of Merlin engines for the 'utterly unsatisfactory' Halifax at a time when the Mark II Lancaster was being fitted with Hercules engines owing to a shortage of Merlins; surely it would be better to use the Hercules for the future Mark III Halifax? In December he turned to the Stirlings, telling Portal of the fearful maintenance problems largely caused by the unreliability of its engines and suggesting that the overheads of 3 Group, which operated the Stirlings, were no longer yielding a worthwhile contribution to the war effort. Then in January 1943, aware that the MAP was starting to think about converting Stirling production to Lancasters, he weighed in by telling the Air Ministry that in his view both the Stirling and the Halifax were already obsolescent and would be completely obsolete by the end of the year. Soon afterwards he was pleased to hear that not only was progress being made in switching over some Stirling factories but that two of the five Halifax factories were also being considered for transfer. He would have liked to see them all go, as he made clear on reiterating the Halifax's shortcomings: its performance was too low, it had vicious handling habits, its exhaust flame damping was unsatisfactory, and the attempts to make it carry the necessary defensive armament rendered it practically useless for operations. Then in April he went to town on the Halifax III which was now being developed. It would have too low a ceiling – a fatal defect in view of the necessity for altitude to avoid crippling casualties from the increasing enemy defences – and it could be expected to reproduce the vicious flying characteristics of its precursors. A six-foot greater wingspan, as previously recommended, would help by raising the ceiling but the result would still be an unsatisfactory aircraft. Losses of aircraft and crews, he concluded, 'will ensue on an ever-increasing scale if we persist in our present policy of sending crews to fight in inferior aircraft instead of converting our production to a type of proved operational efficiency'.[3]

Nor was the Lancaster itself exempt from criticism. As Harris told the Air Ministry, 'Improvements in enemy methods of night interception are making it more and more necessary for our bombers to fly at the maximum possible height obtainable to avoid high losses in heavily defended areas.' The Lancaster I was now barely holding its own at its highest practical operational altitude of 20–21,000 ft; in a year's time 30,000 ft would be required. So, recognising the critical importance of his Lancasters for the future of the strategic offensive, Harris knew that he must resist all attempts to poach them for other purposes and must employ them in the most efficient ways. In February 1943, for example, he enlisted Portal's aid in resisting the MAP's proposal to fit 30 Lancasters to carry the spinning bomb being developed by the scientist Barnes Wallis – a weapon which, Harris wrote, existed so far only in the imagination of those who conceived it. 'With some slight practical knowledge and many previous bitter experiences on similar lines I am prepared to bet that this is just about the maddest proposition as a weapon that we have yet come across.' The enthusiasts could be given one aircraft to play with but he was not going to hand over any more of his precious Lancasters.[4] On this point he soon changed his tune (see p.254).

Harris tried, too, to keep his Lancasters for the most efficient units and was particularly resistant to political pressure from the Poles in May 1943 to allow one of their Wellington squadrons to convert. In his opinion the Poles, though good fighters, were essentially individualists, not all that well disciplined, and made the worst crews for heavy aircraft in which good teamwork was the prime essential. If they wanted a heavy bomber squadron they could have Halifaxes, but Lancasters should not be provided for them until all RAF and Dominion squadrons had been so equipped. Three months later he refused to change his mind, stressing how unfair it would be to the many British and Canadian crews still flying Stirlings and Halifaxes,[5] but this time he was overruled and 300 (Polish) Squadron obtained its Lancasters in April 1944.

Another means of maximising the value of Harris's Lancasters was to use them as little as possible for training, and in the later part of the war most operational training was carried out on Stirlings and Halifaxes, leaving crews needing only short familiarisation courses at a Lancaster Finishing School. Nor did Harris ignore the possibility that the Germans, appreciating the significance of the Lancaster, might try to administer a spot of his own medicine, and at his request Bottomley commissioned a study of the vulnerability to air attack of the main factories involved in Lancaster production. The conclusion accepted by Bottomley and by Air Marshal Leigh-Mallory at Fighter Command suggested that the risks were only slight, but Harris was not so sure: 'I think we are being very complacent,' he told Bottomley. 'The air offensive against Germany is now [July 1943] catastrophic for them and I am sure they will realise sooner or later, and probably sooner, that their best and indeed their only chance of reducing it is to attack the factories.' There would be no warning, he added, and the consequences could be disastrous.[6] On balance, we may judge, the Air Staff's assessment was fair but Harris was not one to fall into the trap of under-estimating his enemy.

Meanwhile the prospects of Harris's other heavy bombers continued to be debated. In June 1943 he told Portal he was 'despondent about the Stirling', which had for some time got away with it at relatively low level but had just suffered 11.8% losses on one raid; it would be useful in other roles but was failing to meet minimum tactical requirements as a bomber. Four months later he went further, announcing his intention to remove it from the front line and use it to replace the Lancaster for operational training in the Heavy Conversion Units, thus freeing the Lancaster for the front line.[7] Nor was he becoming less critical of the Halifax. Writing to Portal in September he pointed out that its losses in that year's Berlin attacks were almost double those of the Lancaster; it carried only half the Lancaster's bomb load (something of an over-statement!); it had been largely disarmed in the attempt to improve its performance; and not only did its aerodynamic vices persist but he had no faith in Handley Page's promise to rectify them. This was a bitter attack on the firm, which Harris described as 'not an aircraft manufacturer, just a financier, with all that implies, and more'. He was no kinder in a formal letter to the Air Ministry in November specifically about the Mark III, which was achieving 'no ponderable improvement over its predecessors and whose continued short range was adversely affecting the employment of the Lancaster when the two types were operating together.' He remained totally convinced that the country must stop squandering resources and concentrate all heavy bomber production on the Lancaster, a plea which he reiterated to Air Marshal D.C.S. Evill, who had taken over from Freeman as VCAS. The culmination of all this was a formal meeting with the MAP on 21 December chaired by Portal, who was less critical of the Mark III Halifax but fully supportive of Harris's convictions about the superiority of the Lancaster. It was clear, however, that only if the war lasted into 1945 could switches of production start to have significant effects, and while the MAP agreed to investigate the possibilities it was clear that in practice Harris would have to operate with the types and quantities of aircraft he already had and was expecting to receive. It remains to be said on this vexed issue that, as Harris had told Portal on 26 October, he hoped he might be mistaken about the Halifax Mark III, and in the later stages of the war it did considerably better than he had feared.[8]

One other aircraft made major contributions to Harris's operations, namely the Mosquito, which he had initially viewed with disdain. In April 1942, when writing to Freeman about the parlous state of 2 Group, which was still equipped with the Boston and Blenheim, he referred to the seriously delayed Mosquito as likely to suffer 'a still grimmer fate than has always been the lot of such naive attempts to produce an aeroplane so much faster than anything the enemy possess that it requires no armament. It will go down in history in consequence as a second "Battle" as far as its bombing role is concerned.' This was one of his less perspicacious predictions, and not one calculated to impress Freeman, the aircraft's principal backer. The 'Wooden Wonder' would prove its qualities as a bomber not only in most other campaigns but also in the bomber offensive itself, notably during the final year of the war, yet in his Despatch Harris recognised the work of the eight squadrons of the Light Night Striking Force only briefly in the Appendices, though he did pay them rather better tribute in his book. He certainly appreciated the Mosquitos' ancillary contributions, particularly in their work with Oboe in the Pathfinder Force and later as intruders and jammers in 100 Group, but he never gave the aircraft the kind of praise that was certainly its due.[9] He was, however, right to oppose the contention that the offensive as a whole could have been better conducted by a much larger Mosquito force than by the slower and more vulnerable heavy bombers; for one thing, as he stressed, the many extra pilots needed could not possibly have been trained in the timescale.

Harris had his own views too about the types of bomb his aircraft should be delivering. He had always been a believer in the superiority of high explosive bombs – the bigger the better – over incendiaries, but by the time he became C-in-C studies of the Luftwaffe's bombing campaign against British cities in 1940–1 had persuaded the Air Ministry of the virtues of heavy incendiary attack and led the Air Staff to urge him to target Lübeck and Rostock. When Freeman subsequently appraised these operations in a letter to Harris he attributed their success, particularly at Lübeck, to the heavy concentration of 4 lb incendiaries which had overwhelmed the defences. 'If we are going to rely on incendiaries for our results,' wrote Freeman, 'we should go the whole hog and not allow the proportion of HE carried to detract from our chances of starting a really satisfactory conflagration.' Harris was not entirely convinced; for one thing Lübeck was an exceptional town, built more like a firelighter than a human habitation. He went on: 'I am always being pressed to concentrate entirely on incendiaries but I do not agree with this policy. The moral effect of HE is vast. People can escape from fires, and the casualties on a solely fire-raising raid would be as nothing. What we want to do in addition to the horrors of fire is to bring the masonry crashing down on top of the Boche, to kill Boche, and to terrify Boche; hence the proportion of HE.' Moreover the damage caused by HE to water mains and other services greatly helped the fires to spread. In his judgement, therefore, the weight of bombs used in city attacks should normally be in the proportion of two-thirds incendiary (4 lb and 30 lb) to one-third HE, mainly big blast.[10]

In practice this ratio was not going to be easy to achieve, as Freeman had to admit in July when telling Harris that his recent large-scale raids had seriously depleted the stocks of incendiaries and asking him to go easy on their use other than when operating conditions were clearly favourable. Harris was not amused. He had repeatedly been urged by DB Ops to increase the proportion of incendiaries still further and been assured that supplies were ample; now he was being blamed for wasting them. Hopefully, he told Freeman, DB Ops' and others' noses would now be rubbed in it and production would be stepped up; meanwhile he would reverse the proportions between the two types of bomb.[11] This was an unfortunate episode. In mid-1942, with the bomber offensive being stepped up, such shortages were probably inevitable – for one thing magnesium supplies were limited – but the failure of the Air Ministry and MAP staffs to get their acts together did nothing to restore confidence in the mind of a C-in-C who was already disenchanted with DB Ops. Eventually, however, the shortages were overcome and Harris was able to say in his Despatch that the 4 lb magnesium incendiary bomb was the mainstay of the Command throughout the war. At the same time, if it was to be effective it had to be properly dropped and in May 1943 he drew attention to the grossly inefficient technique of incendiary bombing. The low terminal velocity and inadequate stowage provisions for these small bombs, together with their primitive release equipment, were major disadvantages whose answer lay in the development of cluster projectiles and by the end of the year the first versions of these were coming into service. Yet as late as January 1945 such were the production problems that he was impelled to write to VCAS about the 'procrastination and incredible technical incompetence' that continued to punctuate this particular story.[12]

Notwithstanding the importance of the incendiaries, Harris remained convinced that HE bombs not only had their part to play in the area offensive but were also essential for the many other types of operations his Command was being called upon to undertake, and he strongly encouraged the development of heavier and increasingly specialised weapons, including the Tallboy and Grand Slam designed by Barnes Wallis. He also appreciated the handling implications of the growing quantity of bigger, heavier and more complicated bombs. As he wrote in September 1943 to John Bradley, one of his more helpful air marshals in the Air Ministry, the irremediable shortage of skilled manpower could be compensated only by the provision of more mechanical aids, and he asked specially for help in obtaining cranes. Soon Harris was telling Bradley how refreshing it was to know that his Command's needs were being investigated energetically and that he (Bradley) was preparing to lay on a bomb handling demonstration which covered much more than cranes. He summarised the outcome to Bradley three weeks later:

> When one is faced, as we are, with a very heavy task, it was irritating to be
> told consistently that mechanical aids could not be provided because of the

shortage of manpower and material. Were it not for your great help we would still be arguing with the Air Ministry Directorates on questions of policy, instead of dealing with the allocation of a flood of useful equipment which has followed as a result of the demonstration.[13]

When Harris dealt with men after his own heart, men who saw where help was needed and were ready to use their power and influence to provide it, he was always at pains to show his appreciation. Sharply critical of authority though he often was, he usually had good cause, and when he came across someone like Bradley, who was prepared to try to move mountains on his behalf, he was ever generous.

Space precludes discussion of other aspects of offensive armament with which Harris concerned himself, and we must turn now to one of the greatest challenges that faced him and his Command, that of enabling his bombers to find their way to their targets, identify them and hit them, usually by night. We have seen how much store he personally had always set by learning and practising the art of aerial navigation, yet up to 1942, like most of his contemporaries, he had remained wedded to the traditional methods. His initial reaction in 1940 to the research that would lead to GEE was one of scepticism and he did not face up to the significance of the German 'beams' (see pp.101 and 110). In August 1941, however, it was decided to fit GEE to all Bomber Command aircraft and by the time Harris arrived the first ten squadrons were ready.

The new C-in-C was rapidly seized of the system's advantages. Based on the measurement in the air of the time difference between synchronised pulses received from three ground stations – a master and two slaves – it enabled any number of aircraft to fix their positions without ground-air communication and regardless of weather, though its range was limited to about 350 miles by the earth's curvature. The implications for his operations in enabling attacks on the nearer targets to be well concentrated and helping the crews find their way home again were considerable; moreover, as a passive system it would not give away the aircraft's position, though it would be susceptible to jamming.[14] Harris was not, however, starry-eyed about it and, as the official historians say, expected no miracles. He certainly did not share the optimism of Bufton and his colleagues on the Air Staff, who considered that he should immediately have undertaken full trials of the system in conjunction with flare-dropping and followed up by developing a target-marking force. In their view he was missing a golden opportunity, but as the man on the spot he was all too well aware of the many other factors influencing his operational effectiveness and of the need to preserve a sense of proportion. To quote a modern commentator, Sebastian Cox, he was right to be sceptical of the more optimistic claims of the Air Staff.[15] GEE, as experience would show, was an excellent navigational aid but could not provide accurate target locations. For this Harris and his Command would have to wait for science and technology to mature.[16]

Connected with the advent of GEE arose one of Harris's hottest disputes with the Air Ministry. Hardly had he taken over command than he received from Portal a copy of a letter from Lord Cherwell suggesting that one of the bomber groups, with an active-minded man of the Slessor type in charge, should be specially tasked with target finding. Portal had told Cherwell that he personally supported the idea and was referring it to Harris, who had 'a very active mind on this kind of subject'. 'I seldom find myself in disagreement with you over such matters,' Harris replied, 'but this time I am. Long ago, in 5 Group, I adopted the practice of sending picked crews first, in order to illuminate the target for the rabbits,' and now he found that all his Groups did this. He could see no way of filling one particular group entirely with superior crews, not least because to transfer such crews from the other groups would have the most appalling effects on the morale of the remainder.[17]

Harris soon found out, however, that this subject was not going to go away and decided to call a meeting with his AOCs and SASOs to which Baker and Bufton from DB Ops were invited. As Bufton later recalled, Harris told them they were there to discuss the very emotive subject of a target-finding force, an idea to which he was fundamentally opposed but on which he wished to hear their views. Not surprisingly, Bufton commented, all the C-in-C's staff supported him and he and Baker returned to London with their tails between their legs. The next day Bufton bumped into the C-in-C outside the Air Ministry. 'Good morning, what are you going to do to me today?' asked Harris. 'I didn't plan to do anything, Sir,' replied Bufton. 'Well, if you've got any ideas, please write to me,' said Harris.[18] So Bufton, described by the official historians as 'a convinced and courageous champion' of the target-finding force, immediately set out the arguments in a carefully-worded letter suggesting the allocation of six squadrons, strengthened by one good crew from each of the other 40 squadrons, to his proposed force. The special squadrons should be based close together to enable them to co-operate and develop their techniques as quickly as possible and thus to exploit the newly arriving aids to navigation and target finding.[19]

At the same time, distrustful of the judgement of Harris's own 'non-operational' staff, Bufton wrote informally to a number of his own experienced friends – many of them in Bomber Command – setting out his ideas and inviting them to complete a questionnaire. Then on 11 April he told Harris what he had done, commented that there was complete unanimity on the need for the target-finding force, and enclosed the replies for him to study. Harris's reply on the 17th was remarkably restrained, given that

Bufton had unashamedly gone behind his back. 'I have a fairly open mind,' he wrote, 'but am not yet convinced,' and at a further conference his senior staff had remained firmly opposed. He was prepared to allow the squadrons in each Group to compete monthly for the honour of being the Group's target-finding force but would not accept the serious disadvantages of a corps d'élite in order to secure some possible improvement on methods which were already proving reasonably satisfactory. On 8 May Bufton returned again to the attack in another long letter which analysed the difficulties of target-finding as demonstrated in recent raids, challenged the alleged morale implications of the corps d'élite, urged the need for a team approach, and argued for more commanders with operational experience to be brought into the running of Bomber Command. This was strong stuff but hardly tactful. The official history, which fully covers the whole of the Harris-Bufton debate, identifies the really fundamental differences that lay behind all this. Whereas Harris regarded area bombing as a means, if properly pursued, of winning the war, a technique which would never require absolute accuracy, Bufton saw it as a preparatory phase on the way to perfecting the techniques of precise attack and was convinced that the key to this lay in his target-finding force.[20]

Certainly Bufton's ideas reflected deep thought and had much to commend them. Clearly his superiors, from Portal and Freeman downwards, were impressed by his analytical qualities and his ability to apply his extensive operational experience to the practicalities of bomber operations, and he would remain persona grata in the Air Ministry for the rest of the war. Yet between him and Harris there was from the start not just a conflict of ideas but a clash of personalities. It was one thing for Bufton to set out his stall when invited to do so; it was quite another to use what Harris could well regard as underhand methods to advance his cause, and as a group captain to go on arguing the toss with a recently appointed, strong-willed C-in-C who was under intense pressure from all sides and ill-disposed towards Air Ministry staff officers who tried to tell him how to do his job. The matters Bufton was raising were central to the conduct of the Command's affairs and he should not have been tangling directly with the C-in-C – or have been allowed to do so – for as long as he did. Harris's irritation finally emerged when he wrote in his Despatch that he, a Commander in the field, had been overruled on this issue at the dictation of junior staff officers in the Air Ministry.[21]

Harris was, of course, wrong to talk of higher authority dictating to him in this way. As he admitted to Churchill on 6 July 1942, it was CAS and the Air Staff who had overruled him. It had taken the intervention of Freeman to bring the impasse over the target-finding force to CAS's attention, and early in June Portal, long persuaded of the need and fully briefed, discussed the subject and exchanged letters with Harris. The C-in-C set out his final case on the 12th, telling Portal that his senior staff remained utterly opposed; the squadron selection process was already providing a target-finding force; regular raid leaders' conferences were being instituted; and it was hoped to introduce a special badge for selected crews. 'My existing raid leader scheme,' he asserted, 'provides all the requirements of the target-finding force fanatic, bar living together in special units.' Portal was not persuaded. Replying on the 14th he pointed out how far Harris had already moved and felt it illogical not to take the final step of welding the selected crews into the closely knit organisation necessary to make their leadership and direction effective. This letter was followed by another meeting at which Harris reluctantly accepted the inevitable. Then on the 19th he outlined some of the practical steps that were needed, requested urgent action on a special promotion scheme and a distinguishing badge for all members of selected crews, and suggested that, for brevity, the squadrons and personnel be called 'Pathfinders'.[22]

Now a commander was required. The charismatic, well known Basil Embry, currently CO of Wittering in Fighter Command – and a former colleague of Harris in Iraq – was mooted, but Harris's preference was for Donald Bennett, whose operational and technical skills, especially in navigation, had so impressed him at Pembroke Dock in 1933. Soon Bennett, now a Wing Commander, called on him at High Wycombe, to be told of his immediate promotion to Group Captain in order to command the force whose formation his new C-in-C said he had fought tooth and nail to prevent. He would not give it DB Ops' proposed name of Target Finding Force, Harris implied, nor would he waste any effort on it, but he would support Bennett personally in every way. As Bennett records, 'this assurance was carried out to the letter and in the spirit from then on to the end of the war', though he did not really give the Pathfinders a fair chance relative to other special units.[23] This was not quite the 'good grace' with which Saward says he accepted them, but neither was it remotely fair for Bufton in retrospect to say that Harris actually hated the Pathfinders. Searby, himself one of the most distinguished Pathfinder pilots and a great admirer of Harris, certainly felt that his acceptance of the new force was less than graceful and that for a long time he remained sceptical of its work. Harris himself was never prepared to accept that his original judgement had been mistaken. As he wrote in his Despatch, his 'contention that each Group should find and maintain its own Pathfinding Force was proved infinitely the superior method when tried out in 5 Group.'[24] This conviction was echoed by Slessor, who as AOC 5 Group had opposed the scheme in early 1942 and judged that the Group's later achievements under Cochrane proved it to have been unnecessary.[25] Yet as Harris made abundantly clear, his reservations in no way reflected on either Bennett or the Pathfinder crews, who did wonders in the face of great handicaps, avoidable and unavoidable.

Moreover, whatever the critics may say, he did much for them. His letter of 6 July 1942 to the Prime Minister on their behalf was one of the best he ever wrote. To set the scene he described, in almost Churchillian tones,

> the 2 o'clock in the morning courage of lonely men, their actions hidden by darkness from their fellows, determined to press home their attacks through fantastically violent defence barrages into the searchlight cones, wherein gunfire concentrates immediately on any aircraft illuminated. Their behaviour cannot be watched, it can seldom even be adjudged by an individual. Only after the event and by results achieved do we ever know how went the fight. We seldom know, except by implication, which crews made the greatest contribution. You would be the first to appreciate how dependent we are on the high courage and qualities of the leaders.

Harris went on to describe the pressure exerted on him to cream-off picked crews for a special force: the decision had gone against him and the challenge now was to attract into it and retain the best men. 'We shall ask indeed much of them,' he wrote, and he wanted them to be rewarded with a special badge and a step-up in rank. While the badge should be forthcoming, neither he nor the Air Ministry could move the Treasury. 'Therefore I ask your intervention towards obtaining this step-up in rank for every member of each crew selected, volunteering and qualified as Pathfinders.' On this occasion Harris had taken the fight to the top and it paid off.[26]

A month later he sent Bennett a stirring message to mark the Pathfinders' first operation:

> Tonight the force under your command makes its debut in the vitally important role for which it has been raised. I am confident that the selected crews under your command will achieve all that skill and determination make possible of achievement. All the crews of Bomber Command now look to the Pathfinders for a lead to their future objectives which will ensure the maximum infliction of damage on the enemy with the greatest economy of force. They will I know not be disappointed. Good luck and good hunting.

Soon afterwards he visited Wyton, as we have seen, and continued in close touch with Bennett, who phoned and wrote regularly to consult him and keep him informed. That Harris appreciated the special demands being made on the crews was illustrated in a letter to Bennett in November: 'I am always against any sort of automatic award. Nevertheless I want you to see to it that no member of any Pathfinder crew who completes the full 45 sorties fails to get an award, unless for some very special reason you consider he has not earned one.' Then in March 1943, by which time the force had become No 8 (PFF) Group, Harris urged on the Air Ministry that its title should revert to 'Pathfinder Force' since people were increasingly referring to it just as 8 Group and losing sight of its special status as the *corps d'élite*. 'The force has already paid a rich dividend,' he wrote, 'by successfully locating and marking out targets and enabling the remainder of the Command to saturate defences and go straight in without spending time searching for their target. It has built up a reputation which can and should be capitalised in order to attract the best material available in the Command.'[27]

For March 1943 this assessment was something of an over-statement. At the end of December Harris had told all his AOCs that over the previous four months a mere 24% of aircraft attacking German and Italian targets were shown by photographs to have bombed within three miles of the aiming point,[28] and only on 5 March did the first really successful Pathfinder-led attack take place – on Essen. Until then it had been a period of frustration, of experimentation, of pressing for improved types of equipment including marker-flares and bombs,[29] and awaiting and preparing for two critically important new radar aids.

The first, known as Oboe, was a blind-bombing system not dissimilar to the enemy's 'beams' which Harris had earlier despised. Relying on two ground stations and a pulse repeater in the aircraft it enabled the crew to be guided to the desired release point with extreme accuracy – 150 yards on average – and it was invulnerable to jamming. Like GEE, however, it was limited by range and a pair of stations could handle only about six aircraft per hour. Its value, as Harris wrote, was that it could be fitted in the high-altitude, fast-flying Mosquito to mark targets for the main bomber force, and in mid-1942 he pressed the Air Ministry to provide six Oboe-equipped aircraft and a pair of ground stations. The result was that 109 Squadron arrived in the order of battle operating alongside Bennett's heavy bomber squadrons, began its work in January 1943, and proved its effectiveness over Essen in March. This specialised target-marking force, gradually expanded, would play a key role in shorter-range operations for the rest of the war.[30]

The second new aid, H2S, carried within the aircraft itself, was in effect the first ground mapping radar. Its narrow rotating beam scanned the ground below and presented the radar returns on an 'echo map' centred on the aircraft's current position. It could therefore be used for navigation to the target area and for homing to the release area, though the map was crude and target identification required much skill. It thus provided a true blind bombing capability, eventually accurate in the best hands to about $1\frac{1}{4}$ miles, and unlike GEE and Oboe it was not limited by range. As with Oboe, 1942 was the key development year, when it was decided to incorporate the magnetron valve, and on 3 July – not long after the 1,000-bomber raids and also the loss in an accident of the Halifax being used to test the equipment – Harris found himself in Downing Street discussing with Churchill and others, including scientists from TRE (the Telecommunications Research Establishment), how to speed production of the new H2S sets so as to equip two squadrons by October as the Prime Minister was insisting. Harris's contribution, as recorded by Bernard Lovell, one of the scientists, was to state that they must be fitted in Stirlings. In the event two of Bennett's squadrons, one Stirling and one Halifax, were so equipped by the end of the year and H2S was first employed against Hamburg for target-marking on 30 January 1943.[31]

By this time Harris was pressing for the remaining two Pathfinder squadrons, both now being re-equipped with Lancasters, to receive H2S, and for Bennett then to be allotted two more squadrons similarly fitted. Yet in April he was having to comment to the Prime Minister, who had set high hopes on H2S and was keenly following its progress, on figures showing that Bomber Command still had only enough sets for two squadrons and that Coastal Command had almost as many ASVs (the maritime equivalent). The net result was that during intensive operations he was lucky to get a dozen H2S Pathfinders marking the target on any given occasion. Nevertheless, progress was being made and Harris made a point of paying tribute to Sir Robert Renwick for his work in the MAP controlling the development and production of all radar systems and equipment: 'Within my experience his efforts are always successful in producing the maximum feasible results.'[32] Three months later, in the series of heavy attacks on Hamburg, the Pathfinders' H2S really proved its worth for target-marking, and by September all six of their squadrons were so equipped.

Harris described in his book at some length the techniques – including the actual marking methods – used in the growing number of long-distance operations in 1943,[33] but did not refer to one occasion when he took the Pathfinders seriously to task. As he signalled Bennett on 23 September after an attack on Hanover:

> it was a complete flop, the worst failure we have had yet. While we cannot always be successful ... the great majority of PFF crews must have discarded their own navigational reckoning and the indications of their aids and followed blindly, if not light-heartedly, on to misleading markers and incendiaries ... no doubt you will take the lesson to heart in determination to preserve the name for skill and efficiency which you have acquired through much toil and bitter experience. Forget it, pull your socks up, and make sure that no careless action of anyone of you individually can in future serve to lead the entire force astray as on this occasion.

This sharp rebuke blended with encouragement prompted Bennett to do some 'stocktaking'. Among other things, he told Harris, he was not getting the pick of the crews that he needed, there were few opportunities for further training, H2S results remained poor, pyrotechnics were inadequate, and he was still not allowed to operate himself. Harris accepted most of his points, though not the last, but the incident demonstrated how much more was yet to be done to bring pathfinding to the level required and enable the bomber force as a whole to do its job properly. Over the next few months, the period of the Battle of Berlin, there were further developments. H2S began to be used for blind bombing as well as target marking, main force squadrons started to be fitted with it, and experiments with an improved Mark III version were set under way. At the same time a new aid which Harris had also encouraged was coming into service: GH, a kind of 'Oboe in reverse' which relied on initial transmissions being made by the aircraft and re-radiated by two ground beacons. This was to prove invaluable for blind bombing of less distant targets, for although limited by range it could be utilised by many more aircraft than Oboe.[34]

While Harris tried hard to cope with the complexity of the constantly advancing technologies on which these and many other types of aircraft equipment relied, not all the experts believed he had the necessary understanding or patience and in April 1944 matters came to a head in relation to the use of H2S. The scientists at TRE had become convinced that the Pathfinders had not made effective use of the Mark III for blind target marking during the campaign against Berlin and were also critical of the failure to conduct a full experimental raid using H2S for blind bombing. Renwick therefore wrote to Harris and was promptly told that TRE should 'mind its own ruddy business. They remind me simply of a bunch of prima donnas squabbling for the limelight.' This, says Lovell, from the C-in-C of a Command that would have been dead long ago without the scientific aids originating in TRE, was too much, and a campaign was launched 'to get rid of him'. A critical paper was circulated, Bufton and Coryton – as ACAS(Ops) – backed it, and on 22 April Bottomley chaired a meeting at which Saundby represented Harris. Three hours later, in no small measure thanks to Saundby's negotiating skills, most of TRE's points had been conceded.[35] For Harris it was not a happy episode. Much as he appreciated what the scientists could do for him he was loath to let them criticise or interfere on operational matters, and understandably insofar as they could not be aware of many of the other factors affecting his decisions. To treat them and their views with disdain was another matter and here he did himself no favours.

Harris also needed to direct his attention to ways of countering the German defences, a further area where the scientists had much to contribute. One such method, known as Window, had been devised before he took over.

It consisted of strips of aluminium foil on black paper which when dropped in quantity interfered with the ground and airborne radars on which the enemy fighter force depended, and in April 1942 the Air Staff persuaded the Chiefs of Staff to authorise its use. Lord Cherwell, however, then pointed out that if the Germans were also to employ it this would reduce the efficiency of Britain's own air defences, and when he met Sinclair and Harris in May they agreed to defer its introduction – a decision subsequently endorsed by Air Marshal Sholto Douglas, C-in-C Fighter Command. At an Air Ministry meeting in November, when Saundby represented Harris, Bomber Command again did not press for using Window, and only at a conference chaired by Portal in April 1943 did Harris come out firmly in favour. Even now there were further delays both on military grounds and because of production problems, and not until a meeting chaired by Churchill on 15 July was the last opponent overruled; Herbert Morrison, Minister of Home Security, had remained fearful of the consequences of renewed German bombing of the United Kingdom in the face of impaired defences. Ten days later Bomber Command used Window for the first time against Hamburg, and with great success.

After the war Harris claimed in his own book that he had continually pressed for its use in 1942 but 'the authorities' considered that the UK was still too vulnerable to attack. On the other hand the official history judges that, curiously, he did not exert himself at this time to secure the introduction of a measure which was expected so greatly to favour the offence against the defence, and implies that thanks to the delay many aircraft were lost which need not have been. R.V. Jones, who consistently urged the release of Window, confirmed that in November 1942 Harris did not wish to press for its use. Saward, writing much later in consultation with Harris, was strangely silent on the whole subject. It was not all that clear-cut an issue and there were plenty of other cautionary voices being raised, but for a man who urged his cause so strongly on many other matters Harris does seem, to echo Max Hastings, to have been slow to respond to this particular technological innovation.[36]

Window, which from now on proved invaluable, was just one of many countermeasures in which Harris interested himself as the bombing campaign intensified. R.V. Jones recalled talking to him in September 1942 about the Kammhuber Line, showing him what had so far been found out about the German defences, and asking for assistance. 'It shows I'm hurting them,' said Harris, and he promised to try to provide two Mosquitos to help establish the operating frequencies of the German night fighters, though eventually Jones had to be content with a Wellington.[37] At the same time Harris was pressing hard for the introduction of Monica, a device for providing bombers with early warning of the approach of other aircraft, and by early 1943 was becoming increasingly frustrated over the delays in getting it fitted; as he told Portal in April, the requirement was urgent but progress was badly held up, with MAP seemingly unable to get its act together.[38] Harris turned to another theme in July, pointing out to Portal the successes achieved in intruder operations by a Beaufighter squadron equipped with Serrate, a device for homing in on the enemy fighters' radar emissions. It should not be impossible, he wrote, for Fighter Command to provide a strong force of night fighters to operate in this role in support of every major attack. Portal took no persuading of the importance of such operations and promised him, inter alia, two more Serrate squadrons equipped with Mosquitos.[39]

Already Harris's mind had been turning to the possibility of establishing a special formation to take responsibility for all operations against the German fighter force, and in August he summarised his ideas to Bottomley. He felt sure that the profound effects of the bombing on the Germans' economy and morale were compelling them to devote constantly increasing resources to their air defences, which in turn were not only inflicting heavy losses but limiting the planning and effectiveness of his own operations. Complementary offensive action to break down and disorganise those air defences was therefore essential in the form of night fighter and bombing intruder operations coupled with radio countermeasures (RCM) against the German R/T system, and the necessary squadrons, including one for RCM, should all be in Bomber Command. Harris followed up with a letter to the Director General of Signals which referred to the limitations of Window and of various RCM devices already fitted into some aircraft and proposed the adoption of 'barrage jamming' of the whole enemy radio system; the project had already been examined by TRE and was technically practicable. The aircraft for this role, he went on, would have to meet a performance specification that pointed clearly to the American Fortress. The Air Ministry had already authorised the formation of 100 Group for the purpose Harris had outlined, but the preliminaries did not move with the speed he was looking for and on 18 November 1943 he urged VCAS to try 'to dispel the illusion' that the new Group did not require high priority. For him it was a matter of operational urgency. Evill lent a hand, and on 1 December 100 Group came into existence under the command of a signals officer with long experience in the world of radio countermeasures, Air Vice-Marshal E.B. Addison. Within six months it was fully organised to employ its wide variety of deception tactics, integrated with the complex and detailed planning of each operation, and to make a major contribution to containing the toll of Bomber Command's losses.[40]

So much for the application of some of the major technologies which engaged a lot of Harris's attention. There were, too, matters of somewhat less moment. One of these arose in February 1943, when Bennett spotted a short article in *Tee Emm*, the light-hearted monthly training journal made famous by the fictional Pilot Officer Prune. According to the anonymous author the solution to predicted flak (anti-aircraft fire) was to make a 90-degree turn every 30 seconds or so, advice that Bennett thought 'might be regarded as an attempt to sabotage the bombing offensive!' Harris totally agreed, asking Air Vice-Marshal Garrod, Air Member for Training, to publish a note cancelling the article and to refer any future ones of similar type to his headquarters: 'I can imagine no better method of ensuring that no bomb ever hits its objective than by executing the idiotic antics recommended.' Garrod, far from accepting Harris's strictures, rose to the defence of his staff explaining in detail who had been involved in writing the article, and suggesting that if Bennett wrote a letter to counter it this would open a valuable discussion. Harris would have none of this: 'I feel very strongly that no article dealing with important aspects of bomber tactics should be published in *Tee Emm* unless it is known to be in agreement with my views or has been passed by some senior member of my Operations Staff.' Garrod too remained firm. In April *Tee Emm* published Bennett's rebuttal of the original piece, albeit without naming him, but in May a further item appeared in which the original line was in part defended, particularly in relation to bombing operations in other theatres of war. This sent Harris through the roof. 'Attempting to avoid flak in heavily flak-ed areas . . . only makes bomb aiming hopeless and renders gun defence against fighters impossible,' he wrote to Air Marshal Peter Drummond, who had just taken over from Garrod. 'I think *Tee Emm* had better give up fooling about with operational matters. I have therefore ordered that it is to be banned on every Bomber Command station . . . until I have your assurance that matters so closely affecting the efficiency of bomber operations are agreed by me.' Fortunately at this point Drummond succeeded in calming the situation by promising to arrange informal consultation on such matters. Harris had won a not insignificant little battle.[41]

It is impracticable to say much more about the vast enterprise that constituted Bomber Command and which Harris and his staff had to run. Its operations depended on a massive infrastructure – much of it outside his own control – that enabled the aircraft to be maintained, repaired, and supplied with fuel, armament and specialised equipment. Equally the crews, those who directed their operations and those who worked to keep the aircraft serviceable had to be housed, fed and provided with a host of supporting services. Harris never lost sight of how much was entailed in enabling his Command to do its business, and as his correspondence files indicate he was always ready to support his specialist staff on subjects where his assistance was likely to be useful. Some of these we have touched on; just one more was so fundamental as to demand at least our brief attention. That subject was airfields.

When Harris took over he had 79 airfields for his front-line squadrons and operational training units; two years later, even after a number had been transferred to the Americans, there were 128. He had therefore had to cope with a major expansion, and also with the need to modernise many of them in order to provide for the new generation of four-engined bombers. One of his great concerns in 1942 was that some of his older but better appointed airfields still had grass runways, and in August 1942 he was having to remind Courtney that such surfaces could not stand up to constant traffic of heavily loaded bombers. He therefore wanted Mildenhall, Driffield, Hemswell, Waddington, Scampton, Marham, Feltwell and Newmarket restored to the list of those scheduled for concrete runways and thought they deserved higher priority for resources than the widening of Western Avenue, which he regularly used on his way to London. Nine months later he was complaining about the length of time being taken to lay the new runways, the failure of others, and delays in completing new airfields and providing accommodation for second squadrons on existing ones. The position was aggravated by labour cuts and over-optimistic forecasts of completion dates. All these factors were combining to prejudice the continued development of the bomber force. While these and other difficulties, such as a shortage of the hangars so essential for winter maintenance, were eventually overcome, they were typical of many of the wider anxieties that affected the Command's operational capability for much of the war and always lay at the back of the C-in-C's mind.[42]

We must now turn to one other major theme which also demanded much of Harris's time and attention: the steadily growing presence in the United Kingdom of the Eighth United States Air Force, preparing for and then taking its place alongside Bomber Command in the air assault on Germany.

Notes

1. Folders H81, dated 14 August 1942; H16, dated 25 August 1942.
2. Harris, *op.cit.* p.102; letter to author from Chadwick's daughter, Mrs Margaret Dove.
3. Folders H66, dated 12 November 1942; H81, dated 27 December 1942; H67, dated 8 January, 21 February and 30 April 1943.
4. Folders H67, dated 10 January 1943; H82, dated 18 February 1943. Here Harris seems to have confused Wallis's two spinning bombs, Highball and Upkeep; see OH vol.II, p.170.
5. Folders H18, dated 8 May 1943; H67, dated 17 August 1943.
6. Folder H47, dated 27 June and 7 July 1943.
7. Folders H82, dated 24 June 1943; H67, dated 30 October 1943.

8. Folders H82, dated 7 September 1943; H67, dated 22 November 1943; H82, dated 21 December 1943.

9. Folder H16, dated 10 April 1942; Harris Despatch, pp.82, 130, 208; Harris, *op.cit.* pp.135–6, 142. Commenting in 1982 to Alan Bramson, who was researching for *Master Airman*, his book about Donald Bennett, Harris firmly defended the line he had taken about the Mosquito at that time: 'When I was told it had no armament, in face of our losses, and relied on running away...!'

10. Folder H16, letters dated 27 and 29 April 1942.

11. *Ibid* dated 1 and 4 July 1942.

12. Folders H67, dated 27 May 1943; H15, dated 17 January 1945; Despatch, pp.94–5.

13. Folder H88, dated 23 September and 9 and 29 October 1943. Bradley, a former Director of Equipment, was now Deputy AMSO.

14. For fuller explanations of GEE see, for example, OH vol.IV, Annex 1; Harris Despatch, pp.65–7; Air Vice-Marshal Hedgeland in RAFHS, *Reaping the Whirlwind*, p.9.

15. OH vol.I, p.385; Harris Despatch, pp.xiii, 9–10, 206.

16. Terraine, *op.cit.* p.498.

17. Folder H81, dated 1 and 2 March 1942.

18. RAFHS vol.6, pp.24–5.

19. OH vol.I, p.420. See folder H53 for Bufton's actual letter.

20. OH vol.I, pp.420–4; Folder H53; AIR 14/3523; Furse, *op.cit.* pp.315–19.

21. Despatch, p.11.

22. OH vol.I, pp.429–32; Saward, *op.cit.* pp.150–3, where part of Portal's letter is quoted; Folders H81; H65. For a strong criticism of Harris on this whole episode see Furse, *op.cit.* pp.201–3, 206–8.

23. Bennett, *Pathfinder*, pp.162–3. See also Gordon Musgrove's *Pathfinder Force* (Macdonald and Janes, 1976) for a full coverage of the Pathfinder story.

24. Saward, *op.cit.* p.153; Searby, *op.cit.*; Despatch, p.11.

25. Slessor, *op.cit.* p.373, and letter to R.V. Jones, 22 June 1973 (copied to author). These sources contradict Bufton's statement to Furse (*op.cit.* p.202) that Slessor favoured the Pathfinders.

26. Folder H65; OH vol.I, p.432, note 1.

27. Folders H57, dated 18 August and 14 November 1942; H67, dated 18 March 1943.

28. Folder H57, dated 31 December 1942. OH vol.I, p.434, implies the percentage was a little higher.

29. On 13 January 1943, for example, he wrote to Freeman, now at the MAP, stressing the urgency of speeding up their production; Folder H57.

30. OH vol.IV, Annex I; Despatch, p.68; Hedgeland in RAFHS, *Reaping the Whirlwind*, p.10; Harris, *op.cit.* pp.124–6.

31. OH vol.IV, Annex I; Despatch, p.71; Hedgeland, *op.cit.* p.11; Lovell, *Echoes of War – The Story of H2S*, p.135.

32. Folder H65, dated 17 April 1943.

33. Harris, *op.cit.* pp.166–71.

34. Folder H57, dated 23 September and 1 October 1943; Despatch, pp.68–70: Harris, *op.cit.* pp.225–8.

35. Lovell, *op.cit.* pp.213–15; Folder H20, dated 29 March 1944.

36. OH vol.I, p.401; vol.II, pp.141–5; Harris, *op.cit.* pp.132–3; Jones, *Most Secret War*, p.377; Hastings, *op.cit.* p.205.

37. Jones, *op.cit.* pp.351, 360.
38. Folder H82, dated 29 April 1943; Despatch, pp.119, 127. Monica was used but never fulfilled its promise and was abandoned in September 1944.
39. Folder H82, dated 3 and 9 July 1943.
40. Folders H67, dated 31 August and 7 September 1943; H16, dated 18 November 1943; Saward, *op.cit.* p.235; Hedgeland, *op.cit.* p.13; Despatch, p.138.
41. Folder H90, dated 4 February and 9 May 1943. Drummond was killed in an air accident in March 1945.
42. Despatch, pp.150–3; Folders H88, dated 18 August and 8 October 1942; H67, dated 25 May 1943.

Chapter 12

Comrades in arms

Before Pearl Harbor, as Harris later pointed out, none could have anticipated the need for the Americans to have airfields in Britain, yet by the time he reached High Wycombe plans were afoot to bring substantial air forces across the Atlantic, and the bomber commander, General Eaker, had arrived. The two airmen were already good friends and Harris insisted that Eaker and his staff must join him immediately at his Headquarters until they could establish one of their own. Eaker was delighted to do so, not least since he had no wish to be dominated by the US Army theatre commander in London, General Chaney. Since one of his initial tasks was to 'understudy' Bomber Command there could be only one place to do it and Eaker and his men were accorded the warmest welcome. There could have been no better way of starting to bond together the airmen of the two bomber forces, and when Eaker began to search for his own 'home' he knew it had to be close at hand so that the co-operation between them could be preserved and developed. The choice fell on Wycombe Abbey School for Girls, which was – with Harris's backing – promptly requisitioned and renamed 'Pinetree'. Its new organisation was modelled largely on that of HQ Bomber Command, and not only did Eaker continue to attend Harris's daily conferences but members of his staff served on some of the more important operational committees.[1] Thus was the scene set for the alliance between Bomber Command and the Eighth United States Air Force which was to play a decisive role in winning the war.[2] Differences there were bound to be but they would be resolved through mutual respect, trust and friendship.

One of the earliest questions was where to accommodate the American bombers. To start with the Air Ministry agreed to allocate some airfields north-west of Huntingdon which were being developed for a new 8 Group, but Harris rapidly became worried that Chaney's plans to expand around these could eventually cut Bomber Command off from most of its own units, with grave control complications. Initially, with Eaker's agreement, he proposed that the American bombers should go up north but when he heard that they would be bringing light bombers and fighters with them he offered in lieu to give them much of East Anglia. Eaker, as he told Slessor in May 1942, was extremely keen on this obvious solution, which was not only satisfactory to everyone except Chaney but could not be better from the practical standpoint. Bomber Command would not be cut up into penny packets and the Americans too would retain their territorial identity. Chaney, Harris's *bête noire* in these matters, did not last much longer, being replaced by General Eisenhower in June, and as Harris then told Courtney, 'Eaker and I and Spaatz [who had taken over as the senior American airman in the United Kingdom] can amicably settle things with the least inconvenience to anyone.'[3] They did so and ultimately the deployment urged by Harris was in broad terms adopted, though the Americans also retained their original bases near Huntingdon.

Meanwhile in May the initial Eighth Air Force parties had arrived, followed by the first B17s on 1 July, and Eaker's forces quickly became the earliest beneficiaries of reverse lend-lease. This took many forms. Real estate was required; British labour was needed to help build the bases; many aircraft, much specialised equipment and other supplies including fuel were provided.[4] In these and a host of other ways immense British resources were made available to the Americans, most of them coming from right across the economy, but the role of Harris and his Command in their willingness to point the way must never be under-estimated. Right at the start, for example, he gave Eaker RAF and WAAF clerks to handle the flood of paperwork, and many specialists were provided for liaison and to help familiarise the Americans with British equipment and procedures. Harris and his staff, like many others, did all they possibly could to assist in these early days, yet inevitably there were critics – notably in the USA. In August Richard Peck drew Harris's attention to an article in the *New York Times* headed 'British US Rift on Planes holding up Air Offensive'; this alleged that the Americans and British were unable to agree on methods or objectives, and Peck asked him to provide some ammunition to scotch this 'enemy propaganda'. Harris, who had recently been told by Eaker 'I shall continue to look upon you as the senior member of our firm – the elder brother in our bomber team', was quick to provide reassurances. He told Peck that he fully endorsed the bombing tactics that the Americans intended to use under present circumstances, that he and Eaker saw eye to eye on the planning of raids, and that Eaker was highly appreciative of the practical assistance he was receiving. He went on:

> I would say that relations between myself and General Eaker are such, and my complete faith in his ideas and ability so strong, that I have repeatedly asked him to exercise command over my Command for a period while I myself do a round of visits to Units. It would be unlikely that I should make such a request if I had not complete faith in his ability and judgement, and the greatest possible regard for him. My attitude to him and his Command ... is that if we possess anything he wants ... everything 'up to the half of my kingdom' is his for the asking. There has never been ... the smallest vestige of

any difference of opinion (between him and myself or Spaatz), excepting only that I have done my best to dissuade them from rushing into wholesale daylight bombing until they have felt their way. This, in fact, they are now doing.[5]

One matter on which they did in fact differ was whether top commanders should fly on operations, and despite Harris's disapproval Eaker flew on the B17s' first operation, against Rouen, on 17 August. 'Congratulations from all ranks of Bomber Command,' wrote Harris, 'on the highly successful completion of the first all-American raid by the big fellows on German occupied territory in Europe. Yankee Doodle certainly went to town and can stick yet another well-deserved feather in his cap.'[6]

From now on Eaker began to build up his offensive, but his force remained small and, since it was equipped and trained only for daylight operations, could operate solely against targets in occupied Europe that lay within range of escorting fighters. Consequently doubts grew on both sides of the Atlantic about the future of the American bombing campaign against Germany itself at a time when there were conflicting pressures for the use of air power in every other theatre of war. The major debates and decisions would be matters for higher authorities, but since Harris and Eaker were constantly sharing their anxieties and their views so often coincided it was inevitable that Harris should try to exert his influence on behalf of Eaker and his colleagues. As Harris put it to Arnold on 14 August, 'we can defeat the enemy if we are not defeated by our friends'. So when a paper written by Arnold to Harry Hopkins came covertly into his hands he equally covertly sent a copy to Churchill on 15 September. Arnold was complaining at length about the widespread dispersion of America's military effort, including her air power, and urging rapid concentration of effort on the bombing of Germany, the number one enemy. To Harris this broad thinking was sound and in sending it on he had in mind his own earlier paper of 3 September (see p.142), where he had expressed somewhat similar sentiments. Churchill was not particularly impressed by what he called 'Arnold's very weak and sloppy survey of the war', though he did agree about strengthening the air attack on Germany and regarding the Pacific as a secondary theatre. What he would like, he told Harris, was 200 or 300 of Arnold's heavy bombers to be adapted to night fighting and sent to expand Bomber Command – hardly a suggestion likely to appeal to the Americans. Nevertheless Churchill followed up with a note to the President, enclosed a copy of Harris's memorandum with the comment that the writer had 'almost unique qualifications to express an opinion on the subject', and pleaded for the American bomber force in Britain to be built up so as to deal a blow at the enemy's air power from which he could never fully recover.[7]

A month later, notwithstanding these representations, nothing seemed to have happened to lift the despondency of Harris's friends and on 23 October he again took up the cudgels with Churchill on their behalf. The US Navy and Army, he said, were doing all they could to scotch the Bomber Plan and were alleging that Churchill himself wanted to use the American bombers on the Atlantic War instead. Harris went on:

> You will please excuse frankness on this matter. My information is that matters have now reached so critical a stage that unless you come down personally and most emphatically on the side of throwing every bomb against Germany, subject only to minimum essential diversions elsewhere, the Bomber Plan, in so far as US assistance is concerned, will be hopelessly and fatally prejudiced within the very near future for an unpredictable period, if not for keeps.

Churchill did not reply on this occasion, but on the 30th the Chiefs of Staff agreed a proposal which had been prepared by Portal for a combined British and American force of 4–6,000 heavy bombers to be built up by April 1944 for the attack on Germany, and this led in January to the Allied decision at Casablanca to undertake the combined bomber offensive.[8]

In practice, however, there remained a long way to go, and Harris became increasingly frustrated by the slow pace of the American build-up over a period when his own Command was at last becoming ready to embark on a heavy and sustained offensive. In November 1942 he let his hair down to the sympathetic Bottomley, reminding him that much of the best flying country in England had been handed over for bases, thus exposing the RAF bomber crews to greater risks and reducing their range over enemy territory. Yet so far, he went on, the Americans had dropped not a single bomb on Germany; they were being employed instead on daylight bombing of targets in France, in particular the Atlantic ports, a task which could be better accomplished from bases in western and southern England. It was high time Washington made clear its intentions about the bombing of Germany and if these were unsatisfactory some or all of the East Anglian bases should be handed back. Shortly afterwards Harris put his concerns to Portal somewhat differently. Referring to the way in which the American bomber force was being concentrated on Operation Torch in the Mediterranean and on fruitlessly attacking the French submarine pens, he was convinced that they ought to be joining the RAF in a joint offensive against the building yards in Germany itself. 'I cannot do it all myself. The Americans must help and make some worthwhile contribution to the war. Eaker is keen enough, but you know his Navy-Army troubles.'[9]

Harris also found himself in direct communication with the War

Department in Washington, where Bob Lovett (see p.121) began consulting him privately about how to put across the bombing message to the Navy and Army. 'Will you lend me a hand and provide me with some ammunition for the battle of Washington?' wrote Lovett on 24 November. Harris, only too pleased to try to help, promised to step up the provision of photographs, films, digests of information and so on in the attempt to supply, through Air Vice-Marshal Evill (now heading the RAF Delegation in Washington), convincing and up-to-date information to people at the top, and over the coming months he and Lovett continued to share confidences and ideas. In the process Harris left Lovett in no doubt of the need for the American reinforcements to arrive in full on the forecast dates; otherwise, and if Bomber Command were to be reduced by diversions for other purposes, 'the Russians would be left to fight Germany virtually single-handed for an indefinite period – a deplorable position.' The two men were in close rapport, and after visiting Harris in May 1943 Lovett wrote of the tremendous kick he got out of 'seeing the plans which we used to talk about in Washington coming into being at long last. With the aid and comfort you have generously given the Eighth Air Force I have no doubt whatsoever of the outcome, and the deep impression made on me by your Bomber Command is something I must try to put into words when I get back home.'[10]

Another of Harris's sources of information and opinions was Air Commodore Bill Thornton, the Washington Air Attaché whom he had come to know and trust in 1941. In December Thornton gathered from Arnold that while he fully accepted the need to concentrate on the bombing of Germany, owing to the British weather conditions it might be better to attack from different directions. Arnold, Thornton told Harris, was constantly up against the Generals and Admirals on the issue of bombing, and Thornton felt that the matter would eventually be forced by public opinion rather than round-table argument. He added that Anglo-American relations did not seem to have improved and the Americans still appeared remarkably susceptible to Axis propaganda; the RAF, however, was not usually included in general criticisms of the British. Harris's response on 21 January 1943 was uninhibited: 'The American Air Force is doing nothing worthwhile and in fact is more of a handicap to our own offensive than an assistance.' They were constantly promising but never performing; maybe some day they would have a worthwhile force and do something with it, for their airmen were all right, but their Army and Navy were seeing to it that the bombing of Germany would not be assisted by the American Air Force while they could be misemployed anywhere else. Such private views were not, of course, reflected in Harris's public statements and only a few days later he warmly congratulated those who had carried out the first United States raid on Germany, which he hailed as the start of a campaign the enemy had long dreaded: 'Let us press past this milestone on the road to victory, assured that between us we can and will bust Germany wide open.'[11]

These were fine hopes but Harris knew they would need time to fulfil, and not least since the Americans would be operating in daylight rather than – like his own bombers – under cover of darkness. Eaker had overcome Churchill's objections on this subject at Casablanca, and while most on the British side, and some Americans also, doubted if the Fortresses would get away with it, all including Harris were committed to backing them in the attempt. First, however, a much greater build-up of the American force was essential, and while Eaker was under pressure from Washington to postpone meanwhile major operations against Germany he knew that he must press ahead on at least a modest scale if he was to retain Harris's backing and allay the many doubts still being expressed at home. Yet with no more than 200 bombers, only half of them serviceable at any one time, he had to avoid heavy losses, and he found both Portal and Harris giving him the strongest backing. Whatever the latter's misgivings on this whole subject, his practical support for Eaker and for the build-up of his force was unstinting. In a letter on 5 March 1943 which Eaker forwarded to Arnold he wrote:

> Our only regret is that the VIIIth Bomber Force, which we know already to be fully equal in quality to the best we can produce, is still too small to take its full share of the attack. Had you the force to operate by day on the same scale as we have done and shall continue to do by night, there would be no hope for the enemy in Europe, who could not long stand against such a weight of combined offensive. The whimperings of the German propagandists at our opening blows in the campaign of 1943 show that the enemy now strives to win the sympathy of the world in his misfortunes. When the Devil is sick, the Devil a saint would be. This change of tone in itself reveals his fear of what is still to come and increases my conviction that, when you can hit him as hard by day as we can by night, the day of reckoning will set on Hitler's Germany.

A fortnight later Harris was delighted to hear of the Eighth's first really successful raid on Germany, carried out by 97 heavy bombers on Vegesack, a submarine building plant near Bremen, for the loss of only two aircraft, and soon afterwards spirits at Pinetree were high at a dinner in honour of Churchill. Reporting on this in a letter to Arnold, Eaker mentioned that General Andrews, the new American commander in Europe, had proposed sending Arnold a cable: 'We are dining together, smoking your cigars, and waiting for more of your heavy bombers. Churchill, Andrews, Harris, Eaker.' Sadly a month later Andrews was killed when his aircraft crashed in Iceland. Harris paid him tribute. 'One of the greatest airmen, he will go down in history as a leading prophet and exponent of air power as doughty in advancing his beliefs in the military and civil application of aircraft as he was a fearless and skilful fighting airman. We have lost one of the great commanders.'[12]

Meanwhile Eaker had been following up the Casablanca Directive by preparing his own plan of action, intended to concentrate his daylight precision bombing offensive on six specific target systems whose destruction would fatally weaken the German capacity for armed resistance, and on 15 April Harris gave the 'Eaker Plan' his blessing. In what proved a remarkably accurate prophecy, he told Eaker:

> The effect of linking up precision bombing of selected targets in daylight by an adequate force of VIII Bomber Command with intensified night bombing by the RAF will unquestionably cause damage to material and morale on a scale which the enemy will be unable to sustain. The necessity under which such an offensive will place him of maintaining still larger day and night fighter forces in the West from dwindling production will inevitably reduce his fighters on other fronts below the danger point and force him to put more and more emphasis on fighter production to the emasculation of his already inadequate bomber force.

Whatever doubts Harris had, the critical issue for him was, to quote the official historians, 'to see the Eighth Air Force vigorously reinforced and actively engaged over Germany'.[13]

Yet for all the bonhomie, all the optimistic planning, the anxieties persisted. On 17 March Harris had told Trenchard of the continuing danger that the main American bombing effort might be diverted elsewhere and asked if he could try to persuade Maisky, the Soviet Ambassador, of the importance to the Russians of getting the American bombers into action in Europe as quickly as possible. Were Russian pressure to be exerted, Harris said, this might be the best means of ensuring that the Americans contributed better than in their present 'ridiculous, futile and useless manner'. Trenchard promised to try. Then early in April Harris was told by Thornton that Stratemeyer, Arnold's Chief of Staff, doubted if the American heavy bomber force in England could be increased to the 300 minimum needed for useful deep penetration raids before the autumn. Soon afterwards, in a message to Peck, relayed to Harris, Thornton referred to a spate of press criticisms of the intention to build up the daylight precision bombing force for use against Germany and urged the need for the RAF to give firm public backing to the concept of the two bomber forces operating side by side. Harris was only too willing to lend his support, telling Thornton that the Americans and British were now far too deeply committed to their respective operational methods to be able to switch. What mattered was to ensure that they complemented each other, and while Bomber Command had 'every prospect of bringing the Germans to catastrophe by night bombing alone in the next six months', it could not do more as long as the daytime remained to them for recuperation. While much of the American bombing, thus far, had been very good, lack of aircraft was preventing it having more than nuisance value, whereas a force of 600 bombers operating against Germany twice a week would render the combined offensive decisive. In so doing it should be able to shoot the enemy fighter force out of the skies at comparatively slight cost to itself. For Harris the issue was clear. He wanted the Americans in alongside him but quickly and in strength; at present, however, they were a liability, not an asset, and unless they gave up their half-hearted approach should get out of the way and give Bomber Command the best chance of doing the job on its own.[14]

These issues were also much discussed with American visitors to Springfield, including Eaker, Stratemeyer, and – of particular importance – Harriman, Roosevelt's special representative in London, and it was at their urging that Harris wrote yet again to Churchill on 22 April. As he reported their views, the many opponents of American daylight bombing were claiming that the British had no faith in it, that the bomber offensive as a whole was useless, and that the European war should yield priority to the defeat of Japan.

> Out of all this chat clearly emerged one demand – urgent and reiterated. My guests all emphatically claimed that neither you, the Secretary of State, nor the Chief of the Air Staff, have ever come out with a resounding declaration as to the need for really strong American bomber forces to complement the Bomber Command offensive from Britain. It has never been put across to America, publicly or officially.

Some such statement, Harris concluded, was essential to convince public opinion of the bomber's role in the war strategy and to ensure that the resources would not be diverted elsewhere. Although Churchill acknowledged this letter he did not comment, but soon afterwards, as he journeyed to the Trident Conference in Washington aboard the *Queen Mary*, there was ample opportunity for discussion with Harriman, one of his travelling companions. On 21 May the whole subject of the combined bomber offensive was considered at the conference itself and four days later, at a joint press conference with the Prime Minister, Roosevelt said that the combination of the day and night bombing of Germany by United States and British aircraft was achieving 'a more and more satisfactory result'.[15] If this was not quite the 'resounding declaration' Harris had called for his aptly timed letter had certainly done no harm and at last, to all intents and purposes, the great debate about Anglo-American bombing priorities was over.

There was still much to do, however, before the Eighth Air Force could achieve its potential, and throughout the rest of 1943, while Harris was taking the war to Germany by night on a steadily increasing scale and often with spectacular results, the American build-up still seemed to him unnecessarily slow. Worryingly too, its first relatively heavy, deep pene-tration raids were often accompanied by losses on a scale that could well prove unsustainable. Nor did it help that some of Eaker's practical problems did not seem to be clearly appreciated in Washington; as Parton comments, 'it looked as if Arnold and Eaker were devoting more time to fighting each other than to defeating the Germans.' Harris, whose dealings with the Air Ministry had given him much experience in such matters, fully sympathised with his colleague, and his supportive attitude was well illustrated in a cable sent by Harriman to Lovett on 28 June arising from one such dispute:

Find Eaker and Harris in complete agreement that outcome of battle over Germany both day and night hinges largely on success of our Fortresses in destroying strength and vitality of German fighter air force before possible new German tactics in defense are developed. The decision will be affected by number of planes we can get into battle during the next two or three months.[16]

Then in early August Harris felt impelled yet again to take up the cudgels on behalf of his American friends, this time in a signal to the equally supportive Portal. Stressing what he saw as the critical significance of the bombing campaign over the next few months he stated that the Americans were still not making adequate effort to build-up the Eighth Bomber Command, so the enemy was being left free to concentrate against his own forces a weight of defence far greater than if the Eighth had received its planned reinforcements. Had this happened they would have knocked out by the autumn the whole German fighter force in the air and most of their fighter factories, whereupon the combined bomber forces could have had a clear run and rapidly knocked Germany stiff, but the opportunity would be lost within six months if the USA persisted in neglecting the Eighth. 'Eaker and Anderson wish particularly to get these facts put over at this juncture,' his passionate plea for Portal's intervention concluded.[17] Bitter experience, beginning over Schweinfurt on the 17th, quickly showed that Harris's assessment of what the unescorted American bombers would be able to achieve in face of the enemy defences was over-optimistic, and not until early 1944 did the advent of long-range fighters enable the crucial air battle to be won. Nevertheless, by the end of 1943 the bombers were at last arriving in the quantities required and Harris deserves much credit for the stubborn, determined way in which he helped the American airmen fight their long, often bitter political battles of 1942 and 1943. Had these been lost their heavy bombers could never have made their immense contribution alongside Bomber Command to the Allied victory in Europe.

There was one consequence of the quickening American build-up which, while it came as no great surprise, did not please Harris. Visiting England in September 1943, Arnold suggested to him – and to Portal – that the Eighth Air Force and Bomber Command should be placed under a single Commander who, it was clearly implied, would be an American. This idea had been previously floated with Portal via the Head of the RAF Delegation in Washington, and Harris told Arnold that he was firmly opposed to the RAF's losing control of its night bombing, with the consequent decline in its prestige. Anderson subsequently passed Harris a copy of a memorandum to Eaker outlining his proposals for a possible single command for all the strategic air forces operating against continental Europe, including those to be based in Italy. Harris sent this on to Portal, making a practical point that needed impressing on the Combined Chiefs of Staff and the Americans in general: namely that the limiting factor on such operations was not the weather in England or Italy but over the targets in Germany, which was the same wherever they started from. By November Arnold had persuaded his American Chiefs of Staff colleagues to support him, but Portal, who already – since Casablanca – had the task of co-ordinating the two bomber forces based in Britain, was concerned lest a new structure should disrupt the excellent relations that existed between them and would not work efficiently between separate headquarters in Britain and Italy. So the idea was in due course abandoned, and though the Americans still decided to place their own strategic air forces in Europe under one co-ordinating authority the day-to-day working ties between Harris and his Eighth Air Force opposite numbers continued unimpaired. As Anderson signalled Harris on 13 December, 'readiness on your part to participate in connection with recent operational plans of this command has made me feel that no Commander anywhere could enjoy a more favorable position with respect to his Allies.'[18]

Harris did, however, make one further significant attempt to influence their policy. We shall see in the next chapter how determined he was in the closing months of 1943 to try to bring about the speedy collapse of Germany through bombing. He missed no opportunity to try to influence those in high places, and when Churchill asked him in November to send Roosevelt copies of his 'blue books' of bomb damage photographs he readily agreed. At the same time he decided to exercise yet again his persuasive powers on the Prime Minister by summarising the destruction and damage which bombing had so far brought about, stating what remained to be done to complete the 'programme', and concluding:

> I feel certain that Germany must collapse before this programme, which is more than half completed already, has proceeded much further. We have not got far to go. But we must get the USAAF to wade in in greater force. If they will only get going according to plan and avoid such disastrous diversions as Ploesti, and getting 'nearer' to Germany from the Plains of Lombardy (which are further from 9/10ths of 'war-productive' Germany than is Norfolk), we can get through with it very quickly. We can wreck Berlin from end to end if the USAAF will come in on it. It will cost us between 400–500 aircraft. It will cost Germany the war.[19]

Harris has been widely criticised over this oft-quoted statement. It ignored both the mounting and critical battle for air superiority and the planned invasion of Northern France which was now central to Western strategy. Moreover, as we now know, it heavily over-estimated the impact of the bombing thus far on Germany's war-making capacity. Yet, as the official historians remind us, Harris was not alone in his claims. Portal certainly was disposed to agree with him, and in November 1943 few were sanguine about the USAAF's chances of driving the German fighters from the sky; indeed, as Parton observes, the American bombers were being increasingly forced into RAF-style area attacks.[20] On the evidence available Harris did have a case for pleading that an all-out assault on the remaining important cities and towns over the winter months might break the enemy, and knowing that the RAF could not do it alone he made his final attempt to bring the Americans into a joint area offensive, with Berlin the prime target.

That Harris's plea would fail was inevitable. Very few men with influence were open to persuasion and in the USA the commitment to daylight precision bombing was absolute. So when he wrote to Bottomley, now DCAS, in December 1943 it was clear he accepted that attacks on the smaller targets, including individual factories, were both highly important and the proper province of the USAAF.[21] The general pattern of the combined offensive was at last clear and in February the seal was set upon it by the success of the Americans' 'Big Week' attacks, carried out under the long-range fighter escort that was at last available and with the co-operation of Bomber Command.

By this time Eaker had left for the Mediterranean and handed over the Eighth Air Force to General Doolittle. None was saddened by Eaker's departure more than Harris. They had been together for nearly two years, learning from, encouraging and helping each other in innumerable ways, fighting battles together, respecting each other's position on matters over which they differed, appreciating each other's company, and forging a relationship between the two bomber forces that would endure not just for the rest of the war but onward into the post-war era. As the *New York Times* wrote on 1 January: 'Whatever the invasion cost in human life may be, it will be less than if General Eaker and his friend and collaborator, Air Chief Marshal Sir Arthur Harris, had not won the battle for a trial of air power first.' On the 7th Portal, Harris and many others dined with Eaker at a special Bomber Night at High Wycombe and when he arrived at Bovingdon a few days later en route for Italy both the Harrises were there to bid him farewell.[22]

Thus were laid the foundations of the contribution that the 'Mighty Eighth' was from now on to make to the victory in Europe, and it must never be forgotten how much its great successes owed to the constant support its leaders received in the earlier days – and later – from its British friends, and in particular Harris. His own reflection on this Anglo-American partnership has been oft-quoted but is so apt – and tells us so much, as well, about Harris himself – that it deserves repetition here:

> If I were asked what were the relations between Bomber Command and the American bomber force I should say that we had no relations. The word is inapplicable to what actually happened; we and they were one force. The Americans gave us the best they had, and they gave us everything we needed as and when the need arose. I hope, indeed, I know, that we did everything possible for them in turn. We could have had no better brothers in arms than Ira Eaker, Fred Anderson and Jimmy Doolittle, and the Americans could have had no better commanders than these three. I was, and am, privileged to count all three of them as the closest of friends. As for the American bomber crews, they were the bravest of the brave, and I know that I am speaking for my own bomber crews when I pay this tribute.[23]

Notes

1. Harris, *op.cit.* p.104; Craven & Cate, *Official History of the Army Air Forces in World War II* vol.I, p.662; Parton, *Air Force Spoken Here*, pp.134–5, 142–3. Parton mistakenly implies that Eaker left Springfield at the end of March.
2. The Eighth Air Force comprised all the air units which were being based in the UK; the bomber elements were all contained in the subordinate formation known as Eighth Bomber Command. The term 'Eighth Air Force' is used here whenever possible so as to avoid confusion with the RAF's Bomber Command.
3. Folders H18, dated 8 May 1942; H88, dated 27 June 1942.
4. Alfred Goldberg in RAFHS, vol.9. p.33.
5. Craven & Cate, *op.cit.* vol.I, p.610; Folder H51, dated 12–13 August 1942.
6. Craven & Cate, *op.cit.* vol.I, p.665.
7. *Ibid* p.594; Folder H65, dated 15 and 16 September 1942; OH vol.I, p.355 (this whole

subject is discussed on pp.353–63); AIR 8/711; see also Saward, *op.cit.* pp.172–4 for the main texts.

8. Folder H65; OH vol.I, pp.366 *et seq*; AIR 8/711; Saward, *op.cit.* p.175; De Groot, *op.cit.* p.197. These and other policy issues relating to the Eighth Air Force are discussed at length, together with the American air operations, in Robin Neillands' recent book *The Bomber War*.

9. Folder H66, dated 12 November 1942; Portal Folder 9 and Folder H81, dated 21 November 1942.

10. Folder H28.

11. Folder H37, dated 10 December 1942 and 21 January 1943; *Daily Telegraph* 29 January 1943. The raid was on Wilhelmshaven.

12. Parton, *op.cit.* pp.221–2, 242–5; Folder H100, E43. For Andrews, see also Lucas, *Out of the Blue*, pp.268–9.

13. OH vol.II, pp.15–21, where the context of the Eaker Plan is discussed; Folder H45, E18.

14. Folders H50, dated 17 March 1943; H37, dated 5, 12 and 13 April 1943.

15. Folder H65, E43 (fully reproduced in Saward, *op.cit.* pp.202–4); Gilbert, *op.cit.* pp.396–7, 412, 414.

16. Parton, *op.cit.* pp.277–8.

17. Folder H82, dated 12 August 1943 (fully reproduced in Saward, *op.cit.* pp.205–6). General Anderson had taken over Eighth Bomber Command from Eaker in June, when Eaker became Commander of the Eighth Air Force.

18. OH vol.II, p.43; Arnold, *Global Mission*, p.218; Portal Papers, Folder 10, dated 21 September 1943; Folders H45, dated 19 September 1943; H100; Dr Richard Davis, quoted in RAFHS, vol.9, pp.8–9. Arnold accepted after the war that his proposal would have caused many complications.

19. Folder H65, dated 3 November 1943; Saward, *op.cit.* p.218.

20. OH vol.II, p.51; Parton, *op.cit.* p.324.

21. Folder H67, dated 28 December 1943.

22. Parton, *op.cit.* pp.344–5; Harris scrapbook.

23. Harris, *op.cit.* p.246.

Chapter 13

From the Ruhr to Berlin

We must now return to the story of Bomber Command during the year in which Harris strove mightily in the attempt to enable it to fulfil what he believed was its ultimate potential. It started on 4 February 1943, when he received a new and particularly important directive, which reiterated the wording agreed by Churchill, Roosevelt and the Combined Chiefs of Staff at the Casablanca Conference in January. This stated that the primary aim of the British and American bomber forces in the United Kingdom would be 'the progressive destruction and dislocation of the German military, industrial and economic system, and the undermining of the morale of the German people to a point where their capacity for armed resistance is fatally weakened.' The directive issued to Harris went on to specify a variety of 'objectives' which would vary in nature and priority from time to time, and added that when the time came to invade the continent the bombers would operate in support. As the official historians comment, the question of how the air offensive was to be conducted was left unsolved and all depended on the way the directive was interpreted. In Harris's view it meant that the area bombing offensive against Germany's major industrial cities – for practical reasons the only worthwhile strategy – must be continued and extended, and for the present the Air Staff were fully behind him. 'His forceful, single-minded and courageous leadership,' they go on, 'had not only infused the whole force with a spirit which, throughout many long and some dreadful nights, was to prove unquenchable, but had also stimulated new confidence among those higher authorities who directed the policy.' In effect, therefore, the broad Casablanca statement of intention became Harris's charter, albeit slightly but significantly amended by him so as to read 'aimed at under-mining' German morale. At this stage of the war he certainly believed this to be vulnerable, and were it to be broken Germany might surrender.[1]

What mattered for the present was to get on with the job. To hand was a much more powerful bomber force than Harris had inherited a year before; while the number of squadrons had risen only slightly almost two-thirds were flying 'heavies' and the process of replacing the Wellingtons, usually with Lancasters, was well under way. Indeed by the end of the year there would be some 65 operational squadrons, mostly flying Lancasters and Halifaxes, and including four of Mosquitos. The effect of this expansion was almost to double the average availability so that by March 1944 Harris

252

could draw on nearly 1,000 aircraft for operations, and all with far greater striking power than in 1942.

In one respect, however, there was to be a reduction. The light bombers of 2 Group – first Blenheims then Bostons, Mitchells and Venturas, and eventually Mosquitos – were also under Harris's command, largely engaged on operations over North-West Europe either to draw the Luftwaffe into battle or to hit short-range precision objectives, of which the Philips Works at Eindhoven, heavily damaged in December 1942, was the most notable. While Harris certainly appreciated and encouraged their work he became increasingly anxious about the quality of their aircraft, telling Portal in March 1943 that he considered them deplorable. He then heard that it was planned to move them all to Fighter Command and in due course to the Second Tactical Air Force for Army support, a switch that he scathingly described to Trenchard as having no connection with the air offensive against Germany.[2] Fortunately when 2 Group departed on 1 June 1943 he succeeded in hanging on to his two Mosquito squadrons, whose performance was enabling them to bomb precise and often remote targets with great accuracy, and they became the nucleus of Bennett's highly successful Light Night Striking Force.[3]

By this time Harris's main offensive was well under way. It had started in March, having been delayed by what he correctly described as the 'completely wasteful' winter offensive against the U-boat bases on the Biscay coast which he had been ordered to undertake at the Navy's insistence (chapter 7), and its first phase, usually referred to as the Battle of the Ruhr, lasted four months. This is not the place to describe it in detail. Suffice it to say that 43 major attacks were mounted, usually by forces of between 300 and 700 aircraft, that the targets were far from confined to the Ruhr, that 4.7% of the aircraft despatched were lost over Germany and a great many more damaged, and that 'the result was a whole series of consistent and pulverising blows among which the failures were much rarer than the successes', to quote the official historians.[4]

Right from the start the new level of achievement was recognised where it mattered. After the opening attack on Essen on 5/6 March Portal signalled that reports and first photographs showed it to have been one of the most successful of the whole war, and as was his wont Harris immediately passed on the congratulations throughout the Command. A week later Portal's praise for a second attack on Essen was equally enthusiastic, describing it as magnificent in terms not only of the damage inflicted on the plant and staff of the world's greatest armament factory but also the effect of the devastation on the morale of the whole of the Ruhr. That Churchill was following the mounting offensive was illustrated in May, when Harris met his request to send him a list of the hundred most important towns in the German war economy. On May 15, however, Harris's own enthusiasm rather got the better of him when he signalled Portal in Washington that in the past ten weeks 'staggering destruction had been inflicted throughout the Ruhr to an extent that no nation could stick for long. If we can keep this up it cannot fail to be lethal within a period of time which in my view will be surprisingly short.' The need now was to get the Americans in on it. Trenchard too was enthusiastic, telling Harris in July that his efforts would greatly shorten the war and save untold casualties, whereupon Harris permitted himself the unusually guarded observation: 'I really feel that lately we have been getting somewhere.' That the Battle of the Ruhr was what Denis Richards' recent account calls 'a major victory' is beyond doubt but Harris's words to Trenchard turned out to be nearer the mark than some of his others.[5]

The most spectacular event in the four-month assault was in fact a 'one-off' in which Harris himself played a key role. The story began in February when he pooh-poohed Barnes Wallis's bouncing bomb and the possibility of using it to breach the Ruhr dams (p.221). He was not alone in his doubts; as Elworthy recalled to him much later, 'your scepticism of what seemed just another crazy idea was certainly shared by your staff.' Yet when the incredulous Elworthy went to be briefed by the inventor he decided he could not entirely dismiss it, whereupon he and Saundby persuaded Harris to see Wallis. It was a most unusual meeting. As John Morpurgo, Wallis's biographer, puts it, Harris had an almost frenetic mistrust of inventors and, until Cochrane persuaded him to the contrary, saw Wallis as just another scientist crazed out of peacetime sanity by the urgencies of war. Yet, as Morpurgo also comments, they had similarities. Both mistrusted politicians, disliked senior civil servants and despised obstructionists; they possessed determination and originality far beyond most of their contemporaries; and between them they had as much diplomacy as a circus prize fighter.

Harris's alleged greeting was typical: 'My boys' lives are too precious to be wasted on your crazy notions.' He himself never accepted that he had addressed Wallis in this forbidding way, and he listened to his visitor and watched the film with patience, cross-questioned with skill and understanding, and admitted that he had not been fully or accurately informed of the details. His farewell was non-committal, though he did say – to Wallis's surprise – that Portal had authorised the conversion of three Lancasters. In fact Harris was sufficiently impressed to back the proposed use of the new weapon, so on 15 March he briefed Cochrane to form a special squadron and nominated Guy Gibson – already well known to him from his own days in 5 Group – to command it. As Elworthy later observed to him: 'Typically, having made your decision, you put all your steam behind it, and notwithstanding your distaste for the *corps d'élite* principle ruled that a special squadron should be formed forthwith. This could never have been done but for the drive you put into the venture.'[6]

We need not recount here the oft-recorded drama of 617 Squadron's destruction of two of the dams on 16/17 May, other than to say that Harris knew for certain where he had to be that night. He, Cochrane and Wallis anxiously followed the various reports arriving in the 5 Group Operations Room at Grantham, and as dawn broke went out to Scampton to greet the returning crews. While they waited Harris told Wallis that he would now be prepared to buy from him a pink elephant, and added: 'For this I'll see to it that you get a K.' Sadly, for all his efforts, Harris was unable to deliver and not until 1968 was honour satisfied.[7]

As we saw in chapter 9, 617 Squadron's achievement was greeted at all levels with the greatest enthusiasm and Harris's desk was inundated with congratulatory messages. In fact the direct damage caused to the Ruhr turned out to be much less than was first thought and had been hoped for, partly because the critical third dam had not been breached. On the other hand the Germans not only had enormous repair work to do but also felt compelled to strengthen the defences of these and other similar targets, and for the Allies – and Bomber Command in particular – the attack was an immense boost to morale. For Harris, however, the real question was 'what next?' Eight out of nineteen of his very best crews had been lost in the first low-level precision attack on Germany by heavy bombers since Augsburg and in the short term were almost impossible to replace, so was it right or even possible to persist with such specialised operations? Would it not be better to concentrate on the normal pattern of main force area attacks that were at last achieving substantial success?

Cochrane's mind, too, was being focused on this subject, as shown in a letter on 2 June. Keen as he was to preserve the squadron for special operations it was still very much under strength and he was making little progress in rebuilding it. Harris, perhaps surprisingly in the light of his earlier misgivings, wasted no time in assuring Cochrane of his support and telling the other AOCs that since the value of 617 Squadron as a specialised unit had been fully demonstrated he intended to keep it for similar tasks in future. Consequently for a start he now wanted two highly skilled and experienced crews from each Group. Inevitably it took time to reconstruct and train the squadron to the standard required, and Harris and Cochrane needed all their resolve to keep it in being – particularly after the loss of five out of eight Lancasters that attacked the Dortmund-Ems Canal at low level on 15/16 September. Cochrane, urging the need for a decision on the squadron's future policy, recommended it should concentrate on accurate high-level attacks, and Harris stated unequivocally that he wanted it retained for occasional operations requiring special training and equipment.[8]

Here then were the roots of his Command's future and increasingly important precision bombing role.

We can only speculate on the possible outcome had the fertile-minded Harris been allowed to use 617 Squadron against Mussolini. In mid-1943 the heavy bombing of the main cities of northern Italy was being seriously considered with the object of encouraging an Italian surrender, and on 11 July Harris suggested that a plan he had prepared in 1942 to bomb Mussolini's office and residence should be resurrected and carried out by what he called his squadron of 'old lags'. They would be routed across France under cover of darkness, attack at 0930, *ie* 30 minutes after Mussolini's normal time of arrival in his office, and continue to North Africa. Portal supported it but the Foreign Secretary, Anthony Eden, turned it down with Churchill's endorsement. In their view the chances of success were slight and if the operation went wrong it could do great harm. So Bomber Command's main contribution to the defeat of Italy took the form of area bombing attacks in August, mostly on Milan, Turin and Genoa, and it needs to be stated that these were not ordered by Harris on his own initiative. They were carried out under firm and close political direction and were intended to help ensure that the Italian government would not only come to terms quickly but would meet the Allied surrender requirements as fully as possible.[9]

Harris was, in fact, never very enthusiastic about bombing Italy; it merely diverted him from the attack on Germany, the main enemy and the primary subject of the directives that governed his activities. By the end of the Battle of the Ruhr he had in theory a new one, agreed by the Combined Chiefs at the Washington Conference in May and after modification spelt out to him by Portal in June. While preserving the essential aim of the combined offensive as laid down at Casablanca (p.252) the Chiefs endorsed the key features of the Eaker Plan (p.245), and stressed the need to mount a preliminary or simultaneous assault on the German fighter strength which was now perceived to be threatening not only American daylight operations but Harris's night offensive as well. The plan thus agreed, referred to as Pointblank, then had to be converted into a formal directive, and the draft circulated by the Air Staff on 3 June stated that the British and American bomber forces based in the United Kingdom were to give first priority to attacking the German fighter forces and their associated industries. It went on to specify various primary and secondary objectives, including submarine yards and bases, ball bearings and oil, but instead of quoting the former primary aim it merely said that the general responsibilities allocated to the bomber forces in the original Casablanca directive still held. The draft bore all the hallmarks of the Directorate of Bomber Operations, where it was increasingly believed that Bomber Command ought to be concentrating on specific types of target rather than on Germany's industrial economy as a whole. Precisely what happened in the next week is not clear, the official historians tell us, but certainly Harris had his say. So in the final Pointblank Directive of 10 June the full Casablanca primary aim was reinstated, the various precise objectives – including the enemy fighter force – were assigned to the Eighth Air Force, and Bomber Command, while being employed firstly in the general disorganisation of German industry, was instructed to complement as far as possible the American operations.[10]

Harris had been in a strong position. At this moment, at the height of the Battle of the Ruhr, he was delivering the goods and everybody knew it; conversely the Eighth Air Force was not only far behind in its build-up but was a long way from even proving its case. So the C-in-C won the argument. His new directive gave him licence to continue his campaign in the way he was convinced it must be fought – and it is hard to believe that in mid-1943 there was any effective alternative.

Nevertheless, Harris remained under pressure from influential quarters to concentrate more on specific types of target whose destruction was deemed crucial to the entire German war effort, and he missed no opportunity to take on those he called 'the panacea merchants'. On 14 April 1943, to take just one example, he wrote to Trenchard, who had asked how to counter those who were asking why the German rubber industry in Hanover was not being targeted. Harris's reply was particularly succinct:

> What your critics say about the rubber industry of Hanover applies with equal force to the rubber industry all over Germany, upon which we have already wreaked considerable incidental damage while carrying out operations of a more general description. I do not believe in 'panacea' targets, eg oil, rubber, ball bearings. Specialising on one such means that the enemy concentrates all his defences, and nothing else in Germany including morale and housing is likely to suffer. If the 'panacea' fails all is lost. Finally I distrust experts and specialists on 'panacea' commodities ... for example a fortnight after we were told Germany was nearly on the rocks for oil she staged the biggest campaign in history [Russia] using billions of gallons. Not even the 'oily boys' attempted to laugh that off. They just hid their heads for a spell and now raise the same song again.

As Richard Overy today summarises Harris's views, he was hostile to panaceas 'because he realised that an enemy economy and social structure could not be dislocated by an attack on just one of its many elements with the prospect of forcing a decision.'[11]

It was the German ball-bearing industry centred on Schweinfurt that formed the principal bone of contention in 1943. Ever since 1941 the MEW had been urging that it be attacked (pp.144–5), and its case was strongly backed by Bufton and his colleagues in the Air Ministry to the extent that by July 1943 they thought they had won the argument. Consequently Bottomley wrote to Harris about the 'imminent' joint RAF and USAAF operation against Schweinfurt and enclosed a special brief for the crews which had been drawn up by Bufton. The operation could prove one of the war's major battles, wrote Bufton, evoking Harris's pencilled comment 'Sez you!' The ball-bearing industry, Bufton went on, had long been established to the mutual satisfaction of the British and American Air Staffs ('but not to mine', wrote Harris) as a vital link in the enemy's whole production chain, and the Schweinfurt factories produced 60% of their requirements ('35% at most', said Harris). This missive cut no ice at High Wycombe, where Harris simply marked his copy 'No action'. In his view the precision bombing required, even if the attack was necessary, was a task for the Americans. So when they claimed after their second – and very costly – attack in October that it had done the job and would not need to be repeated for a very long time it seemed as though that might be the end of the story.[12]

Yet in November the MEW, convinced that much more still needed to be done, strongly recommended a night area attack and Bufton, who needed no convincing, persuaded Bottomley to take it up directly with Harris. The C-in-C was not to be moved. 'I do not regard a night attack on Schweinfurt as a reasonable operation of war,' he replied on 20 December; the target was heavily defended and at night very hard to find and mark. Moreover, not only was he convinced that the Germans had long since dispersed their ball-bearing production but there had been many other examples of the 'infallible infallibility' of panacea mongers, including transportation, the Ruhr dams, molybdenum mines and refineries. If the job was vital, which he believed it was not, the Americans should set the target alight by day so that Bomber Command could follow at night. Otherwise he refused to take it on. Sharp Air Ministry discussions followed this blunt refusal, with Portal giving his staff full backing, and eventually, following a 'Big Week' American attack on 24 February 1944, Harris obeyed the specific order he had been given and sent 734 aircraft to Schweinfurt. While this episode proved a landmark in the growing divergence between Harris and the Air Ministry on the subject of general versus precision area bombing, it vindicated all his scepticism about the value of ball bearings as a critical target. The official historians, who recount the whole saga in some detail, state that 'almost exactly in the way anticipated by Harris, Germany was able to surmount the crisis produced by the Anglo-American attack on her ball-bearing industry.'[13] Oil, his last great 'panacea', would prove a different story.

Harris remained unhappy, too, about the various 'diversions' that continued to be inflicted on him. On some such matters he was absolutely right – not least about the bombing of the French Atlantic ports in early 1943, which he consistently opposed. As he told Portal in March, such operations demonstrated the appalling extravagance and ineffectiveness of the Navy's ideas about using air power. The official history, summarising this winter offensive, has no doubt that his judgement of it was 'precisely correct'.[14]

On other issues, however, Harris was on weaker ground. On 26 April, for example, he protested to Portal about the decision to send three of his Wellington squadrons to North Africa, 'a secondary theatre of war'. At this critical time, he went on, Bomber Command ought to have first call on the RAF's resources of men and aircraft instead of being regarded as a convenient source to meet the real or fancied needs of others. Portal was unmoved. 'It is not a case of failure to recognise the needs or the importance of Bomber Command operations but of balancing conflicting claims to the available resources,' he replied. A month later Harris returned to the charge in the context of the intended despatch of more American bombers to the Mediterranean. Instead of the combined US-British bomber force operating from the UK being increased, 'constant and intolerable additional drains' were being imposed upon it. Portal, while sympathising, refused to accept the assertion that Mediterranean Command was unnecessarily strong for its task: 'I must ask you to accept my views on these subjects as long as I have to do this job.' At the same time he recognised Harris's anxieties about the steady flow of men from his Operational Training Units to the overseas commands, which represented a further serious 'diversion' in terms of both qualified aircrew and training resources. There were other claimants too, as Harris observed to ACAS (Ops) on 15 June when asked to supply 18 trained crews to 38 Wing for the training of glider pilots and parachutists 'for a hypothetical operation which may take place some day'. He went on:

> Upon all occasions when other commands fail to make provision for their commitments they have invariably been allowed to regard Bomber Command as an inexhaustible pool from which to cover all deficiencies. It is apparently regarded as able not only to meet its own foreseen commitments, but also to meet any unforeseen or rapid increase in its strength while at the same time supplying all and sundry with crews for every conceivable purpose with or without notice. It is impossible for this situation to continue.

Harris's exasperation was total. He had been trying to live with these pressures ever since becoming C-in-C and now, with his Command's prospects brighter than they had ever been, he felt it was time for it to be given proper priority. Yet Portal was equally exasperated, for his subordinate's single-minded determination often seemed to ignore the dictates of the rest of the war. As John Terraine rightly reminds us, where else could the heavy, long-range aircraft needed to cover the Atlantic and in the Middle and Far

East come from, if not from Bomber Command, and where else could the crews come from, if not from Bomber Command squadrons or OTUs?[15] Ultimately, however, it all came down to the fact that in war resources are always limited; had Harris not pressed his case further than anyone else in his position would probably have done, Bomber Command might well never have achieved as much as it did.

Increasingly as 1943 moved on the 'diversions' became linked to the preparations for invasion in 1944. One of these was Operation Starkey, intended to simulate an Allied landing in North-East France so as to draw the Luftwaffe into intensive combat. Telling Portal on 9 July how disturbed he was about its likely effects on both his and Eaker's strategic offensives, Harris suggested that Fighter Command would do better to devote its spare resources to lending him a hand, and Portal – who was himself opposed to the use of the heavy bombers for this operation – did his best to provide reassurances. In the event, however, his objections were overridden and on the night of 8/9 September he sent some 250 aircraft to bomb several German coastal gun batteries near the small town of Le Portel, outside Boulogne. In his view these were unsuitable targets and when the Oboe marking went wrong many of the bombs fell on the town causing heavy civilian casualties. It was a sad episode, unfortunate and unnecessary as far as Harris was concerned, though it certainly enabled lessons to be learnt for the future.[16]

Another diversion of his resources which Harris always opposed but was compelled to accept was clandestine operations in support of the Special Operations Executive. As far back as March 1942 he had started objecting to such activities and he never became reconciled to them. To him there was no guarantee of worthwhile return on what steadily became a substantial investment of military resources; moreover, to quote Professor Michael Foot, he had a sound professional reason. 'Aircraft allotted solely to secret work were, from Bomber Command's point of view, part-wasted assets because they had to have moonlight to see where they were going and could only work for 10 or 12 days out of 28.' Sir Lewis Hodges, who operated in this sphere, agrees: 'We were certainly not popular with the boss, who looked upon us as a diversion of effort from the main task of bombing Germany.'[17] Yet, protest as he might, Harris always knew at the end of the day that orders were orders, and in due course, as we shall see, he had to accept the biggest diversion of them all: direct support for the Normandy invasion.

In mid-1943, however, that lay a long way ahead, and while Harris knew that the preparations were in hand he was far more concerned to get on with his own immediate job. By July his initial great assault on the Ruhr was complete and he judged it time to take on Germany's second largest city, Hamburg. He had long had it in mind. But for the weather, it would have been the target of Operation Millennium in May 1942, and in March 1943 Portal had sent him a reminder: 'If you can pull off an 800 raid on a place such as Hamburg, I shall be delighted.' The Admiralty, too, was keen, for the city was the enemy's greatest port and shipbuilding centre. Harris knew that to damage seriously a target of such size would require a sustained assault rather than a single attack, as his message to his crews before the first of these on 24/25 July made clear. In fact over the next ten days four major attacks took place, each by almost 800 aircraft, together with two smaller scale daylight operations by Eaker's B17s. The city's location on the River Elbe not far from the North Sea coast made it relatively easy for the Pathfinders to identify and mark, and the decision to use Window for the first time threw the night fighter defences into almost total confusion to begin with. The consequence was a degree of success that almost certainly exceeded even Harris's hopes and expectations.

In summary, from some 3,000 sorties Bomber Command lost only 86 aircraft, or about 2.8% – well below the rate it had become accustomed to. In return it inflicted damage on a vast scale, and, largely owing to the horrific firestorm unintentionally created during the second attack, caused casualties far greater than in any other of Bomber Command's operations hitherto. Indeed, Hamburg's estimated 45,000 deaths may well have exceeded even those in Dresden in February 1945 (p.320). The immediate effects of all this on the German people and their leaders were enormous, with Albert Speer, Hitler's Armaments Minister, making his oft-quoted statement to his colleagues that another six similar attacks, quickly repeated, would cripple Germany and might well compel the end of the war. In fact Hamburg's recovery (though never complete) came more quickly than Speer had expected and Harris, even if he had known of Speer's fears, could not have repeated the dose elsewhere; most other major targets were further away, would be much harder to find and hit accurately, and would entail considerably greater losses. In any case, his Command was still not strong enough to mount frequent attacks on such a scale. Nevertheless, Harris did know quickly enough from reconnaissance photographs and other sources how much damage had been done, and coming in the middle of 1943, when the war as a whole was very far from being won, the Battle of Hamburg was a remarkable success. To quote the official historians, 'for Bomber Command the victory was complete. In the earlier months and years of the war it was without precedent, and in those that were still to come it was never excelled.'[18]

It was immediately after this that Harris was required to turn his attentions to Northern Italy, but at the same time he was preparing to undertake a very different kind of attack. In June, intelligence sources having confirmed long-held suspicions that the Germans were developing long-range rockets, the Defence Committee of the War Cabinet ordered the bombing of the research and development station at Peenemunde, on the German Baltic coast. In early July, after consulting his AOCs, Harris obtained permission to wait for the longer August nights before tackling such a distant target, and tasked Cochrane to draw up the detailed plan for what would amount to a precision attack by the main force of Bomber Command. Martin Middlebrook, in his excellent account of the operation, brings out the care taken with the planning process and the boldness of Harris's decision to attack at relatively low level in bright moonlight so as to try to ensure that the target was correctly identified and marked. He insisted too that this task be undertaken both by Pathfinders and by 5 Group aircraft using their time-and-distance technique,[19] and the whole assault was to be directed from the air by a 'master of ceremonies', the first time this procedure was employed on a full-scale operation.[20] The risks were high, and Harris tried to deceive the enemy fighter defences by mounting a Mosquito diversion against Berlin.

Six hundred aircraft took off on the night of 17/18 August. For security reasons their crews could not be told the real nature of their target; as far as they knew Peenemunde was developing some highly specialised radar equipment. They were, however, left in no doubt of its importance, for Harris's briefing message stated that if the operation failed it would have to be repeated as long as necessary and regardless of casualties. Many who listened to this remembered how his injunction concentrated their minds; they had never heard anything like it before. In the event 40 of the crews (6.7%) did not come back, which was bad enough, and the losses would have been much heavier had many of the German fighters not been sent initially to Berlin. Nevertheless, the operation as a whole was considered to have achieved its object and it goes down in history as one of Harris's most daring. Earlier post-war assessments were somewhat dismissive of its value in relation to the development of the V2 rocket and of the V1 flying bomb on which work was also being done at Peenemunde, but the relatively recently published *Official History of Intelligence* states firmly that it did immense damage to the installations and killed many of the V2 scientists and engineers, thus delaying the programme by about two months. The wider consequences of this and subsequent attacks on German missile targets in terms of preventing interference with the preparations for D-Day hardly need stating.[21]

By this time, with the nights lengthening, Harris judged it time to restart his campaign against the German capital. With Churchill's strong encouragement he had made his first attacks six months previously. Now, on 19 August, the Prime Minister's views were reflected in a cable from Portal, in Washington, to VCAS asking when heavy attacks could begin: 'In the present war situation attacks on Berlin on anything like the Hamburg scale must have enormous effect on Germany as a whole,'[22] Harris's response was immediate: on the 23rd he despatched 719 aircraft on the first full-scale attack, and two more attacks followed during the next ten days, but they achieved only moderate success and at 7.6% the overall losses were heavy. Consequently – and in particular to give time to try to overcome serious target-marking problems – Harris waited until November before resuming the Berlin offensive, meanwhile devoting his efforts to a series of heavy attacks on other cities, mostly less distant. On 11 October he received a message from Churchill:

> The War Cabinet have asked me to convey to you their compliments on the recent successes of Bomber Command . . . the results of this campaign are not restricted to damage which can be seen and photographed but are reflected with equal significance in the extent to which the German Air Force has been forced from the offensive to the defensive both operationally and in new construction, and compelled to concentrate more and more of its resources on the protection of Germany against bombing attacks, to the benefit of our own and Allied forces on the other European fronts. Your Command, with the day-bomber formations of the 8th Air Force fighting alongside it, is playing a foremost part in the converging attack on Germany now being conducted by the forces of the United Nations on a prodigious scale. Your officers and men will, I know, continue their efforts in spite of the intense resistance offered, until they are rewarded by the final downfall of the enemy.

Almost certainly this message, which Harris immediately circulated throughout the Command, had been triggered by a note from Bottomley (DCAS) to Evill (VCAS) on 21 August urging the need for a special word of appreciation at top level for Bomber Command's recent achievements, and it came as a great and timely encouragement. 'It is an unfailing sense of strength to us,' Harris replied to the Prime Minister, 'to realise that every bomb which leaves the racks makes smoother the path of the armies of the United Nations as they close in to the kill.'[23]

The message also assured Harris that his continuing campaign was still fully supported at the highest level, both in the Air Ministry and elsewhere, and its warmth may have influenced his decision of 3 November to plead with Churchill yet again the case for trying to end the war by bombing alone (see p.249). The Prime Minister did not reply, but Harris remained determined not to rule out the possibility that to inflict a 'Hamburg' on Berlin would prove a shattering, even decisive blow to the enemy. So far the German capital had not been extensively damaged; now, with the long winter nights and better target-finding equipment available, he judged the opportunity right to make Berlin his principal target. Many accounts have been written, most notably by Martin Middlebrook, of the series of 16 heavy attacks that he ordered over the next four months. They involved some 8,700 sorties, from which 500 aircraft failed to return. They were carried out in appalling weather, with crews nearly always having to bomb blind using the Pathfinders' sky markers, and without more than the occasional reconnaissance photograph to indicate what they were actually achieving. Then, at the end of the day, judged by the standards of the Battle of Hamburg, the campaign did not seem to Harris and his staff to have been an overwhelming success, though very heavy damage had certainly been inflicted.[24]

The type of target, of course, was very different from Hamburg. It was spread over a much greater area and further away, the weather was far worse, and the night fighter defences were considerably stronger and more effective. Consequently Berlin was both a less suitable and more difficult target than Hamburg for heavy bombers of that era to take on if the object was to try to force the enemy to surrender, and Harris himself probably started to have doubts well before he called off the assault towards the end of March. In late January 1944 he read 'with much interest' an assessment by 'C', the head of the Secret Intelligence Service, which had been sent to him at Churchill's specific request. In C's judgement, under continued serious bombing of a German city the initial anger of civilians usually turned to hopeless apathy and occasionally to strikes and riots; even Hitler was becoming worried about civilian – but not military – morale, and his colleagues were considerably worried. 'But,' he concluded, 'so long as the morale of the Gestapo and SS troops remains unaffected as it does at present, it is difficult to see how an even more serious decline in German civilian morale can bring about a rapid collapse as in 1918.' The similar view expressed by Harris when writing after the war about German civilian morale suggests that C's words were not lost on him.[25]

We must remember that there was much more to the bombardment of Germany during these winter months than the assault on Berlin. Indeed Harris devoted more than half his effort to 19 major attacks on other large towns and cities, thus keeping up the offensive against Germany as a whole, making the enemy's task of air defence much more difficult, and often complementing the daylight operations of the Eighth Air Force, not least during 'Big Week'. In one of these attacks, on Leipzig on 19/20 February, the losses rose to a worrying 9.5% and in the last operation against Berlin, on 24/25 March, they were almost as great. The enemy defences were exacting increasingly heavy penalties when the bombers tackled the more distant targets, and the worst was still to come.

Harris's decision to attack Nuremberg on 30/31 March 1944 has exposed his operational judgement to more criticism than any other decision he took.

As Martin Middlebrook observes in his excellent book on this raid, March had been a month of largely poor results, and on the 30th – his crews having been rested for three nights – a major raid looked practicable. The choice of target and the route and timing would, as always, depend heavily on the phase of the moon and on the weather, and on this occasion Harris took what was certainly a borderline decision to go for a major, hitherto largely undamaged, industrial city deep in southern Germany. Success would require the presence of high cloud along the outward route, clear skies over the target, precise timing, accurate navigation of the bomber stream through a gap in the Rhineland night fighter defences – and luck. Some of his staff had their doubts about the decision and as the planning proceeded there were differences of opinion about the route. Then later in the day came the final weather forecast, based on the Mosquitos' reconnaissance reports, indicating that cloud was unlikely en route; moreover there was now cloud over the target, though this should clear. Saundby showed it to Harris, expecting him to cancel the operation. He did not.

So that evening 782 Lancasters and Halifaxes took off for Nuremberg. There followed an unpredicted change of wind, which took many off course, and in bright moonlight, nearer to the night fighters; an hour-long battle as the bombers crossed the Rhine and flew east resulted in the destruction of 59 of them – appalling losses. On reaching the turning point towards the city most were too far north, which upset the timing, and they soon found the target area covered in low cloud, which prevented the visual marking that had been planned. In the subsequent confusion, not helped by the absence of a Master Bomber to provide direction, relatively few aircraft hit the target, many bombed nearby towns, villages, and often open country, and 100 actually attacked Schweinfurt, 55 miles away. The final count revealed that 95 aircraft were missing – a shocking 11.6% – and many more damaged. The target, however, emerged relatively unscathed, in no way a worthwhile return.[26]

Bomber Command had thus suffered, says the official history, 'the ill-consequences of unusually bad luck and uncharacteristically bad and unimaginative operational planning' and the blame – if blame there must be – has to rest with Harris himself. As Middlebrook points out, his was the initial decision to mount the raid; the plan received his approval; and it was he who declined to cancel it in face of the revised weather forecast. Yet Middlebrook rightly adds that hindsight gives us no right to be over-critical.[27] Already for two years Harris had taken the awesome responsibility for deciding when to commit his force in pursuit of the objectives he had been given and all too often the arguments had been finely balanced. To be over-cautious would diminish the impact and value of his offensive; to be over-rash would court disaster. The occasional misjudgement was inevitable, and if Harris is to be blamed over Nuremberg he deserves credit for all the occasions when he got it right, including the many when he decided *not* to go. He himself was reticent on this subject. Neither his Despatch nor his personal memoir referred to it; Dudley Saward, writing with his master watching over him, merely mentions it without discussion as Bomber Command's most tragic reverse, and Middlebrook received no response to his request for an interview about it. While Harris did overcome his reluctance when talking in 1971 to Alastair Revie, in 1979 he would still go no further than write that Nuremberg was 'the one real disaster, and we were lucky not to have had a dozen.'[28]

Thus ended the long, cruel winter campaign which Harris always referred to as the Battle of Berlin. The verdicts upon it differ. Hardly anybody – not even Harris himself – has ever considered it an unqualified success, and many have judged it a defeat in the sense that it did not cost Germany the war as Harris had predicted it would. The official history goes further in describing it in the operational sense as a defeat, draws attention to Harris's letter of 7 April 1944 telling VCAS that the growing strength of the German night fighter defences would soon be causing unsustainable losses unless substantial night fighter support could be provided, and considers it fortunate that the Berlin campaign had to be stopped at this point. John Terraine accepts this verdict but in omitting the key qualification 'in the operational sense' appears to imply that the battle was a defeat in a wider sense. Curiously, while unaware of the personal Harris connection (chapter 2), he compares it with Passchendaele. Denis Richards, while rightly noting the qualifications, does not refer to Harris's letter and doubts if the battle can in any way be regarded as a defeat. Dudley Saward rudely dismisses the official history, quotes the Harris letter without drawing a conclusion from it, and simply says that Harris called off his offensive because of the shortening nights and the impending requirements of Operation Overlord. Martin Middlebrook, on the other hand, simply considers the cost too high in relation to the results: 'The Luftwaffe hurt Bomber Command more than Bomber Command hurt Berlin', a view which echoes those of Max Hastings, Peter Johnson, Robin Neillands and other critics.[29]

What we must accept is that in the night air battles over Germany, as Harris said, Bomber Command was by March 1944 coming off second best. But that must not lead us to deduce that he and his men had been engaged in a futile campaign and that their sacrifices were in vain. True, they had not knocked the enemy out of the war, but they – together with the Americans – had been placing the German homeland under intense and growing strain and compelling them to devote resources to its air defence to an extent that would ensure the success of the Normandy invasion and of the other great land campaigns in the later stages of the war. While Harris has been widely attacked for devoting rather too much effort to 'the big city' it is questionable whether a different 'spread' would have made all that much difference to the end result, and his campaign can hardly have found disfavour with Churchill. Having referred to the Berlin attacks in a message to Stalin on 12 January 1944, the Prime Minister was told in reply: 'Our armies have been successful recently, but it is still a long way to Berlin. Therefore you do not have to lessen the bombing on Berlin, but should endeavour to intensify it using all means.'[30]

Nevertheless, it was that concentration on Berlin that brought Harris under increasing censure from the Air Ministry during these winter months and contributed to a direct confrontation with Portal in April 1944. Among his critics, most notably in connection with Schweinfurt, was Bufton, whose new dispute arose initially from Harris's decision to attach three squadrons from Bennett's Pathfinder Force to Cochrane's 5 Group in order to strengthen the latter's ability to operate against specialised targets independently of the main bomber force. Nor surprisingly Bennett was hardly enthusiastic about this scheme and when Harris and Portal discussed it on 11 April at one of their regular meetings, Portal, while agreeing with it, urged that Bufton be kept in the picture. This prompted Harris to comment on Bufton's attitude and on the circumstances under which the PFF had been originally formed, whereupon Portal wrote to him briefly on 12 April in the attempt to set the record straight. He saw no reason to modify his opinion that the credit for the Air Ministry's share in what the PFF had achieved lay with Bufton, and hoped Harris would invite Bufton to his Headquarters to talk about such matters.[31]

The opening of Harris's reply to Portal on the 14th showed his irritation and was less than helpful: 'It has frequently been obvious to me that I am often unable to make myself either clear or even understood when discussing such matters with you.' He went on to defend his original view that the formation of the PFF had been premature, and to assert that its institution as an entirety had not proved either the right or best solution; the better way, he was still sure, had been and still was to form a Pathfinder element in each Group, and for increasingly important tactical reasons he now wanted to go down this route, starting with 5 Group. Then Harris switched to Bufton:

I am astonished that you should ever have misunderstood me to infer that the 'credit' for the formation of the PFF does not belong to Bufton ... my complaint ... is that his ideas on Pathfinders, as on some other matters, have always been and still are rammed down our throats whether we like them or not. I have personally considerable regard for his ability and honesty of purpose and have time and again stressed ... that he should come and discuss things with me and regard himself as a welcome critic here and a Bomber

Command agent in the Air Ministry in addition to being your personal Bomber Operations Staff Officer, rather than as a sort of shadow C-in-C of the Bomber Offensive. In practice he has been a thorn in our side and the personification of all that is un-understanding and unhelpful in our relations with the Air Staff ... his name has become anathema to me and my senior staff.

Concluding, Harris made it clear he did not dislike Bufton; it was his methods he could not stand, and if Bufton would rid himself of his *idée fixe* that he could have the fun of running the bomber offensive his way while the C-in-C took the responsibility, it should be possible to put relations on a proper footing.[32]

Portal can have taken little pleasure from this. Clearly his own Bomber Operations staff were still at loggerheads with Harris, a highly unsatisfactory situation, but if the thought of moving Bufton occurred to him it was quickly rejected: Bufton's skill and experience were far too valuable to him in the Air Ministry. So Portal – not for the first or the last time – had to pour oil on troubled waters. His reply on the 16th was exemplary. Having picked out those of Bufton's qualities that Harris had commended, he sought to secure Harris's agreement to the real point at issue, *ie* the methods Bufton should use. First he should keep in touch with the Command's needs, thought and practice, through contacts at different staff and command levels; second he should use his knowledge to help the Command both in the Air Ministry and elsewhere; and third, he should advise Portal himself in relation to his own higher responsibilities for the bomber offensive. To these ends, Portal concluded, Bufton and Harris should be able to meet and work together.[33]

Two days later Harris sent his reply, accepting Portal's statement of Bufton's functions with a firm proviso: he must accept that he could not carry them out unless he collaborated closely with Command Headquarters and avoided pressing his own theories on its organisation, operations and requirements without prior consultation on their merits. In other words, Harris was not prepared to allow himself and his senior staff to be short-circuited as had happened in the past[34] – a perfectly reasonable position to take. Here this particular correspondence ended and relations eased for a while, though Bufton never visited Harris and the tensions later returned.

The Bufton issue was not the only one to surface at this moment, for another, even more serious, arose from Harris's letter to VCAS of 7 April about the implications of the increasingly strong enemy defences. In this he had also accused the Air Ministry of 'defensive mindedness' in not being prepared to risk the later marks of airborne interception radar falling into enemy hands, and gone on to accuse the Air Staff of never giving Bomber Command proper priority in aircraft, men and equipment. Portal, to whom this letter had been shown, took grave exception to these remarks and wrote to Harris on the 12th (the same day that he wrote about Bufton) picking up these two points. 'It seems to me that your habit of throwing blame wherever possible on higher authority has entirely defeated your sense of logic,' he said about the first. The second, he commented, was utterly untrue. 'I only ask you to display towards the Air Ministry, and towards me, the same loyalty in these matters which you no doubt expect from your own subordinates when you have to disappoint them.' Harris's only proper course, he concluded, was to re-issue his letter with the offending paragraphs removed.

On the 15th (doubtless fired up by his reply about Bufton on the 14th) Harris responded to what he considered a charge of disloyalty. He would not recognise 'loyalty to the Air Ministry' if that meant accepting without question rulings and methods which he judged inimical to the efficient discharge of his responsibilities. As for Portal himself, Harris concluded:

> You infer that I am lacking in loyalty to you personally. That is untrue. For twenty years and more you have had no more loyal supporter than I. But I do not regard loyalty as in any way involving an automatic or unquestioning acceptance of your ideas and still less the ideas or rulings of every or any junior officer on your staff. If in these circumstances you have no confidence in my loyalty I must ask you to relieve me of the onerous duties of my Command at the earliest opportunity which serves the interests of the country.

So now Portal had to face the ultimate challenge. Despite having rejected Freeman's suggestion in July 1943 that Harris's name be considered for command of the Allied Expeditionary Air Force,[35] he had continued to wonder if he was right to keep him at Bomber Command. Indeed, as Denis Richards records, Portal had actually asked for Bufton's opinion about this after the Schweinfurt episode and been advised against making any change; whatever their differences Bufton recognised the quality and value of Harris's leadership.[36] Irritating though his subordinate might be, Portal had no real doubt that Harris must stay put. Not only had he built up his Command and directed it through two years of increasingly important operations but he had become one of the RAF's best known and most prestigious commanders and was at this moment joining the command team for the Normandy invasion. In no way would Portal be able to justify to Churchill a proposal to move him, even if he wanted to – and, of course, Harris knew it.

Portal's answer, like the other he wrote on the 16th, therefore had to be emollient: 'I have always valued your loyalty to me in the sense in which you use the word, and it is not in question now,' he wrote. Harris should certainly go on arguing his case cogently and forcefully, but how much better it would be if the relations between the Air Ministry and Bomber Command were similar to those with the other Commands – who were just as ready to argue for their needs but did it differently. This would not come about, however, unless Harris really tried to see the Air Ministry point of view and 'to refrain from unfair and unnecessarily offensive criticism'. Replying on the 17th Harris agreed to amend his original letter but would not give way to the extent of accepting that other Commands should be treated equally. Bomber Command had been in direct action throughout the war, he stressed, it was still the milch cow, and he resented the sacrifices it was called on to make in order to meet others' needs. Nevertheless, he assured Portal, he did not enjoy these repeated controversies and would be greatly relieved if a more helpful attitude throughout the Air Ministry rendered them unnecessary in future. Of late there had been 'many and welcome signs of improvement in that respect' – a closing comment which Portal was 'extremely glad' to note.[37]

These had been a difficult few days, reflecting in part the extent to which the policies of Bomber Command and the Air Ministry for the strategic bombing offensive had increasingly drawn apart over the long winter months, and also highlighting critical differences of view about the working relationships that should exist between the Air Ministry and Bomber Command staffs. Harris's own convictions were clear. As Commander-in-Chief he was responsible for the efficiency of his Command, for ordering its operations and ensuring their success – and for its failures; it was for the Air Ministry to give him his broad directives and supply the wherewithal but not to tell him how to do his job. Unfortunately the wider 'political' dimension in which the Air Ministry had to live and work was not his scene, as it was Portal's, and he was disinclined to take proper account of it. Yet in many ways it was this single-minded, even blinkered approach that helped make him such a good C-in-C and one of Portal's great achievements was his success in handling his powerful subordinate and keeping him – more or less – in check.

Their relationship would be tested still further towards the end of the year, but right now Harris and his Command were going to work for a different master, General Dwight D. Eisenhower.

Notes

1. Folder H67, E188; OH vol.II, pp.12–15, 91; OH vol.IV, pp.153–4. Harris, *op.cit.* p.144, wrongly states that at Casablanca the subject of morale was dropped.
2. Richards, *The Hardest Victory*, pp.183–4; Folders H82, dated 17 March 1943; H67, dated 12 May 1943; H50, dated 22 May 1943.

3. Harris himself disliked this term and told Bennett so on 13 February 1945 (Folder H70); it gave a false impression of the aircraft's bomb-load and the serious effects of its raids on the enemy.

4. OH vol.II, pp.97–8, 108, 110.

5. Folders H82, dated 7 and 13 March and 15 May 1943; H65, dated 8 May 1943; H50, dated 29 June and 10 July 1943; OH vol.II, p.25; Richards, *The Hardest Victory*, p.173.

6. Letter from Sir Charles Elworthy, CAS, to Harris, dated 9 November 1965, CAS Folder, AHB; Morpurgo, *Barnes Wallis*, pp.241–9; Saward, *op.cit.* pp.198–9.

7. Morpurgo, *op.cit.* p.273. See Sweetman's *Operation Chastise* for a full account.

8. Folders H49, dated 3 June 1943; H59, dated 2 and 4 June, 17 September and 1 October 1943; OH vol.II, p.179.

9. AIR 20/5323; Folder H82, dated 11 July 1943; Portal Folder 4, dated 13, 14 and 16 July 1943; Gilbert, *Road to Victory*, pp.455–6; AHB Narrative vol.V, p.93; Howard, *Grand Strategy*, vol.4, pp.520–1.

10. Folder H47, E57; OH vol.II, pp.23–4, 27–30; OH vol.IV, pp.155–60, 273–84.

11. Folder H50, E44; Overy, *Bomber Command 1939–45*, p.69.

12. Folder H47, dated 25 July 1943; OH vol.II, pp.62–3. Bufton was now Director of Bomber Operations.

13. Folder H47, dated 20 December 1943; OH vol.II, pp.64–70. See also Harris, *op.cit.* pp.220–4.

14. OH vol.II, p.97.

15. Folders H82, dated 15 March, 26 and 29 April, and 27 and 28 May 1943; H67, dated 4 and 15 June 1943; Terraine, *op.cit.* p.471.

16. See Cumming, *The Starkey Sacrifice*, for a full account of this affair.

17. RAFHS, vol.5, pp.11, 22.

18. OH vol.II, pp.154–5. Many accounts have been written of these attacks. The most comprehensive is Martin Middlebrook's, which rather undervalues the success achieved.

19. In essence this was a timed run using the latest wind information from a known position to the weapon release point. For fuller detail see Gordon Musgrove's *Pathfinder Force*, appendix IV.

20. This master of ceremonies (the term 'master bomber' was used later) was the then Group Captain John Searby, a Pathfinder. In the early 1980s, Searby advised Frank Wootton on the painting of the Peenemunde raid which now hangs in the RAF Club.

21. Middlebrook, *The Peenemunde Raid*. See also Harris, *op.cit.* pp.181–4; Richards, *The Hardest Victory*, pp.197–201; Hinsley, *Official History of Intelligence*, p.421.

22. OH vol.II, p.31.

23. Folders H47, E71; H65, E47, 48.

24. Middlebrook, *The Berlin Raids*; Harris, *op.cit.* pp.186–8; Richards, *The Hardest Victory*, pp.208–18.

25. Folder H65, E52; Harris, *op.cit.* p.78. See also Hinsley, *op.cit.* p.407, which mentions ULTRA decrypts of messages from the Japanese Ambassador in Germany as one of the sources.

26. Middlebrook, *The Nuremberg Raid*.

27. *Ibid* p.287; OH vol.II, p.209.

28. Letter to author (as Head of AHB) 9 November 1979, asking me to reply on his behalf to a schoolboy who had written to him for help with a school project on Nuremberg; Harris

felt that the boy deserved all possible help and encouragement but was sorry that he wanted to specialise on this particular subject.

29. OH vol.II, p.193; AIR 24/272; Terraine, *op.cit.* p.557; Richards, *The Hardest Victory*, p.219; Saward, *op.cit.* pp.221, 238; Middlebrook, *op.cit.* p.325; Johnson, *op.cit.* p.203; Neillands, *op.cit.* p.293. Harris, in his own book (p.191), says that in April his Command had the measure of the enemy's defences and had him at its mercy, which does not quite accord with his letter of 7 April.

30. Russian Archives, quoted by Bergander, *op.cit.* p.293.

31. Folder H83, E26. Saward, *op.cit.* pp240–1, reproduces this letter.

32. Folder H83, E28. Saward, *op.cit.* pp.241–3, has a fuller summary of this letter, including the tactical reasons referred to.

33. Folder H83, E29. Saward, *op.cit.* pp.243–4, has the full text. Tedder, *op.cit.* p.509, called Bufton 'an habitual non-conformist'.

34. Folder H83, E30; Saward, *op.cit.* p.244.

35. Portal Papers, quoted by Furse, *op.cit.* p.271. Freeman, although now working in the MAP, was still consulted by Portal on very senior RAF appointments.

36. Richards, *Portal of Hungerford*, p.314.

37. Folder H98 and Portal Papers Folder 11 contain all these letters except for Harris's of 7 April, which (in amended form) is in AIR 24/272. Saward makes no reference to them.

Above: Harris in his office with his Personal Secretary, Flight Officer Peggy Wherry.

Below: Harris with his most senior staff officers, Air Vice-Marshals Graham and Saundby.

Above: Harris with his naval staff, Captain de Mowbray (left) and Lieutenant Commander Haxworth.

Left: Harris, with Jill and General Anderson, outside his office, greeting Air Chief Commandant K. J. Trefusis-Forbes, Director of the WAAF (far left), and Group Officer L. M. Crowther, 1943.

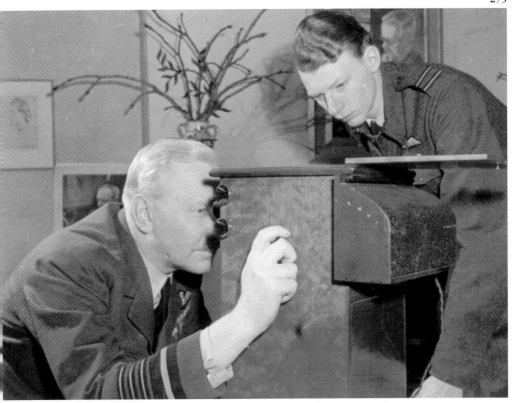

Above: At home Harris's PA, Flight Lieutenant Etienne Maze, assists him at the Stereopticon.

Below: Just occasionally Harris got out and about: at HQ 4 Group he is introduced to members of the staff by the AOC, Air Vice-Marshal Carr, and by Group Captain John Whitley.

Bomber Night 1944 at HQ USAAF VIII Bomber Command, High Wycombe: Harris and Portal are welcomed by Generals Spaatz, Anderson and Eaker.

Opposite page, bottom: The Commander-in-Chief's residence, Springfield.

Below: The family in the garden.

Left: 'Dadn' and 'Jacan'.

Below left: Exhaustion.

Right: Harris is invested by the President of the Polish Republic with the Grand Order of Polonia Restituta, June 1945.

Below: Soon afterwards Harris represents the United Kingdom at the Oslo Victory Parade in the presence of King Haakon.

Left: Harris is entertained in Washington by General Arnold, accompanied by Field Marshal Sir Henry Maitland Wilson, Mr Robert Lovett and Air Vice-Marshal Douglas Colyer, August 1945.

Left: In September Harris and his family land at Eastleigh, Kenya, on their way to South Africa.

Above: Harris is awarded the Freedom of High Wycombe, conferred on him by the Mayor, Councillor C. W. Lance, February 1946, with Air Chief Marshal Sir Norman Bottomley among those present.

Right: Harris is welcomed in Montreal by Air Vice-Marshal 'Black' McEwen, April 1947.

Above: The first of Harris's ships, SS *Constantia*, at Cape Town.

Below: A light-hearted interlude with Henry Mercer (far right) at the Springlake Bathing and Tennis Club, USA, September 1949.

Right: Harris and Jill, dressed for the Coronation of Her Majesty Queen Elizabeth II, 1953.

Opposite page, top: The Ferry House, Goring-on-Thames.

Above: Harris drives the coach *Perseverance* through the streets of Oxford towards Woodstock.

Left: Harris joins many other Anglo-American leaders of the Second World War at a special dinner at the United States Embassy in honour of President Eisenhower, 1959. The President sits at the far side of the table, centre, flanked by Portal and Alexander on the left and Alanbrooke and Ismay on the right. On the near side, Harris sits at the extreme left, with Tedder, Macmillan, the U.S. Ambassador, Churchill and Montgomery to his right.

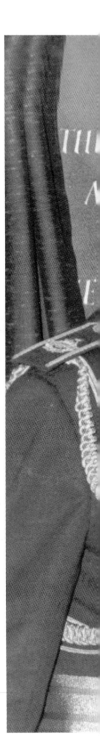

Left: Harris and Winston Churchill (junior) meet at the RAF Museum on the occasion of the arrival of a damaged Halifax bomber to join the Bomber Command collection, 1981.

Bottom left: Harris and Ira Eaker deep in conversation at Grosvenor House.

Below: Her Majesty Queen Elizabeth the Queen Mother meets Harris at the opening of the Bomber Command Museum, April 1983.

Above: Harris and Jill are lunched informally by some of Harris's 'old lags' at The Crown, a local inn near Streatley. Inset is Danny Boon, who took the main photograph.

Left: Harris and Jill at home.

Left: The Memorial Flight Lancaster pays the farewell tribute at Harris's funeral near Goring-on-Thames, 1984.

Chapter 14

Working for Eisenhower

Ever since Casablanca the intention to invade North-West Europe in the summer of 1944 had been built into the Allied planning, and as the strategic bombing offensive mounted during 1943 it became generally recognised as an essential pre-requisite for the success of the invasion – not as a war-winning campaign on its own. Harris, however, was not persuaded. Were he to be given the proper priority for resources, he remained convinced that the British and American heavy bombers ought to be able to compel the enemy's surrender without the need for a high-risk and very costly land campaign in the West. He continued to press his case in his minute to Churchill of 3 November (see pp.249 and 263), at which point Portal himself was still keeping his options open in relation to what the bombers might yet achieve, and on 7 December Harris made his final attempt to convince the sceptics. Setting out to the Air Ministry his assessment of the destruction so far caused in Germany and the critical role of his Lancasters, he argued that immediate concentration on Lancaster production – coupled with improved countermeasures and radio aids – could still enable his Command to force Germany to surrender by 1 April 1944.[1]

Not surprisingly this plea cut little ice in Whitehall and from now on the central issue was how Harris and his Command could best contribute to the success of the invasion and the subsequent land campaign. So on 23 December Portal asked Harris to get in touch with Air Chief Marshal Leigh-Mallory, who had been appointed to command the Allied Expeditionary Air Force (AEAF), in order to plan for the employment of the heavy bombers. Harris, replying on the 27th and accepting the broad commitment, sought assurance on two points. First, he assumed that the general Casablanca injunction for the Combined Bomber Offensive would still hold good, not least since the German fighter force would otherwise be free to concentrate on opposing Overlord; and second, he insisted that any tactical bombing in immediate preparation for the operation would be practicable only if the weather was right.[2]

Soon afterwards, on 13 January 1944, Harris set out his stall in more detail on the basis that 'Overlord must now presumably be regarded as an inescapable commitment.' Stressing the specialised nature of his force he reiterated in no uncertain terms that it could operate only by night in suitable weather conditions and with the aid of some kind of pathfinding technique. Planned scheduling of operations to assist the land forces would not work, the destruction of gun emplacements could not be guaranteed, and his bombers were not suitable for cutting railway communications at critical points. Moreover the cessation of strategic bombing would release enemy resources of many kinds and if it lasted as much as six months would enable a marked recovery in Germany. So, he concluded, the best and only efficient support Bomber Command could provide would be intensified attacks on German industry whenever possible. The alternative, while giving a specious appearance of supporting the Army, would in reality do them the gravest disservice and lead directly to disaster. This lengthy note, circulated among others to Portal, Leigh-Mallory and Montgomery (who had just visited Harris and got on well with him), was received with a generous pinch of salt, and not least by Portal. On 30 January he made it clear that Bomber Command must undertake such tasks as Eisenhower and the Combined Chiefs might decide – after consultation – and to that end must be ready to try out new techniques and tactics.[3]

Eisenhower had been appointed Supreme Commander for Overlord in December 1943 and been joined soon afterwards by Tedder as his Deputy. There followed complex discussions in London and Washington about the top command structure, including Tedder's role in relation to the various air forces involved; while Leigh-Mallory had already taken over the tactical air forces, the status and wider roles of the American and British heavy bomber forces and of their prestigious commanders made it unacceptable to allot them too to the AEAF. Yet their participation in the Overlord operations was considered essential and Eisenhower was insistent that he must have the right to commission their support whenever necessary. The answer, as perceived and strongly argued by Churchill in the face of widespread opposition, including that of the Chiefs of Staff, was to place the Eighth Air Force and Bomber Command – as well as the AEAF – under Tedder. As the Prime Minister put it, Spaatz could take his orders from Eisenhower and there would be no difficulty 'in arranging between Tedder and Harris'. The eventual agreement that the Supreme Commander should be empowered to 'direct' all the air forces he needed was reached on 23 March, and on 14 April, when the new command structure came into being, Harris became answerable, through Tedder, to Eisenhower.[4]

Already Tedder had been busy, and not least on Leigh-Mallory's plan for the interdiction of the enemy's railway communications in France on the run-up to the Normandy landings. Committee-level discussions on this had been getting nowhere in relation to the participation of the heavy bombers without which the plan could not succeed, so at the end of February Tedder persuaded Eisenhower to back him in the attempt to force the hands of the two bomber commanders. A few days later he and Portal received a letter from Harris still pleading the cause of the strategic offensive. 'Any serious reduction of our rate of striking at German production,' it said, 'will inevitably make possible industrial recovery which would, within quite a short period, nullify the results achieved by tremendous efforts during the past 12 months.' At this very moment, however, Portal had decided to put to the test Harris's protestations about the limitations of his bombers. On 4 March orders were issued to attack six French marshalling yards and other targets by night, and over the next three weeks all the yards were bombed – with great success.[5] The lessons were clear. Against such targets Bomber Command could do far better than its commander had predicted, which indicated that it might well be as gainfully employed in direct support of Overlord as in the continued bombing of Germany.

These implications still did not divert Harris from his conviction that the strategic bombers' proper contribution to the success of Overlord was – with only the minimum essential diversions – to continue the assault on Germany's material power, with the German air force the first priority. Therefore, just before a critical meeting to consider the nature of the Allied air campaign in advance of the actual invasion, he set out his views to Portal, asking for a directive giving him full discretion on which German targets he should attack on any particular night. Almost as an afterthought he stated that the Stirlings and some of the Halifaxes could handle the non-German targets in the preparatory period, implying that the Lancasters would remain committed to their normal roles.[6] At the meeting itself, on 25 March (five days before Nuremberg), it quickly became clear that he would have to come into line. Chaired by Portal and attended, among others, by Eisenhower, Tedder, Spaatz and Leigh-Mallory, the meeting was largely devoted to the transportation plan devised by Tedder, Leigh-Mallory and Professor Zuckermann (Tedder's former scientific adviser in Italy). Despite the strong opposition of both Harris and Spaatz, who was firmly championing the attack on oil, it was eventually agreed to submit this plan, centred on the bombing of some 74 key rail centres in France and Belgium, to Churchill and his colleagues, while drawing attention to the risk of causing heavy casualties among the local civilian population. It was during these discussions that Leigh-Mallory is reputed to have expressed his reluctance to go down to posterity as the man who killed thousands of Frenchman, whereupon Harris growled: 'What makes you think you're going to go down to posterity at all?'[7]

Harris's private thoughts at this juncture were reflected in a personal letter to Lovett, in Washington, a few days later. 'Our worst headache has been a panacea plan devised by a civilian professor [*ie* Zuckermann] whose peacetime forte is the study of the sexual aberrations of the higher apes. Starting from this sound military basis he devised a scheme to employ almost the entire British and US bomber forces for three months or more in the destruction of targets mainly in France and Belgium.' Thankfully, Harris went on, the worst features of the programme had now been taken out and the strategic air forces would still be able to perform their proper functions, though even in modified form the plan might cost 200,000 lives (sic). Fortunately, he added, Tedder had 'entirely sound views about the importance of strategic bombing and would not agree to its abandonment in favour of slogan and panacea warfare.'[8]

Thanks particularly to the anxieties of Churchill and others about civilian casualties, which Harris shared, it took some while for Eisenhower and Tedder to obtain the top-level agreement they needed. By 15 April, however, Harris was under their direction and Tedder – armed with the evidence of Bomber Command's March attacks, together with a series of small-scale night precision raids previously carried out against French targets by 5 Group Lancasters – was able to give Harris his 37 railway targets. The rest were allotted to the Eighth Air Force and the AEAF. Two days later Tedder issued the strategic air forces with their new directive (drafted for him by Bottomley). This stated the overall mission as the progressive destruction and dislocation of the German military, industrial and economic system and (significantly) the destruction of vital elements of lines of communication. In the subsequent specific instructions to Bomber Command Harris's main aim was stated as the disorganising of German industry and his operations were to complement those of the Americans in reducing the Luftwaffe and disrupting rail communications.[9] Thus, while the continued offensive against Germany retained pride of place within his terms of reference, he was also required to tackle communications targets in order to assist the Allied Armies in what was described as 'the supreme operation for 1944'.

So Harris had his orders. However vigorously he might have opposed the transportation plan and doubted the ability of his bombers to achieve the extraordinary precision needed, that was now in the past. There was a job to be done and he would spare nothing in the attempt to do it properly. The first attack on the marshalling yards, at Juvisy, was launched the next night (18/19 April) and on the 20th Bottomley told him how well the Defence Committee had received Portal's report of the 'extraordinary measures' taken, including the special marking technique employed to ensure accuracy. The Prime Minister, he added, was greatly relieved to know of the care being taken to avoid heavy civilian casualties. And thus it continued, with some 60 attacks up to D-Day leading to two-thirds of the 37 targets being put out of action for at least a month and at a cost well below the 10,000 civilian casualties that Portal had hoped not to exceed. Unknown to Harris, Zuckermann later wrote in his diary: 'The amazing thing is that Harris, who was even more resistant than the Americans to the idea of AEAF domination, has in fact thrown himself whole-heartedly into the battle, has improved his bombing performance enormously, and has contributed more to the dislocation of enemy communications, etc, than any of the rest.'[10] Zuckermann's 'etc' was important too, for a variety of other 'tactical' targets were also most successfully bombed during the run-up to the landings.

While all this was happening Harris was drawn increasingly into the high-level decision making. On 2 May Eisenhower invited him and Spaatz to attend the weekly Commanders-in-Chief meetings to discuss Overlord problems, and in accepting Harris arranged for Air Vice-Marshal Oxland – his representative on all strategic and tactical bombing specifically connected with Overlord – to accompany him. From June onwards these conferences became almost daily events. While occasionally Saundby stood in for him, Harris himself attended 76 of them between 23 May and 31 August, often travelling in his Auster from the airstrip at Lacey Green, not far from the Headquarters. Just after the first of these Eisenhower came to spend a night at Springfield and was most impressed by the evidence of the photograph albums. 'I would feel derelict in my duty,' he wrote on the 25th, 'if I did not tell you ... of the appreciation and gratitude which I and all of us hold for the contribution of Bomber Command toward eventual victory. Now, by combining the efforts of air, sea and ground forces, I hope we can capitalise on the work already done and press on soon to bring the Hun to his knees – and keep him there.' These were sentiments which Harris immediately applauded. He and his new boss were firmly 'on net'.[11]

Harris was on good terms too with Montgomery, as shown when he addressed a meeting at Headquarters 21 Army Group on 15 May. Never one to miss an opportunity, he told his audience what the strategic offensive had so far achieved and that the question now was whether and to what extent they wished the enemy's weapons to be struck out of his hand before he could use them, or whether they would have to wrest them from him in direct combat. A dividing line therefore had to be drawn within Bomber Command's total resources between strategic bombing and direct tactical assistance in emergencies. 'It can be stated without fear of contradiction,' he went on, 'that the heavy bomber is a first-class strategic weapon and one of the least effective tactical weapons.' Whether his listeners agreed with him is not recorded but he was certainly on firm ground with them when he outlined his Command's achievements thus far in the transportation plan and the many other roles it would be playing in support of the landing operations.[12]

The great variety of operations Harris and his men were now being called on to undertake marked a major turning point in Bomber Command's war. No more – at least for the present – were they concentrating mainly on large-scale attacks on relatively distant area targets. Instead they were often being required to divide their forces so as to tackle simultaneously objectives of many different types, such as railways, aircraft factories, airfields, military depots and coastal batteries. Such operations, usually at fairly short range, called for new, specialised skills and equipment, and to Harris it made good sense to encourage his Groups to operate independently on occasion and to that end develop their own precision marking and bombing methods. In effect he was at last going down the route he had been keen to pursue two years earlier when the PFF had been formed. Then it had been almost certainly right to concentrate the expertise and Bennett's men had done much to ensure the success of Harris's 1943 offensive. Now it was different. Ever since the Dams raid, Cochrane's 5 Group, strongly encouraged by Harris, had been showing the way in the independent use of small numbers of heavy bombers against precise targets, and in 1944 its efforts were to be amply rewarded.

It was on 6 April, immediately after an extremely successful attack on an aircraft factory at Toulouse led by Wing Commander Leonard Cheshire, who marked the target at low level in his Mosquito, that Harris told Cochrane that 5 Group was to be employed as a separate force and ordered the attachment to him of three Pathfinder squadrons (see p.267). Bennett was not a happy man. He had just asked the C-in-C to protect him from the waste of effort involved in sending personnel on 'the eternal and ever-increasing number of courses they were required to attend' and been firmly put in his place.[13] Now, to make matters much worse, his monopoly of pathfinding itself was under threat and on 30 April he lodged his first protest, though at this stage only in terms of the competition between the PFF and 5 Group for specialised equipment and stores. A fortnight later Cochrane reported to Harris on the great improvement in his Group's bombing resulting from the Mosquitos' low-level marking and attributed recent successes largely to the three PFF squadrons. Harris's reply was suitably encouraging: no doubt the crews deserved much of the credit, he commented, but 'an equal share in their success is due to those who, under your direction, have not been content with things as they are but have given a great deal of time and trouble to thinking out new ideas and new tactics.'[14]

Soon afterwards arrived another letter from Bennett, complaining about the loss of his squadrons and its adverse effect on morale, alleging that they were not operating effectively in 5 Group, criticising Cochrane's means of getting his own way, and requesting the squadrons back. As Harris already knew, these two strong personalities (he considered them, said Tomlinson, the most ruthless men in the RAF) did not hit it off, but he needed them both and was quick to talk to Bennett and try to placate him; there was still much for the PFF to do. As for Cochrane, Harris had no doubts whatsoever. On 23 June Portal asked for him to join his staff as ACAS (Pol), where he needed a really first-class man for post-war planning, but Harris was immovable. Describing Cochrane as 'the best operational commander we have today' his reply concluded:

> I should have thought and hoped that Cochrane would have had a very high Command in the Japanese war if not in this one before it is finished. I had personally envisaged him as the obvious relief for me. I hope therefore you will reconsider the proposition, particularly because I am quite certain it would have a very adverse effect on the conduct of the war at this present juncture.

Portal backed off – for the moment – and at the same time Harris, asked by Cochrane to adjudicate on whether Bennett's squadrons should be returned (Bennett had been to see Cochrane about it), stated quite simply: 'I have no intention of returning these squadrons to the Pathfinder Group for the present or as far as I can see for an indefinite period, if at all.' The way was clear for Cochrane to continue his experiments on new techniques so that his 5 Group attacks could continue on the longer nights, and in due course Harris would also give Harrison's 3 Group a specialised role, this time in blind bombing with the use of GH (see p.232).[15]

By now the Normandy campaign was well under way. Later Harris would say it had been obvious to him that the heavy bomber offered the only conceivable means of breaching the Atlantic Wall, a statement that hardly accorded with his previous and clearly stated reservations. Nevertheless his bombers certainly made major contributions, using maximum effort against coastal gun batteries, laying mines and carrying out deception operations on D-Day itself, and continuing afterwards with heavy attacks on railway and other targets as required by SHAEF. Within days, however, irritated at receiving Air Ministry advice on targeting, he curtly told ACAS (Ops) to address such correspondence to SHAEF. Then on 13 June he reminded Bottomley that requests for him to resume strategic attacks, specifically against oil production, should properly be submitted through Tedder. Now that Harris was working for SHAEF in no way was he going to allow the Air Staff to breathe down his neck. Yet on 20 July he felt impelled to protest again, this time to Evill, about continued attempts to instruct him about targets and priorities. As Eisenhower had confirmed, he wrote, the only proper way for him to receive operational orders was through Tedder, to whom he copied his letter. Evill took his point and from then on 'the proper channels' were observed. When Tedder later wrote that Harris co-operated most loyally, this was doubtless one of the aspects he had in mind – though he did add that Harris was at times irritated by delays in receiving targets.[16]

Much more annoying and frustrating was a new diversion that Harris was forced to accept. A week after D-Day the enemy launched their V1 flying bomb campaign against London and Eisenhower quickly agreed that operations against the launching sites and depots should become second in priority to direct support of his land forces. All his air forces were accordingly directed to contribute to Operation Crossbow, and for the next two months Harris devoted 40% of his effort to the task. He was not particularly happy about it. In his opinion to switch major resources to defensive measures was to play into enemy hands. He made his views clear on 11 July when forwarding to Bottomley a letter from Addison at 100 Group protesting against the recent transfer of his two AI-equipped Mosquito squadrons to ADGB (Air Defence of Great Britain) for defence against the V1. These aircraft, specially equipped and trained for bomber support operations, were exactly what Harris had long been pressing for and he despairingly told Bottomley: 'I do not regard the shooting down of a few flying bombs as any fair exchange for the deprivation of my hard-pressed and hopelessly under-armed bombers of their miserable ration of night fighter support and nothing that can be said on that subject is likely to convert me.'[17]

Then on the 18th he reported to Tedder and to Duncan Sandys, Chairman of the government's Crossbow Committee, on the effectiveness so far of his attacks on the flying bomb and rocket sites. He had no doubt about the need to bomb the V1 supply sites and the V2 launching sites – against the latter the new 5-ton Tallboy bombs were proving particularly valuable – but against the other types of target his bombing was having little worthwhile effect. It was merely a major diversion, which, coupled with the attack on invasion targets, had taken nearly all his Command's efforts away from Germany for three and a half months and largely negated most of its last three years' efforts. He was therefore opposed to most forms of defensive bombing and wanted Bomber Command and the American heavy bombers to resume their assault on Germany's resources and facilities in a combined and concentrated offensive. The longer the return to this campaign was delayed, he concluded, the more difficult and more costly it would become. Harris also copied his paper to Eisenhower with a covering letter reiterating his convictions, and on the 27th the Supreme Commander wrote back.

> I hope I have never left any doubt as to my desire to return all the Strategic Air Forces to the Bombing of Germany to the greatest possible extent and at the earliest possible moment . . . Of course we always have the emergencies of the battle front and, most of all, the necessity of beating down CROSSBOW. If at any time you believe that we are uselessly neglecting opportunities for striking the German in his own country, do not hesitate to tell me about it. I am quite sure that you, Tedder and I are all in complete agreement as to the

overall requirements. The only possible question could be the very occasional ones of immediate priority.

Here was the supportive, understanding, balanced view, simply stated by a man for whom Harris already had the greatest respect. The C-in-C could ask for no more and, whatever his personal misgivings, would continue to give his superior all the help he needed.[18]

Eisenhower already had good reason to appreciate Bomber Command's direct support in the Battle of Normandy. Its biggest commitment was the continuing attack on enemy communications; there were fuel and ammunition dumps to deal with; there were enemy Channel ports such as Le Havre and Boulogne – Harris's first large-scale daylight attacks; and there was close battlefield support, a role he had never considered suitable for his heavy bombers. Denis Richards summarises the eight occasions on which they joined in, including two when over a thousand RAF bombers, together with many other aircraft, took part. The most remembered has always been the attack on Caen on the evening of 7 July, delivered at Montgomery's request in order to prepare the way for the capture of the city. Harris's crews did what the Army had requested. The bombing greatly impressed the soldiery and enormous destruction was caused in the city, but the troops did not follow up soon enough and when they did found the roads made virtually impassable by rubble. The bombing was certainly spectacular but not what the Army actually required. Yet at the time Montgomery himself was full of admiration, signalling the thanks of the Allied armies to Harris and his Command for their magnificent co-operation. 'We know well that your main work lies further afield and we applaud your bombing of German war industries and the effect this has on the German war effort, but we also know well that you are always ready ... to co-operate in our tactical battle. When you do this your action is always decisive.'[19] Like Harris, Montgomery could go over the top on occasion, but his sentiments were certainly appreciated.

Harris also welcomed a tribute from Major General Crawford, of the War Office, who watched from the ground the biggest attack of all, on 18 July in support of Operation Goodwood, and then flew in a Lancaster in another 'thousand' operation on 7/8 August to help the Canadian First Army open the way towards Falaise. He had been tremendously impressed by the skill and accuracy of these attacks. While the soldiers must beware of thinking that this terrific weapon could always be wielded on their behalf, Crawford had no doubt of the tremendous value of such operations to the Army; they were clear proof of the flexibility of the Air Arm. It had been a privilege to fly with one of Harris's aircrews and witness their skill, determination and team spirit – a real education for a soldier.[20]

Not always, however, did things go entirely according to plan. On 14

August, in Operation Tractable, Harris despatched 800 aircraft in daylight
to support a further Canadian attempt to close the Falaise Gap, and 77
bombed short, killing 65 soldiers, with many more wounded and missing.
Harris took this incident most seriously and having had it fully investigated
circulated a personal report on the 25th. He began by reminding his readers
that close, direct support was very different from the type of operations his
force had been trained for; he had consistently pointed out the risks entailed
and the Army had always accepted them in exchange for the decisive effects
of such bombing. He himself had studied the Army's request on the previous
evening and carefully considered the line of approach in the light of danger
to the ground troops and also to his own aircraft. He then described the
sequence of events and identified two principal causes of the errors: first,
failure to pay proper attention to the stipulated timed run from the coast;
and second, confusion between the yellow target indicators used by the
Pathfinders and similar ones used by the soldiers to indicate their own
positions to friendly aircraft. No blame, he believed, attached to the master
bombers – overall the attack had gone very well – or to those briefing for the
operation. Indeed AOC 6 Group ('Black' McEwen), some of whose Canadian
crews were involved, had gone out of his way to ensure that the time check
was properly emphasised. Had those concerned, however, made adequate
effort to maintain their time checks the errors would not have occurred and
their failure to do so was inexcusable.

Harris concluded his report with a series of precise instructions designed
to prevent any recurrence and in circulating it stated that the two PFF crews
involved had lost their badges and acting ranks, the squadron and flight
commanders had relinquished their commands and acting ranks, and all
crews had been 'starred' so as not to be employed for the present on further
such operations. This was a firm response. Regardless of whether he agreed
with his bombers being employed in this way Harris was doing his utmost to
ensure that they did their jobs properly and amid the heat of battle there was
no room for half measures. General Crerar, commanding the First Canadian
Army, one of the recipients of Harris's report, clearly agreed. 'I appreciate
the very thorough manner in which you have investigated these unfortunate
mistakes,' he wrote on the 29th. While the errors were highly regrettable,
the main bomber support was so accurate and valuable that it had contributed greatly to the success of his Army's breakthrough, and he remained
a strong advocate of the use of heavy bombers in closely integrated support
of the Army when attacking strong and co-ordinated enemy defences –
provided the target-marking and recognition procedures were compatible.[21]

Harris was much annoyed by another aspect of the Tractable affair. As he
wrote in his report, a sensational story had appeared in the press stating that
wholesale disaster had been averted only by some Army-controlled Austers

firing red verey lights over the area being mistakenly bombed. Their intervention, he observed, had merely added to the confusion and in any case ought not to have been made known outside Service circles. Indeed, the totally wrong implication was now abroad that the Austers had prevented the rest of the bomber force from committing the same mistake. 'I regard the emanation of these sensational and untrue accounts through officially controlled channels as deplorable.'

Deep down Harris's chief concern in the sphere of publicity continued to be the effects on his men's morale of either adverse reporting, as in Tractable, or the lack of any reporting at all. On the whole, as we saw in chapter 9, his Command's work in earlier years had been reasonably well represented, but once the invasion was under way it had become a different story and by the end of June his frustrations were clear. As he said to Evill on the 30th 'we can't keep the morale of our forces going when they open their papers every morning and see the wonderful things that the Army and Navy and the Yanks on the ground are doing when we know that we [ie the RAF] are doing two-thirds of the battling, and that our casualties are infinitely higher than anybody else's.' Next day Harris wrote to Portal, having discussed the subject with Douglas, Coningham, Leigh-Mallory and Hill at an AEAF meeting (Tedder was not there). They were agreed on 'the hopeless inadequacy of the publicity and of the official credit given to the Air Force for their part in this battle, which is in fact so far mainly an air battle'. After quoting his own Command's casualty figures and describing the significance of the overall air effort, he concluded:

> It is not possible for ever to maintain the morale of our first-class fighting crews [ie of all RAF Commands], who have put up such an amazing contribution in this operation, if they are to be denied continuously, as they have been so largely denied in the past, any tithe of recognition officially or publicly, of the vast and successful efforts they are making ... I have no personal ambition that has not years ago been satisfied in full. But I for one cannot forbear a most emphatic protest against the grave injustice that is being done to my crews.

Portal accepted there was much in what Harris was saying and hoped more could now be done through the Public Relations Staff. Meanwhile Harris had already touched on the subject in discussion with Churchill and sent him estimated casualty figures. These showed that over the three months of Overlord operations up to the end of June Bomber Command had probably lost 4,587 men killed, compared with 2,736 British and Canadian Army killed since 6 June and 4,868 American. 'I feel the RAF is not getting full acknowledgement of the brunt which it bears. If you have any opportunity for stressing their great contribution, most of which is given beyond the visual horizons of the ground forces and is largely outside the understanding of the public, it will be very good for the aircrews' morale.'[22]

While in July and August the work of his bombers did receive slightly more publicity Harris remained deeply disturbed. Trenchard too was far from happy. On 13 September he told Harris how appalled he was at the way people had forgotten the work and fighting entailed in winning air supremacy and the struggle still needed to maintain it; indeed he wondered if the true history would ever be properly written. In his prompt reply Harris laid the blame at the door of the Air Ministry's press relations organisation, described the absence of recognition of the Air Force contribution in North-West Europe as a disaster of the first magnitude, and illustrated his point by criticising the press handling of the capture of Le Havre on the previous day. The Army commanders, he said, were enthusiastic in their praise of the bombing, not least since it had kept down the soldiers' casualties to less than 400, yet even the *Daily Telegraph* – usually so sound on air power – was describing the experiment of using heavy bombers to prepare the way immediately ahead of the ground assault as only partially successful. As Harris wrote separately to Crerar, *The Times* was even worse, giving the entire credit for the Le Havre success to the ground forces and dismissing the bombing as a meaningless sideshow. 'What is going on in the press with regard to bomber support to your Army is arousing feelings of grave indignation and resentment among my crews and indeed in my Command generally and in me personally.' Harris's concluding words to Trenchard summed up his thoughts at this moment. 'Everything you have given the whole of your life for, and (I and many others feel) we have given ours for, is being either thrown overboard or allowed to go by default. I personally am in despair, and particularly in despair of any improvement.'[23]

There were other sources of anxiety too. One was the Warsaw Rising. For much of August the Polish Home Army had been fighting the Germans while the Russians passively watched, and Churchill had been trying his utmost to respond to the Poles' impassioned pleas for help. Slessor's bombers in Italy did what little they could and by the beginning of September the use of Bomber Command at greater range was being considered. On the 1st, Air Vice-Marshal Izycki, representing the Polish C-in-C in London, met the sympathetic Harris to plead their case, and the Poles followed up with a letter indicating the desperate urgency of the situation. Already, on the 3rd, Portal had discussed the matter with Churchill, and although the latter seemed persuaded that the operation was impracticable possible plans were considered for at least another ten days. Harris himself thought in terms of using 100 Lancasters to drop containers and return afterwards via Italy. The results, however, would in his view be infinitesimal and unlikely to influence the situation in Warsaw; less than 20% of the containers would reach the

Poles, he estimated, and losses would probably be 10–15%. Certainly he would have tried, if so ordered, but in his view it was simply not a realistic operation of war – though the Americans did actually make an attempt on the 12th.[24]

Nor was Harris without his staff worries. On 6 September, for example, he was furious when told that Oxland, his representative with Tedder, was wanted immediately by the Air Ministry as Chairman of the Permanent Commission Board. It was *absolutely impossible*, he wrote to Evill, for Oxland to be spared. With so much happening and communications between High Wycombe and SHAEF 'parlous in the extreme' Harris needed someone on the spot who understood the Army's organisation and habits, and on whose judgement and decision-making he could totally rely. Tedder gave him strong support. Yet the Air Council immediately tried again and this time Harris went over the top, expressing himself as flabbergasted at its persistence. Oxland's almost unique experience had made him ideal for his job; to pitchfork someone new into 'the maelstrom of action and disorganisation that exists at present over the other side and expect him to find his way about solving on the spot ad hoc problems fired continuously at him while keeping a correct balance between what is practical and what is not, is asking the impossible'. Harris's conclusion revealed him at his firmest and least compromising, and perhaps, too, the stress was showing:

> I really must ask to be relieved from further pressing of this preposterous demand. I am rapidly getting to the stage where the constant necessity to conduct protracted argument for bare essentials, in an atmosphere which I am coming to regard as almost invariably unhelpful where Air Ministry is concerned, is getting me down. I have a tremendous load to carry and there is a limit to additional straws. I protest, and with justification, that it is not right that I should be badgered and heckled to the extent I have been badgered on this subject with such persistence at a time when my Command is under twice and thrice the normal pressure of operational work in exceptionally difficult and complicated conditions. I really can't stand for it and, in my circumstances, neither would anyone.[25]

Despite all the immediate pressures Harris still found time to think about the future. As a case in point he wrote a thoughtful, far-sighted letter to AMP on 24 June expressing his anxieties about aircrews' low standards of discipline and behaviour on the ground; for the immediate future major measures would be difficult but after the war he wanted to see changes in commissioning procedure, proper training for potential officers and NCOs in their future duties and responsibilities, and the removal of pay anomalies. On 13 July he raised the subject of pensions, pointing out that some officers who had been commissioned before the war were going to be treated worse than some commissioned during it. On 11 September he took up the cudgels on behalf of unmarried WAAF personnel who became pregnant and were required to be immediately discharged; he thought it quite wrong for the Service to accept no official responsibility for their subsequent welfare.[26] On such matters – and there were many more – Harris was continuing to demonstrate his career-long concern for the well-being of those he commanded.

Nor did he ever forget those of his men who had fallen into enemy hands, one of them his own former PA, Peter Tomlinson. On 1 June he had told AMP how upset he was at officialdom's failure to tell him anything about the shooting of 50 prisoners-of-war who had escaped in March from Stalag Luft 3, many of whom must inevitably have been men from Bomber Command. The press had made much of the story but so far he knew nothing more.[27] The omission was quickly remedied and on 29 June Harris and his wife attended the moving service of tribute at St Martin in the Fields.

In September 1944 the Eisenhower period drew to its close. On 29 August, with France liberated, the Supreme Commander had written to his Cs-in-C setting out his intentions from then on. The future tasks of the American and British bomber forces were simply stated: 'In addition to carrying out their primary missions against strategic targets, they will always be prepared to support the effort of the Ground Forces.'[28] This critical change of emphasis returned the bombers' first priority to the strategic role, and it followed that the command chain needed revision. Accordingly on 14 September – while close contacts were to continue between their respective Headquarters – Harris ceased to answer to Eisenhower and reverted to the direction of Portal, who also took over with Arnold, on behalf of the Combined Chiefs of Staff, joint responsibility for co-ordinating the American and British heavy bomber operations.

For Harris this was in many ways a sad moment. At Eisenhower's express invitation he had on the 8th attended the special ceremony at the Arc de Triomphe to present a plaque of the SHAEF insignia to the City of Paris, and on the 21st he wrote to his former chief assuring him of Bomber Command's continuing commitment to his support. At the same time he thanked Eisenhower for his unvarying helpfulness, encouragement and support: 'It has been an honour, as indeed a delight, to serve under you through these historic weeks,' he went on. 'I hope also that you will realise the very great admiration, regard and indeed affection that we feel for you personally.'[29] Harris's letter crossed a similarly warm one from Eisenhower, but the latter's judgement was probably even better conveyed in a direct letter to General Marshall in Washington on the 25th.

> In view of earlier expressed fears that Harris would not willingly devote his Command to the support of ground operations, he actually proved to be one

of the most effective and co-operative members of this team. Not only did he meet every request I ever made upon him, but he actually took the lead in discovering new ways and means for his particular types of planes to be of use in the battlefield. He keeps his representative right here in my headquarters, and it is because of the perfection of our past association that I have no real fears for the future. When the great battle occurs for the real entry into Germany, he will be on the job.

Without doubt Tedder shared his master's views. On 14 June he had written in his diary: 'Harris co-operates magnificently', and later in his own book he recalled assuring Eisenhower that if Harris was ordered to carry out specific jobs he would do them loyally: 'My estimate of Bomber Command's work, and of its commander, proved correct.'[30] These judgements were openly recognised in October, when Harris heard that President Roosevelt had awarded him the Legion of Merit for his great services to the Allied cause during Operation Overlord.

Harris's own views on this period are reflected in what is written in his memoir. In 1946 he sent to John Lawrence, who was helping him, some extra text which he wanted incorporated, saying that it was *most* important. Most of this was included, albeit re-arranged, but two closing sentences were not. The analogy may be questionable, but as a good example of original Harris prose and an indication of how he felt deep down it deserves to be recorded here:

I was saddled personally, throughout my tenure of command, with the additional most wearying and exacting task – on top of my other sufficiently onerous duties – of attempting to keep a straining ship on something of a constant course through a sea so confused by every wind that could blow as to require the services of a Master of all Mariners, and a Hoogly pilot to boot, if progress in any recognisable direction and security against hazard were to be achieved. As the harassed mate of this sorely beset vessel, engaged mainly in keeping the sails filled and the rigging taut despite the galaxy of ever-changing captains and amateurs temporarily at the wheel, I recall only one period of calm sailing in those $3\frac{1}{2}$ bitter years – a veritable centre of the hurricane – when all went well, when all pulled together, when there was at last continuity of contact between the compass course required and the lubber line – and that was during the all too short period when Eisenhower was Admiral and Tedder the Captain on the bridge.[31]

Notes

1. OH vol.II, pp.51–8, reproduces this letter in full and appraises it.
2. Portal Papers, Folder 11; Folder H82; Saward, *op.cit.* p.234.
3. Folder H104; Richards, *Portal of Hungerford*, pp.315–16; OH vol.III, pp.24–7, discusses Harris's paper at length.

4. OH vol.III, pp.16–20.
5. Folder H83, dated 2 March 1944; OH vol.III, p.27; Richards, *The Hardest Victory*, p.226.
6. Folder H83, dated 24 March 1944.
7. Story told by Air Chief Marshal Sir Kenneth Cross, RAFHS, *Reaping the Whirlwind*, p.60.
8. Folder H28, dated 3 April 1944.
9. OH vol.III, pp.35–7; OH vol.IV, pp.167–70.
10. Harris, *op.cit.* p.197; Folder H47, dated 20 April 1944; Richards, *op.cit.* pp.227–8; Terraine, *op.cit.* p.623.
11. Folder H55; Saward, *op.cit.* p.254; Hodges conversation.
12. Folders H55; H106.
13. Folder H57, dated 31 March and 8 April 1944. Harris, always a believer in thorough training, told Bennett to think the subject through and stressed particularly the need to teach ordinary aircrew members to become competent leaders or instructors, and to enhance powers of command, leadership and administration in those who needed, but often lacked, such attributes.
14. Folders H57, dated 30 April 1944; H59, dated 15 and 25 May 1944.
15. Folders H57, dated 31 May 1944; H83, dated 23 and 27 June 1944; H59, dated 28 June and 3 July 1944; OH vol.III, p.172. Hastings, *op.cit.* pp.282–5, discusses these matters sympathetically, as does Morris (Cheshire's biographer), *op.cit.* pp.130, 134–6, 155–6, 166–7. According to an unconfirmed story (recounted by John Brown, 467 Squadron) Harris, concerned about his alleged favouritism of 5 Group, called a special senior commanders' meeting to try to convince them of his impartiality and restore harmony. Thinking his efforts successful he stood the first round of drinks in the bar and seeking a non-contentious topic for conversation seized on a current item of press speculation: 'I wonder whom Princess Elizabeth will marry?' From the back came a muffled voice: 'I expect it will be somebody from 5 Group.'
16. Harris, *op.cit.* p.196; Folder H68; Tedder, *op.cit.* p.564.
17. Richards, *The Hardest Victory*, pp.242–3; Folder H47.
18. Folder H55; Saward, *op.cit.* pp.255–7, summarises Harris's report at some length.
19. Richards, *The Hardest Victory*, pp.237–9; Harris, *op.cit.* pp.211, 213. A similar tribute from Montgomery was published in the press after a previous army-support operation on 1 July.
20. Folder H104.
21. Folders H55; H104. The RCAF Official History, pp.816–20, has a fuller discussion of this episode; it states that 126 crews, including 46 from 6 Group, bombed in error. Long afterwards, on 29 November 1979, Harris commented on the subject to Murray Peden (see p.409).
22. Folders H15; H83, dated 1 and 12 July 1944; H65, dated 3 July 1944.
23. Folders H50; H104.
24. Slessor, *op.cit.* pp.618–20; Gilbert, *op.cit.* p.928; Folders H55; H68.
25. Folder H15, dated 6, 13 and 15 September 1944. Oxland stayed.
26. Folder H68.
27. *Ibid.*
28. Folder H55, E38.
29. Folder H55, E36/7. Saward, *op.cit.* p.239, reproduces Harris's letter in full.
30. Saward, *op.cit.* p.258; Tedder, *op.cit.* p.502.
31. Harris, *op.cit.* pp.214–16; Lawrence papers, letter dated 7 August 1946. See also p.359.

Chapter 15

Finishing the job

During Harris's five months under Eisenhower and Tedder the war situation had changed dramatically. In the West the armies had liberated most of France and now, in September, stood on the borders of Germany. In the Mediterranean Rome and central Italy had been captured. Most significantly of all, the Soviet forces on the Eastern Front had swept forward several hundred miles to reach the River Vistula, in central Poland. The stage seemed set for the combined land assault on the enemy homeland. Yet the sheer extent and pace of the Allied advances meant that they needed time to prepare for this and the fierce resistance they would encounter . The winter, too, lay ahead, when campaigning would be more difficult, and Montgomery's attempt at Arnhem to take the enemy on the run and possibly force him to surrender had just ended disastrously. Inevitably another winter of war still lay ahead and there would be plenty more work for Bomber Command in preparing the way for the finale in 1945.

Harris set out his own thoughts in a note to Churchill on 30 September. The Prime Minister had sent him an 'Ultra paper', *ie* an intercepted Japanese report of Germany's current prospects,[1] and Harris accepted its general tenor. He was sure 'the Boche would fight his damnest when driven back onto his own frontiers' and noted the report's emphasis on the importance the Germans were attaching to retrieving the air supremacy which they had lacked in Normandy. They had recently been given 'considerable breathers' from the bombing and full advantage must now be taken of the vast Allied air superiority to 'knock Germany finally flat' and thus prepare the way for the armies in their 'final and perhaps prolonged and desperate battles'. Churchill responded immediately: 'I agree with your very good letter, except that I do not think you did it all or can you do it all. I recognise however this is a becoming view for you to take. I am all for cracking everything in now on to Germany that can be spared from the battlefields.'[2] Here was the top-level encouragement that Harris was hoping for and which would strengthen his personal convictions during the policy arguments that were soon to begin.

To carry out his tasks Harris now had greater striking power than ever before. In October 1944 he could produce on average nearly 1,400 operational bombers per day, 300 more than six months previously; by April 1945 the total would be 1,600, and as an indication of the supporting effort entailed he quoted in January 1945 the figure of 230,000 personnel serving in his Command. There were also benefits accruing from the regaining of France, as illustrated in an exchange of letters in mid-October. As DB Ops observed in a paper forwarded by Portal, the enemy had lost his coastal early warning system and his forward fighter bases, the RAF's bomber support forces could be deployed further east, and the radio aids used for precision bombing and marking could be used far more deeply into Germany. Harris accepted such points and their implications but disagreed that French air-fields could be made usable in the short term for other than fighter refuelling and emergency use, and – not surprisingly – strongly opposed the sugges-tion to transfer to French bases the two Halifax Groups currently based in northern England. Surely, he observed, Bufton could have saved time by discussing these matters directly with him, since most of his ideas were already fully appreciated. What his Command really needed, Harris went on, was more escort fighters and better defensive armament, particularly gun turrets; he was still anxious about his crews. Yet much lower casualties had been evident on recent operations and only a few days later he took pride in telling Portal that only nine aircraft had been lost out of 1,043 attacking Stuttgart and Nuremberg on 19 October: 'Early indications were that the German air force were in complete confusion again.' Portal was greatly encouraged.[3] Most of the signs were indeed propitious; the real question, however, remained. How was Bomber Command to be best used?

Harris had been sent his first directive under the changed regime on 25 September (just before his letter to Churchill). It was issued by Bottomley, as DCAS, who – to Harris's irritation on grounds of seniority – would be acting on Portal's behalf on such matters. Bomber Command's overall mission was stated as the progressive destruction and dislocation of the German military, industrial and economic systems and the direct support of land and naval forces. Within this the oil campaign was to be given first priority, followed by transportation, tank production and motor transport. Counter air force action received no definite priority, land and naval operations were included, and industrial areas were to be attacked when weather and tactical condi-tions were unsuitable for the priority targets.

So oil was firmly at the top of the list, its importance greatly accentuated by the Russians' capture of the Rumanian oilfields in August. Yet for Harris it remained the 'panacea' it had always been. He was still deeply suspicious of the prognostications of the Ministry of Economic Warfare; synthetic oil production was spread over many plants, often small, in different parts of Germany, and up-to-date intelligence about them was hard to obtain; the Germans under Speer were adept at dispersal and repair; and effective attack required a degree of accuracy which he was far from convinced his aircraft could achieve, especially against more distant targets. His colleague Spaatz, on the other hand, had already started to tackle major oil plants with bombers from both England and Italy during the run-up to the invasion, and with the Air Ministry taking its cue from the Americans Bottomley had asked Harris on 3 June to consider attacking ten synthetic plants in the Ruhr as soon as possible after the landings. The subsequent loss of 11% of the 832 bombers despatched in the course of three separate operations (including a horrifying 27.8% on 21 June) had done nothing to convince him that they were sensible targets. A second group of attacks in July, however, proved more successful and less costly and in August Air Staff opinion had moved strongly towards making oil Bomber Command's first priority.[4] Yet not until September were Harris's commitments to Army support and Crossbow sufficiently reduced to permit the full-scale resumption of the offensive against Germany, and he believed it high time to return the emphasis to the assault on its industrial system as a whole.

Consequently October witnessed a much heavier weight of attacks than Bomber Command had ever before devoted to the area offensive. Yet at precisely the time when the intelligence assessments indicated – correctly, as it would later be found – that Germany's oil situation was at its most desperate, a mere 6% of its bomb tonnage was aimed at oil targets, and the Eighth Air Force, with 10%, did little better. There were many factors affecting this imbalance, as would be highlighted in the subsequent debate between Harris and Portal, but the official historians judge that more could and ought to have been done. Such was the hitting power of the Anglo-American bomber force and so weakened were the enemy defences that it should have been possible, they contend, to deprive the Germans of virtually all their remaining oil production if the effort had been much more strongly concentrated upon it in the autumn months. On the other hand, as the BBSU Report states, the weather in this period was very poor, there were few occasions when oil targets could be visually bombed, and not many tactical opportunities for attacking them were in fact missed (a point echoed by the Australian historian). The USAAF official history makes similar points, observing that by the end of November the weight of Bomber Command's oil attacks was exceeding that of the Americans and they were proving generally successful. Overall, it goes on, the joint oil offensive in the closing months of 1944 produced spectacular results which were 'more effective in terms of destruction than most Allied experts had dared to hope.'[5]

The strong conflict of views that lay behind this situation at the time was to be brought out in a long series of demi-official letters which Harris and Portal exchanged over the early winter months. That two such busy men should devote so much time to writing lengthy missives to each other rather than meeting occasionally to air their differences seems incredible to later generations, and we can only assume, as Denis Richards suggests, that both wanted their positions to be firmly and explicitly stated in the unmistakable and permanent terms which only the written word could provide.[6] They have certainly proved of great interest to historians, though Harris himself later opposed the use in this way of what he had intended as entirely private correspondence (see p.383).

The saga began with a memorandum which Tedder sent to Portal on 25 October criticising the patchwork pattern of the strategic air offensive and urging precedence for a campaign against the German transportation system, with oil in effect part of it. A copy of this went to Harris and on 1 November, the same day that Bottomley sent him another directive again giving oil the first priority, he set out his views on these matters to Portal. Having summarised his Command's role in the war thus far he discussed the decisive effect of weather and tactical factors (including the need to keep the enemy guessing) on target selection; the principle he followed was that 'bombing anything in Germany was better than bombing nothing'. Even so, while he resented the revised pressure from the 'panacea merchants', he was attacking the Ruhr and the oil plants whenever possible, but he remained worried lest the 15 major German cities that remained intact (one of them Dresden) were to be left intact. The completion of the city programme would do more towards accelerating the defeat of Germany than the armies had yet done or would do, he asserted.

Replying on the 5th, Portal told Harris how worried he was by the enemy's recovery in October and insisted that the oil offensive offered the best hope for a speedy victory. Indeed the whole war was poised on oil, 'as on a knife edge', and he wanted to understand Harris's targeting policy and reasoning so as to be able to follow his operations intelligently, and to explain and defend them to others in Whitehall. Harris replied immediately, assuring Portal firmly that he not only understood the importance of the oil war but had impressed this on his staff. At the same time, he observed, the oil targets were small and usually outlying; while he was trying to go for oil whenever possible he had always to assess the chances of achieving worthwhile results in the prevailing conditions. It would help, he added, if he knew whether the oil plants were to be obliterated, at high cost in effort and casualties, or merely seriously hindered from manufacturing.

A week later Portal took up Harris's earlier advocacy of further city bombing with a sharp criticism: 'I have at times wondered whether the magnetism of the remaining German cities has not in the past tended as much to deflect our bombers from their primary objectives as the tactical and weather difficulties which you describe ... if I knew you to be as wholehearted in the attack on oil as in the past you have been in the matter of attacking cities I would have little to worry about.' Oil must be attacked, he went on, even if the chances of success were less than on lower priority targets, and the aim must be the complete destruction of the plants, *ie* putting them out of action for at least two to three months. Here was the heart of the issue that divided the two officers, but not until 24 November did Harris re-enter the debate and then only while commenting on an ADI (Science) report on the eclipse of the German night fighters. This emphasised the fact that Bomber Command's recent low losses were not due to its ability to fight and defeat the German defences but to its success in evading them, and Harris – reluctant to see loss rates returning to 3–4% – wanted to keep it that way. He told Portal he needed freedom to go on spreading his attacks so as to keep confusing the enemy.

Not until 6 December did Portal pick up these points. Applauding Harris's current successes but reminding him that the Allied aim was to win the war by early summer 1945, he stressed that the bombers would make their greatest contribution through attacking firstly oil and secondly enemy communications behind the fighting front. Moreover overall losses were still low (1%), but if concentration of effort where it would hurt the enemy most were to help shorten the war a rise to 3–4% would be a price worth paying: this was not the time to pull punches. At the same time Portal recognised Harris's case for spreading his attacks on occasion: the most distant oil plants would obviously serve both purposes, and his directive also provided for the attack on 24 industrial centres throughout Germany, including Breslau, Dresden, Chemnitz and Munich.

Meanwhile Harris's Operational Research Section had been working on the Oil Plan in the light of Portal's injunction to destroy the plants and on 12 December Harris advised him that 9,000 sorties per month would be needed, 6,400 of them at night against the targets in central Germany, and the Eighth Air Force would have to do most of the long-range work. His closing paragraph made it clear that, contrary to his earlier statements, he had now reverted to considering oil as one of the MEW's 'panaceas', and on the 22nd this evoked from Portal a stern reply. He saw no reason why the oil task should be beyond the capacity of both air forces, especially if the main effort was concentrated on the most important targets – the 11 synthetic oil plants in central Germany. It was essential not to waste the previous efforts and to press on. So he was 'profoundly disappointed' that Harris felt oil to be just another 'panacea'. 'Naturally while you hold this view you will be unable to put your heart into it,' he wrote; nor was it easy to believe that Harris's staff could be devoting maximum thought and energy to it. The Command had achieved so much already in the attack on oil that it would be a tragedy if, through lack of faith or understanding on Harris's part, it failed to take the greatest possible share in completing the task. Losses as high as 5–10% could be worthwhile against certain targets, he concluded.

This stung Harris on the 28th into his first really strong letter on the subject. He began by slating the MEW – yet again; he described the 1944 attacks on the German fighter forces and industry as the outstanding example of the futility of panacea seeking (a fair point, given the way they had expanded); and he unequivocally described oil as another panacea. 'But you are quite wrong,' he continued, 'to say that if I hold that view I will be unable to put my heart into the attack on oil. It has always been my custom to leave no stone unturned to get my views across, but when the decision is made I carry it out to the utmost and to the best of my ability.' Nor did he accept Portal's comments about his staff: 'I do not give them views, I give them orders. They do and always have done exactly what I tell them to. I have told them to miss no opportunity of prosecuting the oil plan, and they have missed no worthwhile opportunity.' As for losses, if 5–10 % were to be regularly accepted the oil plan would be the only thing, and the last, that Bomber Command would do. There was much more to this letter, which concluded 'you may think I feel strongly – indeed I do.'

In retrospect Portal might have done better to wind down the dispute at this point. Bomber Command was in fact doing a great deal both against oil and in many other directions – not least in support of the Ardennes battle which was at its height – and with so much happening there was not that much point in increasing the aggravation between the two men. Yet on 8 January 1945 he made another attempt to convince Harris that the oil policy was sound; well though Bomber Command was doing, the oil offensive would be even better conducted if he and his staff really believed in it. He therefore came to the defence of the MEW and with the aid of a dossier of intelligence reports tried to explain the reasons for concentrating on oil. He challenged Harris's suggestion that no policy of selective attacks could succeed and all the bomber force should be directed to area attacks ('not strictly true' commented Harris). He defended the 'selective attacks' on the German fighter forces. Now, he concluded, the vital element in the enemy economy was oil; if the oil plan was firmly adhered to the operational effectiveness of the German armies and air forces would be decisively restricted, but the Allies must be determined to do the job, and '*your* determination matters more than that of all the rest of us put together.'

Harris was very far from persuaded, as his letter of the 18th made abundantly clear. After complaining at length about the lack of consultation between him and the Air Staff he again threw cold water on the panaceas of the past and refused to accept that the enemy would be so foolish as to allow vital bottlenecks to persist, even at this stage of the war. He simply did not believe it was operationally practicable to deprive the Germans and keep them deprived of that proportion of their oil production which was actually essential to maintain the fight. The oil offensive, if it failed to achieve its object, would achieve nothing, and Germany's central and eastern industrial areas, now the mainspring of their war production, would remain intact. He would not share responsibility for a decision he was convinced was utterly wrong. He finished by referring to Portal's insinuation that he had been disloyal in carrying out to the best of his ability policies which had been laid down:

> I will not willingly lay myself open to the charge that the lack of success of a policy, which I have declared at the outset – or when it first came to my knowledge – not to contain the seeds of success is, after the event, due to my personal failure in not having really tried. That situation is simply one of heads I lose tails you win, and it is an intolerable situation. I therefore ask you to consider whether it is best for the prosecution of the war and the success of our arms, which alone matters, that I should remain in this situation.

Portal's reply of the 20th was calm. For the present they must agree to differ over oil, though the evidence of an acute shortage was clear now and the two air forces were actually doing very well against such targets. He defended his own staff, particularly Bottomley and Bufton, and promised better consultation. As for the future, given that the enemy's power of resistance had already been seriously weakened, the oil plan must continue, but he hoped there would still be enough effort left to flatten some at least of the cities Harris had been naming. On the subject of loyalty, he wrote:

> I willingly accept your assurance that you will continue to do your utmost to ensure the successful execution of the policy laid down. I am very sorry that you do not believe in it but it is no use my craving for what is evidently unattainable. We must wait until after the war before we can know for certain who was right and I sincerely hope that until then you will continue in command of the force which has done so much towards defeating the enemy and has brought such credit and renown to yourself and to the Air Force.

Two briefer letters of damage repair were exchanged on the 24th and 25th, with Harris accepting unreservedly that he had mistaken Portal's meaning and greatly regretting that there should be any disagreement between them, and both looking for ways of improving the staff consultation – notwithstanding Harris's continued fulminations against the 'impossible' Bufton. It was high time they got back to the actual business of the war, rather than 'bothering about somewhat academic arguments' (Portal's words), and already Dresden was on the agenda.

It has often been asked whether the differences reflected in this long confrontation were so fundamental that Portal ought to have bitten the bullet and dismissed Harris. Max Hastings and others contend that he should, essentially on the grounds that Harris's failure to concentrate on the oil policy to the extent being required of him was effectively lengthening the war. The official history, describing Harris's prestige as greater than that of anyone else in the RAF, concludes that at this stage of the war dismissal would have been a remedy worse than the disease, a view which John Terraine calls 'undoubtedly correct'. Denis Richards picks up other important factors from the official history, including Harris's dynamic leadership of his Command and his intimate relationship with Churchill, and adds Portal's own later reflection:

> His offer of resignation (by no means the only one I had from him) was not, I knew, intended seriously, but was made in a moment of exasperation. His good qualities as a commander far outweighed his defects, and it would have been monstrously unjust to have tried to have him replaced on the grounds that while assuring me of his intentions to carry out his orders he persisted in trying to convince me that different orders would have produced better results.[7]

Under all the circumstances this seems right. Maybe Harris did not share his master's enthusiasm for oil but he was in fact getting on with it as well as he could (and more effectively than some of the critics thought) while at the same time doing a great deal to support the land and sea campaigns, and also – with Portal's own encouragement – maintaining his attacks on more distant area targets. Though the European war was obviously approaching its final stages there could be no certainty about precisely how it would be brought to an end, but there was everything to be said for continuing to hit the enemy as hard as possible in the attempt to do it quickly – and none was more determined about this than Harris. It is very hard to see what purpose would have been served had he been removed at this time, except maybe to provide some comfort to the Germans. Indeed as Michael Howard observes, the whole row between Harris and the Air Staff over area versus 'panacea' bombing was in fact largely irrelevant, 'for whatever we targeted in Germany in the winter of 1944/5, we were bound to do an immense amount of damage.'[8]

Nevertheless, as Harris himself later recognised, oil did prove more critical then he had judged at the time. Influenced by the views of Albert Speer, Hitler's Armament Minister, he wrote in 1947 that in the final weeks of the war all the German armed forces had been immobilised for lack of fuel, rendering the triumph of the oil offensive complete and indisputable. It was the one 'panacea' that actually paid off.[9]

It remains to consider whether one further step might have been taken in the attempt to persuade Harris of its significance. He had repeatedly questioned with Portal the sources and validity of the information on which the MEW based its assessments, but when Portal referred to 'the irrefutable evidence of Sigint' there is no indication that Harris actually knew where this came from. As Hinsley's official history of British Intelligence shows, much of the best evidence for Germany's growing oil shortage and the way it was restricting the Wehrmacht's freedom of action came from ULTRA, which was based upon the interception and decryption of the German ENIGMA cyphers. For perfectly good reasons of security knowledge of the basis for ULTRA material was limited to those who needed to make direct use of it and, as Ralph Bennett tells us, Harris was not among them.[10] He himself, asked the question in 1982, answered: 'I was never told of the ENIGMA source, but any relevant information from it was sent to me.'[11] He did hear eventually of a special security category called 'Ultra', but he did not know where it originated and therefore what significance to attach to it.[12] To quote Bennett (a fierce critic of Harris and Bomber Command in many ways), 'the matter is critical for an assessment of the grave differences of opinion between them about the advisability or otherwise of a concerted attack on Germany's oil industry during the second half of 1944.'[13] It is understandable that in 1942–3 Harris did not need to be 'on the list', but in late 1944, when Portal was determined to leave no stone unturned in the attempt to convince him about oil, it seems surprising that arrangements were not made to have him suitably briefed. Hinsley agrees that Portal could reasonably have made the attempt.[14]

Throughout these months Harris had continued to despatch his bombers in ever greater strength against a wide variety of targets. In support of the naval war the minelaying campaign had continued, German seaports along the North Sea and Baltic coasts had been heavily targeted, and on 12 November 9 and 617 Squadrons had at last sunk the *Tirpitz*, eliciting warm congratulations from the King, the Prime Minister, the Admiralty and many others, together with excellent press publicity. Harris was particularly pleased to hear from Lovett in Washington, who said he had been engaged in a running argument with the US Navy about the unsinkability of 'modern' battleships. This 'superb piece of bombing' had provided just the evidence he needed. Harris answered in the warmest terms, describing the operation in some detail and praising the Tallboy bomb that had made it possible. The big battle wagon was now a busted flush in the face of air power, and Lovett's sailor friends should 'go build their new battle wagons of rubber, self-sealing tank principle.'[15]

There had also been much help for the Army, not least in the two-month long autumn campaign to capture the island of Walcheren and open the sea route into Antwerp, and many of Harris's targets in the Ruhr and elsewhere in western Germany were linked to the communications system that Tedder was so keen to have attacked. Montgomery, for one, applauded Bomber Command's activities. 'Your chaps are doing grand work in the bombing of

Germany that is now going on,' he wrote to Harris on 9 December, 'keep it up!' Such encouragement was more than welcome amid Harris's mounting arguments with the Air Staff. Soon afterwards had come the Germans' unexpected Ardennes offensive, when Harris responded to Eisenhower's urgent appeals for assistance by bombing tactical targets, especially railway yards, during the month-long battle. So bad was the weather that at times it was only Bomber Command's GH-led Lancasters that could operate at all, and after his aircraft had attacked the rail centre nearest to the front, at Trier, on 19 December Eisenhower sent his congratulations on this 'magnificent performance. The decision to take-off despite increasing conditions of fog at base, and the determination of the crews to reach and hit the target, whatever the weather, illustrate again how ready is the response of the RAF to the needs of the battle on the ground.' Harris's reply was succinct. 'You can count on us in any weather short of the impossible.'[16]

Not always, however, had things gone right. On 4 January, on the orders of SHAEF, Harris had sent 350 aircraft to Royan, a town on the French Atlantic Coast still held by the Germans. The French authorities had asked for the attack and stated that all the French had gone. In the event not only had the town been largely destroyed but some 1,000 French civilians were reported dead. Harris, asked by Portal for the background to this disaster, expressed his deep concern, while observing that it was not for him to question Army support targets which were sent to him by SHAEF and that 'clearance' must be their responsibility. Such mistakes had happened before, he added – at Le Havre in September 1944, and at Limburg, where his bombers had attacked a marshalling yard which – unknown to them – was only 600 yards away from an American prisoner-of-war camp. For Portal, Harris's view was absolutely correct, and SHAEF took steps to correct the system.[17]

Another matter worrying Harris had been the poor publicity that Bomber Command, and indeed the whole RAF, was continuing to receive. As he told Trenchard on 2 January 1945, a *Times* supplement reviewing the year 1944 had been particularly poor, giving far too little credit to the Air Force for its many contributions to the Normandy victory. In part he ascribed such failings to the 'utter ineptitude' of the Air Ministry's press and publicity department, as exemplified in incompetent handling of the story about Aachen, the first German city to be captured by the Allies. Consequently, he wrote, 'the whole world now knows that Aachen was destroyed not by Bomber Command but by United States artillery and tactical air force bombardments during the siege.' For himself he cared not, but for his crews and the future of the RAF he cared a great deal.[18]

Many practical problems, too, continued to arise, with the supply of bombs one of Harris's particular anxieties. In October 1944 he told Portal of his disappointment on hearing that the programme for the production of the ten-ton Tallboy Large bombs (later known as 'Grand Slam') and the modification of a full squadron of Lancasters to carry them was being heavily curtailed, and he was much relieved to hear that this was untrue since most of the bombs needed were to be produced in America. On 9 January 1945 Harris wrote about the increasing shortage of the invaluable 1,000 lb bombs, which could well necessitate 'a partial and deliberate return to the area bombing of cities with incendiaries' and thus affect target selection. Here Portal could offer little comfort: supply of these bombs was unlikely to improve and priority in their use would have to be given to Army support and, of course, oil. Harris was upset too by the continued poor provision of 4 lb incendiary clusters; the use of unaimed incendiaries had not only reduced the effectiveness of the industrial area attacks but also caused much loss and damage among other bombers. As he told Evill on 17 January 'the procrastination and incredible technical incompetence' evidenced by this story called for serious and immediate action.[19]

Harris was thinking too about his manpower situation. Writing to Portal on 2 December he referred to Churchill's warning that the German war might not end as soon as the 'early' summer. Maybe, Harris suggested, the RAF was being over light-hearted about cutting down training and over-generously distributing bomber crews to other Commands, adding that the Canadian aircrew replacement programme, entailing the loss of many experienced men, was particularly worrying. Portal's guarded reply did not really allay Harris's fears and on 30 January he protested to Evill about plans to switch some 100 recently OTU-trained crews to 2 Group for light bomber duties. Soon afterwards Harris decided to extend the first operational tour of his crews from 30 to 36 sorties, a reasonable move given the small losses now being incurred. The Canadians were not happy but after much discussion eventually accepted a points system which Harris proposed should apply to all his Main Force crews. In the event this never needed to be put into effect.[20]

In such matters Harris had long had in mind that Bomber Command's war would not end when the shooting stopped in Europe. As far back as October 1943 he had urged on Portal the development of a 'big bomber' capable of enabling the RAF to take its place alongside the USAAF in the long-distance assault on Japan, and by September 1944 he was well aware that plans were afoot, partly at Churchill's instigation, for Bomber Command to play a part once the German war was over. Even the press were speculating, with the *Evening News* going so far as to say that a large part of the Command might go to the Pacific before very long with Harris in charge. The Air Ministry's plans were more modest. In November, after consultation with Harris, Air Marshal Sir Hugh Lloyd was appointed

Commander Designate of a force of Lancasters and maybe their Lincoln derivatives which would go to the Far East once the German war was over, and from then until April 1945 he and his Tiger Force staff were located at High Wycombe, where (as Lloyd wrote) Harris and his colleagues gave them all the help they needed with 'thoroughness, efficiency and above all willingness'.[21]

Portal had at first tried to persuade Harris to accept Lloyd as Cochrane's successor at 5 Group, where he could learn the business before going to the Far East, but Harris was still highly reluctant to lose Cochrane, whose departure during the next few months would be 'a serious factor towards postponing the conclusion of the European war'. If, however, Cochrane had to go soon his successor must have prolonged and right up-to-date experience of Bomber Command's work, which pointed to one of the 'outstanding youngsters', such as Constantine or Elworthy. Lloyd would learn the job better as an 'extra hand' attached in turn to 5, 8 and 3 Groups. In the event Harris had his way. As he said to Sutton, AMP, in January 1945 in connection with a major set of senior postings: 'The time is here, if not somewhat past, when operationally experienced youngsters should be commanding all the operational groups.' Many years later Air Chief Marshal Sir Hugh Constantine recalled working for the C-in-C at the end of 1944. He had just gone to bed after a long day when the telephone rang. It was Harris: 'I want you to come and see me.' Constantine complained that he was in bed. 'Did you hear what I said? Come and see me and bring your wife.' The Constantines got dressed and drove to Springfield, where Harris awaited them in his green dinner jacket with Jill alongside him. The ladies moved aside and Harris said to Constantine: 'I want you to take over 5 Group tomorrow. Can you do it?' As a young Air Commodore this was the last thing Constantine had expected, though he knew that Harris had been refusing to take any of the more senior officers the Air Ministry was offering him.[22] So it was Constantine who led 5 Group for the rest of the war, when it played a leading role in many of the Command's operations and not least in the attack on Dresden.

The destruction of the historic capital of Saxony — hitherto virtually untouched — on the night of 13 February 1945 has come to symbolise in countless minds all that was dreadful about the bombing of Germany in the Second World War. In particular the degree of devastation caused has since been widely perceived as unnecessary at a time when, it is claimed, the war was virtually won. The historian Anthony Verrier, to take just one example, writes that the attack 'expressed to a stupefying degree the use of an instrument of major war for purposes even more elemental than even those who forged it could have dreamt. It was selected for no reason which anyone who fought in the strategic air war can justify.'[23] While the rationale of

Bomber Command's campaign in earlier years is normally understood, Dresden is often seen as 'a city too far' and the finger of blame is all too frequently pointed at Harris, the man who directed the attack and was bound to be seen publicly at the time as responsible for it. What many of the critics fail to consider, however, is how the war situation actually looked to those involved in the key decisions and how those decisions were actually reached.

In the second half of January the Allied leaders still had many anxieties. On the Western Front the Rhine barrier was uncrossed, the recent Battle of the Ardennes had shown that the Germans remained a far from spent force, and nothing was more certain than that their Army would fight bitterly in defence of the Fatherland. In the East the Red Army was just starting a new offensive in central Poland and encountering fierce resistance in its efforts to break through towards the German border. The enemy was still coming up with new weaponry which might be difficult to counter, notably the ME 262 jet aircraft and the schnorkel submarine. There was even the possibility of the Germans producing an atomic bomb, something which Harris himself thought might happen. In Great Britain itself the euphoria of 1944 was being to some extent replaced by a mood of weariness and despair as the war dragged on and a steady stream of V2 missiles continued to cause death and destruction in London. From Germany were coming increasingly horrific reports of what was taking place in the concentration camps, coupled with desperate pleas to the Allied leaders for urgent action; Auschwitz was overrun by the Red Army on 27 January. Nor would victory in Europe even end the war, for in the Far East lay Japan and the prospect of further ferocious conflict. The Allies would win for sure, but how long would it take and at what cost? We, with the benefit of hindsight, know the answers. Those with the responsibility did not. As the German historian Götz Bergander reminds us, 'who was really sure that the war was now in its last phase?' The official historians issue a similar caution in relation to the often criticised continuation of city bombing as a whole in the early months of 1945. 'While we now know that the armies were able to advance and that Germany did surrender in 1945, had they been checked or Germany resisted for a longer period, the criticism might well have been applied in the opposite sense.'[24] The Allied leaders, Harris included, should not be condemned for their determination to use all the means at their disposal in order to bring the whole ghastly war to its end as quickly as possible.

It was in this atmosphere that on 22 January the complex discussions leading to the Dresden attack began, just as Harris and Portal were beginning to mend fences after their bitter argument (see above). It was Bufton who set the ball rolling by suggesting to Bottomley that the new Soviet advance might offer the opportunity to implement Operation

Thunderclap, a plan originally put forward in August 1944 to deliver a catastrophic blow against either Berlin or some other major city hitherto largely undamaged. The Joint Intelligence Committee took up the theme on the 25th, stressing the value to the Russian offensive of the great confusion that would result from the sustained bombing of Berlin. Bottomley immediately discussed the JIC's ideas with Harris, who suggested that not only Berlin but also Chemnitz, Leipzig and Dresden should be attacked; all would be housing evacuees from the East and were focal points in German communications behind the Eastern Front.[25] There was nothing surprising about this proposal. These three cities, with others in eastern Germany, had long been on the list agreed with the Air Ministry for area attack when circumstances were right and Harris was merely drawing attention to their significance in this particular situation. The real impetus for such operations was about to come from elsewhere.

The story of the Prime Minister's critical intervention has been often told. On the 25th he asked Sinclair about plans for basting the Germans in their retreat from Breslau, on the 26th he received a guarded response, and immediately, in a sharp minute to Sinclair, he made himself totally clear: 'I did not ask you about plans for harrying the German retreat from Breslau. On the contrary I asked whether Berlin, and no doubt other large cities in East Germany, should not now be considered especially attractive targets. Pray report to me tomorrow what is going to be done.'

There could be no further hesitation in the Air Ministry, even though there had been as yet no time for the essential consultation with the USAAF – whose participation would be essential – or with Tedder at SHAEF. Knowing that Churchill was preparing to depart for the Allied conference at Yalta, accompanied by Portal among others, Bottomley went ahead and gave Harris his orders. In essence, he wrote on the 27th, Bomber Command was to attack Berlin, Dresden, Leipzig, Chemnitz and any other cities where a severe blitz would not only cause confusion in the evacuation from the East but also hamper the movement of troops from the West. The particular object was to exploit 'the confused conditions likely to exist in these cities during the successful Russian advance.' On 2 February Bufton, as Chairman of the Combined Strategic Targets Committee, said he felt the attack on these cities had been ordered, not merely because of their communications value or for any other specific object, but because any additional chaos which could be caused at this juncture would make the German administrative and military problems, already immense, still more difficult.[26]

At High Wycombe, surprising though it may seem, doubts were beginning to surface. David Irving, in his comprehensive study of the whole subject of Dresden, discussed this aspect at length with many of the senior officers involved, including Harris, and concludes that there were widespread misgivings. For one thing the Intelligence Staff had far less information about the city than for most other potential targets, which made them wonder how strong was the case for the attack. For another Dresden was a particularly long way to go, the winter weather could make the operation very hazardous, little was known about the enemy defences, and much could go wrong; indeed, the target was not all that far from the old Czechoslovak frontier and the Soviet front line. As Harris, Saundby and their colleagues studied the operation the less they liked the look of it and, Saundby later recalled, they decided to question whether Dresden was intended to be bombed.[27] It took some time for their doubts to be resolved. Since the operation would be a joint one with the USAAF General Spaatz had to be involved; Eisenhower's headquarters had a major interest; and since Churchill, Portal and many others were at Yalta conferring with the Russians the subject was bound to feature in their discussions. Here General Antonov, the Red Army Deputy Chief of Staff, speaking on 4 February, emphasised the need for Allied air operations to prevent the Germans moving troops from other theatres to the Eastern Front. While the formal records indicate that the only individual targets he specified were Berlin and Leipzig the British Chiefs of Staff's own interpreter is certain that Dresden was also requested, not just by Antonov but also – strongly – by Stalin himself. In any case, when the Russians were subsequently told of the many operations being planned in their support, including attacks on Berlin, Leipzig, Dresden and Chemnitz, they raised no objections.[28]

So by 8 February all the key figures were in the picture and the Combined Strategic Targets Committee issued a new directive listing ten towns selected because of their importance for the movement of refugees from the East and for military transportation to the Eastern front. While Berlin, already attacked by the Americans on the 3rd, was still first priority, Dresden came second and Harris and Spaatz were ordered to attack it at the first oppor-tunity. Yet even now, Irving tells us, Harris told Saundby to double-check Dresden's inclusion and not until the 13th, when the right weather forecast at last arrived, did Harris seek formal agreement to the operation from SHAEF and order the attack. 'With a heavy heart,' said Saundby later, 'I was forced to lay the massive air raid on'; and some of the Group Commanders recalled 'the distinctly reserved note in Harris's voice when he confirmed the order, gaining the impression that he was dissatisfied with the whole affair.'[29] When referring to the decision in informal conversation in later years, Harris used to say that the order had come from SHAEF.[30] In the sense that SHAEF had to give final clearance for all Harris's major operations this was true, but without doubt the real decision was the result of much discussion at the highest levels of command, with Churchill himself the prime mover. Martin Gilbert goes so far as to call the raid a direct result of the Yalta agreement – to make emergency use of Anglo-American air power in order to disrupt German reinforcements moving eastward to the Russian front.[31] Harris himself made but one comment for the record: 'The attack on Dresden was at the time considered a military necessity by more important people than myself.'[32]

Once the decision had been taken and confirmed it was a different story. Whatever Harris thought about the orders he was given, once the die was cast – as he had so often shown in the past – he would spare no effort to do the job properly. Since his task was to exploit the confused conditions in Dresden in order to assist the Russians he would use to that end the methods his Command had perfected, bearing in mind that the Americans would be operating too by day in the attempt to disrupt the communications system. Those who contend that it was unnecessary, indeed wrong, to attack the city centre ignore the practicalities of trying to bomb with high precision at great distance and in conditions that were not only hard to predict but might conceivably lead to another Nuremberg. If the job was to be done at all it was essential to go for the city as a whole and in choosing a two-wave attack led by the specialised 5 Group Harris sought to reduce the risks of failure to the minimum. Already the joint plan had gone awry, when the initial American daylight attack against the transport system in the city outskirts had to be postponed to the next day because of the weather, so Harris's men found themselves opening the assault. In the event his own plan worked perfectly. The weather did exactly what the forecasters had said it would, the enemy defences were fooled by the three-hour delay between the first and second phases of the attack, as well as by a separate attack on the oil refinery at Böhlen, the crews of the 800 aircraft involved demonstrated great skill, no more than six Lancasters failed to return, and the heart of the city was destroyed in a fire-storm unparalleled in the European war other than in Hamburg. Of the million or more people thought to have been in Dresden at the time up to 200,000 were initially reported to have died, and numbers of this order are still quoted from time to time. Modern research, however, puts them far lower. While Irving in his recent revised book considers the figure to be at least 60,000, Bergander, who has researched the whole subject in depth over many years, places it between 35 and 40,000, certainly not more than in Hamburg in 1943. But whatever the toll – and nobody will ever know for certain – it was a truly horrifying event and, to quote Saundby, 'a great tragedy ... one of those terrible things that sometimes happen in wartime, brought about by an unfortunate combination of cir-cumstances.'[33]

So what if anything did the destruction of Dresden achieve in military terms? The combined attacks of the RAF and the USAAF damaged but did not ruin the railway system that ran through it. While they had a considerable impact on local industry, much of this had never been of major importance for war production. On the other hand, as Denis Richards points out, they did wreck the city as a potential main administrative and control centre for the German armies fighting farther forward.[34] There was a deeper significance too. Bergander writes:

> It is right to say that the shockwave triggered by Dresden swept away what was left of the will to resist, as the Germans now feared that such a catastrophe could be repeated daily. Awareness of the inevitable defeat increased and the belief in miracles disappeared but, above all, there was the growing realisation that it would be better if the end came soon ... better to have a terrible end than endless terror.[35]

There was a contrary reaction in the Allied camp, sparked off by a despatch from a war correspondent at SHAEF based on an ill-advised briefing by an RAF intelligence officer on 17 February. The despatch stated that Allied air chiefs had made the long-awaited decision to adopt deliberate terror bombing of German population centres as a ruthless expedient to hastening Hitler's doom, and it was widely publicised in America, though quickly barred in the UK. The Germans were thus handed a major propaganda advantage, and as the message inevitably leaked out the Allied air commanders – with Harris by implication one of the foremost – were quickly cast as the villains. Then came the press reports from neutral countries about events in Dresden, and with the bombing campaign continuing apace the critics of the area offensive were quick to take full advantage. The issue was raised by one of Bomber Command's most persistent critics, Richard Stokes, in the House of Commons on 6 March, when he quoted a report in the *Manchester Guardian* about the Dresden fire storm, referred to the alleged decision by the Allied air chiefs and asked whether 'terror bombing' was now part of British policy. He did not receive the reply he presumably hoped for, but three weeks later there was action behind the scenes.[36]

It was on 28 March, in a war situation much changed since his original note sent two months before, that Churchill wrote his oft-quoted minute to the Chiefs of Staff.

> It seems to me that the moment has come when the question of bombing German cities simply for the sake of increasing the terror, though under other pretexts, should be reviewed. Otherwise we shall come into control of an utterly ruined land ... the destruction of Dresden remains a serious query against the conduct of Allied bombing ... I feel the need for more precise concentration upon military objectives rather than on mere acts of terror and wanton destruction, however impressive.

This document, which ignored Churchill's long-term support for the area bombing campaign, his personal role in setting up the Dresden attack, and the very different war picture six weeks later, so shocked the Chiefs of Staff that Portal, backed by Sinclair, urged the Prime Minister to withdraw it. So on 1 April, recognising the validity of their arguments, he substituted a much more guarded and acceptable note.[37]

Before challenging the Prime Minister Portal had felt he should seek Harris's views, so on the 28th Bottomley had written summarising the original and outlining the Air Staff's objections to it. Harris replied immediately, calling the allegations of terror bombing an insult both to the Air Ministry's bombing policy and to the way Bomber Command had executed it. He had no doubt that the destruction of the enemy's industrial cities had fatally weakened their war effort and was enabling Allied soldiers to advance into the heart of Germany with negligible casualties. It would therefore be wrong to give up such attacks now unless it was certain that they would neither shorten the war nor preserve the lives of Allied soldiers. 'I do not personally regard the whole of the remaining cities of Germany as worth the bones of one British grenadier.' Moreover there was still Japan: were vast military casualties to be preferred to bombing their cities flat and giving the Armies a walk-over?[38]

This was a robust, no-nonsense response, marked Personal and Top Secret and written without any thought that it might one day be open to public gaze. The comparison between Germany's remaining cities and the bones of a British grenadier needs to be seen in that light, as does another widely quoted observation: 'The feeling, such as there is, over Dresden could be easily explained by any psychiatrist. It is connected with German bands and Dresden shepherdesses. Actually Dresden was a mass of munitions works, an intact government centre, and a key transportation point to the East. It is now none of those things.' This statement, emotive and inaccurate, has done Harris's reputation no good. It probably reflects the haste in which it was obviously penned, his extreme annoyance at the way in which Dresden was being so widely seized upon as a symbol of the worst aspects of area bombing without regard to the reasons for it, and his refusal to try to conceal his own convictions. Yet he need never have said it and in doing so gave many of his later critics a powerful tool with which to try to lay the responsibility for Dresden at his door. What must be remembered is that whatever Harris said about it afterwards – and on the whole he said very little – the attack was ordered elsewhere, he had considerable misgivings about it, and it might well never have taken place at all had the decision been his alone.

Coincident with Dresden was a further exchange between Harris and Portal, who on his return from Yalta expressed hopes of being granted operating facilities for Bomber Command behind the Eastern Front. Bottomley therefore wrote to Harris on 14 February asking for his views about using Soviet-controlled airfields for emergency landings and also shuttle bombing. Harris quickly wrote off shuttle bombing as totally impracticable on a scale that would make it worthwhile but agreed that facilities for emergencies and for GEE/GH stations in Russian-occupied Germany would be invaluable. A few days later Portal suggested that the C-in-C might actually visit Russia to plead his case for these facilities and at the same time show Stalin his photograph books and explain what his bombers had done towards the destruction of Germany. Harris was not enamoured of this idea. He was reluctant to leave his Command to others at this stage of the war. He did not believe the Russians would be open to persuasion that their achievements on the Eastern Front owed anything to the strategic bombing offensive, and not least since the British themselves had long failed adequately to publicise its value. Nor would he want to be put in the position of having to expound the virtues of the oil offensive in which he did not believe – a point which he ill-advisedly developed in language as strong as that of some of his January letters to Portal. If required to go, however, he would of course try his best. The whole idea, Portal now realised, was a non-starter, though he did tell Harris that he believed Stalin would have been tremendously interested and was big-minded enough to give the Command the credit it deserved.[39] That was probably true, but equally true was Harris's judgement that the Russians would, in the longer term, never acknowledge their indebtedness to Bomber Command.

Nor, Harris still felt, was anyone else properly recognising his Command's work – or, indeed, that of the Air Force as a whole. Trenchard, as always sharing his concerns, had requested information to help him match the Navy's far better publicity about its work since D-Day, and on 21 February Harris included in his reply a sharp criticism of the Air Ministry's publicity department. In the end, he wrote, the Americans and Monty would win the war in Europe and the navies in the Far East, with the RAF mainly making noises off. His fulminations continued:

Tedder and his RAF saved the rout in North Africa and made the subsequent victory virtually a walk-over for the Army. Monty gets the GCB and is made a Field Marshal. Tedder gets nothing, until I personally incur Winston's wrath at his own dinner table by suggesting that Tedder deserved both far more. Then he gets a grudging and belated GCB after the public have forgotten. Tedder is selected by Eisenhower – who knows who and what he wants – as Deputy Supreme Commander. The Army retaliate by making Monty, Alexander and Wilson Field Marshals, thus completely undercutting Tedder's standing. It has never of course entered the Air Ministry's head to make Tedder a Marshal.

There was more in this vein before Harris made it clear that what he really cared about was for the RAF to have its just, and so hardly earned, place in the sun – but it was not going to get it. In a postscript he added Jimmy Doolittle's remark that the US air force would get no credit out of this war; the rest of their Army would see to that.[40]

Soon afterwards, still despairing of the Air Ministry, Harris decided to seek help elsewhere. With Eisenhower's land forces advancing fast his own bombing efforts were increasingly being devoted, directly or indirectly, to their assistance and he was maintaining close contact with Tedder, particularly by attending his weekly Air Commanders' Meetings at SHAEF. At Harris's invitation Tedder had also just visited 5 Group and written a most warm and appreciative letter of thanks. So on 2 March Harris wrote to Eisenhower expressing his concern about the almost entire lack of credit to the bomber force coming from the correspondents working with the armies, most of whom were asserting that the urban destruction they observed had been caused by the artillery. 'Unless we are given adequate credit for our share in the campaign as a whole *now*, it will be much too late for us to claim it or be awarded it hereafter.' Harris quoted several examples, referred to the bitterness being felt by his crews, and asked for Eisenhower's war correspondents to be properly instructed. 'I have no doubt,' Harris concluded, 'that unless you personally take a hand in this matter the destruction of Cologne and Dusseldorf . . . will again be attributed to our guns and tactical air forces. Please help me in this matter.'

Eisenhower quickly came up trumps. He asked his Army Group Commanders to ensure their PROs were fully briefed and he sent Harris and Spaatz excellently worded letters suitable for both internal and external publication.

> As the Allied Armies advance into the former industrialised area of the Rhineland they are everywhere confronted with striking evidence of the effectiveness of the bombing campaigns carried on for years by Bomber Command and, since 1942, by the 8th Air Force ... the effect on the war economy of Germany has obviously been tremendous, a fact that advancing troops are quick to appreciate and which unfailingly reminds them of the heroic work of their comrades in Bomber Command and in the United States Air Force.

Harris could have asked for no more and on 10 March responded with a letter of his own, also suitable for publication. Thanking Eisenhower for his tribute and summarising the work of his crews in preparing the way this concluded: 'The reward we have sought is to know that in [the ruins of Germany's major war industrial areas] the Armies already recognise a major cause of their own comparative immunity from the long drawn agonies and the fearful casualties of the last war.'[41]

Three days later these two letters were widely published in the press – and also read in Germany, where Doctor Goebbels in his diary referred to the writers as 'supergangsters' and called their letters 'disgraceful'. On the 15th the *Daily Telegraph* followed up with a strong leader, stating that no operational policy had contributed more, not only to the shortening of the war but to the saving of life. Over the remaining weeks of the war Harris could have no complaint about the media treatment of his Command's activities, with extra ammunition being provided by spectaculars such as the destruction of the Bielefeld Viaduct by Barnes Wallis's Grand Slam bomb and the attack on the German forces in Wesel in support of Montgomery's operation to cross the Rhine. In their letters to Harris, published in the press, General Dempsey described the bombing of Wesel as 'wonderfully accurate', and Montgomery called it 'a masterpiece', a decisive factor in the capture of the town. Then on 3 April, armed with material issued by the Air Ministry (now taking full advantage of its opportunity), the *Daily Mail* among others described how Harris had broken all records for any air force in the previous month by delivering 67,500 tons of bombs on targets inside Hitler's Germany. By this time the war correspondents were able to witness the devastation caused in some of the enemy's towns and cities for themselves; on 18 April, reading a report written by H.S. Woodham, Harris side-lined one particular comment. 'I had tended to be a sceptic about bombing but my tour of the Ruhr towns has convinced me that it has done more than was ever claimed for it. The real thing is far worse than the photographs revealed.'[42]

Meanwhile Churchill's revised minute about city bombing, issued on 1 April, had led the Air Staff to order the end of the area offensive, other than when required specifically to support the land and sea campaigns, and Harris was told this on 6 April. Ten days later Portal signalled him an order of the day intended for circulation in the Command and stated that there was no objection to its wider publication. To his surprise Portal then discovered that the order had not been passed to the press and that in a similar order published by Spaatz to his forces a reference to Bomber Command had been excised. He was not best pleased and sought explanation, whereupon Harris told him that he was still not prepared to relax his security measures. To tell the Germans that Bomber Command would no longer attack large industrial centres and would be concentrating on army and naval support would be to simplify their defensive problems and thus risk increasing his own casualty rates, now extremely low. For that reason he had decided not to publicise Portal's message outside his Command and had asked Spaatz to limit to the Americans the applicability of his own message. With the

European war clearly in its dying moments this may sound like nit-picking but Harris, ever mindful of the interests of his crews, was even now not prepared to endanger unnecessarily more of their lives.[43]

A week later arrived the letter which probably touched Harris more than any of the multitude he was to receive once the war was over:

> Words are of little use but I would like to try. Your great task is over and by your relentless efforts you have succeeded. I know no man that could have been more determined to carry out what you did. I know no one who could have combined such determination with technical and operational knowledge. I give all credit to your staff and your wonderful air crews and maintenance crews and all. But it was your leadership and knowledge that made the 'Bomber Command' the magnificent force it was. The world should thank you.
>
> Words I cannot find to say what I feel about the part the Royal Air Force has played in this war. Forgive an inadequate letter.
>
> TRENCHARD[44]

Notes

1. This is the first of only two 'Ultra' references in Harris's papers. See note 12 below.
2. AIR 14/3507; Folder H65. Saward, *op.cit.* pp.263–5 quotes this correspondence at some length.
3. OH vol.III, pp.124, 197; Folders H70, dated 2 January 1945; H83, dated 13, 20 and 23 October 1944.
4. OH vol.III, pp.46–7; OH vol.IV, pp.173–4; Richards, *Hardest Victory*, pp.236, 240.
5. OH vol.III, pp.66–7, 84 (note 3); BBSU Report, p.24; Craven & Cate, *op.cit.* vol.III, pp.641–5, 670; Herington, *op.cit.* p.217.
6. Richards, *Portal of Hungerford*, p.318. The letters are discussed and quoted from at length by many authors, including Richards, Saward and the official historians. The originals of Portal's letters are in Folder H83 with copies of Harris's letters. The correspondence is also in Portal Folders 11, 12.
7. Hastings, *op.cit.* pp.334–5; Furse, *op.cit.* p.210; Neillands, *op.cit.* p.349; OH vol.III, p.93; Terraine, *op.cit.* pp.676–7; Richards, *Portal of Hungerford*, pp.328–31.
8. Professor Sir Michael Howard, RAFHS Journal, vol.14, 1994.
9. Harris, *op.cit.* p.233.
10. Hinsley, *op.cit.* chapter 54; Bennett, *Behind the Battle*, pp.57, 164.
11. Interview by Group Captain (now Air Vice-Marshal) Tony Mason, 1982.
12. See note 1 above; the second reference is in Portal's letter of 8 January 1945.
13. Bennett, *op.cit.* p.164.
14. Discussion with author, 10 November 1997.
15. Folders H28, dated 14 November 1944; H70, dated 24 November 1944.
16. Folders H104; H55.
17. Folder H84. The casualty figures at Royan proved to be less than first thought.

18. Folder H50.

19. Folders H83; H84; H70; Harris Despatch, pp.94–5.

20. Folders H83; H70; H84; Canadian OH, pp.104–5.

21. Portal Papers, Box C, File 2, E6; Folder H82; Lloyd Despatch, p.6. See also Probert, *op.cit.* pp.291–5, for an outline of the Tiger Force story.

22. Folders H83, dated 17/18 November 1944; H84, dated 16 January 1945; RAFHS Proceedings, vol.6, p.32.

23. Verrier, *The Bomber Offensive*, p.301. See also McKee, *Dresden 1945*, p.116.

24. Bergander, *Dresden im Luftkrieg*, p.348; OH vol.III, p.279.

25. OH vol.III, pp.99–100.

26. OH vol.III, pp.101–4; Gilbert, *op.cit.* pp.1160–1; AIR 2/8011. Saward, *op.cit.* pp.281–8, reproduces many of the official papers.

27. Irving, *Apocalypse 1945*, pp.105–6.

28. OH vol.III, pp.105–6; Bergander, *op.cit.* pp.299–301; Gilbert, *op.cit.* pp.1177–8; Hugh Lunghi, in *The Spectator* 6 August 1994, and in conversation with the author, 2 March 2000. Captain (later Major) Lunghi attended all the Chiefs-of-Staff meetings with the Russians in 1945.

29. Irving, *op.cit.* pp.105–7, 123; AIR 2/8011. Air Chief Marshal Sir Wallace Kyle, questioned by the author in 1987 (as one of Harris's senior staff officers), said quite definitely that the Air Ministry was asked to confirm the order.

30. Harris would refer to Tedder's *With Prejudice*, p.659, and in a 'personal and confidential' memorandum (written long afterwards) implied that the main impetus for the attack came from SHAEF, which was eager to close the route along which Hitler's government might try to move south from Berlin to the 'National Redoubt' in the Bavarian Alps.

31. Gilbert, *op.cit.* p.1219.

32. Harris, *op.cit.* p.242.

33. For full accounts of the whole story see Irving, *op.cit.*, and (for readers of German) Bergander, *op.cit.* For brief accounts see the many Bomber Command histories, *eg* OH vol.III, Richards, Hastings, and Neillands. See also Johnson, *op.cit.* p.232. The debate over the Dresden casualty figures featured in the libel case between David Irving and Deborah Lipstadt in 2000 (published by Penguin Books in *The Irving Judgement*).

34. Richards, *The Hardest Victory*, p.274.

35. Bergander, *op.cit.* p.349.

36. OH vol.III, pp.113–14; Irving, *op.cit.* pp.254–5, 263–5; Hansard, 6 March 1945.

37. OH vol.III, pp.112–13; De Groot, *op.cit.* p.204.

38. Folder H9, dated 29 March 1945. Saward, *op.cit.* pp.290–4, contains these letters in full.

39. Folders H9, dated 14 and 17 February 1945; H84, dated 22 and 25 February 1945; Richards, *Portal of Hungerford*, p.324.

40. Folder H50.

41. Folder H55.

42. Harris family papers. The Command's total effort over the last four months of the war is summarised in OH vol.III, p.198, which quotes the Bomber Command Review to show that 36.6% of the 182,000 tons dropped were used against cities, 26.2% against oil, and 29.8% against troops, defences and transportation. See Richards, *The Hardest Victory*, pp.276–86, for an account of these operations.

43. OH vol.III, pp.117–19; Folder H84, dated 18 and 21 April 1945.

44. Trenchard to Harris, 29 April 1945, family papers.

Chapter 16

Assessment

The verdicts on Bomber Command's contribution to the Allied victory have been many and varied; only a few can be mentioned here. The views of some of the fiercer critics are echoed by Max Hastings. 'The cost in life, treasure and moral superiority over the enemy tragically outstripped the results it achieved,' he writes, and he strongly criticises Harris's fixation on continued area bombing in the final period of the war. In an emotive Australian television film Harris's Command in 1945 is described as a 'runaway juggernaut' and the 'subsequent revulsion' in Britain towards its work is welcomed on the grounds that it provides hope for the future. The official historians, on the other hand, in their thorough and balanced appraisal of the whole strategic offensive, conclude that 'cumulatively in largely indirect ways and eventually in a more immediate and direct manner, strategic bombing and also in other roles strategic bombers made a contribution to victory which was decisive' – which can be taken to mean that without their work the war could not have been won. And Albert Speer, who had had ample time for reflection, wrote in prison in 1959:

> The real importance of the air war consisted in the fact that it opened a second front long before the invasion in Europe. That front was the skies over Germany. The fleets of bombers might appear at any time over any large German city or important factory. The unpredictability of the attacks made this front gigantic; every square meter of the territory we controlled was a kind of front line. Defence against air attacks required the production of thousands of anti-aircraft guns, the stockpiling of tremendous quantities of ammunition all over the country, and holding in readiness hundreds of thousands of soldiers, who in addition had to stay in position by their guns, often totally inactive, for months at a time. As far as I can judge from the accounts I have read, no one has yet seen that this was the greatest lost battle on the German side. The losses from the retreats in Russia or from the surrender of Stalingrad were considerably less.[1]

In 1976 Speer sent Harris a personal copy of his book (see p.404), with a note referring to this page: 'I hope it will please you to read these facts which are always underestimated.'

Perhaps only one thing is certain in all this: the controversy over the bombing of Germany in the Second World War – and therefore about

Harris – will for ever continue. Already, however, the passage of time, coupled with continued research drawing on additional documentation, is enabling new perspectives to emerge, and we need to consider these in relation both to Harris's own views and to those that prevailed in the more immediate post-war years.

So, as Harris himself posed the question: were the results worth the lives of the 55,000 aircrew, and others, who died in Bomber Command? To this must be added: did the results justify Bomber Command's 7% of the manpower effort directly absorbed by the British fighting services during the war? Harris first set out his summary of these results in his Despatch, circulated to officialdom in 1946, though one particularly important point was not brought out until his personal memoir was published in 1947. Here he stressed the extent to which, as compared with the 1914–18 war, his campaign had saved countless lives elsewhere in all three Services, and also among British civilians.[2] Though incapable of proof this has to be a fair judgement.

Harris expounded the principal achievements in both his Despatch and his memoir. His first key point was that the main attack of 1943 forced the Luftwaffe to switch increasingly to home defence, thus weakening its ability to support the German land forces. His second was that the Germans were obliged to divert more and more guns from the land war to the defence of their industrial cities. Then he referred to the unprecedented devastation caused in these cities, which reduced every form of war production, prevented the development of many new war weapons, and required an army of two million men to be engaged on repair work. Next came the many-faceted support for the invasion, the return to the assault on the cities, the offensive against communications, and the attack on oil. Finally he mentioned the great value to the war at sea of minelaying and the destruction by bombing of surface forces, including several of the enemy's heaviest warships. It is hard to dispute most of this, and the great debate over bombing policy has really centred on just one – albeit very important – aspect: city bombing. It must be remembered that, as Harris made clear, while 45% of his Command's bombing effort was devoted to this 55% went on the many other roles it was required to perform. He accepted, too, that not until the last year of the war did the bombing really begin to affect the whole German war machine. On the other hand, had his Command possessed in 1943 the force available to it in 1944 and been able to use it without interruption alongside the whole American bomber force, he was convinced that Germany could have been defeated outright.[3]

The Despatch, sent round for comment to the Air Ministry staffs and to certain officers elsewhere who had been involved in the bombing campaign, aroused mixed reactions, not least in relation to area bombing. Air

Commodore Pelly, formerly SASO at Headquarters AEAF and then commander of the British Bombing Survey Unit which had recently completed
its report, disputed Harris's conviction that the bombing of Germany's
industrial cities was the soundest method of reducing her capacity to wage
war: 'Later BBSU studies concluded that the effects on war production of
town area attacks were slight.' As for Harris's speculation that bombing
might have ended the war without need of an invasion – whether right or
wrong – this, he said, was based on no reasoned argument. Group Captain
Bufton, who produced a lengthy critique largely devoted to defending the
policies advocated by his own Directorate, stated that it had always been
intended that Bomber Command should return to precision targets as soon
as tactical capabilities permitted. In his view the enemy could well have
sustained city bombing at the tempo achieved by Bomber Command more
or less indefinitely – say two years – as far as war production was concerned:
'Of the two million tons of bombs dropped by the RAF and US strategic
bomber forces the 9% directed at oil were decisive, the 24% against
industrial cities were not.'

Air Commodore Baker, also from a DB Ops standpoint, thought Bufton's
strictures went too far. In his judgement Harris had certainly not been out of
line with Air Ministry policy in the earlier years, and in a well-balanced
response he reminded his readers how easy it was to be wise after the event.
'It would be a great pity,' he wrote, 'if we failed to give Harris full credit for
his immense personal contribution in building up the bomber offensive in
face of such immense difficulties.' Let the final word here come from Ralph
Cochrane, who was now C-in-C Transport Command. He considered the
Despatch a very fair summing-up and believed its concluding paragraphs
could not be seriously gainsaid. Nor was it unreasonable to think that had
bombardment on the scale of 1944–5 begun a year earlier a result similar to
that against Japan could have been achieved.[4]

Under all the circumstances, however, Overlord was an inevitable component of Allied strategy. Given all the conflicting pressures on Allied
resources the strategic bomber forces could never have been given anything
approaching the absolute priority for resources that Harris had urged in the
hope of rendering the invasion unnecessary or at least enabling it to be
mounted on a far smaller scale. That he genuinely believed, until the end of
1943, that bombing, properly applied, might win the war is certainly true.
Equally true is that long afterwards he spoke of being very glad that the
invasion did take place. 'Had Germany collapsed as a result of bombing – as
it would have done – the Russians would have come right through,' he
admitted in 1979.[5]

So much, for the present, for Harris's own views. Between the compilation
of his Despatch and his publication of *Bomber Offensive* the British and United

States Strategic Bombing Missions had been at work, and since their reports would come to constitute prime sources of information for later historians they need some mention here. The American survey was commissioned in late 1944 and with top-level support was established on a lavish basis; the British survey, however, emerged only after much difficulty. Ideas for it had been discussed at Air Ministry level in 1944, in November Harris formed his own small group to make a start in one or two areas of Germany already under Allied control;[6] and in December Churchill's authority for a full-scale Mission was requested. In January 1945, however, the Prime Minister surprisingly refused to sanction anything more than a very small team and not until June was the size and structure of the Mission agreed. The work was done over the next year, drawing its statistical information mainly from the American teams, and the final confidential draft was submitted in June 1946. Yet while the Report was eventually made available to historians not until 1998 was it openly published. Sebastian Cox, in his introduction to it, explains how Solly Zuckermann came from SHAEF to become the BBSU's Scientific Adviser and its most influential member. His previous conviction that transportation was the key target system for strategic bombing came with him and was to influence markedly the overall tenor of the Report.

In his invaluable commentary on the Report itself Cox observes that its description of bombing policy tended to reflect the views of the Air Staff rather than those held at High Wycombe, and that it presented the entire strategic bombing offensive up to March 1944 as largely ineffective because the German economy was not fully mobilised on a war footing – a false assumption, Cox suggests. During the final year of the war the Report gave strategic bombing far greater credit in destroying the enemy's economy, but essentially on the grounds of its effects on the transportation system; the complementary value of area bombing in setting a limit on that economy, in handicapping rationalisation and in forcing dispersal, did not, however, receive due credit. Nor did the Report take proper account of the immense quantities of manpower and other resources needed for the repair of bomb damage, much of it caused by area attacks. There is a great deal more in Cox's critique, much of it complimentary to the Report's authors, but his final comment is amply justified: its most serious shortcoming was its underestimation of the effect of Harris's area attacks.[7] As for the United States' survey, it is worth mentioning the later criticism directed at it by their own official historians: 'Its deprecating tone about the RAF contribution did not reflect a judicious appraisal of the RAF effort . . . and Harris took spirited exception to some of its conclusions.'[8]

Four years later Hilary Saunders and Denis Richards wrote their Air Ministry sponsored history of the RAF in the Second World War, and while this covered the entire RAF story, built into it was the first 'official' account

of the strategic bomber offensive. The authors were free to consult most of
the relevant documents, including Harris's Despatch and the BBSU Report,
but not to refer specifically to them, and although the offensive was ably
described in some detail it was not practicable – or indeed permissible – to
offer a major appraisal. They did refer to the main charge laid against
Harris's conduct of the strategic bombing campaign, namely that the results
achieved were too small in comparison with the effort expended, and they
touched briefly on some of the specific achievements, but they did not
directly address the most controversial issue – that surrounding area
bombing. Indeed when they wrote 'the really decisive blows, those against
oil and communications, fell towards the end of the war', they were in a sense
echoing the judgement of the BBSU.[9]

It was another six years before the four-volume official history appeared,
written by Sir Charles Webster and Dr Noble Frankland. This publicly
referred to many of the significant official records and identified the British
and United States bombing surveys not only as its main providers of
statistical material but also as among the major sources of its conclusions.[10]
It needs to be remembered that this history was intentionally concentrated
upon the strategic offensive; it was not a history of Bomber Command's or
Harris's war, so much of which was undertaken in support of other campaigns. The authors did refer to the Command's many wider activities in
order to place its strategic bombing role in its broader context, but it was left
to the various bi-service or tri-service campaign histories to cover these in
detail. As a result, while this was in no way the fault of the authors (who
were simply following their Cabinet Office remit), the official history helped
to strengthen public perceptions that Harris and his Command had been
essentially engaged in the attack on the great towns and cities of Germany, a
strategy which had not yielded sufficient rewards to justify it.

Certainly the official historians were not uncritical of the bombing surveys
but their guarded judgement of the value of the area bombing campaign did
reflect to a fair extent that of the BBSU. The achievements of Harris's 1943–
4 offensive were thus called, for example, meagre and disappointing, for
German war production continued to increase despite the heavy pressure on
it, the German people remained loyal and obedient, and the German armed
forces continued to fight with great bravery and efficiency. Then, while the
results of the final assault of 1944–5 were described as something far greater,
it was the destruction of whole vital segments of Germany's oil production
and the dislocation of her communication system that were given the main
credit as Bomber Command's contribution to the final victory – not area
bombing, to which too much effort had been devoted.[11]

It must be said here that the official history does not deserve the obloquys
that some have subsequently heaped upon it, especially in the earlier years

after its publication. Most historians now regard it as a remarkable exercise in balance and objectivity, much superior to the other official campaign histories of the Second World War, but what it needs is thorough and thoughtful reading, something which it all too rarely receives. Even its most absolute judgements are nearly always qualified, enabling the reader to appreciate the often conflicting factors that influence them, and it has become the most important single source of reference for all who study the British strategic bomber offensive. Yet as Dr Frankland describes in his recently published memoir,[12] most of the initial reactions in the press went to extremes, often being based on superficial first impressions and relying heavily on selective quotation. Some used the history in order to try to demonstrate that the bomber offensive had been a complete waste of effort, and thus were applauded by the many critics. Others represented it as a total failure to do justice to Harris and his men. In fact neither view was remotely justifiable, but the passions had been aroused and sadly he himself was not immune to them.

We shall return to Harris's views in chapter 19, but at this point it should be remembered what Webster and Frankland themselves wrote about his qualities as Commander-in-Chief of Bomber Command. Referring to 1942 they spoke of 'his forceful, single-minded leadership infusing the whole force with a spirit which was to prove unquenchable.' In relation to 1944 they described him as 'inspired and dynamic', the recipient of his men's absolute obedience and confidence, a commander held in awe and also affection, a man whose power of command and unshakeable determination distinguished him as a giant among his contemporaries. At the same time they did not spare the criticism. His prestige did not depend upon a reputation for good judgement; he made a habit of seeing only one side of a question and then exaggerating it; he often confused advice with interference, he saw all issues in terms of black or white. Their closing reminder to their readers, however, should be re-stated:

> Regularly, and sometimes several times within a week, the C-in-C committed practically the whole of his front line to the uncertain battle and occasionally he committed almost the entire reserve as well. On each occasion he had to take a calculated risk not only with the enemy defences but also with the weather. On each occasion he might have suffered an irretrievable disaster. The enduring courage, determination and conviction of Sir Arthur Harris, who bore the responsibility for more than three years, deserves to be commemorated.[13]

What Harris himself thought about these attributes when he eventually decided to read the book is not recorded, but the insight and balance that the historians demonstrated in their appraisals of him are a good example of the overall quality of their work. Nevertheless, the impression they gave that the results of the area offensive did not fully justify the effort which Harris devoted to it has stuck, and he himself never changed his mind about the way in which this critical part of his campaign had in his opinion been undervalued.

In recent years, however, the research and writing have continued and new perceptions are appearing. Some historians remain highly critical. Max Hastings' view has already been quoted. Peter Johnson, at the end of his recent thoughtful reflections on his part in the bomber war, considers that from April 1943 area bombing was unjustified. Professor Donald Watt wrote in the context of the bombing during the Kosovo crisis: 'The ghosts of Trenchard and Harris with their profound contempt for all civilians, have still to be exorcised.'[14] For a deeply researched and considered modern view, however, it would be hard to better Professor Richard Overy, who in several books has examined the fundamental political, military and economic factors underlying the Second World War, and in the process reassessed the significance of the bomber offensive against Germany.

Overy's contention is that its overall value has been generally underestimated and not least because earlier assessments were unduly conditioned by statistics relating to industrial production – the main type of information that was readily available in the months immediately after the war when the bombing surveys were conducted. In his view there are many other factors to be considered, usually inter-related but more difficult to quantify, and he suggests that the cumulative effect of the bombing was considerably greater than initial judgements suggested. He tells us that in early 1942, at the time when Harris took over Bomber Command, 'the Allies faced the worst case scenario' and that it was during the next two years of attrition that the Allies actually won the war. Observing that in this phase of the bombing campaign the rain of bombs on German and Italian cities eroded once flourishing industries to a greater extent than was first thought, especially in key areas such as aircraft and tank production, he lists its central achievements. It speeded the re-entry of Western forces into Europe; it helped open a Second Front in 1942–3 by diverting large quantities of German manpower and equipment from the Eastern Front to home defence; it created the conditions for the defeat of the German Air Force; and it prevented the effective development of a European superpower. Moreover, while so doing, it served a crucial political purpose to the Prime Minister in his relations with the Soviet Union. To suggest, therefore, that Harris's achievement up to 1944 was of relatively little value is very far from the truth. Even though German military output trebled between 1941 and 1944 it would assuredly have expanded far more in a bomb-free environment.

There has been less argument about the physical effects of the offensive in the final period of the war and much more about the targets at which it was directed, but here we need to consider the overall impact of the bombing – American as well as British – on Germany's military potential as it mounted in 1943 and reached its climax in 1944–5. Overy places its effects in three categories, first of all those that were intended. The increasingly lower ceiling it imposed on German weapons production steadily reduced the quantity available to the front-line forces, not least those opposing the Russians. The system of distributing weapons was seriously affected, as were research and technological innovation; the supply of oil and chemicals was particularly heavily hit. Added to these were the effects of area bombing in disrupting essential services, causing massive diversions of resources to damage repair, and forcing dispersal of different elements of the production processes, with consequent far-reaching implications for transportation. Then there was the workforce, whose productivity was hard to sustain and even harder to increase in the face of air raid alarms and absenteeism. Management too, constantly being enjoined to raise production, had somehow to cope with the endless disruption being caused by bombing. To add to the toll there were the social effects, not least those occasioned by the official and unofficial evacuation of civilians from larger towns and cities – nine million of them by January 1945, according to the German historian Groehler.

Next, Overy says, there were the diversionary consequences. Most important was the extent to which the bombing compelled the Luftwaffe to concentrate unduly on its fighter force and employ it very largely in home defence. Consequently the whole pattern of aircraft production was distorted, German offensive air power was greatly restricted, and their land forces on all fronts increasingly lacked air cover and air support. Also there were the demands of anti-aircraft defence, including by 1944 some 55,000 guns and 900,000 men. The further 1.2 million men employed on damage repair were another major charge on the economy.

Thirdly came the subsidiary effects. These included Hitler's insistence – despite Speer's opposition – that key parts of German industry should go underground; the consequent huge construction task involved half of Germany's building workers, imposed a huge extra load on the transportation system and therefore entailed a colossal extra economic commitment. Another such burden was created by the development of the various V-weapons, seen by Hitler as the best means of retaliating against the bombing. Himmler, who undertook responsibility for providing the resources for these various projects, had no hesitation in using all the power of the police state for his purposes and in the later stages of the war Speer was increasingly sidelined.[15]

No wonder Speer wrote as he did about the air war over Germany being her greatest lost battle, and when in later years Harris sought to answer the question 'what did the bombing achieve?' he would simply refer his listeners to the most knowledgeable of his customers, Albert Speer. While he may at times have seized somewhat too readily on such of Speer's statements as confirmed his own convictions, on the whole Speer's judgements were sound, and it is fair to say that Harris's views of what the strategic attack on Germany accomplished in physical terms – particularly as expressed in his personal memoir – can now be seen to have largely stood the test of time.

This subject would be incomplete without consideration of another major aspect of Harris's campaign, namely the extent to which it fulfilled one of its particularly important early aims, *ie* to break the enemy's morale. We have already seen how strongly this objective was being supported by higher authority, both before Harris appeared on the scene and then well into 1943, with both Churchill and Stalin firmly behind it. Harris expressed his own views after the Battle of the Ruhr when drafting an article for the RAF Journal. Many people, he said, regarded German civilian morale as of little importance; given the power of Hitler's SS they would think twice before staging any kind of revolt. He was not so sure: there could come a point when conditions would be unbearable. He would make no prophesies. 'I will only say that our raids on the Ruhr are making conditions there progressively worse. They will become worse still – much worse. We shall see whether the morale, courage and endurance of the German people are equal to the fortitude of the people of London and Coventry.'[16] By the end of 1943, however, the doubts were spreading, and although Harris himself was disinclined to share them publicly he probably did so privately. As he wrote in 1947:

> The idea that the main object of bombing German industrial cities was to break the enemy's morale proved to be totally unsound; when we had destroyed almost all the large industrial cities in Germany the civil population remained apathetic, while the Gestapo saw to it that they were docile, and in so far as there was work for them to do, industrious.[17]

The BBSU Report delivered a similar message. Referring to the original assumption that the intangible effects of bombing, coupled with de-housing, would demoralise the civilian population and the industrial workers to the extent of forcing Germany's rulers to capitulate, it judged in the light of experience that morale, in the sense of a tendency of the individual to break down and fail to respond to firm authority, was not likely to crack under air attacks. So morale never reached breaking point, even the mounting toll of casualties failed to destroy the hold of the Nazi Party, and insofar as the offensive against German towns was designed to wreck civilian morale it clearly failed, even in the closing period of the war. Nevertheless the authors

of the Report did accept that the issue of morale remained a field for con-
jecture. Harris agreed, saying that it had needed to be regarded during the
war as an imponderable factor; possibly a break in it might have led to the
enemy's collapse, but more probably bad morale would merely add to the
loss of production caused by air raid damage.[18]

Such views were carried forward into the official history and have been
widely echoed since. Speer, who wrote of Hitler's fears in 1943 that continued
city bombing would crack people's morale irreparably, afterwards gave his
personal judgement succinctly: 'Bombing did not weaken morale.' Max
Hastings writes: 'German morale never came near to collapse until the very
end.' Michael Howard agrees, saying that morale did not prove the soft target
that pre-war theorists had believed. However much German civilians may
have disliked the Nazi regime they became increasingly reliant on it to enable
them to survive; they came to hate the bombers and became more and more
involved in fighting the war.[19] Richard Overy, while describing bombing as a
uniquely demoralising experience, considers that the naive expectation that
bombing would produce a tidal wave of panic and disillusionment and wash
away popular support for the war was exposed as wishful thinking. As the
same time, however, he stresses the disruptive effects of bombing on German
society and accepts that the sharp decline of morale in 1944 had severe
consequences for the enemy's production performance.

Thus the conventional wisdom in Great Britain has been that German
morale did not prove to have been a worthwhile objective, contrary to what
Harris among others had originally hoped. The same view has not surprisingly also prevailed in the United States, where the thinking of some British
and American air leaders about the likelihood of enemy morale cracking
under bombing has been recently described by a leading Air Force historian
as myopic.[20] From some of today's German air historians, on the other hand,
rather different views emerge. One of these is Horst Boog:

> If the morale of the civilian population is defined as their will to continue to
> work for the war effort, then German morale was not broken. But it was
> certainly weakened, as recent studies have revealed, especially in cities suf-
> fering heavy attacks. People continued to do their duty in a fatalistic and
> apathetic mood, and this did not increase their devotion to the political cause
> and to productivity. It was not morale in this sense that kept them on the
> ball. Rather it was the desire to survive – which, under the circumstances of
> the political surveillance system, also meant doing what one was told and not
> shirking in the presence of others – and the hope that one day their dreadful
> existence and experience would be over.[21]

Another is Götz Bergander, who has done much research in his determination to put the Dresden story into its wider context. He draws an

important distinction between private morale and war morale. The former was never broken, *ie* the will to live, based on personal, family and vocational aspirations and generating inventiveness, stubbornness and the desire to assert oneself. The latter, reflected in people's ability to think about future prospects, was on the other hand severely damaged – much more than first thought:

> In reality, the air raids on cities and industry shook the foundations of the war morale of the German people. They permanently shattered their nerves, undermined their health and shook their belief in victory, thus altering their consciousness. They spread fear, dismay and hopelessness. This was an important and intentional result of the strategic air war, of this warfare revolution.

Analysing the reports of the Reich Security Service on the effects of the air war, Bergander records the change of attitude after Harris stepped up the air offensive in 1942, and particularly after the terror raid on Cologne. From now on, and on a growing scale, these reports reflected consternation among the entire German people, fear of the future level of such raids, feelings of insecurity, war weariness and much more. After the Hamburg attacks one of these spoke of rumours of apparent unrest in the city spreading throughout the Reich and leading to a kind of 'November mood' (reminiscent of November 1918), as the Germans could not tolerate these raids in the long term and were rebelling against them. 'If Sir Arthur Harris could have read this at the time,' writes Bergander, 'it would have been triumphant confirmation that he was on the right path with the area night bombing', though he goes on to quote this report as saying that most people still trusted the Führer somehow to find a way to victory. Finally came the climax at Dresden, when the will to resist, he says, was at last broken.[22]

While the effects of the attack on morale must remain unquantifiable, it does now appear that they were substantially more worthwhile than was previously thought, and that they constitute a significant argument in favour of the area bombing campaign, including its continuance in 1944–5. The morale factor had a pervasive influence on Germany's warmaking potential and needs to be set alongside the more specific objectives that Harris addressed in the course of the strategic campaign. What this and the American offensive achieved fell short of securing the Allied victory, but their critical contribution proved very much in line with Harris's own hopes under the actual circumstances of the time.

As Overy writes when summarising why the Allies won: 'Underlying everything was the bomber offensive, whose far-reaching effects on German economic potential and on the German home front were sufficient to limit the expansion of German military might to a point where the Allied ground forces (on all fronts) could fight on more than equal terms.'[23]

It remains to pose one more question. Was it morally right for Bomber Command to devote almost half its effort to attacking Germany's towns and cities and thus in effect to be targeting the civilian population? There were some critics at the time, most notably the Bishop of Chichester (see p.193, Note 14), and there have been many since; it was unarguably a dreadful way in which to have to fight a war. Moreover, as we have seen, none of those in authority were prepared to admit publicly what they knew privately, namely that the bombing of cities – the strategy they were ordering the C-in-C to carry out – implied the deliberate targeting of the men, women, and children who lived in them.

Harris was, however, far too honest and blunt to connive at what he considered a deception; in today's jargon he might even have called it spin-doctoring. In his view, if bombing was specially wicked because of its consequences for civilians, it was no different from other methods of waging war, such as blockade in the First World War or siege and bombardment of cities in earlier wars – and indeed the present one.[24] As he had written to Arthur Street in December 1943 (see pp.193–4), it would be a waste of effort to attack children, invalids and old people who were economically unproductive and, as consumers, a handicap to the war effort, but the cities of Germany including their working population, houses and public utilities were literally the heart of her war potential, which was why they were being deliberately attacked. To his mind there was no fundamental difference in total war, *ie* a war of survival, between the uniformed soldiery and that vast number of men and women who, while wearing civilian clothes, were engaged directly or indirectly in enabling the military to do their jobs. When Speer wrote about the cruelty and effectiveness with which the Western Allies extended the war to those he called 'non-combatants' he seems to have been trying to preserve such a distinction, but he did accept that the Allies' desire for destruction was no greater than that of the Germans, and observed that in 1940, when predicting that London would become a rubble heap, Hitler stated that he lacked the slightest sympathy for British civilians.[25] Harris, who at that time had watched London burn, similarly had no qualms about the dictates of total war.

Not surprisingly, therefore, Harris did want to terrify the Germans, a point which Peter Tomlinson was at pains to stress and which he himself made on occasion. Michael Howard makes exactly this point when discussing Bomber Command's attempts to destroy morale: 'Our adversaries called it terror bombing, which it was; we were indeed trying to terrify the German population.'[26] Terror bombing was, and remains, a highly emotive phrase, one whose use seems almost automatically to trigger the worst of reactions to Harris and his campaign. During the war the enemy used it for some of their best propaganda; in public the British, apart from a few brave critics, denied its validity. Yet deep down Harris was one of those who recognised that the ability to strike terror into the heart of one's enemy had throughout history been a weapon of war. The fact that there was now a new means of doing this made no difference to the concept: he was under orders to take the fight to the enemy in order to help win the war and there was no point in ignoring or not admitting its potential in assisting the enemy's defeat. Those who criticise him should forever remember that he was essentially an honest man, a realist who understood the implications of what he was being required to do and was never prepared to conceal the truth as he saw it.

Two brief quotations will serve to round off this discussion. First, on whether it was morally right to conduct the strategic bomber offensive as it built up under Harris's leadership, Dr Noble Frankland, speaking in 1961: 'The great immorality open to us in 1940 and 1941 [and in 1942 and 1943, adds John Terraine] was to lose the war against Hitler's Germany. To have abandoned the only means of direct attack which we had at our disposal would have been a long step in that direction.'[27]

And finally Leonard Cheshire, one of Harris's greatest bomber pilots, speaking in 1993: 'I am convinced that without the bomber offensive as he ran it we would not have prised Fortress Europe open enough to let the armies in.'[28]

Notes

1. Hastings, *op.cit.* p.352; TV film *Wings of the Storm*; OH vol.III, p.310; Speer, *Spandau – The Secret Diaries*, p.399.
2. OH vol.IV, p.440; BBSU Report, p.38–9 (in 1943–5 the percentage was higher – 12%); Harris, *op.cit.* pp.268–9.
3. Harris, *op.cit.* pp.262–6; Despatch, pp.39–40 (published by Frank Cass, with invaluable introductions by Sebastian Cox and Horst Boog, 1995). See also pp.353–4.
4. AIR 2/9726. Bufton and Baker, like so many other wartime senior officers, had now reverted to their substantive ranks.
5. Interview with Dewar McCormack.
6. Johnson, *op.cit.* pp.267–312, describes his experiences in this work in mid-1945.
7. Official Report of the BBSU, published by Frank Cass, 1998, with introduction by Sebastian Cox. See also OH vol.IV, pp.40–58, for a valuable commentary on the British and US Surveys.
8. Craven & Cate, *op.cit.* vol.III, p.791.
9. Saunders & Richards, *Royal Air Force 1939–45*, vol.3, pp.381, 387. This was first published in 1955.
10. OH vol.IV, p.40.
11. OH vol.III, pp.288–9.

12. Noble Frankland, *History at War*, pp.114–25.

13. OH vol.II, p.91; OH vol.III, pp.78–80, 286.

14. Johnson, *op.cit.* pp.332–3; *Daily Telegraph* 15 April 1999. For a useful American view, also somewhat critical, see paper by Tami Davis Biddle, entitled 'Bombing by the Square Yard: Bomber Harris at War', published in *International History Review*, Canada, September 1999.

15. This brief summary of Overy's views is based on *Why the Allies Won, Bomber Command 1939–45*, and talks at the RAF Historical Society (1993) and in Canberra (1995, published by Alan Stephens of the Air Power Studies Centre).

16. Folder H106, E10. This paragraph on German morale was not published, having been deleted by ACAS(G) in the Air Ministry.

17. Harris, *op.cit.* pp.77–9. He made an exception in the case of Italy's northern cities.

18. BBSU Report, pp.67–8, 97, 164; Harris, *op.cit.* p.88.

19. Speer, *Inside the Third Reich*, pp.262, 278; Hastings, *op.cit.* p.349; Howard, RAFHS Journal, vol.14, p.16.

20. Major General John Huston, in his Foreword to the BBSU Report.

21. Dr Horst Boog, until recently Chief Air Historian at the Militargeschichtliches-forschungsamt, Freiburg, in RAFHS, *Reaping the Whirlwind*.

22. Bergander, *op.cit.* pp.312–15. Bergander also reminds us how the Russians exploited the bomber offensive in propaganda leaflets delivered to German troops on the Eastern Front. They were told of the way their home towns were being destroyed and their families suffering in the hope that their own morale also would suffer.

23. Overy, *Why the Allies Won*, p.322.

24. Harris, *op.cit.* pp.176–7. See Neillands, *op.cit.* chapter 18, for a valuable recent discussion of the moral issues.

25. Speer, *The Secret Diaries*, p.45.

26. Author's discussion with Tomlinson; RAFHS Journal, vol.14, p.15.

27. Lecture to the RUSI, 13 December 1961; Terraine, *op.cit.* pp.507–8.

28. RAFHS, *Reaping the Whirlwind*, interview by Mark Laity.

Chapter 17

Enough is enough

When the war ended Harris was 53. He had just spent over three years amid all the strains and stresses of directing Bomber Command, he had taken no proper leave and had been away from his working duties for only the very occasional few days when his chronic duodenal ulcer was playing up badly. No wonder he was exhausted and in need of a total change of scene. Portal knew this full well when he wrote personally to 'my dear Bert' on 9 May 1945 telling him how deeply and sincerely grateful he felt for the 'magnificent' work he and his Command had done. He went on:

> I also want to thank you for never letting the inevitable differences of opinion in a long war affect our personal relationship, and I would like also to say how tremendously I admired the way you refused to let ill-health affect your grip and mastery of your great three-year battle. For the support you have always given me, and for your tremendous personal contribution to the achievements of the RAF in this war I can never adequately thank you.

To this warm, totally genuine message Harris immediately replied in a letter which, as Denis Richards says, perfectly illustrated the 'bigness' of character which Portal always saw and admired in his subordinate:

> Thank you for your letter – which I do not deserve, altho' my crews and others do. If we had differences of opinion they were not personal – and in the outcome you were always right on the things that mattered. The burden which you have so well supported far exceeded mine, but I am of the lesser stature. I regret indeed occasions on which I have been crochety and impatient; I was the closest to the urgencies of my Command and, frankly, borne down by the frightful inhumanities of war. Thank you for all you did for us and the Country.[1]

There was still plenty to be done before Harris could take his leave. From 29 April to 8 May his bombers had turned their attention to a mission of mercy, the dropping of food to the starving people of Holland in Operation Manna, and between 26 April and 6 June he directed another much publicised operation, equally satisfying to him and his crews: the flying home of some 75,000 released prisoners-of-war, some of them his own men. Sinclair had written to him about this and while totally supportive was somewhat anxious about the risk of accidents; he hoped strict instructions were being given to ensure that safety was the prime consideration. Harris assured him that this was the case: the crews were being carefully selected, there was no overloading, and operations would be stopped if weather conditions were unsuitable. Inevitably, however, he realistically went on, there were risks in using wartime aircraft in this way and the occasional accident was unavoidable – there had been one already. If safety was absolutely overriding it might be better to establish a shipping service from Antwerp, but his crews would certainly do their best and not be rushed by any considerations of delay, inconvenience or disappointment. The operation continued.[2]

One airman who came home by this route in early May was Peter Tomlinson, who with a colleague – Ian Bourne – decided on arrival in England to make his own way to London. To their surprise the train stopped at High Wycombe so they got off and Tomlinson asked a WAAF railway transport officer for the phone number of Bomber Command. 'Just ask for Southdown,' she said. On getting through Tomlinson boldly asked to speak to the C-in-C. 'Harris,' came the almost immediate reply. 'Sir, this is Peter.' 'Peter who?' 'Peter Tomlinson.' 'I've had an aircraft on standby for you for ages. Where are you?' 'High Wycombe station.' 'Stay there – don't move.' A short while later the C-in-C's car screeched to a halt, with himself at the wheel. Jackie's godfather was back. The story did not stop there, for Harris was already looking for a successor to his PA, Walter Pretyman, who was keen to retire and get back to his civilian career in Brazil. Arrangements were quickly made, so Tomlinson went off for a spot of leave before returning to take over from Pretyman and rejoin the Harris family at Springfield.[3]

At the forefront of Harris's mind at this time was the need to pay his personal tribute to the men and women of Bomber Command. This he did in an excellently worded, at times moving, Special Order of the Day issued on 10 May. He outlined the course of the bomber war, listed his aircrews' many achievements, and acknowledged the contributions of the countless men and women without whose work both in and outside his Command the job would have been impossible. Two brief quotations must here suffice. Having spoken of the grievous casualties incurred, he went on:

> To you who survive I would say this. Content yourselves, and take credit with those who perished, that now the 'Cease Fire' has sounded countless homes within our Empire will welcome back a father, husband or son whose life, but for your endeavours and your sacrifices, would assuredly have been expended during long further years of agony to achieve a victory already ours. No Allied Nation is clear of this debt to you.

Then in conclusion:

> To all of you I would say how proud I am to have served in Bomber Com-
> mand for $4\frac{1}{2}$ years and to have been your Commander-in-Chief through more
> than three years of your Saga. Your task in the German war is now com-
> pleted. Famously have you fought. Well have you deserved of your country
> and her Allies.[4]

Already, however, Harris was becoming incensed at the absence in the
wider world of recognition of his Command's work. As he told Portal on 12
May, neither he nor any single member of his Command had been invited to
any of the recent ceremonies accepting the enemy surrender. He himself had
no personal pride in such matters but he felt jealous both for his Command
and for his Service. While the omission was no doubt unintentional he
considered it a gross discourtesy, and the presence of Spaatz on these
occasions had ensured that the whole American bomber force was receiving
due credit. He made similar points to Trenchard, adding that he blamed the
Air Ministry for not insisting on his Command being invited; neither the
War Office nor the Admiralty would have let such a thing happen under
similar circumstances. Indeed, the comments of Kesselring, Rundstedt and
Goering from the enemy side had in recent weeks done more to indicate
Bomber Command's achievements than anything the Air Ministry had
attempted. Portal's somewhat lame response on 16 May was to send a copy
of Harris's letter to Tedder, observe that the ceremonies were entirely
matters for the Supreme Commander, and presume that Tedder had been
considered the RAF representative.[5]

Meanwhile there had been something far worse. On the afternoon of 13
May Churchill broadcast to the nation and next day this 'VE Speech' was
fully reported in the press. Harris and Eaker listened to it together with
mounting incredulity. It reflected on the early days of the war, the Battle of
Britain, the 'blitz', the value of Northern Ireland, the work of the Royal
Navy and Merchant Navy in the Battle of the Atlantic, the Mediterranean
battles, the entry into the war of Russia, Japan and the USA, the liberation of
France, the measures to combat the German V-weapon campaigns, the final
land operations in Europe, and the challenges of the future. Of the strategic
bombing campaign, or indeed in specific terms of any other bombing
operations, there was not one word – apart from a single oblique reference to
damage done in Berlin. It was as though the bomber offensive had never
been.[6]

To Harris this was incomprehensible. He and Churchill had been partners
in conflict. Whereas without the Prime Minister's backing the whole
offensive might well have been a non-starter, with it the campaign had not

only contributed enormously to victory but also served vital political purposes. For Churchill now to ignore it seemed totally unjustified and out of
character, and although Harris always retained his admiration and affection
for his old friend he never forgot the slight on his men and never understood
how it could have occurred. Insofar as historians have tried to explain it they
have usually linked it with the views Churchill expressed after Dresden,
when he seemed to recoil from the consequences of the destruction of
Germany's cities by the Allied bomber forces. Enough was enough, he
appeared to be saying: it was time now to concentrate on how to prepare to
meet Germany's post-war needs. This was an admirable sentiment but it
hardly explains the absence of any public mention of what the bombers had
actually done. Might it also have been that Churchill had developed pangs of
conscience about the death and destruction that had been caused and did not
want to risk being portrayed as glorifying or gloating? This too is possible,
but it is hard to believe that it was beyond the power of such a master of the
English language to devise a form of words which would have acknowledged
Harris and his Command in some acceptable way.

Neither of these reasons seems sufficient and one wonders if some other
factor may have been at work, something specific to the moment when
Churchill actually spoke. Harris himself had understood for some while his
friend's fears about the future. Late one February evening at Chequers, soon
after Dresden, Churchill was speculating about what would happen when
Harris had finished his destruction of Germany; what, he mused, would lie
between the white snows of Russia and the white cliffs of Dover? Perhaps the
Russians would not want to sweep on to the Atlantic or something might
stop them as the accident of Ghenghis Khan's death had stopped the horsed
archers of the Mongols, who retired and never came back. 'You mean now
they will come back?' asked Harris. 'Who can say?' replied Churchill. 'They
may not want to. But there is an unspoken fear in many people's hearts.'
When three months later, on 20 May, Harris dined for the last time at
Chequers and the conversation occasionally turned from pressing election
matters to the future of Germany and the Russian peril, he was again
reminded of the Prime Minister's deep anxieties.[7]

Long afterwards, in December 1954, Churchill summarised them in the
House of Commons. 'In those days of victory, the thought that filled my
mind was that all the efforts we had made to free Europe from a totalitarian
regime of one kind might go for naught if we allowed so much of Europe to
fall into the grip of another totalitarian regime from the East.' He was at that
moment facing criticism for having said in a speech to his Woodford con-
stituents that he had telegraphed Montgomery in May 1945, 'directing him
to be careful in collecting the German arms, to stack them so that they could
easily be issued again to the German soldiers whom we would have to work

with if the Soviet advance continued.' Later Montgomery confirmed in his memoirs that he had received this order. Alanbrooke went further, recalling in his diary that the Prime Minister had instructed the Chiefs of Staff and their Planners to report on the 'unthinkable war'. In other words, in the event of trouble what were the military possibilities of driving the Russian bear back home before the Western Allies had demobilised their forces?[8] Much more recently the report itself has come to light. Delivered to Churchill on 22 May, this showed not surprisingly that the whole concept was indeed unthinkable. Nevertheless, among the assumptions on which it was based was that Britain and the USA would be able to count on the use of German manpower and what remained of their industrial capacity, and in considering how Germany might contribute the Planners discussed the possibility of rearming up to ten German divisions under a re-formed German High Command.[9] The report had been commissioned on or about 8 May, just a few days before Churchill spoke to the nation. May it be that at that moment he was so anxious about the immediacy of the Russian threat that he did not wish to prejudice the chances of obtaining German support in the event of conflict? We are unlikely ever to know for certain whether this was why his speech ignored Bomber Command – and if Harris mentioned the subject to Churchill on 20 May he never spoke of it afterwards – but it is not easy to think of any other sufficiently compelling explanation.

Maybe significantly the public distancing from the bomber offensive that Churchill had just exhibited was not reflected in the message he sent to Harris only two days later, on 15 May. This referred to the deep sense of gratitude felt by all the nation for Bomber Command's glorious part in forging the victory, summarised its many achievements, and assessed its contributions to Germany's final defeat as decisive. Its massive achievements would long be remembered as an example of duty nobly done. Harris's reply, immediately circulated with Churchill's message throughout the Command and reported in the press, stressed the Prime Minister's personal understanding of the Command's needs in its darkest hours, his unfailing encouragement, his inspiring determination to hold to the course through everything: 'You were foremost of the Pathfinders.' Yet when Harris wrote to Portal a month later he made it clear that he still regarded the omission of Bomber Command from Churchill's 'eulogy to the Services' as a bitter affront to him and his men.[10]

There was a second 'affront' committed by the Prime Minister to which Harris referred at the same time, namely his leading part in preventing the award of a campaign medal for the men and women of the Command. Harris had long been worried on this score. Back in October 1944 he had warned Sinclair about the muddles and anomalies which were already arising between airmen (and soldiers and sailors) serving in overseas theatres and those serving in operational commands at home. He hoped that sufficient thought was going to be given so as to ensure either that the discriminatory award of campaign medals would be avoided altogether or that such medals, if issued, would go to all personnel involved in a particular campaign in any operational command. He was specially concerned about his own ground-crews, who had been working harder, longer and under similar discomfort and personal risk to those in France, Italy or Africa and were receiving nothing. Sinclair broadly agreed but had to tell Harris that the subject was one for the tri-Service Honours and Awards Committee and finally for the Prime Minister. Later, in March 1945, Harris wrote to Portal about the situation of his aircrew, whose activities had extended to just about every campaign in the European theatre but seemed unlikely to receive full recognition. This was not just a problem for the present; it could become even greater in future as aircraft ranges increased and enabled even more distant targets to be attacked from home bases. In lighter vein he pointed out that under the regulations he as the Commander-in-Chief would not qualify for the relevant campaign medal.[11]

By the end of May it was clear that Harris's pleas on behalf of the ground personnel had been rejected, and on 1 June he launched his most powerful broadside on the subject. The recipients were Sinclair, Portal and (for information) Trenchard. As Harris read the situation, while his aircrew were to receive the appropriate campaign stars few of his staff would do so and everyone else, including all the ground personnel, would be awarded only the Defence Medal. Even the terminology was wrong, he said; his Command's role had been 'offence'. These men and women had laboured up to six years under often terrible conditions, buoyed up by their determination to maintain the offensive and try to secure the safety of their crews, and many had been killed or injured in the line of duty. There were countless anomalies, Harris went on to say, when one compared their conditions and responsibilities with many from the other Services and other parts of the RAF who had happened to be based outside the United Kingdom. To deny them their campaign medal was a slight to them, a contemptuous gesture in return for their service and devotion – a slight which underlined the Prime Minister's omission of any reference to the strategic offensive in his victory speech, 'which was of itself an insult not to be forgotten, if it is forgiven.' While he appreciated the difficulties in deciding such matters he therefore urged reconsideration on the basis that medals should be awarded for operational connection with a campaign. His solution was to follow the example of the 1st and 8th Armies and award the relevant campaign medal with 'B' for Bomber, 'F' for Fighter and 'C' for Coastal. He concluded:

> I must tell you as dispassionately as possible that if my Command are to have the Defence Medal and no 'campaign' medal in the France-Germany-Italy-

Naval War then I too will have the Defence Medal and no other — *nothing else whatever*, neither decoration, award, rank, preferment or appointment, if any such is contemplated or intended. I will be proud indeed to wear the Defence Medal and that alone — and as bitter as the rest of my personnel. I will not stand by and see my people let down in so grossly unjust a manner without resorting to every necessary and justifiable protest which is open to me ... I therefore ask to be saved the embarrassments that will certainly ensue if I am to be the recipient of honours while my people — who have given for so long such devoted service — are denied any recognition beyond the gesture so far made.

To Trenchard he added a postscript: 'I started this war as an Air Vice-Marshal. That is my substantive rank now. With that and the "Defence" medal I shall now leave the Service as soon as I can and return to my country — South Africa. I'm off.'[12]

Harris's views, totally understandable and totally justifiable, were far from unsympathetically received. Sinclair, now out of office, told him how the Air Ministry had tried and failed to unblock the ruling that campaign stars for those serving on the ground could only be given for operations from overseas bases, though he understood that the fight was continuing. Harold Macmillan, who had succeeded Sinclair in the Caretaker Government, promised to do all he could. Evill, on behalf of Portal, echoed Sinclair's comments about the Air Ministry's efforts thus far and said there was general agreement that some new approach must be made. He was not, however, optimistic of success.

A fortnight later, in a private letter to his former Personal Staff Officer, Harry Weldon, Harris made it clear where he really thought the blame lay: with Churchill. He added that there were half a million good voters who had passed through the operational commands in England; while they might swallow one gratuitous insult in the Victory speech, they were unlikely to be favourably influenced by a repetition. Harris's views on these matters did not, however, reflect any loss of faith in Churchill's qualities as the nation's leader, for on 28 June, as the Prime Minister departed on holiday to await the verdict of the General Election, Harris sent his good wishes. 'I trust you bask in sunshine and will return here well rested to take up the further tasks which I am confident the confidence of the country will consign to you.'[13] It was not to be. On 26 July Churchill knew that he had been defeated and Harris knew that Attlee was now Prime Minister.

Meanwhile, on 13 June, Harris found he had been awarded the GCB in the Birthday Honours, and following on his stated intention to refuse all further honours he immediately wrote to Portal about the extreme personal embarrassment and distress this had caused him. He realised that since the

King was the final fount of honour in such matters he could not with propriety extricate himself from this situation but asked Portal to ensure that as long as the injustice to his men and women persisted he would never again be placed in a similar position. 'Please bear in mind that I can neither forget nor forgive the affront and the injustice that has been done to my people in the matter of the campaign medals and that consequently this high honour that has now fallen to me personally, even as a mark of appreciation of Bomber Command's part in the war, becomes dust and ashes to me.' He also sought the backing of Bracken, now 'Caretaker' First Lord of the Admiralty, drawing his attention to the political significance of the medals issue. In Harris's view Churchill's decision on this was causing much ill-feeling among many Service people, not just from Bomber Command, and the great man must not be allowed to persist in this 'very naughty and expensive error'.[14] In the event the policy remained unchanged, for the new Labour Government saw no need to overturn the decision agreed by Churchill's wartime Coalition.[15]

It was this issue that lay at the heart of one of the great controversies surrounding Harris: why, unlike the other top British commanders of the Second World War, did he receive no peerage? In a confidential note written some years after the war Harris said he had heard that he had in fact been put forward for a peerage by the Labour Government but that it had been stopped at the instance of Lord Stansgate, the Secretary of State for Air, and John Strachey, his deputy. Strachey happened to be one of Harris's *bêtes noires*. A former Mosleyite, Labour politician and left-wing propagandist (a strange mix), he had gradually modified his extreme views in the late 1930s and, keen to do his bit against Hitler, joined the RAF for administrative duties in 1940. As Adjutant of 87 Squadron in 1941 he was a great success, recalled his CO, Denis Smallwood, but when he went to work on public relations at 5 Group in 1942 he fell foul of Harris, who had no time for 'communists', particularly in his own Command. For the rest of the war Strachey served – to Harris's annoyance – under Bufton in DB Ops, partly as Secretary of the Combined Strategic Targets Committee, and became nationally known for his regular 'Air Commentaries' after the BBC News. He had, in fact, done a good job for the RAF before being re-elected to Parliament and joining Attlee's government, but Harris, ever reluctant to change his mind on such matters, remained convinced that Strachey was an arch enemy of him and Bomber Command. His views were eventually taken on board by Saward, who in effect accused Strachey of using his official position to revenge himself against Harris.[16] As a result of this, and of some of Harris's own statements in later life, the 'Strachey explanation' has since gained wide currency.

Yet in allowing Saward to use it Harris seems to have ignored the wise counsel of a trusted friend. In 1973 he told Maurice Dean that he was convinced Strachey was responsible for his not getting a peerage and for the absence of a campaign medal for Bomber Command, whereupon Dean read up the subject and wrote to him. 'If you have irrefutable evidence that Strachey did in fact take this action, well and good (and I don't mean hearsay evidence). But my judgement is that nobody in the Establishment would have given a damn for Strachey's opinion. He was a very small minnow indeed, and I cannot believe that Attlee would have paid the slightest attention to his views.' Dean therefore advised that Harris should forget about Strachey, but if Saward had to make a statement on the subject in his book it must be capable of instant and irrefutable proof. Sadly the allegation was made but no proof was offered.[17]

Peter Tomlinson, shown this letter in 1996, commented that Harris could be a wonderful friend but a terrible enemy. Tomlinson admitted that he had always taken what Harris said about Strachey as gospel, but he would not now dispute Dean's view: 'He was such an objective man.' Tomlinson also drew attention to a letter he himself had written to the *Cape Argus* in 1983 stating precisely that Harris *was* offered a peerage by the Labour Government but turned it down, his real reason being that he had always intended to return to Africa and the sunshine, where a 'handle' would not be an advantage. This letter followed closely on Tomlinson's last private discussion with Harris in 1982, when Harris said he had been approached unofficially about a peerage and had declined it simply because he did not want it. The fact that it would have been a Labour peerage did not influence him at all, and he did not think Attlee had been involved.[18]

Another key witness in this regard was Harris's Personal Secretary, Peggy Wherry, who remained with him until his departure from Bomber Command and was privy to all his 'state secrets'. In 1989 she read an article by Tim Heald in the *Radio Times* about Don Shaw, the script-writer for the film in which John Thaw portrayed Bomber Harris, and this included statements that 'there was no peerage for Harris' and 'his name was off the list'. Having stayed silent on all 'secret and confidential' matters for so long and now in advanced years, she decided to place the truth, as she remembered it, on record. This, in a letter to the Editor, was that Harris refused all recognition unless and until the ground crews were equally recognised with the air crews. 'His name was undoubtedly "on the list" but acceptance should be on his terms.'[19] This, from a source far more reliable than most, not only confirms Tomlinson's evidence but fits in with Harris's stated intention in 1945 to refuse all further honours.

So why, we must ask, did Harris himself not come clean in public on this subject and try to place the blame elsewhere, particularly when Saward was writing about him long after the main sensitivities had departed? In 1946, given all the privacy rules that always surround public honours and awards, in no way could it have been stated that he had been offered and had declined a peerage. So when Churchill wrote to Attlee on 6 January that year expressing his surprise at Harris's omission from the recent honours list, he received what struck him as a dusty answer. Churchill had paid Harris a most glowing tribute, expressing the greatest admiration for his work and asserting the cardinal importance of the bombing offensive in shortening the war, but Attlee merely replied that the List had to be limited in size and that Harris's promotion to Marshal of the Royal Air Force on 1 January was not an inadequate recognition of his great services. Some weeks later Churchill returned to the charge, referring to the widespread feeling among the high American airmen about 'the slighting treatment' of Harris, but Attlee was not to be moved.[20] Under the circumstances the Prime Minister could have said little else. Harris himself did not know what Churchill had written but he was certainly aware of his friend's anger. When they lunched together on 6 January with Alanbrooke and others, Churchill had launched a tirade against all and sundry for leaving Harris out of the list: 'I won't have it,' he went on and on. Harris, who reported this occasion to Tedder (just appointed CAS),[21] could, of course, say nothing to Churchill or anyone else about having declined a peerage and the impression quickly spread that it was Attlee and his government who had it in for him, a fiction which Harris could not correct – and in some ways may not have wanted to. He had never liked the Labour Party and it was not difficult for him to go along with the many criticisms of the new government, and particularly of the new Air Minister and his Deputy, Strachey. So to portray Strachey as responsible for his omission from the List may have become a convenient way of blotting out, at least in public, the real reason, and Harris seems in later years to have almost convinced himself of its truth. Peter Tomlinson sensed this confusion when he commented that Harris was never quite straight on the whole subject. While further research may one day throw more light on all this there seems little doubt that it was not the Labour Government that denied him his peerage but he himself, essentially for the best of reasons: his loyalty to the men and women of Bomber Command.

Whatever doubts Harris may have had about leaving the RAF at the end of the war had therefore been rapidly dispelled; indeed, as early as May 1945 his superiors knew that he wanted to depart and were considering what arrangements to make for him. In conversation with Slessor, now AMP, he made it clear that he was ready to depart at any time but could not afford to do so without a job to go to, and on 17 May Slessor sent Sinclair and Portal his thoughts on the subject. Pointing out that the C-in-C had hardly any private means and was worried about his family's financial position, he stressed that as one of the war's great commanders Harris deserved special consideration, and while it would take time to work out the long-term solution there was an immediate problem. Harris was far from well, he was suffering from an understandable reaction after the years of pressure, and his staff were having difficulty in getting him to busy himself sufficiently in his Command's affairs now that the spur of active operations had gone. He should therefore be sent on leave and then, perhaps for a few months, on a special mission to South Africa or the USA before retirement.[22] This idea found no favour, but in June Slessor was asked to comment on the possibility of Harris continuing in the Service as Inspector General. Slessor had no doubts about this one, as he told Portal. Harris would not look at it, and in any case would do more harm than good. He lacked the balance and judgement needed for such a post and could prove a pernicious influence. 'No one appreciates his qualities more than I do,' continued Slessor, 'but I don't consider the Service owes him anything.' He should retire and the Service should do everything possible to get him a suitable job afterwards – though his own 'violent and intolerant personality' was his worst impediment in that respect.[23] While there were elements of truth in this slating assessment it was both overdone and unnecessary.

The truth was that there was no further post suited to Harris in the post-war RAF and if there had been he would not have accepted it. As he reminded Churchill himself later, he was actually offered and declined the Military Governorship of the British Zone of Germany (the post which Sholto Douglas took in May 1946). It may have been about this that the new Foreign Secretary, Ernest Bevin, hinted when they dined together on 19 August. Writing to him afterwards, Harris referred to 'the further tentative suggestion as to my future employment you asked me to think over', and said that the direct reason for his refusal to accept another Service appointment was the repeated official denials in the House of Commons during the bombing campaign that his instructions were to destroy German cities. He had then sworn that while he would continue to do his duty during the war he would in no circumstances accept any further appointment.[24] All one can add here is that a less appropriate incumbent of the Germany post would have been almost impossible to imagine.

It was in September that Harris bade farewell to Bomber Command, and in the interim there had been much to do. Ever mindful of those who had worked with him, he was determined to do his best to ensure they received their just deserts. Among the first members of his own staff to be thanked were his Royal Navy representatives, to whom he issued a special message on 10 May. Referring to the Command's anti-shipping campaign, carried out by both bombing and minelaying, he praised highly their efforts, skill and devotion to duty, and wished them good luck for the future. Bomber Command would always retain a soft corner in its heart for its 'tame' sailors.

To Captain de Mowbray he added: 'For your personal help to me I cannot thank you enough.' But Harris wanted more than this. For some time he had been urging the Admiralty to recognise their efforts, but without success, so on 23 May he told Portal of the brick wall he always encountered when tackling the Admiralty through normal channels on behalf of de Mowbray and Lieutenant Commander Haxworth, his deputy. Portal immediately approached Cunningham, the First Sea Lord, who fully took the point – though not until June 1946 did de Mowbray receive his CBE. Sadly Haxworth went unrewarded.[25]

Harris's warm thanks went also to all the personnel from overseas who had served or were still serving in Bomber Command: Australians, Canadians, New Zealanders, Rhodesians, South Africans, Czechs, French, Norwegians and Poles among them. Letters went too, to take just three examples, to the General Post Office for its running of the Command's landline communications, to Maintenance Command for all its tireless and unremitting work, and to Lord Camrose for the enormous help which he and the *Daily Telegraph* had given the Command throughout the last three strenuous years. There was correspondence as well with Eisenhower coincident with the award to Harris of the Distinguished Service Medal and the winding up of SHAEF. 'This past year of war,' Harris wrote, 'has proved that wherever the life and liberty of our two nations are threatened they can and do forget that there are British or American peoples.'[26]

There were plenty of ordinary matters too. Some with which Harris concerned himself were connected with the preparation of Tiger Force to depart for the Far East, as when he drew attention to the dangers to security of careless press publicity. Another related to the unfair way in which the pay of RAF prisoners-of-war had been docked in exchange for virtually valueless tokens issued to them by the Germans – a topic doubtless raised by Tomlinson. He also drew on his memories of 1919 by reminding his commanders of the importance of keeping people usefully occupied in the immediate post-war situation, and he fully appreciated the significance of such measures as the Educational and Vocational Training Scheme which the Air Ministry was implementing. At the same time he sensibly drew Slessor's attention to the difficulties of conflicting priorities and shortage of resources – not least the deplorable situation as regards Education Officers, many of whom were intending to resign in the absence of proper conditions of service.[27]

His main office task during this period, however, was to set in hand the writing of the Despatch on Bomber Command's wartime operations which the Air Ministry requested of him on 21 June. In agreeing to do so he made it clear that this would cover his own time as C-in-C but not the periods of his predecessors; if these were to be covered that was a task for them.[28] The Despatch took just under six months to prepare, and inevitably virtually all the work was done by his staff, some of it after he had left High Wycombe. Indeed, in a letter to Churchill's Private Secretary, Anthony Montague-Browne, he stated: 'Apart from its four-para covering letter the whole Despatch was prepared by my OR civilians and my air staff and never seen by me until I signed it' (in December 1945).[29]

There was also much going on away from the office. While Harris had no wish to take a look at Germany for himself and never did one of the 'Cooks' tours' that were laid on to enable many of his personnel to witness from the air the damage they had caused, towards the end of May he did fly out to meet Marshal Zhukov. This was no more than a social occasion, recalled Tomlinson, who went with him, and since they had not taken their own interpreter they had to rely on a Russian who conveyed Zhukov's lengthy remarks in unduly brief terms. Tomlinson remembered nothing significant being said: the two commanders just wanted to meet each other and they departed on excellent terms with the assistance of a good lunch and plentiful vodka.[30] On 16 May Harris also met the Russians at the Victory Reception laid on at their Embassy in London. At about the same time he flew up to Middleton St George to bid farewell to some of his Canadian crews as they set off for home; 'if when you get home you're asked what you did in the war,' he told them, 'tell them you won it.' Then on 7 June he and his wife visited the Polish Embassy, where he was invested by the President of the Polish Republic with the Grand Order of Polonia Restituta. On the 12th they attended the ceremonies at Guildhall and the Mansion House when Eisenhower was invested by the King with the Order of Merit – an occasion when Harris himself received a tremendous public ovation. The next day he was at Cranwell with many other RAF dignitaries for the King's visit to mark the College's Silver Jubilee.[31]

Harris's visit to Honiton on 21 June was entirely different. Addressing the staff and pupils of Allhallows, his old school, he spoke of the challenge that his own 'lads' in the bomber crews had faced up to and told the boys not to be misled by the word 'security'. Though a good enough word in its way it should not be used as a banner under which to march out into the world. He would give them a much better slogan: Adventure. 'Nail that to your mast, not in the spirit of buccaneering but as a working idea, and you will find it will not fail you,' he concluded. A further comment made by the anonymous Honitonian who wrote afterwards to the school magazine (p.26) is worth quoting here:

There is something else about him, difficult to define, that as a boy I should not have fully appreciated, but which must have left a deep impression on my mind, for when, on Speech Day, after many long years, he returned to the School, trailing clouds of glory, the memory of a simple, kindly manner returned to me, and as I watched him giving the prizes, as though to the manner born, with a kindly word to each boy, this recollection so in tune with reality was all the more impressive.

No sooner was Harris back than he was invited to do the honours at the Victory Celebration in Oslo. According to the Foreign Office the King of Norway was much concerned at the lack of public appreciation of the part played by the three main Allies in the liberation of his country, and he wanted a really well-known military figure from each of them to join him at the Victory Parade he was organising. When Harris heard that his name was being suggested he expressed himself more than willing to attend. So on 28 June his personalised Dakota, piloted by Squadron Leader E.V. Smith, escorted by a Lancaster and welcomed by 12 Norwegian Spitfires, landed at Gardermoen, and on the 30th he represented the United Kingdom on the Reviewing Stand, together with General Bradley and General Ratov, and took part in the associated functions. He remained in Norway until 2 July, after which he spent three days on an unofficial visit to Sweden, where he was warmly welcomed by the Swedish Air Force and attended two memorial services for British airmen buried there. It was a different story a fortnight later, when he protested to the Air Ministry about the absence of Bomber Command representation at the Victory Parade in Berlin:

> I read that inter alia the Navy was there. Bomber Command also took some part in the defeat of Germany. Unless our hundreds of visits to Berlin prior to VE Day are accounted our share of such parades and celebrations in which we are otherwise repeatedly and consistently ignored, I find it hard to understand why Bomber Command is never invited.[32]

23 July saw Harris again at Honiton, this time to receive the Honorary Freedom of the Borough and in the process to deliver his first full post-war address to a public audience about the work and achievements of his Command.[33] Almost immediately he was on his way abroad again, this time to South America. The Brazilian Ambassador had already sounded him out on the possibility of taking a Lancaster to Rio de Janeiro to participate in the nation's victory festivities, and very quickly the Air Ministry gave its authority and the official invitation was issued. Consequently on 25 July three tropicalised Lancasters commanded by Wing Commander C.C. Calder took off from St Mawgan and after night-stopping at Bathurst and Natal landed at Rio on the 27th. Accompanying Harris were Peter Tomlinson, now firmly entrenched as his PA, and his predecessor Walter Pretyman, whose previous Brazilian connections, including his proficiency in the language, made him an ideal liaison officer. Harris had perceived that Pretyman, together with his four-year old daughter (he was a widower), would

much appreciate a free flight home to Brazil and it was 'fixed' for the girl to travel with her father. Her name was not mentioned on the nominal roll.[34]

Tomlinson recalled the great success of the visit, assisted not least by their method of arrival. The aircraft were planned to land at Santa Cruz airfield, some distance from the city, but Harris would have none of this: they would touch down where everyone could see them, on the short runway at Santos Dumont, the central airport. The local Americans, whose B17s could not use it and who had said Lancasters would never make it either, were furious. Harris and his party were then put into open cars and driven to the Copacabana Hotel through packed streets and up to their necks in flowers. For the next ten days, partly in Rio and also in Porto Alegre and Sao Paulo amid wide publicity, they were royally treated and Harris claimed afterwards to have met most of the leading people in the country, from the President down. Such was the impression it all made upon him that on his return home he wrote cordially to Stafford Cripps, now President of the Board of Trade. The Brazilians, he said, were enthusiastically pro-British and keen to turn to the United Kingdom rather than the Americans for their industrial requirements. The country had enormous potential and offered the most attractive and lucrative avenue for the re-establishment of Britain's export trade that he had ever seen.[35] Whatever Harris's general views of the new Labour Government he was not averse to urging the cause of 'UK Limited' with his acquaintances in the corridors of power.

On 7 August, accompanied by Tomlinson, Harris departed for Washington, where he spent the next ten days largely on informal visits (see chapter 18). There was time on the 15th, however, to attend a small reception arranged in his honour by Hap Arnold.[36] Then on the 18th he paused on his flight home in an American Fortress to take a look at Bermuda, where there was a possibility that he might become Governor. He was back in time to stand with Eaker at the unveiling of the Memorial presented by the RAF to the USAAF at Bushy Park. Then a week later his impending retirement from the Service at the age of 53 was announced in the newspapers and he gave his first post-war press interview, talking not just about his wartime campaign but also the implications of the atomic bomb, the hottest topic of the day.

Soon afterwards, this time accompanied by his wife and daughter, Harris was off again on his travels, prompted particularly by invitations from Godfrey Huggins to visit Southern Rhodesia and from Field Marshal Smuts to stay as his guest in South Africa. They departed in the Dakota, escorted by a Lancaster, on 4 September, and made their way via Malta, Cairo, Khartoum, Nairobi and Lusaka to Pretoria, where having paused several times en route they arrived on the 12th. During their week in South Africa, when they spent several days with Smuts at his official residence, Groote Schuur,

Harris's activities – including speeches, interviews, visits, and attendance at the opening ceremony of Cape Town's new Graving Dock – were widely publicised. He was also reported as likely to be settling in Kenya, Rhodesia or South Africa, and – in lighter vein – as being keen to find a country where there were no telephones, no motor cars, no aeroplanes and no bureaucrats. On the 20th they flew north to Southern Rhodesia, the country Harris still regarded as his own, where they devoted ten days to sightseeing and engaging in nostalgia; for the first time in four years he was able to enjoy some leave. The return journey took them via Rome, where they spent three days seeing something of the city and visiting the opera, before reaching home on 6 October. By this time Norman Bottomley had been occupying the C-in-C's chair at Bomber Command for three weeks, and it merely remained for the Harrises to move out of Springfield and go to stay with the Tresfons at Felden Lodge, Boxmoor.[37]

Harris had known for two months not only the date of his departure but also that he would be retiring from the RAF on 15 November. He had also been told by Slessor on 11 July that he would be several months short of qualifying for the full pension of an Air Chief Marshal and there was no hope of the Treasury changing the rules. Harris's reaction was predictable. 'With pensions grossly inadequate by any standards, after carrying on my shoulders the full weight of this Command for over $3\frac{1}{2}$ years and in my present rank for over $2\frac{1}{2}$, I am deprived of some £60 a year of the full pension of that rank,' he replied on 24 August. He would certainly not leave the matter there, and not only on his own account, for such anomalies were just as serious for many other Servicemen. Both Attlee and Bevin, to whom he had mentioned the problem, thought that it must be put right. In due course it was – for Harris himself – though not in the way he was looking for.

It was the inadequacy of the RAF pension that was in prospect, with or without the extra £60, that lay at the heart of Harris's retirement situation. Simply to make ends meet, given his family commitments and lack of private resources, he had to obtain further employment, and he already knew how impracticable this was likely to prove in the United Kingdom. As far back as June 1944 the Home Secretary, Herbert Morrison, had invited him to become Metropolitan Police Commissioner when the European war was over and after careful thought he had declined it. For one thing he doubted his ability to do the job, particularly in the uncongenial London environment. For another he had always hankered after returning to Africa either as a government official or in a private capacity; here, he believed, he could do much more to serve the British interest. The finances, however, were critical. The bank statement he obtained indicated that out of the Commissioner's £3,000 salary and the £1,120 retired pay he would receive he would be left with little more than £2,000 to live on after paying tax and alimony. So the job was a non-starter, he explained to Morrison.[38]

Another possible appointment – far more appealing – had come Harris's way at about the same time. Godfrey Huggins, Prime Minister of Southern Rhodesia, visited him at Springfield in May 1944 and subsequently the British Government was asked if he could become Governor at the end of the year. Huggins was keen to have a 'Rhodesian' in that post, rather than a British establishment figure, and Harris would have fitted the bill. Sadly the timing was wrong. Churchill was not prepared to let him go at that critical point in the war, nor would he himself have willingly departed. Nevertheless, he greatly regretted missing the opportunity and on 2 June 1945 he set out his stall in a letter to Huggins. If the Governorship happened to become available again he would still like to be considered, but since this was obviously unlikely he wondered if any other Rhodesian appointment might be open, maybe working for the government, for example in aviation business, or possibly in politics. 'If I have deserved anything of my country – Rhodesia – it would delight me to have opportunity to serve her further.' Huggins' reply on 16 July was sympathetic but frank. By the time a new Governor was needed Harris would be too close to the age limit. While there might later be a suitable opening in aviation, this could depend on the far from certain outcome of the April 1946 General Election, and to enter politics he would have to reside in the country for six months and then nurse a constituency.[39] This was all very nebulous and although Harris subsequently met Huggins during his September visit he had to accept that Southern Rhodesia was impossible.

Two more Governorships were also discussed. One, that of the Isle of Man, Harris dismissed without ceremony as being ideal for Billy Butlin. The other, Bermuda, seemed to him both practicable and acceptable. Its possibility had been mentioned to him by Churchill and later by Attlee, and during his August visit he had viewed the Governor's Residence. This prompted him to ask Slessor to press for ex-RAF governors to be given an element of RAF staff assistance similar to that allotted to their Navy and Army counterparts; Harris was already considering the practicalities of the job. Yet he had now heard that the Colonial Secretary was pressing for a 'civil' Governor on the grounds that the locals were insisting on one. Having been told precisely the opposite while visiting Bermuda Harris duly asked the sympathetic Ernest Bevin on 19 August to intercede on his behalf. Thereafter things went quiet until Attlee wrote on 11 October telling Harris that after consultation with the Colonial Secretary he could hold out no hope of offering him the job – though he would bear Harris's name in mind should other suitable vacancies arise in the public service. The disappointed Harris wrote stressing that he needed something straight away, but the

Prime Minister was not to be moved.[40] So with all other options gone Harris now knew that he must concentrate his attentions on the private business career in South Africa that he had long been considering. We shall return to this in chapter 18.

Meanwhile there was a more urgent matter, for when Harris got back from Africa he at last agreed to seek medical advice about the condition that had troubled him ever since his time in Palestine. A doctor friend, Air Vice-Marshal T.J. Kelly, had advised him to go to the RAF Hospital at Halton for a short period of investigation and then to undergo a medical board before retiring; this might show that, in view of the great strain under which Harris had worked during the war, he had a case for a disability pension. Consequently on 10 October he was given an initial medical board. This confirmed that he was still suffering from the duodenal ulcer first identified in 1939 and recommended that he be treated at Halton, where he spent the whole of November before returning home. His retirement was consequently deferred to 4 February and a board on 9 January reported him as considerably better and fit to go to 'temperate climes in Africa'.[41]

During the autumn Harris also turned his attention to the writing of his personal memoir. Its essential purpose was to set out to the world at large his own views of the bomber offensive, while at the same time earning him some much needed income. That it could be published as early as January 1947 was to a great extent thanks to the work of Harris's former Press Officer, Wing Commander John Lawrence, whom Harris, in July 1945, persuaded to become his PSO and then in September, on leaving the RAF, to work for him privately. Between then and February 1946, when Harris left for the USA, they spent much time together at Boxmoor, accompanied by one of his wartime typists, Betty Quihampton. As she remembers these long sessions, they talked their way through the story, often drafting orally, while she recorded their discussions and produced the first typescript. At the same time Sir Walter Layton, publisher of the *News Chronicle* and *The Star*, had agreed to handle the book and for tax reasons Harris waited until his arrival in South Africa before signing the contract. From then on Lawrence continued his editing and sent the draft chapters to Harris for comment and approval. He also obtained – quite easily – the necessary clearance from the Air Ministry.

Only with Churchill was there any real difficulty. Knowing how upset he was by comments about him in several other books already published, Harris insisted to Lawrence that he would make no reference to the former Prime Minister without his express permission, so when Lawrence sent the relevant extracts to Churchill on 14 June 1946 he wrote:

> In referring to you Harris had but one aim in view, to show how much he and others depended on you for inspiration and support. He included, of course,

some details as might help to make his sketch more alive and his view of you more convincing to the general public. In doing so he was above all anxious that nothing should appear in print of which you might in anyway disapprove or consider a breach of hospitality. For this reason he wrote freely, knowing that nothing was going to appear unless you saw and approved it first.

Lawrence told Harris a few days later that Churchill was decidedly unhappy about references to his ability to talk incessantly without listening to what others were saying. A month later, however, Lawrence could report that Churchill had become more amenable and what eventually appeared in the book was exactly what Harris had originally drafted. Writing to Lawrence on this subject, Churchill said:

> Our friend should be very careful in all that he writes not to admit anything not justified by the circumstances and the actions of the enemy in the measures we took to bomb Germany. We gave them full notice to clear-out of their munition-making cities. In fact they had very good shelters and protection, and the position of the civilian population was very different from that of London, Coventry, Liverpool etc when they were bombed in the second year of the war.

So by late summer the book was taking shape and a title was needed. Lawrence suggested *War against Cities* or the less inspiring *The Air War with Germany*. Harris proposed *Carry War to the Enemy*, adding that the publishers could call him Bomber Harris as long as they did not call him 'Ginger'. The publishers themselves then came up with *Bomber Offensive*, which he accepted despite still preferring his own choice. So under this title the book was first serialised in *The Star* during the autumn of 1947 and then published by Collins, though not with a Foreword by Trenchard as he had hoped.[42]

It did, on the other hand, use Harris's new title, for on 1 January 1946 he had been promoted to the highest rank his Service could bestow, that of Marshal of the Royal Air Force. Hitherto no officers other than the Chiefs of Air Staff had ever held that rank and while one other – Sholto Douglas – was similarly recognised on that day none has been since.[43] This was the Royal Air Force honouring its own, as Portal – quoting the *Daily Mirror* – made clear in his letter of congratulation: 'this *was* a war honour'.

Harris did not initially see it in this light. Back in October Portal had sent him a fulsome pre-retirement letter referring to the outstanding example he had always set, his magnificent leadership of Bomber Command as it helped bring the Germans to their knees, and his personal support and loyalty throughout the war. In reply Harris spoke of having abandoned hope of any worthwhile official appointment, implying that the Colonial and Dominion Secretaries were against him, and referred to press assertions that the bomber offensive had been an expensive failure and he was being sacked because of a tremendous row with Portal. 'For myself,' Harris went on, 'I care not a button and am taking the very earliest opportunity of leaving this grateful country and returning for keeps to my own. But for the Service it appears that something should be done to put the bomber offensive and its results properly across.' Portal, far from convinced that this hostility was widespread, commented that if anyone was rash enough to put anything in the papers suggesting that Harris was 'sacked' he would have a perfectly good remedy, and short of this the Air Ministry would instantly deny it.[44]

For Harris, however, this issue was not going to go away and to begin with his totally unexpected (and in some ways unwanted) promotion merely served to fuel the flames. On 2 January he wrote to Tedder, who had just taken over CAS's chair, first to congratulate him and then to seek his advice. Having decided, as a retired officer, to take up a good business appointment in South Africa, he needed assurance that this would be unaffected by his remaining on the active list – as all Marshals did, albeit on half pay. Here, of course, there would be no problem. Only a few days later, however, when Harris reported to Tedder on his meeting with Churchill on 6 January and quoted the latter's tirade against the Air Ministry and the Labour Government for washing their hands of him, sacking him, and so on, he came back to the 'extraordinary gaucherie' of the announcement of his retirement issued by the Air Ministry in September while he himself was in Africa. He went on:

> The overwhelming impression is that I was 'sacked' indeed and that my promotion *after* retirement was a 'contemptuous sop' thrown after me. It has caused me much hurt in the market place, great mischief indeed. My telephone and reporters have driven me mad, and my 'no comment' has resulted in them drawing their own conclusions and writing them up. I am now widely regarded by wishful thinking as the bad boy who was rightly snubbed in public by the Air Ministry and the government and thrown out. I do not know what I have done to deserve it. I only wanted to go in peace back to my own country.[45]

At the same time, following up their meeting, Harris wrote to Churchill personally, spelling out even more fully the shameful way in which his retirement had been handled. 'If it was intended to promote me, it might with more thoughtfulness and spontaneity have been done before announcing my retirement in that manner – or at all. An odd process, to retire an officer first and then promote him!' It would not have been difficult, he added, to still the speculation with a few official words in the right quarters, but nothing had been done and as a result he had been much hurt.[46] Harris was certainly keen to give Churchill the information necessary to support any efforts he might wish to make on his behalf, but as Harris admitted to Tedder he also knew that in reality nothing could now be done. Without doubt these matters were ill-handled by officialdom, though when the finger is pointed it must always be remembered how much else was going on at the time – just as was the case when Dowding was approaching the end of his time at Fighter Command in 1940.

Yet as Harris before long came to appreciate, his promotion had practical advantages over a peerage. As he later wrote, a Lord in South Africa was a joke, as out of place as a hippopotamus in Trafalgar Square; if he was to make his way there he would do much better without a title. Moreover promotion meant greatly improved pay for life, and given his financial circumstances this was much more useful than a peerage which would carry no remuneration and entail extra expense.[47] So possessed of his new rank he and Jill prepared to leave initially for New York and subsequently Cape Town. They were first able to fit in two special ceremonies. One was in the Town Hall at High Wycombe, where on 4 February Harris was admitted as an Honorary Freeman. This was to have been a joint event for him and Ira Eaker, but owing to his imminent departure it could not be arranged and Eaker was similarly honoured later. The second ceremony was at the French Embassy, where on the 12th Harris was invested as a Grand Officier of the Légion d'Honneur. A third ceremony came too late, so it was *in absentia* that Liverpool University awarded him the honorary degree of Doctor of Laws on 4 March.[48]

There were many farewells and letters of good wishes, of which two particularly merit quotation. One came from the Deputy Prime Minister, Herbert Morrison, after they had talked one evening at dinner:

> I was sad to hear of your disappointments in certain matters and I wish I had known earlier though the matters you raise are not within my power directly. I need hardly assure you that I wish your desires had been met. It has been a very great pleasure to know you and Lady Harris so well and to have had happy evenings at Bomber Command. I am a great admirer of your work and of the men who served under you, and it was always a real pleasure to come along. Please accept my very best wishes to you both, and of course, to the lovely little daughter.[49]

By no means all Labour politicians were anathema to Harris.

A letter from a Dutchman may have remained even more firmly in Harris's mind as, in the company of 12,000 returning Canadian servicemen, the family set sail from Southampton aboard the *Queen Elizabeth* on 14 February 1946. He and his wife were thanking the Harrises for the friendly way in which their son had been looked after on holiday in their home, and he added:

We shall never forget the nights when your squadrons passed us in the dark on the way to Germany. The mighty noise was like music for us and it told us about happier days to come. Your passing planes kept us believing in coming victory, no matter what we had to endure. We have suffered much, but Britain and the RAF did not disappoint us, and we have to thank you and with you the British nation for our living in peace again.[50]

Notes

1. Misc Folder 8; Richards, *Portal of Hungerford*, p.327.
2. Folder H80, dated 3 and 10 May 1945.
3. Tomlinson to author; Folder H75, dated 10, 16 and 19 May 1945.
4. Folder H84.
5. Folders H84; H50.
6. Dean, *op.cit.* p.292.
7. Colville, *The Fringes of Power*, pp.563, 601.
8. Gilbert, *Never Despair*, pp.1070–2, 1078–81, covers the Woodford speech controversy; Montgomery, *Memoirs*, p.358; Lewis, *Changing Direction*, pp.242–3, discusses Lord Alanbrooke's recollections.
9. Article by Ben Fenton (based on PRO documents in CAB 120/691 released in 1998), *Daily Telegraph*, October 1998.
10. Folder H84; Messenger, *op.cit.* p.197, quotes Churchill's message in full.
11. Folders H83, dated 20 and 25 October 1944; H84, dated 27 March 1944.
12. Folders H84; H50.
13. Folders H80; H84; Misc 8; Gilbert, *Never Despair*, p.51.
14. Folders H84; H70. Misc Folder 9 contains many of the letters Harris received congratulating him on his GCB, together with his replies. Field Marshal Montgomery and Admiral Horton were the only other Service commanders similarly honoured on this occasion.
15. The documents of the Honours and Awards Committee, which met under Treasury chairmanship, show that much attention was devoted in 1944–5 to the award of campaign stars to ground personnel of RAF operational Commands in the UK (and to similarly placed personnel of the Navy and Army), that Churchill opposed it, and that the final and very strong Air Ministry submission was almost summarily dismissed by the Chairman on 19 July 1945 (PRO, T300/53).
16. Misc Folder 5 (Harris's paper is undated but was probably written in the late 1950s); Hugh Thomas's biography of Strachey; author's discussion with Air Chief Marshal Sir Denis Smallwood, 1997; Saward, *op.cit.* pp.326–30.
17. Misc Folder 22, letter dated 20 September 1973.
18. Author's discussions with Tomlinson, 1996.
19. This letter, dated 5 September 1989, was not published, but after Miss Wherry's death in September 1998 a copy was sent to the author by her niece, Mrs S.K. Goodman.
20. Gilbert, *Never Despair*, pp.178–9, 192–3.
21. Harris to Tedder, Tedder Papers, courtesy of Dr Vincent Orange, who is currently researching the life of Lord Tedder.
22. Slessor Papers, courtesy of Dr Vincent Orange.
23. Portal Papers, Box D, File 6, dated 20 June 1945.

24. Misc Folder 11, dated 6 January 1946; Harris's undated paper, see note 16 above. See also Folder H23, dated 20 August 1945.
25. Folders H70; H84. Harris also sent a note about this to Lawrence on 27 June 1946 in the hope it could be included in *Bomber Offensive* (Misc 13/1).
26. Folders H70; H55.
27. Folders H70; H75.
28. Folder H69. See chapter 16 for comment on the Despatch itself.
29. Misc Folder 20, dated 18 February 1964.
30. No documentary evidence of this meeting has come to light, but Tomlinson, a reliable witness, was quite firm about it.
31. Harris family scrapbook.
32. Folders H23; H104; H70; Misc 8. Before joining Harris's Communications Flight at Halton in August 1944 Squadron Leader Smith, DSO DFC AFC, had flown Mosquitos on Pathfinder operations with 109 Squadron.
33. *Western Morning News* and Folder H70. See Folder H106 for the full notes used for this speech.
34. Folders H69; H75; AIR 24/322. Wing Commander Calder, DSO and Bar, DFC, had commanded 158 Squadron and then served as a Flight Commander in 617 Squadron. It was he who dropped the first ten-ton bomb on the Bielefeld Viaduct in March 1945. Flight Lieutenant Norman Ashton, one of the aircrew selected for the Brazil trip, recounts it in detail in his personal memoir, *op.cit.* pp.132–68.
35. Tomlinson discussions; Misc Folder 8 (Visit Programme); Folder H44.
36. Arnold, *Global Mission*, p.259, says this took place on the 10th but Washington newspapers say the 15th.
37. Folders H70; H84; Tomlinson discussions; family scrapbook. The Tedders were in Cape Town at the same time.
38. Misc Folders 8, 10. Saward, *op.cit.* p.324, wrongly implies that this offer was made at the end of the war.
39. Folders H70; Misc 8; discussion with Air Vice-Marshal Bentley.
40. Tomlinson discussions; Folders H70; H75; Misc 8.
41. Misc Folder 8.
42. Folders H70; Misc 13/1 (this contains the drafts); Gilbert, *Never Despair*, p.259; author's discussions with Ann Lawrence, Betty Quihampton and Peter Tomlinson. Strangely, Trenchard later said he would have written a Foreword had he been asked.
43. Douglas was promoted in advance of becoming C-in-C Germany. Tedder, too, was promoted to Marshal of the Royal Air Force in advance of being CAS. Only Harris was promoted when on the verge of retirement.
44. Misc Folder 8; Portal Papers, Box A, File 3.
45. Tedder Papers, courtesy of Dr Vincent Orange.
46. Misc Folder 8.
47. Misc Folder 5; Tomlinson discussions.
48. Misc Folder 15.
49. Misc Folder 8, dated 5 February 1946.
50. Misc Folder 11, dated 24 January 1946.

Chapter 18

Safmarine

The venture on which Harris was now engaged had its origins in 1941, when he had been working in the United States (chapter 6). Among the American businessmen to whom his cousin, Ian Elliot, had introduced him was Henry Mercer, President of the States Marine Corporation, and the two of them told him how keen they were to see a South African shipping line formed after the war in co-operation with Mercer's own company. Harris already appreciated the advantages that South Africa could gain by developing direct trading links with North America, as compared with the traditional routes which compelled her – in the absence of a shipping line of her own – to rely for her overseas trade largely on the Union Castle dominated services via the United Kingdom. Perceiving that such a project might one day offer a useful opportunity to live and work in South Africa, he expressed interest and the two men kept in touch, assisted by the good offices of Elliot. In April 1945, with the war nearing its end, Elliot and Mercer prepared a proposal for a South African company to be established to provide a joint service with States Marine between the USA and the Cape, and the plan was sent to a group of enthusiastic South African industrialists, led by Dr H.J. Van der Bijl of the Iron and Steel Corporation. As a result the leading players met in England in July 1945, when Harris, already being thought of by Mercer as the potential Managing Director of the new company, joined in some of the discussions. By November, with other options gone, and after preliminary meetings both in New York and South Africa during August and September, he had decided to take the one job he really wanted.[1]

So in February 1946 Harris and his family arrived in the USA, where he spent a month in New York being briefed and joining in local negotiations, and finding time on 4 April to be presented by Eisenhower with the Distinguished Service Medal. Another month was spent on holiday with Mercer in Florida, some of it deep-sea fishing, before the family departed aboard a States Marine vessel, the *African Star*, for Cape Town, where Harris was initially to be that company's representative. So when he arrived on 18 May he already knew that his immediate task would be to set up the new local company, soon to be known as the South African Marine Corporation, *ie* Safmarine. Next the first three ships necessary to commence the service would have to be obtained and prepared for use, and then they would have to earn their share of the market. To face these challenges he knew that he needed the active help and support of a trusted aide – just as when he had exercised high command in the RAF – and who better than Peter Tomlinson? Delighted and flattered to be asked, Tomlinson had resigned his commission and would arrive on 25 June, Mercer having agreed to take him on the payroll as Harris's Freight Manager. At the same time Tomlinson would doubtless assist with some of the 'family' responsibilities, such as house hunting, furnishing, staffing and travel. To begin with, while the family were staying in the Mount Nelson Hotel, these would not be too onerous; later, when they started occupying private residences, the commitments would be much greater.

The first part of Harris's task was quickly under way. Van der Bijl and other key local figures undertook to raise the money and try to float a company if he or Mercer could obtain the three ships, whereupon Harris cabled Mercer outlining their proposals and offering to run the business. Mercer immediately agreed, Safmarine was registered on 21 June, and the ensuing press announcement made it clear that the Corporation had 'the express purpose of enabling South Africa to build up a merchant marine and to carry an increasing proportion of her imports/exports in South African bottoms.' Harris, it said, would be managing director. Inevitably there was hostility in some quarters, notably from other shipowners and in the South African Parliament, but Van der Bijl and his colleagues were far from deterred and when Safmarine's first board meeting took place on 3 July Harris was authorised to manage its affairs, to charter ships through States Marine, and to purchase Victory ships from the United States Government, also through States Marine. A week later the Board agreed that he should hold office for five years and indefinitely thereafter until termination by six months' notice on either side, and the next day he was appointed Chairman. The historian of Safmarine, Willie Le Roux, refers to innumerable matters requiring attention over the next few months, and not least the provision of office accommodation. For this 'a piece of Old Cape Town, a quaint two-storied building at 72 Keerom Street, adjacent to the Houses of Parliament', was acquired, which was to serve as a fine home for Safmarine until 1961. Typically Harris involved himself in much of the detail, down even to the design of the colour scheme for the ships' funnels, and Le Roux refers to some of the qualities he demonstrated: 'As in his military career, Sir Arthur was a quick worker, determined and clear thinking.' The historian writes too of the consistent records of success of Harris and the other key figures in Safmarine. 'The fact that these early leaders identified themselves with Safmarine provided the guarantee South African business executives needed for giving their blessing and support to this courageous endeavour.'

That Harris's name, reputation and contacts were important assets was particularly evident when it became necessary, in December 1946, for him to return to New York. Mercer seemed to be getting nowhere in his efforts to persuade the United States Maritime Commission to release any of its wartime Victory ships; ostensibly the Commission was arguing that since South Africa had lost no ships during the war no replacements were needed. This was a specious argument since South Africa had possessed no major ships of her own anyway, and the real reason was that American shipping companies were opposed to the encouragement of foreign competition. To make matters worse the government attitude was hardening. So on arrival Harris immediately put his weight behind Mercer, first by bending the ear of one of Mercer's friends who held a senior post in the State Department in Washington, and then by tackling one of his own wartime allies, Averell Harriman, who was now Secretary for Commerce and therefore nominally responsible for the Maritime Commission.

The paper Harris wrote to Harriman following up their conversation bears comparison with some of his better wartime missives. Having succinctly set the scene he argued strongly that Safmarine's intention was not to compete against the American merchant marine but to retain the trade between the USA and South Africa in their own hands so as to prevent it returning to British and foreign monopolies; it must therefore be in the American interest to give it full support. As he wrote in his conclusion:

> In sum. The South African Marine Corporation is closely affiliated to American interests. It can be irrevocably committed for the future if America so wills. It has every moral right to be permitted and encouraged to participate in American/South African seaborne trade. It offers great material advantages to both countries. It stands four-square for American/South African collaboration in the limitless industrial expansion now imminent in South Africa. It is the only organisation which can avert the reversion of a large proportion of American/South African seaborne trade to outside organisations and monopolies – British and foreign – neither South African nor American. It is owned in its South African manifestation by the leading industrialists in South Africa, who are adamantly determined that South Africa shall have her own merchant marine. To that end they seek and hope for the fullest American collaboration. For these reasons, therefore, the South African Marine Corporation asks equal consideration and equal priorities in response to her application for American Victory AP-3 war-built vessels – for which they are prepared to pay in full on delivery.

Le Roux calls this 'a treasured document in Safmarine's records', one which testifies to Harris's clear thinking and his straight-talking, fearless approach. There is little doubt that it was only thanks to Harriman's personal support that the way was cleared for Safmarine's ships to be allocated, and that it was Harris's persuasiveness which secured it. The 15,000-ton former troopships were, in fact, the last three to be delivered to foreign countries under the post-war American legislation.

Acquiring the vessels was one thing; doing battle over the legal detail with the minions of the Maritime Commission was quite another. Then they had to be converted to carry cargo and a small number of passengers, and crews had to be obtained from England for each ship's initial voyage to South Africa. Well aware of the need for close supervision of the whole complicated and often technical process and determined to travel back home with Jill and Jackie aboard the first ship, Harris eventually had to extend to eight months what had been originally intended as a trip lasting eight weeks. By the time the *Constantia* sailed from New York on 1 August 1947, her departure finally delayed by local labour troubles, both he and Jill had taken close interest in the ship's preparation, even down to the decor and fittings of the passenger accommodation, including the cutlery, crockery and glass. When a passenger on the second vessel, the *Morgenster*, wrote in November calling her one of the smoothest ships she had ever sailed on and describing her stateroom as the best she had ever had, including her trip on the *Queen Elizabeth*, it seemed that the Harris attention to detail would pay dividends – as it needed to given the small take-up of Safmarine shares the previous June and the general state of the market.

The *Constantia* docked in Cape Town on 22 August to a warm welcome suitably reported in the local press, and Dr Van der Bijl paid Harris tribute for 'bringing home the bacon'; he hoped Harris's future work with Safmarine would be less trying than the difficulties he had faced in America. Harris himself summarised the achievement: 'We obtained three vessels valued on the market at well over one million pounds each for somewhat less than one million pounds the lot – a not unsatisfactory conclusion.' It was now time for the Harrises to try to settle down into a more normal family life. While they had been away Tomlinson had been looking after Kenwick, their rented house in the Claremont district of Cape Town, and handling their financial and other domestic affairs. Immediately, therefore, they were able to take up residence again and when the lease ran out in November they moved to White Cottage, in Wynberg. Harris had plenty to occupy himself as the company's business expanded and the organisation built up, and he was particularly pleased when Jean Tresfon came out to become Managing Director of Anglo-Vaal Industries, which having underwritten Safmarine's shares was now saddled with them; a year later he would join the company's Board. Meanwhile in May 1948 Harris, accompanied as usual by his family, was off to North America again, this time to negotiate the time-chartering of several States Marine ships to augment Safmarine's sailings to the USA, and also to discuss the introduction of an extended service into Canada. As a result the *Morgenster* opened a new service from Montreal four months later.

On their return the Harrises moved into their third and final Cape Town residence, Glen Dirk, a large Cape Dutch house in Constantia which, Tomlinson recalled, they made into a very comfortable home. Grander than Springfield and commanding a wonderful view, it lent itself to stylish living and with five or six servants – including 'Cooker John', a big, cheerful African – it was ideal for one of Harris's great delights, the entertainment of guests. Over much of the next three years it witnessed many dinner parties which helped put him and Jill on the South African social map. He was less enthusiastic about accepting the frequent return invitations, for he was always happier at home in a relatively small gathering where he could play host and demonstrate his great talents as a raconteur. For weekend relaxation he would drive Jill, Jackie and Peter around the beautiful nearby countryside in the De Soto station wagon given him by Henry Mercer, and on occasion he would go deep-sea fishing in 'Clemmie', an ex-RAF rescue launch made available to him by the financier Alfred Beit. This life style was facilitated by his being better off than at any earlier stage of his life. As MRAF he was on half pay, he had received £10,000 for his book, he was being paid a salary in South Africa, he was entitled to director's fees from States Marine, and since many benefits were provided in kind there were relatively few expenses. Tomlinson bought him Safmarine shares when there was money to spare, though he showed little interest in them.

For the family, then, it was a happy existence, though with Harris in town all day – he usually lunched at the Nederlandsche Club, near his office – Jill found it a little lonely. So she in particular enjoyed the contrast afforded by their lengthy visits to New York, where they first lived in an apartment in the Pierre Hotel near Central Park, and later in rented apartments. Jill, still at heart a city girl, loved the atmosphere, the shops, the theatres, and when not at school Jackie was in the safe hands of Miss Barber, a governess. Harris himself enjoyed being alongside Mercer in the Big Apple, the centre of the action, and the comfortable, relaxed, 17-day voyages in his Safmarine ships also had their appeal, not least in enabling him to get to know the men who were working for him.

The family's next trip to New York was in 1949, when Safmarine – not to mention Harris himself – was getting an increasingly favourable press for the standards of its ships, the facilities for its passengers, and the quality and treatment of its crews. The most important topic for discussion on this occasion was the desirability of extending its operations to the United Kingdom and Europe. For this it was essential for Safmarine to be admitted to the Conference of Lines, the 'club' which had for many years regulated such trade routes, and in January 1950 – after sometimes stormy negotiations at the Mount Nelson in which Harris played a key role – the object was achieved. So when the *Morgenster* left Cape Town on 16 May with the Harris family and their car on board her destination was Liverpool. She docked on 2 June, giving him six weeks back in the UK before returning to Cape Town aboard the *Constantia* on 15 July.

Since leaving in 1946 Harris had maintained few formal RAF connections, though in South Africa he had always been supportive of the Royal Air Forces Association, as in July 1946 when he became President of its new Cape Town Branch and a year later when he attended its Ball in Cape Town City Hall. He was also touched by the moving tribute paid to him by Lord Dowding at the RAFA's Festival of Reunion in the Albert Hall on 22 September 1946: 'How Sir Arthur Harris hated the work he had to do, with what inflexible determination did he carry it to its conclusion, and how magnificently was he supported by his bomber boys. Truly if Fighter Command's Calvary was measured in months, theirs was reckoned in years.'[2] Then in April 1947 Harris had taken advantage of his Canadian visit to speak at the first Reunion Dinner of the 6 (RCAF) Bomber Group Association in Montreal, and two years later, on 12 March 1949, he had sent a personal message to the first Bomber Command Annual Reunion in the Albert Hall. For the second reunion a year later his stirring message, this time tape-recorded, assured his enthusiastic audience that he had certainly not forgotten them.

Now, in 1950, Harris was back at last, albeit primarily on Safmarine business, and on 19 June he was entertained at a private dinner organised by the Pathfinder Association at the Dorchester; present among others were Trenchard, Slessor (now CAS), Ludlow-Hewitt, and members of his former staff. On 6 July he was at Grosvenor House at the Annual Dinner of the Chamber of Shipping and heard Montgomery refer to him in his speech on behalf of the guests: 'I doubt whether any single man did more in winning the war than he did. I doubt whether that is generally realised.'[3] Two days later Harris was an official guest at Farnborough for the RAF's first post-war flying display. The home country, though he would not have so described it, was beginning to exert its pull as he met old colleagues again, and among them Churchill, to whom he had regularly sent parcels of Christmas 'goodies', always warmly acknowledged. Just two months later Harris was invited by Churchill to represent him at the funeral in South Africa of their mutual friend, Jan Smuts. Writing afterwards to 'Dear Bert', Churchill said: 'I am proud and honoured to have acted, through you, as one of the Pall Bearers at this farewell to a great friend and comrade.'[4]

So by August, when Harris arrived back in Cape Town, he had overseen the start of Safmarine's European service and the Company dividend was about to be raised from 5% to $7\frac{1}{2}$%. Sadly, however, storm clouds were gathering. While Mercer's States Marine (on its way to becoming the largest United States shipping company) owned 40% of the equity, the rest was split between a substantial number of South African shareholders. With other companies, especially a Greek line, starting to sniff around, Harris decided to try to build up a holding company in order to acquire a controlling interest and thus ensure that Safmarine would always remain in friendly hands. What actually happened was that Mercer, opposed to this scheme, himself acquired further shares for States Marine, which by the end of 1950 held 52%. Harris, who had always considered Mercer's hands friendly, later felt obliged to apologise to the Safmarine Board for misleading them into accepting assurances which he had accepted in good faith; he would accept no more, he told them. Meanwhile, having gained the controlling interest, Mercer pressed Safmarine to establish permanent representation in New York, a far better location than Cape Town for handling world-wide shipping business. To that end he would like to see Harris himself based in New York, and in March 1951 the Board agreed to this. Consequently from June onwards Harris lived and worked in New York, with brief visits to Canada and, in January 1952, the United Kingdom, and only in June 1952 did he and the family return for a few weeks to Cape Town and a flat at Sea Point.

For Harris this had been a very difficult period as the Company grappled with complex organisational problems and as individual personalities – mostly much younger – competed for key positions in the developing business. Le Roux tells the story in detail; suffice it here to say that by the end of 1951 Safmarine had two managing directors, one in South Africa and Harris in New York, and States Marine and Clan Line had gained between them 70% control. Among the casualties in this process were Peter Tomlinson and his brother Paul, who had also joined the Company. Remaining in Cape Town they had become increasingly isolated from their master and utterly frustrated by States Marine's spate of criticism of their freight marketing methods and achievements. Replying on 1 August 1951 to Peter Tomlinson's letter of resignation, Harris wrote of how his hopes for Safmarine had been dashed as States Marine had taken control: 'I can see no future here for people like you – the sooner you strike out for yourselves the better – and the more I'll be relieved, having unwittingly led you up the garden path.' At the same time he told Tomlinson of his own decision to get out. He would never come back to South Africa except perhaps on business once per year; he would like Tomlinson (who would soon be working in Cape Town with Tresfon) to look after his local business interests. Nor had he any wish to remain in New York, which he now called 'the dirtiest city in the world', and where it cost the earth merely to exist.

The disillusionment was clear and there were strong personal factors too, as Harris explained to his co-managing director on 31 July 1952. He was worried about his status as a serving RAF officer were he to remain in a South Africa that appeared increasingly likely to become a republic; he therefore believed it essential to assert his British citizenship. He needed also some permanency in his home life as opposed to living in hired apartments, rented houses and hotels. 'I am getting no younger,' he wrote, 'I am a sick man and neither my health, finances nor patience will stand much more.' There were concerns too about 13-year-old Jackie's education and future, and Jill, who had been far from happy in South Africa, longed to go home. So while he could give the present arrangement a year's try-out he reserved his position for the longer term, and in May 1953, having continued to fight Safmarine's corner in New York in face of ever-increasing difficulties with States Marine, he tendered his six months' notice. He had finally had enough. As Peter Tomlinson later put it: 'in Bomber Command he was God, but in South Africa [and the USA] the smart businessmen outwitted him. Mercer, with whom his personal relations remained good, kept him out of harm's way and ensured he was reasonably well provided for, but the important decisions were eventually being taken over his head.'

Yet even in his final months at Safmarine Harris was looking to its future interests, for example when he arranged for Donald Bennett to prepare an outline plan for an airline to operate the Comet II between South Africa and the USA. At that time such a scheme was quickly perceived as impracticable. On the other hand his role in ordering Safmarine's first new owned ships in 1953 was to prove of great significance for the company's future. Then following his retirement he remained on the Board for part-time duties in Europe and North America and on relinquishing his seat in 1960 became a consultant and received a life pension. At the same time he and Jill were allotted the 'perk' of travelling from England to South Africa once a year with the use of the owner's suite. They were to take full advantage of it.

Over more recent years, having merged first with the Clan Line and later with Union Castle, Safmarine has become a major container company operating world-wide, and it continues to acknowledge the debt owed to those who fought the critical battles in its earliest days. Its historian observes that Harris's success in obtaining the three United States vessels at a premium price set Safmarine on its course to become the internationally accepted success of today. Had these not formed the basis for solid development, that might have been the end of the dream. Furthermore his constant battle for more owned vessels and his unflagging vigilance in steering share acquisitions ensured that control ultimately remained in friendly hands.

Notes

1. This chapter is based primarily on Willie le Roux's *History of Safmarine*, which itself relies heavily in its earlier chapters on Harris's own extensive Safmarine papers preserved at the RAF Museum. The other sources are Misc Folder 14/1, the family scrapbook 1946–53, Ian Elliot's memoir, and the author's discussions with Peter Tomlinson.
2. *Daily Telegraph*, 23 September 1946.
3. *Liverpool Journal of Commerce*, 13 July 1950.
4. Misc Folder 11, dated 27 September 1950.

Chapter 19

Back to base

By 1952 there were further constraints affecting Harris's decisions about his future, the most important of them being Churchill's victory in the General Election of October 1951. Writing immediately afterwards to Brendan Bracken, whom he knew still to have the Prime Minister's ear, he issued a reminder of Churchill's earlier promises to try if possible to right the wrongs done to the men of Bomber Command by the post-war Labour Government. Bracken undertook to relay his message. Then the possibility of a peerage was quietly reopened, but as Harris explained to his son, Anthony, on 26 December, 'I am adamantly opposed to tagging a lordship on to my name which would be a great handicap and expense to me and you, and indeed an infernal nuisance. I have signified as an alternative my willingness to accept a baronetcy which should have the desired result and satisfy other interested parties without altering ostensibly or ostentatiously my present style and title.'[1] So in effect Harris was now accepting that his 'medal campaign' was unwinnable and there was no point in maintaining his original stance of refusing all further honours (see chapter 17). As he subsequently explained to Bracken, such public recognition by Churchill, as Prime Minister and Minister of Defence at the time, would once and for all still the widespread and embarrassing allegations that he had been struck out of the Honours List and forced to resign and leave the country. At the same time – and much more importantly – it would remove the gross insult these allegations implied to his 'bomber boys'.[2]

So on 7 April 1952 Churchill, as a mark of the great esteem in which he had always held Harris – and to the consternation of the Honours Committee – pushed through the baronetcy, and on the 22nd Bracken wrote to Harris, 'Your wishes have been fulfilled. They are below your merit, but I can see what an embarrassment it might be to you to join the mausoleum in which I am now interred.' Yet almost immediately Churchill had to tell Harris that since Dr Malan, the new Prime Minister of South Africa, objected to any citizen or resident receiving honours, his name could not go forward while he lived there, and in a further message received by Harris at sea on his way back to Cape Town Churchill confirmed that, according to the South African government, he did possess their nationality and citizenship. On 30 May, however, Harris was able to reply that he would notify them on his next departure that he was abandoning domicile.

'Thereafter the action which you propose in the New Year would be agreeable and indeed, emanating from you, highly gratifying to me.'[3] The public announcement was made on 1 January 1953.

Another significant 'pull' back towards Great Britain had been exerted in December 1951, when Harris was invited to occupy one of the Stalls allotted to the Knights Grand Cross of the Order of the Bath in King Henry VII's Chapel in Westminster Abbey, and on 2 January 1952 he wrote from New York to accept. There followed over the next couple of years much correspondence and the occasional meeting with Garter King of Arms about various heraldic matters connected with this, and also with the baronetcy. These deliberations duly culminated in the grant of a coat of arms which was emblazoned on the support above his Stall. At the same time a territorial designation was required for the baronetcy, and when Harris proposed Wycombe, the town most closely associated with his wartime headquarters, Garter recommended for clarity's sake the fuller name, Chepping Wycombe.[4]

In February 1952 a major national event also influenced Harris's plans: the death of King George VI. Remembering how widely remarked had been his absence from the Victory Parade in March 1946, he knew that the ensuing Coronation of the new Queen was a ceremony he must attend. As early as June 1952, a year ahead of the event, he was asking about shipping reservations from New York to England; in September he wrote to Sir James Barnes, now PUS (Permanent Under Secretary of State) in the Air Ministry, about seating arrangements in the Abbey, dress requirements, and the method of transportation. While he assumed that most of the present Air Council would not know the southern end of a horse from the other he himself was quite prepared to sit a horse if required; any other form of conveyance would also be acceptable provided he was not expected to walk, something he was not very good at. Eventually, after some more light-hearted banter, he was told that he would be riding in a landau, a new No 1 uniform was ordered, and – with every possible London hotel already fully booked – Maurice Dean promised to put him and Jill up at home in Wimbledon. By 4 May, when they arrived at Southampton aboard the *Queen Mary*, the plans were complete. The national press, which in January had widely applauded his baronetcy, now reported his homecoming, albeit temporary as they thought. Four days later he attended his first bomber reunion, the annual dinner of the Pathfinder Association, and on the 22nd he took part in the first of several well publicised Coronation rehearsals in readiness for the Great Day on 2 June. As he rode in the RAF's First Carriage with three fellow Marshals, Douglas, Slessor and Tedder, Harris was for the first time in his proper place, a position reinforced on 15 July when at Odiham he attended the Queen's Review of the Royal Air Force. The *Daily*

Express wrote simply of this day: 'Bomber Harris seems to have made his peace with the RAF.'[5]

To a large extent this was true, but Harris knew only too well that the controversies over his wartime role were not going to go away. At the Pathfinder Dinner he had referred to the official history of the bomber offensive that was being written, saying that the authors had already made up their minds and he reserved the right to reply. He had first become aware of this subject the previous November, when Professor Charles Webster, who had been appointed in 1950 by the Cabinet Office to write the history, called on him in New York. Dr Noble Frankland, who had become co-author, records what Webster noted in his diary: the warmth of his welcome by Harris and his wife, the quality of the lunch, and the two-hour discussion of the bomber offensive, during which nobody could have been more frank and willing to discuss the problems the historians faced. Writing to Frankland about this visit immediately afterwards, Webster expressed his pleasure at how it had gone. Yet only two days later Harris wrote informally to Ralph Cochrane asking 'who the devil is Sir Charles Webster?' and seeking enlightenment about the roles of the War Cabinet (sic), the Ministry of Defence, and the London School of Economics – to which Webster belonged and for whose left-wing politics, as he described them, he had no time whatsoever. He followed up on the 25th with similar requests to James Barnes and Maurice Dean. Gradually Harris elicited the background, and when Webster visited him again early in December he had been warned in a letter from Frankland about how Harris was privately reacting.

Even so, their second meeting proved from Webster's point of view to be equally pleasant; they seemed to have much in common, Webster told Frankland afterwards, in their attitudes to the world at large, and when Harris wrote to Barnes thanking him for detailed information about Webster and Frankland and about the official history programme Harris replied 'I like the old boy.' He went on, however, to call him prejudiced and an unfortunate choice by the Air Ministry (which of course had not chosen him, as Barnes had just explained), and also to call Frankland 'a disgruntled Navigator from Bomber Command' (a totally unfair description of a Flight Lieutenant who had completed a full operational tour and earned the DFC). The essence of Harris's complaint lay in his subsequent statement: 'I should have thought that the historians should at least have been thoroughly acceptable personally to the Service department concerned and that they would somewhat carefully have watched in defence of their own interests who was appointed.'[6] Most unfortunately the official history was off to a bad start as far as Harris was concerned and – as on various other issues over the years – once he had made up his mind he was rarely willing to change it.

So for a whole variety of reasons Harris was being pulled back to England.

At one stage, in early 1953 during a visit to Canada, he did consider trying to settle somewhere near Vancouver, where he and Jill spent a month on the recommendation of a long-standing friend, James Duncan, President of the Massey-Harris Company in Toronto. They had already decided that Duncan would be their first choice as Jackie's guardian should circumstances so dictate; Ira Eaker would also be high on their list. Yet much as they were taken with British Columbia, all the practicalities were pointing in the opposite direction and once the Coronation celebrations were over they began to look for a permanent abode. For this they based themselves as guests of Jill's sister Marjory and her husband, John Prideaux-Brune at Prideaux Place, their fine Elizabethan house in a beautiful position just outside Padstow.

Harris recorded the search in a series of letters to Peter Tomlinson in Cape Town. In July 1953 there was 'no dream house yet'. In October they investigated Salcombe and showed interest in an old mill at Bosham. In January they were following up ideas in Sussex, Buckinghamshire and Kent, but almost despairing of finding a house they wanted at a price they could pay. In February, after their offer of £10,000 for Longbridge House near Warminster had been accepted, it was found to be infested with beetle and rot. Then on 10 April, having rustled through a packet of agents' recommendations and picked one at Goring-on-Thames with no hope whatsoever that it would be any good, they viewed it and bought it. As Harris described The Ferry House it was set in six and a half acres, with beautiful gardens, a paddock abutting the towpath, and a private backwater with wet and dry boathouses. The village was charming and the house could not be overlooked, as the river was on one side and the church on the other. The building itself was apparently in beautiful order; there were five modern bathrooms and nearly all the seven or eight bedrooms had a private bath or private access to one. They were both delighted, Harris told Tomlinson, and could move in almost immediately.[7] He might have added – had he known at that moment – that Oscar Wilde was among the former residents. So in June 1954 The Ferry House became their final home.

The news of where Harris was living quickly spread, and at precisely this time the publication of Denis Richards' and Hilary Saunders' history of the RAF in the Second World War was putting the spotlight, among other things, on his wartime role. The press picked particularly on the clear statement that in the area bombing campaign he was acting not on his own authority but on the orders of the Air Staff, with the ultimate sanction of the War Cabinet.[8] Not surprisingly he was soon on the receiving end of invitations to ceremonies and to functions of many other kinds, requests for interviews, advice to authors, support to good causes, and much else. With the house inevitably making heavy demands on his energies and his health still worrying him he knew he must avoid being at everyone else's beck and call. In any event, having stated his position in his own book, he remained determined to distance himself from the continuing arguments.

Nevertheless there were major events, especially those with Bomber Command connotations, which Harris felt impelled to attend and would keep him to some extent in the public eye. He had been present at the opening of the Runnymede Memorial in October 1953: in May 1954 he was at Lincoln Cathedral for the unveiling of the Memorial Window to the 55,000 men killed in Bomber Command; and November 1955 saw him at York Minster in connection with the Thanksgiving Memorial. In 1956 he was a Pall Bearer at the funeral of Lord Trenchard in Westminster Abbey in February, spoke at the dedication of the Cambridge American Military Cemetery in July, attended the unveiling of the Smuts Memorial in Parliament Square in November, and a few days later (suitably briefed by Maurice Dean) was installed with seven other holders of the GCB in the Henry VII Chapel at a service attended by the Queen. The highlight in 1957 was the Guildhall Reception for the Commonwealth Prime Ministers; in 1958 it was the RAF's Fortieth Anniversary Dinner at Bentley Priory in the presence of the Queen, before which he had consulted Dean on whether he really needed to foot the bill for a new mess kit that he was most unlikely ever to need again; and in 1959 it was the special Dinner that President Eisenhower gave at the United States Embassy in honour of Churchill and other top Allied military leaders of the Second World War.

Such great occasions apart Harris generally turned down invitations to RAF functions in the 1950s, though he did join the Air Marshals' Club, continued to support the Pathfinder Association club (he declined to become its President), and attended two very special squadron ceremonies. One was at Wyton in 1957 when 58 Squadron, which he had commanded at Worthy Down, received its Standard. The second was at Scampton in 1959, when the Queen Mother did the honours for 617 Squadron. Otherwise his attitude towards such activities was well summed up in 1958 in a letter to Sir Robert Renwick, who tried hard to persuade him to attend the Radar Association Dinner. 'I have given up public speechifying ... I have refused so many invitations to speak that whenever I have been bullied into doing so ... it has created soreness amongst some to whom I have sent refusals. Moreover I am now getting much too old and out of date and gaga to be bothered or able to prepare any more speeches let alone deliver them.' In addition, even if he was not expected to speak, there were the practicalities of getting to and from functions, especially at night.[9]

There was, however, one Service request to which one feels Harris should have responded. In 1956 CAS, Sir William Dickson, wrote to tell him (and many others) about the launching of an Appeal to rebuild St Clement Danes

to serve as the central church of the RAF, and he was subsequently asked to
allow his name to appear on the list of supporters. Declining the request he
wrote: 'As an agnostic I am perhaps naturally not in favour of the use of
funds which in my opinion could be used in more pressing directions than
the rebuilding of one of the many surplus London churches.'[10] Certainly, as
Harris himself concluded, he was entitled to his own opinions, and his reply
was, as ever, totally honest. Yet it is disappointing that, regardless of his
religious views, he seems to have given no thought to the value of this
project, so widely backed among his contemporaries, in preserving the
traditions and collective memory of the RAF, and not least of his own men.
Nevertheless, in later years he did come to appreciate the significance of this
new RAF institution, not least when he was there in 1968 for the dedication
of the Polish Air Force Memorial, and again in 1971 when he delivered the
address at the Memorial Service for his much esteemed colleague Robert
Saundby. There were other occasions in later years, especially in connection
with the Aircrew Association (see chapter 21).

Many appeals for help came from elsewhere. There were authors and
publishers seeking information or advice, some of whom – like Andrew
Boyle and Ralph Barker – Harris was disposed to help, and others to whom
he replied uncompromisingly. Cassells, for example, having asked him for
observations on the proofs of a new book, were told 'I neither comment upon
nor read war books', which was not exactly true. He certainly read Joubert's
book *Rocket*, for example, and complained to the publishers over 'derogatory
and untrue statements' about wasted bombing effort, his relationships with
Bennett and the Pathfinders, and his resentment of 'diversions'. He read too,
this time with great pleasure, Sir Arthur Bryant's *The Turn of the Tide*, with
its author's inscription on his personal copy: 'For MRAF Sir Arthur Harris
whose Command made Victory possible'. Bryant made clear in his covering
letter how much he admired Harris's own book, which he had found of great
help. Occasionally Harris could even be persuaded to write a Foreword, as he
did in 1956 for Geoff Taylor's personal memoir, *Piece of Cake*, or to provide
advice on films, such as *The Dambusters*, and *They saved London*, a portrayal of
the flying bomb story.[11] For every request he accepted, however, far more
were turned down. Inevitably, too, there were many personal appeals which
he generally tried to answer sympathetically. To take just two examples, he
did what he could to encourage a 14-year-old schoolgirl seeking advice on
the possibilities of a flying career, and to 11-year-old Master Victor Wade,
engaged on a school project, he wrote in 1953:

> I am only too glad to return you my autograph, and hope your efforts to
> compile a record will be successful. Incidentally, thank you very much for
> enclosing a stamped addressed envelope. Most of the many thousands of

people who write to me from time to time, generally on their own affairs but
entirely unknown to me, never send me a stamped envelope as you did. If
they did so I would be a much richer man today. I have signed it twice, once
on each side so that you can cut off the signature on one side and swop it for
what you can get, if anything! Good luck to you.[12]

If on most matters Harris was eager to maintain a low profile, the affairs
of South Africa provided an exception. Still a member of the Safmarine
Board, he remained in close touch not just with its shipping activities (in
December 1954 he attended the launch on the Clyde of a 12,500-ton cargo
liner), but also with the South African High Commission in London. He was
therefore well informed about the activities of Father Trevor Huddleston,
who, in his book *Naught for your Comfort*, castigated the Union Government's
apartheid policy and urged South Africa's expulsion from the Commonwealth. So when the High Commissioner took Harris up on his offer to help
counter Huddleston's campaign he agreed to lend a hand. He did so in a
carefully measured letter to *The Times* on 30 April 1956. This pointed to the
dangers in an unstable world of campaigns of interference in the internal
affairs of other nations; these served only to harden attitudes and helped
nobody. He went on:

> In nearly 50 years of close connection with South Africa and South Africans I
> am convinced only that British and Dutch South Africans alike are earnestly,
> sincerely, and indeed desperately trying to find a solution to a uniquely
> complex problem, of fearful import, the nature and implications of which
> most people in these islands cannot even begin to understand. Moreover, if
> they did understand it, they would also realise how large a part of South
> Africa's present difficulties arise from our own past mistakes when South
> Africa was under direct British rule, and humble themselves accordingly.

Inevitably this earnest plea for moderation aroused its share of criticism, not
least from Huddleston himself, and some columnists tried to contrast
Harris's support for a modern police state with his attitude towards a former
police state, Nazi Germany. Elsewhere, however, his view was frequently
welcomed as a valuable and influential contribution to a very complex
debate.

Two years later Harris returned to the fray, again at the prompting of the
High Commissioner, whose major social functions he and Jill often attended.
On 24 January 1958 in *The Times* he contrasted the attitude of the 'do-
gooders' towards South African detainees with their view of other people
recently arrested by the authorities in Kenya. It seemed, he suggested, that if
those who were so vociferously fund-raising for South African prisoners felt
so strongly they ought to be showing their concerns much more widely. This

letter aroused the ire not only of Huddleston but also of many members of Christian Action, including Canon John Collins, and in a further letter on 31 January Harris stressed what he saw as the key issue: was it right for citizens of one self-governing Commonwealth country to support financially the citizens of another who might be indicted for treasonable activities? Harris's final public contribution to the debate came on 4 January 1960, when in a good letter to the *Daily Telegraph* he pointed out many of the practical consequences for the ordinary inhabitants if the Labour Party and TUC were ever to implement their proposed boycott of South African goods. He was, in fact, writing from up-to-date knowledge, for he and Jill had returned the previous March from their first holiday visit to the Union, courtesy of two of Safmarine's vessels and their comfortable owner's cabins.[13]

In November 1960 Harris became involved in a partly public argument of a different kind, this time prompted by a *Sunday Times* feature based on the forthcoming memoirs of Earl Attlee. Here, in presenting his views of the top wartime military commanders, Attlee was reported as never thinking Harris 'frightfully good', and not believing that a lot of his bombing was really worthwhile; he should have concentrated it more on 'military targets', particularly oil, than on attacking cities. Hardly surprisingly this stung Harris, who immediately wrote to Attlee at some length pointing out that his comments implied that city bombing was his (Harris's) policy and that Attlee had disagreed with it. The truth was otherwise, he went on. The policy had in fact been decided by the Government and War Cabinet and as a prominent member Attlee shared the responsibility. Having reminded his reader of other facts about the attack on morale and the oil campaign, Harris concluded:

> I am more than weary of the repeated attempts, by commission and omission, that have been made since the war to saddle me, and me alone, with the bombing policies ordered and approved by HM Government, of which you were a leading member, and I am not prepared to take any more of it lying down. Perhaps you will now be good enough either to justify the allegations ... or to inform me that you were misreported and will now disown them.

Attlee's reply was apologetic and emollient. He fully accepted his own responsibility for the bombing policy, admitted the dangers of failing memory, commented that he had merely been trying to convey an impression of his feelings at the time, and undertook to have his book suitably amended.

Harris answered briefly, accepting Attlee's comments but requesting that 'out of respect to those who were lost in these operations and the feelings of their surviving relatives, and in the interests of historical accuracy' he would publish in the *Sunday Times* a statement correcting the erroneous impression he had given. Attlee's response showed some irritation. While he reiterated his promise to alter the text of his book he told Harris that he saw no reason to conceal the opinion of bombing policy which he had formed at the time. 'In view of the discourteous and peremptory character of your letter I do not propose to write to the *Sunday Times*. If all criticism is to stop because of the feelings of surviving relatives, military history could not be written at all.' Tempers were becoming frayed on both sides and Harris's riposte not only complained of discourtesy but also stated his intention to pursue the historical and legal implications if a suitable public statement was not forthcoming. Attlee was not to be moved, telling Harris that what he had said in recording the impression made on him at the time was a matter of historical fact. 'All of us in public positions are liable to be criticised but we learn not to be hyper-sensitive.' There the correspondence ended, and a brief letter from Harris was published in the *Sunday Times* on 22 January 1961, simply making clear where responsibility had lain for the wartime decisions about bombing policy.[14] It had been an unedifying exchange which showed neither man at his best and indicated two differing views of the purposes of history.

The contrasts were soon to be brought out much more strongly and publicly with the publication of the official history. The draft had been completed in 1958 and in November Webster had written to Harris, among others, asking whether he would care to look at it if it was sent to him unofficially; he and Frankland 'would naturally pay the greatest attention' to any comments he might wish to make. Saundby, who had been most helpful, had also promised to read it. While Harris might disagree with some of the conclusions he hoped he would find them based on all the available evidence. 'I hope,' Webster concluded, 'you will find that the book shows how great were the achievements of Bomber Command and, if I may be allowed to say so, of its great Commander-in-Chief.' Replying on 23 December from his holiday address in South Africa, Harris thanked Webster for the offer and said he would indeed be interested. He thought it odd, however, in view of his role in the campaign, not to have been invited officially to consult with the historians, and he was not therefore prepared to assist 'unofficially'.[15]

One can see Harris's point of view. The attitude of many military commanders in both the First and Second World Wars was that officially sponsored histories of the campaigns they had been engaged in should record and interpret the facts in a way that would explain and in general justify their actions. Harris belonged firmly to that school of thought, and not least out of loyalty to his men's reputations. Webster and Frankland, on the other hand, appreciating the complexity and uniquely controversial nature of their subject, were convinced it had to be tackled objectively by looking at the facts and seeing where they led; in this they were backed by the Cabinet

Office, which was responsible for the whole official history programme and keen to ensure that the lessons of this particular campaign were identified for the future. Had Harris been allotted an official role this would have given him the right to intervene on matters with which he disagreed, and without the freedom to draw their own unhindered conclusions Webster and Frankland would never have accepted their appointments.[16] Certainly they would not have ignored Harris's unofficial views had he been willing to offer them, but it was not in his nature to stand back at a distance and discuss such matters with objectivity. Sadly there could only have been confrontation.

So during 1959, when the draft was being extensively considered by a variety of Service and civilian experts, by the Cabinet Office advisory panel on official histories, and by interested government departments, Harris was not party to the discussions. Maurice Dean, however, was. As PUS he was central to the deliberations in the Air Ministry, where the main concerns about the draft were to be found, and was therefore able to keep Harris informed on some of the issues. One of the most significant of these was whether it was permissible for the authors to make direct use of the demi-official (DO) and personal correspondence between Portal and Harris without their concurrence; the draft contained many quotations and reproduced in full the letters they had exchanged in the winter of 1944–5 (see p.308). The authors regarded this material of great importance in establishing the relationships between the two personalities and the reasoning that lay behind their intentions and discussions, and all the documents were in any case available on the official files to which they had been given full access. They were not therefore going to be moved and once a series of possible legal questions had been cleared it seemed that the Air Ministry could do little more. However, when Portal's views were sought he stated his conviction that nothing of what he had written demi-officially in the course of duty and which the gutter press might then exploit should be published during his lifetime.[17]

Then, on 10 October, Harris entered the fray in a letter to Dean. In his view DO letters provided for the exchange of tentative ideas, information and confidential proposals between two particular individuals. They were often hurriedly written under stress of work pending official, carefully phrased versions. He had not been asked to give permission for his DO letters to be published, nor would he now do so. If they were published without his permission it would be a most serious breach of confidence and custom and the authorities should not be surprised at the action he would take. Having given at some length his version of the events relating to the official history he ended by criticising the Air Ministry for handing over the correspondence in the first place. Dean's brief reply promised that he and the

Ministry were doing all they could, though he could not be sure of success. Eventually the authors were persuaded against printing the Portal-Harris letters in full, but few of the many textual changes which the Air Ministry had requested were incorporated. Given the major differences which remained and could not be resolved between the authors and the Air Ministry, and in view of the widespread interest and probable controversy the book would arouse, the Cabinet Secretary felt bound to refer the matter to the Prime Minister, Harold Macmillan, who accepted on 20 February 1960 that the risks entailed in publishing the book as it now stood were outweighed by those entailed if it became known, as it surely would, that the authors had in effect been gagged.[18]

Now Harris could merely wait for the storm to break, his anxieties unallayed when Saundby told him on 3 March that the efforts to get the history amended had been insufficient and the whole thing was 'past praying for'. Harris's reply implied that he might not bother to do anything about the book, entirely blamed the Air Ministry, and stated that 'the whole thing went back to Stansgate and Co and the time when he asked the Air Ministry to clear suspected Communists out of contact with Bomber Command's operational affairs' (see pp.349–351).[19] Regrettably Harris does not emerge well from this affair. He allowed preconceived ideas to dominate his whole approach and, like others, failed to appreciate the long-term importance of objective history and the dictates of writing it. It does seem unfortunate that nobody had thought to have him briefed before Webster came to see him in 1952; had this happened at least some of his misconceptions might have been avoided. Yet it is hard to think of anyone of authority – except perhaps Sir Arthur Bryant – to whom he would have listened with the necessary attention. There was an inevitability about Harris's hostility to the way the official history was compiled that reflected the set of his mind and the unshakeable conviction that he was right.

The four-volume history was published on 2 October 1961, shortly after Webster's untimely death. Rarely do 'official histories' make headlines but this one did. The *Sunday Telegraph*, alerted in advance, headed its front page on 1 October: 'Row Breaks Over Last-War Bombing – Sir Arthur Harris's Retort to Charge of Costly Failure'. The ensuing report quoted Harris's answer to the charge. He commented first on the choice of authors: 'Surely if you are going to get it fairly treated you don't appoint people who have already made up their minds. Their history [which he had not read] exaggerates our errors and decries our victories.' Then, following the lines of his own book, he discussed a variety of his Command's achievements, most of which differed little from those discussed in the history itself. He was in fact being asked to answer a charge that the history did not make, for the book's only specific mention of 'costly failure' appeared in its quotation of Harris's own statement in 1943 that attempts to carry out low-level attacks with heavy bombers had almost invariably proved to be costly failures. But if this report was in most respects a defence of Harris the accompanying review article by the MP Richard Crossman took a very different line. Reminding his readers of the shadow of public disapproval that had lain over Bomber Command ever since VE Day he praised the magnificent way in which the official historians had now destroyed the legend of the Command's victories. He accepted that Harris, a fanatical believer in terror bombing, was fully backed by the Government, but accused him, like Haig, of having been wrong on almost every major decision. 'The irony of Bomber Command,' he concluded, 'was that, although its offensive was a substitute for Passchendaele, its consequences were very much the same.' So, without using the actual term, Crossman was strongly supporting the 'costly failure' verdict and attributing it to the official history.[20]

Over the coming days and weeks the argument spread through the media in many parts of the world. Harris was interviewed, Donald Bennett, other senior commanders and some of Harris's old crew members entered the fray, and Frankland – now having to take the flak alone for the historians – also found himself in the thick of it. Yet hardly any of the critics could have done more than skim the four volumes, and only when the *Times Literary Supplement* published its review on the 20th did the first properly balanced appraisal appear. Written anonymously (as custom required) by Michael Howard, another official war historian, this pointed out – among much else – the authors' carefully considered judgement of Harris's diverse qualities, their assessment that he was quite often right and the 'experts' hopelessly wrong, and their view that only after Overlord could his policy be seriously faulted.[21] Harris himself certainly read this article, although his reaction is not recorded. From now on, with Howard having set the tone, the official history was to acquire its just recognition in considered circles, but superficial, ill-informed judgements would long continue. Harris himself did eventually come to appreciate that the book had much to commend it and – as he indicated in a private letter to Elworthy in 1965 – accepted that its authors had not judged his campaign a costly failure. Yet, influenced partly by the tone of the initial debate, he never became enthusiastic about it. In particular he felt that many of his 'old lags', as he called those who had served under him, were hurt by what they believed to be an unfair verdict on their efforts, and he started to become more inclined to take up the cudgels again on their behalf.

In so doing Harris must have welcomed encouragement from an unexpected quarter. Lord Morrison (previously Herbert Morrison), who had seen the 'unjust and dispiriting' remarks about Harris in the official history press notices, wrote a short article in *Today* and sent him a copy. In this Morrison defended the area bombing policy for which the Churchill Government, of which he was a member, was responsible, and for which Harris was the executant. He believed that Bomber Command's persistent attacks seriously damaged the German war effort, affected their morale and shortened the war. 'Of course it was a brutal business but, after all, the Nazis started it. We were fighting for our lives and liberties. We had to win. I believe that the brave efforts of Bomber Command were not wasted. And I believe that Bomber Harris was a really great commander.'[22]

Notes

1. Misc Folder 22/1; Rosemary Harris, for the letter to Anthony.
2. Misc Folder 22/1. Saward, *op.cit.* pp.331–2, reproduces part of this letter.
3. Colville, *op.cit.* p.644; Misc Folder 22/1.
4. Misc Folder 15; Harris was installed in the Bath Chapel on 15 November 1956.
5. Misc Folder 16/1; Family scrapbook.
6. Misc Folder 17; Frankland, *History at War*, pp.85–9, covers this subject in detail.
7. Tomlinson discussions; family papers.
8. Richards & Saunders, *op.cit.* vol.2, p.118.
9. Misc Folders 15, 16/1, 16/2, 22/1; family scrapbooks.
10. Misc Folder 11.
11. Misc Folder 19/2.
12. Misc Folder 22/1.
13. Misc Folder 14/2; family scrapbooks.
14. Misc Folder 20. In *A Prime Minister Remembers*, pp.49–50, Attlee's comments clearly take some account of Harris's strictures.
15. Misc Folder 17; Saward, *op.cit.* pp.329–30, reproduces Harris's letter in full; Frankland, *op.cit.* p.99.
16. RAFHS Proceedings, vol.2, pp.56–7, author's comments.
17. Frankland, *op.cit.* pp.103–8, covers this whole episode in detail.
18. *Ibid* pp.109–13; Misc Folder 22/1.
19. Misc Folder 17; Harris letter to Lawrence, 23 August 1961, courtesy of Ann Lawrence.
20. Misc Folder 17; Frankland, *op.cit.* pp.114–16.
21. Misc Folder 17; Frankland, *op.cit.* pp.116–26, covers the press controversy in detail. Crossman had been the wartime Director of Psychological Warfare.
22. Misc Folder 17, letter from Morrison dated 6 December 1961.

Chapter 20

The Ferry House

By this time the Harrises were well settled into their Thames-side residence in rural Oxfordshire. There had inevitably been frustrations, not least those occasioned by the English climate, so very different from that of South Africa. Delectable The Ferry House might be in summer, but winter invariably brought its problems, not least the flooding of the garden. Then there was the never-ending battle with the taxman. In 1958 Harris told Tomlinson that his bank's tax expert had been trying unsuccessfully for five years to agree with the Inland Revenue how much he ought to pay. Admittedly the situation was complicated by his earned and unearned incomes from the UK, USA, South Africa and Canada, but 'when thieves fall out what is an honest man like myself to do and how the ordinary man is expected to understand his income tax form is quite beyond me'. As for the country as a whole, he wrote in 1957 in the aftermath of Suez, it was 'hopeless and rapidly getting worse' and 'the Conservatives were as bad as the Labourites'. England was 'a good country to keep out of' and when Jackie had finished her education they would be away again.[1]

The possibility of uprooting themselves once more was never meant seriously and it was the fairly regular winter trips abroad which from 1958–9 onwards provided the changes of scene that they craved. Jackie, now completing her studies at Winkfield Place, the Finishing School run by Constance Spry, accompanied her parents on the first of these holidays but from then on was committed elsewhere, for in November 1959 she became engaged. Her fiancé, Nicholas Assheton, was the younger son of one of the longest-standing family friends, Lord Clitheroe, who as Ralph Assheton MP had been associated with Harris both before and during the war. The couple were married three months later in the Henry VII Chapel, where Harris was able to exercise his privileges as holder of the GCB.

The grandchildren who started to arrive in 1961 were not Harris's first. In 1946 his eldest daughter Marigold had married Robert Armitage, who subsequently worked in insurance, and after the Harrises returned to England the Armitages with their family frequently came to stay at The Ferry House. Other regular visitors included Jill's relatives the Prideaux-Brunes, and through the 1960s and into the 1970s there would, to Harris's delight, be constant invasions of growing children – not just 'family' – for whom the house and its surrounds were ideal. Many observers have spoken of his love of children. Vivienne, Ian Elliot's daughter, commented that no child ever had any fear or him and his gruff manner; James Denny, a neighbour in Goring, said 'my children loved him – he was never intimidating to them'; and Charles Milner, with whose family the Harrises stayed in South Africa, mentioned, for instance, how much he enjoyed throwing coins into the swimming pool for the boys to dive after when they were saving for a canoe. There were, too, ample opportunities for him to go on indulging his penchant for bestowing nicknames – Peanut, Roo and Doodlebug, for example – and often they stuck into adulthood. A long-lived survivor from his original family was also in evidence in these later years – his sister Maud Onslow, now widowed and living just opposite. She shared his sense of humour and they thoroughly enjoyed reminiscing together.[2]

Sadly this picture of happy family relationships did not always extend to Harris's other two children by his first marriage, nor to Barbara, with whom he occasionally exchanged letters on financial matters. She had been widowed in 1953 and resided in Hampshire until 1964, when she came to live with Anthony and Rosemary in Chelsea, remaining there until her death in 1986. Anthony, who had left the Army after serving well during the war, now worked in the antiques business, and Rosemary was achieving considerable success as a writer. They had both kept in touch with their father during the war, but while he was abroad there was little contact, although they did meet him and Jill occasionally during their visits to England and in 1960 attended Jackie's wedding. In their view he was not of a temperament to understand how difficult they found the divisions created by the divorce and his remarriage and, wrapped up in his new young family and his many wider responsibilities, turned a largely blind eye to their equal need for encouragement and support. Not until the 1970s did Rosemary start visiting The Ferry House and rebuilding a relationship with her father, and by this time Jackie was using her influence to try to bring the two families at least a little closer together.

It is hard to believe that Harris himself was happy about this situation: all his four children were important to him. Unhappily, however, he and his son possessed such contrasting personalities that after Anthony outgrew childhood there was never any real rapport between them. Harris, unwisely but like many other fathers, had probably wished for a son and heir cast in his own image; Anthony, a charming, gentle, kindly man of artistic temperament and not physically robust, did not match his hopes. To put it simply, they were on different wavelengths. There was more than this, however, to the distancing that occurred in Harris's retirement years. Jill had never been able to accept the implications of her husband's first marriage, partly because she herself was little older than the children themselves but mainly on account of her Roman Catholic upbringing. Nevertheless during the war –

and afterwards in South Africa and the USA – there had been position and social responsibilities most unusual for someone so young, and she had coped with these not only remarkably well but also with great enjoyment. Now, all of a sudden, life was almost totally different. There were occasional major functions but not many, and at the age of 40, when most women would be approaching their most active and influential years, hers were largely past and her much older husband was feeling his age. To open new doors, to take new initiatives, however, was not for her. Nor was it easy for her or her husband, both of whom had been brought up as semi-orphans, to show or discuss their deeper feelings on such matters. So while she remained polite towards Anthony and Rosemary there was always an 'atmosphere', with Harris terrified that Jill would be upset if he tried to improve matters. He had always been protective towards her but never more than now.

These attitudes were well symbolised in the early 1970s when Saward wrote Harris's biography and ignored his first marriage. Only after his death, when the book was published, did Barbara and her family – or anyone else – find this out, and they were devastated to discover that according to their husband/father's 'authorised biography' they did not exist. Saward must have known about them and it can only be assumed that Harris instructed him to exclude all reference. Might it be that Harris, knowing all too well Jill's sensitivities about the subject and that only she would be around when the book eventually appeared, was almost obsessed by the need to spare her feelings?

Most of Harris's attention at The Ferry House was, of course, devoted to far more mundane matters, particularly in the early days. At the age of 62 he had come into possession of the first home he could call his own, and he welcomed the opportunity to apply again some of his practical skills. While the major tasks were beyond him he always kept a critical eye on the various builders and maintenance men who came to ply their trades. Usually (well supplied with coffee or beer) they got on well with him, particularly those who knew their jobs, but he gave short shrift to the less competent and often argued the toss with those he considered to be overcharging him. He was remarkably adept in mechanical matters, a talent which went right back to his earliest days in Rhodesia, and would not only complain but try to offer constructive ideas when appliances he had bought failed to work properly.

The purchase of a water softener in 1954 gave rise to one particularly long-running saga. Harris first complained about the way the salt clogged and the size and weight of the packs in which it was delivered; then he turned to the machine's declining efficiency and the constant attention it needed, supporting his comments with considerable technical detail. The manufacturers, doubtless realising they were dealing with an expert, replaced the machine, whereupon Harris commended them for their sense of responsibility towards their customers. From now on, while conducting a parallel dialogue with ICI about the suitability and method of delivering their salt, he carefully monitored the softener's performance. At first this seemed satisfactory, but he did tell the manufacturer that the overflow pipe ought to be re-designed and suggested how this might be done. The ensuing letters became even more lengthy and technical, extending to the nature and pressure of the local water supply, and culminating in Harris reporting (with detailed figures) that the output of the second softener was now much less than it should be. The correspondence had throughout been amicable, and the firm – probably learning quite a lot from him about its products – offered to take back the existing appliance for testing and fit a third. By the end of 1956 Harris at last was able to declare himself satisfied and to write: 'I cannot speak highly enough of your firm's attitude throughout, which is most refreshing in these days when so many firms still incline towards a take it or leave it attitude vis-à-vis their customers.'[3]

Harris's innovative mind also engaged itself in the garden, especially in the attempt to ease the task of mowing his extensive lawns. In 1955 he acquired a new motor-mower about whose assembly and serviceability he was soon complaining. At the same time he wrote to the managing director urging his firm to produce a small rider-mower suitable for the ordinary garden. On receipt of a friendly reply Harris offered some ideas on design, stressing the position of the seat, the importance of its being quickly and easily detachable, and the possibility of also using the machine to drive a lawn sweeper and maybe other labour-saving devices. The top-level contacts continued and in 1956 Harris (or his gardener) was not only riding on a trailer behind his existing mower but also using the contraption to sweep the leaves.[4]

Another of Harris's bright ideas was sparked by a letter in September 1955 from an old wartime friend, Roy Dobson, Chairman of AV Roe in Manchester. Dobson asked if Harris would provide a brief personal tribute to the work of the Lancasters for inclusion in a colour film his firm was making about the new Vulcan bomber. Harris was quick to agree: 'I am always prepared to do anything I can to help you and your Company.' Then he added: 'I have a backwater on my property here which requires re-bridging with a single span. Have you anywhere lying about an old main spar, or better still a pair, for which you have no use? I would be happy to pay the usual scrap price.' In November his bridge was delivered and in December he went to London to do his bit for the film.[5] Later he and Bill Hooper – an ever-welcome visitor – enjoyed constructing together two bridges and a large fruit cage, and rebuilding a big garden shed.

While Harris was not personally very keen on the actual gardening, most of which he left to Luker, the gardener, and to Jill, he certainly took an interest in the vegetable produce and went so far as to keep chickens. These he acquired from his friends at Gawdy Hall in Norfolk, with whom he discussed in some detail the best methods of feeding, and in due course they congratulated him on the way he was managing his flock and the encouraging results he was achieving. So the grounds met at least some of the needs of one of his favourite hobbies. He had always enjoyed cooking but had rarely had sufficient time for it; now at The Ferry House there was time, so countless visitors – the author included – were surprised and delighted to find that their lunch or dinner or both had been cooked by their host. The kitchen was not Jill's scene; it was very much his. He built up over the years an extensive collection of recipes, many reflecting his travels in foreign parts, and if occasionally his dishes were too rich or highly spiced for some of his guests they were generally greeted with warm approval. Nor was he averse to taking over someone else's kitchen. When staying in South Africa with the Milners, to take one example, he would spend anything up to four hours there on his own – Liz, the cook, having wisely fled – and prepare a wonderful meal. Invariably, however, Liz commented long afterwards, he had used just about every dish and implement in the place and left all the washing up for her! At home his own kitchen was impeccable, always equipped with the most recent devices and gadgets, and with a place for everything. Perhaps surprisingly he was no great authority on wines, but he would always find something suitable – almost invariably South African – to accompany the cuisine. His own favourite tipple was whisky and there was never any shortage of liquid refreshment for the guests he so loved to entertain. Smoking, however, no longer interested him. An inveterate smoker in earlier days he gave it up for health reasons in 1952 and actually commented in 1955 that after Churchill had entertained him to lunch and insisted that he smoke a cigar it had literally made him sick.

Nobody who visited The Ferry House could have had any doubts about the nature and significance of Harris's career. He and Jill had brought with them a mass of books, papers, photographs, souvenirs and mementoes – most of which had been to South Africa and back – and the house was full of reminders. Indeed, his study was converted into virtually a personal museum whose contents ranged from models and photographs of many of his aircraft to a fine collection of toy soldiers, press cuttings, autographed photographs presented by many of the wartime 'greats', and many books. He was particularly proud of the bugle presented to him by the Rhodesian Army in 1975 to replace the one he had buried in South-West Africa in 1915. Visitors would usually be shown round, and those with whom he judged it worthwhile to talk 'Bomber Command shop' were also introduced to the comprehensive card index which he used to refresh his memory. With most guests, however, he steered clear of the great wartime issues; the war was simply 'taboo' and there were plenty of less controversial things to talk about.

The subject was certainly on the agenda, however, when old wartime colleagues came along. Ira Eaker and Tooey Spaatz were early arrivals, and Eaker – who just outlived Harris – came again and maintained regular correspondence. They were always great friends and totally frank with each other. Writing after a visit to The Ferry House in 1972, Eaker said he thought Harris 'less changed by the passing years than any of us. You always had the reputation, according to Portal, of being slightly cantankerous, but I admired your refusal to compromise with principle so much that I followed your example as best I could.'[6] Another whom Harris was particularly pleased to see visited him in 1955: the Canadian 'Black Mike' McEwen, whose work in command of 6 Group in 1944–5 had, in Harris's view, never been adequately recognised.[7] Some of his RAF contemporaries visited too from time to time, notably Saundby and Cochrane, both of whom lived not far away and shared his concerns about the ways in which the bombing controversies were developing. A long-standing Army friend from Camberley days, Lieutenant-General Sir Henry Pownall, was a further regular guest, as was the widow of Captain de Mowbray, Harris's trusted Navy representative at High Wycombe. Maurice Dean and his wife too were ever welcome.

The 'family' relationships with Harris's former PAs were also well maintained. Whenever Peter Tomlinson came over from Cape Town he would stay, and his brother Paul and the rest of the Tomlinson family, including the actor brother David, also appeared. Walter Pretyman came at times from Brazil, and his daughter Christina (the unregistered passenger from Harris's Lancaster, and nicknamed Doodlebug) stayed frequently when she was studying at Winkfield with Jackie and later when working in London. Harris's other PA, Etienne Maze (nicknamed 'Feets' because of his large feet), kept in touch too; he had been a most valuable member of the initial Bomber Command Survey Team in 1945. The Harrises attended his wedding in 1954, and it was thanks to him that in 1944, at Springfield, they had first met one of Harris's closest friends of the post-war years, Etienne's own father. Paul Maze, a Frenchman with strong English connections, had made a name for himself in the First World War as a soldier and then as an artist on the Western Front, where he first met Churchill. Between the wars he had done much to help Winston develop his painting skills, and when Maze and Harris met their Churchill connections immediately created a common bond. In the later 1950s Maze stayed several times at The Ferry House, his visits usually coinciding with the Henley Royal Regatta, where Harris had become a member of the Stewards Enclosure. He had his own boat, Paul sketched, Jackie and her friends joined in the action with enthusiasm, and a good time was had by all. Harris himself, however, became increasingly irritated by the size of the crowds and after a polite exchange of letters with the Chairman, Harold Rickett, resigned in 1960. By this time Maze, already well into his 70s, was becoming increasingly reluctant to leave his home in Sussex, but he and Harris continued to exchange lengthy and frequent letters. While many were on day-to-day matters some discussed Harris's wartime work, which Maze would treat with sympathy and understanding, and in others they shared their misgivings about post-war society and Britain's declining situation in the modern world. If Harris ever had a soul mate it was probably 'Pauli' Maze, and when in 1973 Brigadier (now General Sir) Michael Gow wrote to Harris asking him to support an attempt to secure an honour for Maze in recognition of his unique contribution to Britain's national heritage Harris was only too ready to oblige.[8]

In the 1950s Maze had also taken advantage of his friend's hospitality as a coach passenger. Ever since his youth Harris had been keen on horses and at The Ferry House he was only too willing to allow neighbours to keep their animals in his own paddock. Among his new friends was one George Matthey, who not only kept horses but also maintained a nineteenth-century stagecoach, Perseverance, at South Stoke. Matthey, who sometimes used his coach to convey tourists between Oxford and Blenheim Palace, soon realised that Harris possessed the driving talents he needed, and the invitation to join his team of volunteers was readily accepted. So for several years Harris was a familiar Oxford figure as he drove his coach and four in great style through the city and out to Blenheim and Woodstock. Sometimes he had personal friends on board – Henry Mercer was one, Lord Clitheroe another – and his skills were generally admired, not least by John Seabrook, the American who in 1965 was to win the championship four-in-hand at the Royal Show. On one occasion in 1959, widely seized upon by the press, Harris's trip to Blenheim was planned to coincide with a visit by Churchill, who was surprised and delighted to greet his old wartime colleague and find him engaged in such a nostalgic enterprise. Unfortunately Harris suffered a slipped disc in 1960, which put an end to his coaching days.[9]

The Ferry House paddock came in useful in other ways as well. In 1954 Harris readily agreed to the Goring Gap Bowmen continuing to use it during the summer months subject to paying a 'peppercorn' rent of one arrow a year and insuring him against third party risks. At the same time he, Jill and Jackie became honorary members, though he declined the invitation to become President; while he would certainly continue to assist he would take no official role. Occasional questions that arose subsequently over such matters as mowing the grass, locking the gate, and admitting guests of the Club were always settled amicably; Harris was all for helping a local

organisation which conducted its affairs in a responsible manner. He was
pleased too to let scouts come and camp. A Brighton vicar brought his troop
in 1955 and his warm thank-you letter elicited an equally warm reply,
commending the boys for leaving the place spotless and looking forward to
seeing them again. Their visits continued. In 1959 the Sea Scouts from
Cheadle, near Manchester, spent what they called 'a memorable week' in
which Harris and his family had played 'a wonderful part', and followed up
by offering him life membership of their Group as their Honorary Group
Scoutmaster. This offer he accepted. Other Scout Groups in London and
elsewhere also got the message and drawing on his experience Harris
compiled a little note of things his visitors must not do. They must never, for
example, throw rubbish or anything except another scout into the river;
there must be no shouting after 9.00 pm *please*, 'but certainly sing if you feel
like it'; and:

> Please do not feed Rastus, our bull terrier, even if he tells you he is allowed
> camp hand-outs. He is not very truthful in that regard. Do not allow him
> near garbage pits or cookhouses, or he will help himself and he has already
> had to be operated on for Scout camp bones stuck in his interior. He will eat
> anything except a scout.

Here was Harris using his sense of humour and skill with words, suitably
tailored to his audience, to get his message across. They loved it, they did
what he told them, and they observed his final injunction: 'Enjoy yourselves.'[10]

Not all who had dealings with the owner of The Ferry House were as
enamoured. Local shopkeepers who failed to meet his exacting standards
often found themselves in trouble, and he was particularly irritated with
drivers who obstructed the lane near his gate. He even wrote via the AA on
one occasion to one of its members who had blocked his entrance for much of
a day, and threatened to sue him; fortunately the abject apology that
promptly arrived softened his heart. Brian Cooke, who ran the local garage
in Goring and got to know Harris well in the 1960s and 1970s when driving
him on many of his longer journeys, comments how naughty he often was
about so-called 'unauthorised parking'. Indeed he was not beyond using his
own car, the Chrysler he had brought back from South Africa or the Bentley
which he later bought, to push some offending vehicle out of the way.

Brian Cooke remembers his long association with both Harris and Jill
with great affection. Their journeys together would usually be to some
official function: Harris liked to sit in front, and when he was not swearing at
the idiots on the road would be talking most knowledgeably, and
humorously, about the history of the towns and villages they were going
through. He was always concerned for Cooke's well-being and not least

when arriving at their destination; totally typical was his first question on reaching Finningley for the Royal Review in 1978: 'What happens to my driver?' As Cooke also testifies, despite his advancing years Harris never lost his personal enthusiasm for driving, and after damaging his Bentley and later writing it off in South Stoke he took possession of a Jaguar and continued to take the wheel in the local area until almost the end of his life. In these closing years Cooke became a highly trusted family aide, often called upon in emergencies, such as when Harris telephoned for help in getting a huge turkey out of the oven and they first had to carve the legs off.[11]

Harris had not long been in Goring before his concern about its roads led him to add his support on a significant local issue: the need for traffic lights at a crossroads in nearby Streatley. This he described in a letter to the Berkshire County Council as one of the most dangerous in the country and he subsequently strongly challenged their complacent reply. Eventually continued local pressure, Harris's – and Jill's – included, achieved its desired effect. Never reluctant to take on bureaucracy – shades of his earlier battles with the Air Ministry's civil servants – he also had a go at the Postmaster General in 1957, protesting at length at attempts to inflict on the residents of Goring a new postal address implying that they now lived not in Oxfordshire but in Berkshire in a mere suburb of Reading. On this he achieved nothing but in 1961 he extended his battle on behalf of his fellow citizens by calling on the Oxfordshire County Council to 'defend Goring' against the Berkshire County Council's unwarranted erection on the Oxfordshire side of the Thames bridge of a sign announcing 'Now Entering Royal Berkshire'. His spirited conclusion called on the Oxfordshire authorities 'to defend us against these wrongs and trespasses and should any question of a punitive expedition against the high-handed Authorities concerned be contemplated I shall be pleased to raise at my own expense, and lead, a half troop of horse, a hand ballista battery, or a Chinese stinkpot platoon. But by any means let's get up at 'em.' Having just signed the letter he heard that the notice board had been moved to the Berkshire side, possibly by the Goring Maquis![12]

Nor did the providers of the train service between Goring and London escape Harris's attentions, and the General Manager of British Rail's Western Region at Paddington was the regular recipient of letters containing a wide mix of complaints and suggestions relating to the rolling stock. Its general condition and maintenance were criticised, the design and provision of the luggage racks were discussed, the quality of the cleaning was castigated, the positioning of the first-class accommodation was considered inconvenient, and the inadequacies of the heating system were frequently identified. Sometimes the trains were overheated, at others they were bitterly cold, and when Harris was told that cold weather was to blame for the failure of the heating in the first-class coaches he lost no time in asking the obvious question: what is heating for? The correspondence was always courteous but the General Manager in the late 1950s must have felt somewhat apprehensive each time another 'Bomber Harris' letter appeared in his in-tray.[13]

Yet while Harris often took up the cudgels with private businesses and public authorities on both his own behalf and that of his fellow citizens he did not become a prominent local personality in the more public sense. Though he received frequent requests to officiate at such events as school speech days and to address Rotary Clubs, Round Tables, Old Comrades Associations and so on, invariably he turned them down. As he told Upper Basildon School in 1955, if he accepted even half his many invitations he would do little else, and for obvious reasons he could not accept some and refuse others. Nor would he agree to take on honorary posts, usually Vice-Presidencies, with clubs and societies. Goring United Football Club were told, for example, that he would never accept any office unless he could take active interest in their activities, and he had had no personal interest in football since giving up playing rugby over 30 years before. He did, on the other hand, agree to become Vice-President of the South Chiltern Scout Association in 1963, doubtless reflecting the active help he was giving visiting scouts, and while not taking any official role he and Jill supported the local Conservative Association in some of its fund-raising activities, especially at election times. Indeed, in 1958 he actually put in a public appearance in Streatley as the mystery celebrity in an Association version of the BBC panel game 'What's my Line?' As the *Bucks and Oxon Advertiser* reported: 'Sir Arthur gaily entered into the spirit of the game, and disguising his voice and speaking in French, Dutch and German (which he translated to the Chairman to the amusement of the audience) completely baffled all the efforts of the panel to discover his identity.'[14]

That Harris did, in fact, become reasonably well-known was demonstrated long afterwards on 6 June 1980, when he delivered the address at the memorial service for Mr Richard Wilson in Goring Parish Church. Wilson, his solicitor and a close personal friend, was an important and popular figure in the village life, and the church was packed. In outlining his life and career Harris spoke of the respect and affection in which he was held, of the involvement with so many people and their affairs which had made him so widely loved and respected, and of the enormous interest he took in both the young and the old. It was a most moving tribute which Harris concluded with a reference to Pilgrim's Progress, for Wilson, not least in his attitude to his final illness, reminded him of Mr Valiant for Truth. That Harris could deliver such a fine address in his late 80s bore testimony not just to the respect in which he himself was held in his own community but also to his continued mastery of an audience.[15]

It was also typical of Harris that he did not forget his old school, All-hallows. In 1952 he agreed to endow the Geography Prize – and with some pleasure, for he had always been interested in the subject and had also 'had a little to do here and there with altering the map and therefore making life harder still for the average student'. While he subsequently felt obliged to decline the Presidency of the Old Honitonians Club he did in 1966, and again in 1976, allow his name to be used as a Patron of two School Development Appeals, with their emphasis on improving the facilities for youngsters, a cause always close to his heart.[16]

Nor, of course, could he and Jill ignore the pull of South Africa. From the winter of 1958–9 to that of 1981–2 they made the sea journey from England to Cape Town roughly every other year, their visits timed to take them away from England's winter weather into the warm, sunny climate of the Western Cape. Sometimes they travelled further afield, including South-West Africa on one occasion, but usually they divided their time between the Mount Nelson Hotel in Cape Town, the farmstead belonging to the Tresfons at Rooshoek, near Wellington, and the picturesque eighteenth-century Cape Dutch house owned by Sir Mordaunt Milner in the winelands to the East. The two families had met through their daughters Georgina and Jackie, and they all quickly became good friends. If at all possible Harris would take his own car with him (another Safmarine privilege), enabling them to get around easily, and Peter Tomlinson, with whom they also stayed occasionally, would often accompany them – still the PA![17]

Usually there would be one or two Safmarine events, such as a special luncheon held in Harris's honour by the Chairman and Directors in 1965 and the ceremonies four years later when two former Union Castle liners were transferred to the South African flag. One major event, however, he did not attend. Having accepted an invitation to the 21st Anniversary cele-brations in 1967 Harris spotted an advance article in the *Cape Times* which, based on an interview given by Peter Tomlinson, expounded on the wartime role of the Company's first Chairman. Ever mindful of the continuing pro-German sympathies of many in South Africa, Harris was furious. He con-sidered it totally inappropriate to join in Safmarine's celebrations in an atmosphere where he personally was liable to be accused of seeming to revive the old Bomber Command issues. He immediately cancelled the visit and put Tomlinson in his place. Fortunately the fences were soon mended and future visits were arranged in lower key.

There was, however, always one occasion on each visit when Harris could let his hair down: the Annual Dinner of the RAF Officers' Club, held at the Mount Nelson and timed to coincide with his stay in Cape Town. Invariably he and Jill were warmly welcomed and he would speak, at length and without notes, about the wartime days. One of the last letters he ever received, dated 27 February 1984, came from the Secretary, Gordon Jefferys, telling him how much he and Jill had been missed that year as the Guests of Honour; many had been the tributes, formal and informal, from his 'old lags'.[18]

Notes

1. Except where specifically stated this chapter is based partly on discussions with members of Harris's family and friends, including Peter Tomlinson, and partly on scrapbooks and other material held by Jacqueline Assheton.
2. Maud outlived her brother and when she died in 1986 her grave was placed alongside his.
3. Misc Folder 24/1.
4. *Ibid.*
5. Misc Folder 11.
6. Misc Folder 7.
7. *Ibid.* In June 1959, hearing that McEwen was very ill, Harris wrote to the Canadian High Commissioner urging that he be given some suitable honour; Harris also told Mrs McEwen that responsibility for the omission had lain between the Canadian High Command in the UK and the Air Ministry. Misc Folder 11.
8. Misc Folders 22/2, 23. See also Johnson, *op.cit.* p.269. Maze died in 1979 aged 92.
9. Family scrapbooks; Misc Folder 23.
10. Misc Folder 23.
11. Author's discussion with Mr Brian Cooke.
12. Misc Folder 24/2.
13. *Ibid.*
14. Misc Folder 23; family scrapbook.
15. Misc Folder 23; discussion with James Denny.
16. Misc Folder 23.
17. Discussions with Peter Tomlinson and Charles Milner, the son of Sir Mordaunt Milner.
18. Misc Folder 14/2.

Chapter 21

The old lags

It was not just in South Africa that in Harris's later years his old lags were increasingly demonstrating their affection. Indeed, wherever significant numbers of them were to be found – whether in the United Kingdom, Canada, Australia, New Zealand or elsewhere – they were coming together to talk of their wartime days in Bomber Command, to remember their fallen comrades, and not least to try to pay their respects to 'Butch', the revered Commander-in-Chief who continued to show such remarkable powers of survival.

Yet back in the 1960s, once the furore over the official history had abated, it had seemed unlikely that Harris would ever again return to the public stage other than for the very occasional formal function. Certainly his letters to Peter Tomlinson suggested that he was feeling his age. In 1961, despite recovering from his slipped disc, he said The Ferry House was becoming too much and he was thinking of moving out of the Thames Valley to a small *pied-à-terre* with no garden. Two years later he wrote that he and Jill had been hibernating mentally as well as physically in England's coldest winter for 223 years; 'I am very lazy in my old age.' In 1965 he complained about his continuing skin problems. In 1966 life was 'very quiet these days but for the occasional weekend party and visits by Jackie and the kids', and in 1968 he was finding difficulty in standing for any length of time, as exemplified at a recent Bath Service in the Abbey.[1]

Over these years he was compelled to witness the steady departure of many of his great wartime contemporaries. Usually he played his part in the appropriate ceremonies, but for the most important of them all, Churchill's funeral in St Paul's Cathedral in January 1965, he was absent, for he and Jill happened to be aboard ship en route for South Africa. Otherwise he would assuredly have accepted the Churchill family's invitation to act as a Pall Bearer. His public statement about the great man, published in the press, deserves recording:

No one can pay adequate tribute to Sir Winston Churchill because no one can comprehend the vast scope of the catastrophe or the endless miseries which would have overwhelmed Europe, and indeed most of the civilised world, had victory gone to Hitler's Nazi Germany. But for Winston Churchill victory would not have been ours.

In 1967 and 1968 came the deaths of Lord Tedder and Sir John Salmond, and in 1969 at the funeral of Lord Douglas in Westminster Abbey Harris represented the Queen – Portal, who customarily officiated at such RAF ceremonies, was now in failing health. Afterwards Harris told Tomlinson about his 'royal' treatment, including being taken in the Queen's Rolls Royce complete with Crown and no number plates, but added that 'this ex-bugler-boy takes no pride in such things and has long since learnt to weary of the load of gee-gaws one has to wear on such occasions.'

That year also saw the departure of one of Harris's closest American colleagues, former President Eisenhower, for whom a Memorial Service was held in St Paul's. The two had always kept in touch and in 1964 Harris had been particularly pleased to receive a personal letter to mark the 20th Anniversary of D-Day. Addressing Harris as one of his closest associates in Overlord, Ike had referred to his professional skill and selfless dedication to the cause, adding that 'no historian could possibly be aware of my obligation to you'. Now, five years later, standing with Anthony Eden (Lord Avon) outside the Cathedral after the service, Harris was the RAF's only top wartime commander on parade. He was there again in 1970 for General de Gaulle, and then in July 1971 came the Memorial Service for Lord Portal. As Denis Richards records, 'among those in uniform from what seemed by now the almost legendary past was Sir Arthur Harris, more than eighty years old but still tall and erect, and still wholehearted in his praise for Portal.' Joan Portal had previously told Jill how well 'dear Bert' had spoken about 'Peter' via the BBC just after his death, and the obituaries department of *The Times* had written to Harris about the number of people who had praised their obituary of Portal. The parts of this which their correspondents said they liked best, and which rang the truest, were the comments on his character and temperament. These, the writer stated, had in fact been written for *The Times* by Harris himself back in 1964 and he wished to say thank you for this splendid help.[2]

As the years went by Harris's advice was also sought by historians working on the lives of some of his contemporaries. One such was an American, Dr Alfred Chandler, who was preparing Eisenhower's private papers for eventual publication; Eisenhower wrote personally to Harris in 1965 requesting his help and when later thanking him for his generous assistance reported on the great success of Chandler's visit. Another historian was Martin Gilbert, working on the official biography of Churchill and convinced that he must deal fairly and objectively with the whole controversial problem of the bombing of Germany; his instinct, he told Harris, was entirely in sympathy with what he and Churchill were doing. A third was Beaverbrook's biographer, A.J.P. Taylor, with whom Harris was soon on friendly terms, and in 1972 Denis Richards paid the first of several useful and enjoyable visits in connection with his biography of Portal.[3]

Meanwhile, with the press continuing to protest on occasion about such matters as the absence of a peerage, there were other questions to cause Harris annoyance. In February 1967, for example, to mark the 25th Anniversary of the Channel Dash by the German battleships *Scharnhorst* and *Gneisenau*, the *News of the World* published a feature severely criticising the Navy and the RAF, and included Harris and Bomber Command among the culprits. He was not best pleased, since he had not even taken over as C-in-C at that time, and proceeded to sue the newspaper for libel. As a result the *News of the World* not only published an apology but to his delight paid him £2,500 plus costs.

A longer running saga began about the same time, when Sir Laurence Olivier and Kenneth Tynan decided to stage at the National Theatre the play *Soldiers* by the German author Rolf Hochhuth. The play centred on an allegation that the death of General Sikorski, the Polish Commander-in-Chief, in an air crash at Gibraltar in 1943, resulted from an assassination plot hatched up by Churchill, but the story ranged much more widely and was to include the impersonation of Harris. Since he was still alive, however, this would not be legal without his permission, and when the script was belatedly sent to him there was very little time for him even to read it. Realising that there was much to object to about him personally he enlisted the aid of Richard Wilson, his local solicitor, and his views were quickly registered. Soon afterwards the Board of the National Theatre decided not to stage the play but over the next few years attempts to produce it on television and elsewhere (as well as in book form) continued, accompanied by a series of legal battles. In the process the impersonation of Harris was removed, but a number of statements about him remained, and the legal advice he received indicated that some at least were defamatory. Just one example must suffice: 'It is unprecedented that a General should want to back out of history after setting fire to half a million civilians in order to get into it.' In December 1968 Harris told Sir John Grandy, CAS, that he would sue for libel if necessary but was tired of fighting the battle to protect the RAF and Bomber Command single-handed, at very considerable personal expense, and with the risk of further financial liabilities. He felt it time the Air Force Board lent a hand. Grandy, who considered the play was not defamatory to the RAF, was not to be persuaded but the saga dragged on. Eventually in 1972 Prchal, the pilot of Sikorski's aircraft, won his libel case against Hochhuth, and Harris exchanged letters of relief with the young Winston Churchill, who himself had been greatly exercised on his grandfather's behalf.[4]

Over these years Harris continued to attend occasional major RAF functions which kept him to some extent in the public eye. In 1964 he was at

Buckingham Palace when the Queen presented a new Colour for the RAF in
the United Kingdom, and in 1968 he was back at Scampton for the Ceremony to mark the stand-down of Bomber Command and the formation of
Strike Command, an occasion he viewed with mixed feelings, not least since
he thought 'Strike' an awful name – common! That same year witnessed the
Queen's visit to Abingdon to mark the RAF's Fiftieth Anniversary, another
occasion when the Service's 'greats', past and present, were gathered in force.
These events apart, his RAF-connected activities were limited to visits to
nearby RAF Benson for an Air Display and an 'At Home Day' and to
attendance at some of the Pathfinder Dinners; in 1968 he was presented by
Donald Bennett with a gold replica of the Pathfinder Badge. He also supported a new venture being organised by Squadron Leader Tony Iveson, a
wartime pilot in 617 Squadron, who wrote in 1966 inviting Harris to a
Reunion Dinner for its wartime members. The function was backed, Iveson
stated, by Mick Martin (one of the Dambusters, now Air Marshal) and
Leonard Cheshire, and Ralph Cochrane and Barnes Wallis were also being
invited as guests. For Harris, despite his general reluctance to extend his
activities, this was not an opportunity to miss, and buoyed up by its success
the squadron helped to organise a special Dambuster event at Scampton a
year later, followed by a third occasion in London to mark the 25th Anniversary of the Dams Raid in 1968.[5]

It may have been these gatherings with some of his 'old lags' that
caused Harris's mind to turn towards the need for a biography, something
which would help 'set the record straight', not just about him personally
but also about what his men had achieved. Back in 1959 he had turned
down flat a suggestion by London International Press that he should
write his memoirs, but in 1966 a letter from Jock Colville, Churchill's
wartime Private Secretary, may have started Harris thinking again, for it
invited him to bequeath his papers to Churchill College to be housed
alongside those of Winston himself. As Colville wrote, 'He had the
greatest affection for the C-in-C Bomber Command, whom he thought
was abominably treated, but I think it would have given him pleasure to
feel that you might have been willing to let your papers rest alongside
his.' While Harris did not take up this suggestion, soon afterwards Jill
tried to persuade him to agree to a family friend becoming his biographer.
Gerald Pawle, a former *Sunday Times* journalist who had served in the
Navy during the war, had with his wife got to know the Harrises during
their regular voyages to Cape Town and they visited The Ferry House
several times in the 1960s.[6] Jill, increasingly convinced that Pawle would
be a good man for the job, exchanged letters with him in the attempt to
persuade her husband to discuss it, and when Harris was approached in
October 1967 for a similar purpose by Andrew Boyle, Trenchard's bio-

grapher, and replied that the commission was already promised elsewhere, he was almost certainly referring to Pawle.

Boyle had argued strongly. He felt Harris's case had somehow gone by default, partly through people's fickle readiness to forget the atmospheric, political and many other strains and pressures which had to determine policy in times of national crisis. As a result Harris had suffered much, quite unnecessarily and for too long, and Boyle wanted not only to set the record straight but to do it with Harris's own co-operation. Ralph Cochrane, he added, would certainly give an objective and independent opinion. Cochrane was, in fact, exchanging views directly with Harris on historical matters, telling him that it must be nearly time for an official reappraisal of the war and Bomber Command's part in it; there was still a powerful body of opinion which was quite ignorant of the facts as Harris had set them out. Moreover he sometimes wondered if Harris knew how much he was looked up to by the aircrews; though personally unknown, he was a very real person to them. Cochrane also told Harris: 'I think you know that we all thought you personally were treated disgracefully in comparison with other Commanders, not only because of what the force did but [also considering] the way you maintained morale in the face of continuous losses.'[7]

In the event it was neither Boyle, whom Cochrane would have liked, nor Pawle who got the job, but Group Captain Dudley Saward, Harris's former Chief Radar Officer at Bomber Command. Saward wrote to Harris in April 1968 inviting him to a small ceremony at de Havillands in support of the RAF Benevolent Fund, and their renewed friendship eventually led Harris to suggest that he might like to take it on. Saward had already made a name for himself by writing *The Bomber's Eye*, a history of the use of radar by bombers in the Second World War, and Harris must have felt that he had better credentials for the task than Pawle. Saward was also more likely to follow his old master's directions. By 1970 Harris was consulting friends on the subject, and in January 1971 Saundby – who said he had himself been under some pressure to contribute to, or even undertake, such a work – wrote offering to collaborate with whoever was appointed. At the same time he firmly advised against publication during Harris's lifetime, and when the formal documents were exchanged between Harris and Saward on 20 August a clause was inserted to that effect.

Saward did his work over the next two years. He talked to Harris at length on tape, he consulted some of Harris's personal papers though by no means all, he studied a good many official documents, he interviewed some of the important surviving Germans, but sadly he seems to have met few of the many witnesses who were still available elsewhere. In 1973 Sir Arthur Bryant willingly agreed to write the Foreword, and the draft, after some amendment to meet Harris's own suggestions, was passed to Saward's literary agents in May. There ensued a two-year battle with them and the potential publishers, who pressed very strongly the case for going ahead as soon as possible. The book was of great importance, they argued, its story needed to be told now rather than later, the public interest and therefore the potential market would probably decline, and other related books such as Denis Richards' biography of Portal were already on the stocks. Saward himself saw the force of such arguments and although he told Harris that he did not mind either way he knew that the delay was bound to leave him personally out of pocket. Harris, however, was immovable. Under no circumstances would he permit publication until after his death, and so not until 1984 did the book appear.[8]

Among the Germans whom Saward had consulted was Albert Speer, Hitler's Armaments Minister and now released from Spandau, and at Saward's first meeting with him Speer signed Harris's copy of his book *Inside the Third Reich*, published in 1970. His inscription read: 'To Air Marshal Sir Arthur, who caused me so many sleepless nights of despair – now, but only now, best wishes for many times of good luck and of satisfaction'. On 19 February 1972 Harris wrote to thank Speer and added: 'Those were sad days indeed for us all and one can but hope that the nations will show more sense in the future – and less attention to demagogues. It is always the Big Mouths that cause the world's troubles!' On 20 May Speer replied:

> Your kind letter was one of the very few delightful events of my lifetime. In those years of Spandau I often thought, what surprises will happen to me after release. I imagined many good – and bad things, which partly came true, but certainly never a letter from you. I liked to contribute to Saward's biography and I hope it will help to show things in a true way.

In September Harris wrote again, this time to tell Speer that he and Eaker were arranging for the return of the citation for a Gold Medal presented to Speer in 1938 and subsequently looted and taken to America. Speer, in a warm letter of thanks, said how pleased he was to hear from Saward that Harris would like to meet him. 'So do I,' wrote Speer. 'Possibly that is one of the rare occasions to show without much ado that we are living in a new world.' They never did meet, although in 1973 Speer met Saward again, this time in London when being interviewed for the *World at War* television series. In 1976, however, Harris wrote to thank Speer for sending him a copy of his just published *Spandau: The Secret Diaries*, and told him it absolutely confirmed his own constant message to his Army friends: 'The diversion of guns, ammunition and soldiers to air defence was *the* major strain on the German armies in the field . . . and probably the major cause of that outcome of the war. I am very grateful to you for your generosity and helpfulness –

especially in view of the harsh manner with which you were treated after the war.'[9]

Peter Tomlinson made a related point when saying that Harris had disapproved of the Nuremberg trials and was particularly sympathetic towards Speer, and even to a limited extent towards Goering. In no way did this imply that before the war or during it Harris had had any time for Germans, or 'the Boche' as he called them. His opinions had been typical of those of the great many British people who in the wake of the First World War regarded the only good German as a dead one. After the Second World War, however, perceptions gradually changed and Harris's own views became less extreme, although he had few direct contacts with Germans before exchanging letters with Speer. Curiously it was at that time, in October 1972, that he was called upon to undertake the most exalted ceremonial task of his life in the presence of the Queen and of her guest, President Heinemann of the Federal Republic of Germany (an Honorary GCB). The occasion was the Ceremony of the Installation of Knights of the Order of the Bath, held in the Henry VII Chapel, when Harris – as the Senior Holder of the GCB – acted as Representative of the Great Master, the Duke of Gloucester, who was unwell. Harris, wondering how the President would react to him and having attended no fewer than three rehearsals of the elaborate ceremony, carried out his duties impeccably and five Knights were installed, including Earl Mountbatten.

A month later Harris was again meeting the Queen, this time in a less formal but for him far more evocative situation. The opening of the RAF Museum at Hendon by Her Majesty on 15 November demonstrated the determination of the modern Royal Air Force to pay proper regard to its lengthening history and of all the RAF's top wartime commanders only Harris had survived to witness it. Having previously signed with Barnes Wallis 850 prints in support of the Museum Appeal he was undoubtedly delighted to find that two of his Command's greatest aircraft, the Wellington and the Lancaster, were included in the extensive range of aeroplanes on display – though he did feel that the occasion called for the wearing of uniform rather than plain clothes, and told CAS as much.

Such occasional events apart, Harris remained reluctant to re-engage in controversy. Paul Mann, a local journalist who interviewed him on his 80th birthday, wrote of this former man-at-war – stout, silver-haired, possessing immense dignity and wit – watching his grandchildren at play and now every inch a man at peace. He still possessed a sparkling irreverence and despite physically registering the burden of the years retained a formidably agile intellect and would express thoughtful opinions on a host of modern issues. He would not, however, discuss his years as C-in-C Bomber Command.[10] This attitude had been demonstrated a few months earlier when he refused the historian Corelli Barnett's invitation to take part in the BBC's series of documentaries on *The Commanders*. The programme on Harris was shown in November 1972. Harris himself – who disliked the way the BBC had treated him in the past – was reported as 'not interested' in appearing, and at least some of the critics felt it lacked a clear personal picture of the man, who remained a distant figure. He was not averse, on the other hand, to helping at least some of the authors who approached him. Alastair Revie in particular, when writing *The Lost Command* in 1971, not only consulted him but obtained many helpful comments on the draft; then after *The People* serialised it the Deputy Editor wrote to Harris telling him how many letters had arrived from his former airmen, almost all insisting that they would hear no ill of 'Old Butch'. The message that his old lags really cared about him was beginning to get through.

Most of Harris's direct contacts, however, were still limited to the officers, including the members of the Headquarters Bomber Command Association of Officers, who held their Annual Reunions in the Mess at High Wycombe. While he had attended some of these over the years he had never addressed the assembled company, but in 1974, following a talk by Sir Denis Small-wood, C-in-C Strike Command, Harris suddenly said he would like to speak to them all. The anonymous recorder of what he said to the 70 members referred to it as 'vintage Bert'; no mere prosaic summary could begin to convey its impact. He spoke for an hour without notes about things he wanted some of the old lags to know and about untruths he wanted to correct while he could still do so. Encouraged by the 'deplorable official history', the post-war press had deliberately campaigned to denigrate Bomber Command's achievements, and only in more recent years had evidence come from the Germans, notably from Speer, to show that the bombing had never been given credit for the results obtained. Harris then discussed the many consequences of area bombing for war production and diversion of weapons from the land fronts, and went on to stress his Command's many achievements in aid of the Navy and Army, frequently quoting statements by Allied and German Commanders in support.[11]

Two years later, on 8 September 1976, Harris spoke again at Strike Command, this time formally when unveiling a plaque during ceremonies commemorating the wartime collaboration between his own Command and the Americans. His audience, including Ira Eaker and Jimmy Doolittle, heard him reiterate the achievements of the bombers as perceived by Speer and the military commanders of both sides. He particularly stressed that the major factor in the success of the Normandy invasion was the absolute air supremacy won by the Allies, and that the bombers had played a critical part in ensuring the victory at sea. He was, as always, listened to with rapt attention.

Meanwhile, on 3 May 1976, Harris had taken up a special invitation from Sam (now Lord) Elworthy, who had arranged for some 70 members (including wives) of 463 and 467 RAAF Squadrons to hold a reunion party at Waddington, the station he had commanded when they were serving there in 1943–4. The Australians were wondering if Harris could possibly join them, whereupon Elworthy suggested that he and Jill, rather than come all the way to Waddington, might like to meet them at Runnymede and then at Windsor Castle (where Elworthy was Governor). Afterwards Lady Elworthy wrote to Jill: 'I don't need to tell you how much your presence and his meant to all those chaps and their wives – to whom he was a legend. I think the chaps could hardly believe their Bomber Chief could be, at 83, so essentially the same person. Sam, at Waddington, heard this said over and over again – "with loving admiration".'[12]

Shortly before this Harris had welcomed a new visitor to The Ferry House. Ray Callow was a former airman who had trained as a Wireless Operator/Air Gunner towards the end of the war, served then as a Flight Mechanic, and left the RAF in 1947. He had since become an avid collector of wartime memorabilia and a leading figure in the Air Gunners' Association, for which he was a keen fund-raiser. Spotting a press photograph of Harris at Runnymede, Callow telephoned to ask if he would sign a copy for him, whereupon Harris said 'come and see me'. From this meeting emerged the idea of a fund-raising dinner in the RAF Club which Harris would attend and Callow would organise, hopefully with the help of other 'Bomber Greats', including Mick Martin, Donald Bennett and Leonard Cheshire.[13] It all happened in 1976. Harris, who had suffered pneumonia just beforehand but insisted that he would be there, spoke impromptu for 40 minutes and was subsequently chosen by the Guild of Professional Toastmasters as 'The Best After-Dinner Speaker of the Year'. This was some achievement for a man who 20 years before had declared his speech-making days were past. For Harris it was a turning point. James Denny, who as his neighbour knew him well and had found him alarmingly bitter and cynical, says that the warmth of the reception he received moved him greatly and entirely changed his attitude.

Building on the success of this occasion, Callow and his colleagues, some of them very high-powered, decided to go for a much larger scale event in 1977 and in consultation with Tony Iveson, who happened to be the public relations officer at Grosvenor House, a dinner for over 700 Bomber Command air and ground crew was organised there on 2 May. Again Harris spoke at some length, without a script, telling the airmen and airwomen that they had never been given adequate recognition for their decisive part in the defeat of Hitler. Afterwards he wrote to Tomlinson: 'My bombers – all ranks – gave me a wonderful dinner; some even from Canada, the USA, Australia;

a very moving occasion.' He also wrote the warmest of thank-you letters to Callow, saying how astonished he was at the enormous amount of sheer hard work that must have gone into it: 'My feelings were too nearly out of control to enable me to express them adequately on that evening to you personally. I will never forget it – or you.' After such a start it was no surprise that the Grosvenor House dinners became annual events, continuing until after Harris's death. Sir Michael Beetham, one of Harris's distinguished wartime pilots and for several of his final years Chief of Air Staff, referred to them in his address at Harris's Memorial Service:

> Over the last few years of his life, a particular pleasure were the annual Bomber Reunion Dinners at Grosvenor House. At these, Arthur Harris would always give a pungent and witty after dinner speech – 20 minutes without a note, captivating his audience. We hung on his every word and afterwards he would sit late into the night with a word for everyone and outlasting most.[14]

The 1977 Reunion also provided the initial impetus for an entirely new society. Among those attending from Dorset were several members of the Wool Branch of the Air Gunners' Association, who were so impressed by the atmosphere that on returning home they arranged a rally to test the potential interest in an organisation to embrace all aircrew from all three Services. Encouraged by the results, they held on 8 September a formal meeting in Wool to establish this body, which immediately became known as the Aircrew Association. The word spread quickly, new Association branches were formed, and by the end of 1979 some 500 members were enrolled. Harris himself had taken little persuading of its significance, for when John Williams, the Chairman of the Wool Branch, nobbled him at the 1978 Grosvenor House Dinner and explained the Association's purpose to him he immediately agreed to become its Patron. Then on 4 April 1979 he wrote to Geoff Burwell, the first Secretary, saying he was 'honoured and delighted' to accept the invitation to become President.[15] Invariably in the past he had declined the many such offers; now at the age of 87 he was so impressed by the enthusiasm not just of his own old lags but of many others too that he was only too ready to take this one on.

For the next few years Ray Callow and Danny Boon, the new Secretary, regularly arranged for small groups of members to visit Harris and Jill at The Ferry House and then take them to lunch at one of the local riverside pubs. These were happy occasions. There were, too, various formal functions such as the first of the continuing series of annual services at St Clement Danes, at one of which, in June 1982, the Association's Colour was dedicated. But the most memorable event was the Banquet held by the Association at Guildhall on 4 September 1982 to honour their President in the year of his 90th birthday. Among the after-dinner speakers at this great gathering were Douglas Bader, Donald Bennett and Air Marshal Sir John Curtiss, who had recently commanded the RAF formations taking part in the Falklands War and some of whose aircrew were present, bridging the generations.[16] Yet it was Harris himself who dominated the occasion with what would prove to be his last great public speech. Finally, in a totally hushed hall, all heard another of Harris's great Pathfinder pilots, Hamish Mahaddie, recite in his moving Scottish lilt Noel Coward's evocative poem *Lie in the dark and listen*.[17] Sadly that night's drama was not quite over, for Douglas Bader too had made his final speech. He died of a heart attack on his way home.

These were busy days. On the previous evening Harris, with Jill, attended a party in the Mess at High Wycombe for past and present officers of Bomber Command, followed by a dinner at Springfield, and a week later he was in Oxford at a major dinner for former prisoners-of-war. On the 24th there was yet another dinner, this time in Sussex to mark the 90th birthday of Barnes Wallis, whom Harris called in his excellent speech 'our number one wizard'. The demands on his time had been building up for some while and partly to escape nuisance calls he had felt compelled to go ex-directory. Nevertheless he remained willing to lend a hand to reputable historians. In 1975 he had helped Montgomery Hyde in his work on the RAF between the two World Wars; in 1977 John Sweetman, researching for *Operation Chastise*, his book on the Dams Raid, found him most supportive; in 1978 Norman Longmate, working on an in-depth discussion programme for Radio 4 entitled *The Bombers*, not only secured a valuable interview from him but also received helpful observations on the draft script; and in 1982 when Long-mate was working on the associated book (published in 1983) he again provided invaluable corrections and suggestions. Another author whose work Harris admired was the Canadian pilot, Murray Peden, whose book *A Thousand Shall Fall*, about his experiences in Bomber Command, he read in 1979. In a letter he subsequently wrote to Peden he called it 'not only the best and most true to life "war" book he had read about the war, but the best about all the wars of his lifetime, from the Boer War onwards.' He added what he called a criticism: 'At times it made me so sad that I found it hard to retain the moisture within my eyes.'[18]

Harris kept in touch, too, with Andrew Boyle in whose just published book *The Climate of Treason* the spies Burgess, Maclean, Philby and Blunt were exposed. Aware of Harris's convictions regarding John Strachey and puzzled at the absence of any reference to this subject in Hugh Thomas's biography, Boyle was keen to establish whether Harris had any written evidence which might suggest a Strachey connection with one or more of the traitors. He was also curious about how Strachey had managed to influence Attlee and Stansgate over the treatment of Bomber Command and its

C-in-C. Harris could not enlighten Boyle on these specific points but he did seize on the hint that Strachey might have actually been a traitor and, despite the absence of any significant reference to Strachey in Boyle's book, alluded to it in a letter to Sir Michael Beetham in October 1980. Harris's main purpose in this letter was to recommend Boyle for the task of reappraising Bomber Command's wartime achievements, something the historian himself was keen to undertake. There for Harris this particular story finished. Right to the end of his days he remained convinced that Strachey had done him great damage and that Webster and Frankland had failed to do full justice to his men's achievements.[19]

Yet in these final years Harris was not always totally scathing about the official history. For example, when he agreed to be interviewed for the record at the Imperial War Museum in 1977 he repeated his comment to Elworthy (p.385) and stressed that it was the selective quotation from it by the press that had caused the real hurt. He also paid tribute to Frankland, who had done very well as one of his Command's navigators; he was certainly not angry about what the historian had written. A year later, in writing the Foreword to Maurice Dean's book *The Royal Air Force and the Two World Wars*, he must have been aware of his friend's highly complimentary verdict upon it. This particular subject was not, however, raised when Harris spoke again for the record in 1982, this time at the RAF Staff College. Carefully and thoroughly questioned, he gave his views on many of the issues he had faced as Commander-in-Chief, expressing himself clearly and succinctly and still revealing an excellent memory. For a man of 90 it was a superb performance. A year later he was again on form when giving a short filmed interview for a Dambusters documentary being compiled by Yorkshire Television. Leonard Cheshire, who also took part, congratulated him afterwards for all the trouble he had taken to be available despite the effects of a chest infection; the series was aimed, Cheshire said, at a new generation of Germans who were ill-informed about the war and in particular Bomber Command's role, and Harris's interview was bound to make a big impact.[20]

There were further activities in these last few years. In 1977, for example, Harris represented the Order of the Bath at the Memorial Service for a fellow Marshal of the Royal Air Force almost 30 years his junior, Sir Andrew Humphrey. In 1980 he visited the RAF Staff College at Bracknell for one of CAS's briefing days for senior retired officers, and in 1982 he spent a nostalgic day at Camberley. The invitations from more distant parts, however, invariably had to be turned down, including one from the RAAF to speak at a Dinner in Melbourne and several from RCAF squadrons to attend reunions in northern England. Yet always he sent messages, usually in fairly standard wording summarising their achievements, but also containing phrases such as 'warmest regards and greetings to our great Canadians who did so much to secure victory for our armies', and 'all those who really matter have confirmed again and again that you, and your like, in the British, Canadian, Commonwealth and USA Strategic Bomber Commands did more than anyone or anything else towards the defeat of the enemy'. Among the Allied and German witnesses whom he was now including in his list of those whose views mattered was Dr Goebbels, further parts of whose Diaries had just been published.[21]

Harris had never had more reason to appreciate the affection in which he was held by his old lags and by their successors than on his 90th Birthday on 13 April 1982. Of the many messages he received two may speak for all. One came from the 428 members of the recently formed Wickenby Register (the Association of 12 and 626 Squadrons):

> The passage of time has not dimmed our memories of the long war years when we were privileged to serve under you in the sure and certain knowledge that you would lead us to the ultimate victory. Few of us met you in those days but we hope you were aware that your messages which were read to us in the briefing room stirred many a young heart and strengthened many an apprehensive young airman. In the years which have followed, we have been grateful for the way you have spoken for us and for our comrades who did not survive the struggle. We are grateful for all you have done to remind those who would prefer to forget what we did and what we achieved and of the enormous cost. We are aware of your affection for us and want you to know that you are remembered with affection and admiration by us all.

The other came from the present-day Royal Air Force at the time it was preparing to contribute to the Falklands War. The message was delivered in the form of the Lancaster of the Battle of Britain Memorial Flight flying low over The Ferry House in salute. Writing afterwards to the CO, Squadron Leader C.S.M. Anderson, Harris thanked the Flight both for this and for other 'Bomber Command occasions' when it had appeared. 'May you long keep flying.'[22]

One further important matter still lay on Harris's mind. Always a great supporter of the RAF Museum he had become increasingly concerned that it was devoting insufficient attention to the work of the bombers – and particularly since the fighter boys had received special recognition with their own Battle of Britain Museum, opened in 1978. His views were widely shared; the subject was often discussed at the growing number of bomber reunions, and on 16 June 1980 Mick Martin wrote referring to recent conversations both at Grosvenor House and at CAS's Bracknell briefing day. Stressing the large number of Bomber Command airmen who would like to leave money, mementoes or both to a Bomber Command Museum of proper status, he wished to establish Harris's own views. Would he wish such a

Museum to be a separate entity or should it comprise a dedicated Hall within the main fabric at Hendon? Martin's approach was conveniently timed, for only a week later the key players were all on site for the unveiling of a small display about Harris himself. Dr John Tanner, the Director of the RAF Museum, put his views to Harris on paper, pointing out that the prime exhibits, *ie* the big bombers, were already part of his main collection and urging that further support on behalf of Bomber Command could best be directed to Hendon.

Harris quickly replied to Martin and Tanner. His own wish, he made clear, was for a Bomber Command Hall within the Museum, but account must be taken of the feelings of his old lags, many of whom were fed up with the much greater recognition awarded everywhere to the Battle of Britain boys as compared with them. His men would not back such a project if it was to be a mere side-show; to succeed it would require as much effort as had been put into the Battle of Britain Museum and it might not be easy to finance this in the short term. On such a subject Harris's personal views were bound to be critical. The practical constraints urged by Tanner were heeded, Martin and his colleagues, including Callow, brought the old lags into line, and, as recognised by Harris, a most important role was played by Marshal of the Royal Air Force Sir Neil (later Lord) Cameron, as Chairman of the Trustees of the RAF Museum. The Duke of Edinburgh, too, as Patron of the Museum, was highly supportive. Harris himself gave the whole process much attention, insisting on being consulted on the building programme, the detailed plans for the layout of the aircraft and the galleries, and the problems over finance. He personally signed 'hundreds of begging letters'. Finally, as the work neared completion, Her Majesty Queen Elizabeth the Queen Mother agreed to open what was now to be known as the Bomber Command Museum on 12 April 1983, the eve of Harris's 91st birthday. Her Majesty afterwards told him how particularly pleased she was that he himself, who would always be identified with the wonderful achievements of his Command, was able to be present.[23]

By this time, thanks in large part to the Museum project and the continuing success of the Grosvenor House Dinners, moves were afoot to compile a Bomber Command Register, with Sergeant Harry Pitcher playing a leading role, and late in 1983 Harris was asked informally if he would become the first President of a new Bomber Command Association. He said he would be delighted to do so and the Association was duly set up with its Headquarters alongside the RAF Museum, and Doug Radcliffe became its indefatigable Secretary. Sadly the first President could never be installed in office, but the Bomber Command Association of today owes a great debt of gratitude to him, just as do the other two institutions that he helped to inspire in his closing years, the Aircrew Association and the Bomber Command Museum.[24]

Sir Arthur Harris died quietly at home in Goring-on-Thames on 5 April 1984, eight days before he would have celebrated his 92nd birthday. His funeral service on the 11th took place with military honours in the nearby parish church, and was attended mainly by his family, local friends and a number of his old lags. Then, as interment followed in the Burntwood Cemetery on the brow of the hill overlooking the village, came the Lancaster, flying unbelievably low, to pay the RAF's closing tribute. Thus departed the last of the Royal Air Force's great captains of the Second World War, properly described by Sir Michael Beetham in his address at the Memorial Service in Westminster Abbey on 24 May as certainly the greatest of them.

Of Harris's leadership talents there is no doubt. They were apparent in his youth; they were well demonstrated in his career between the wars; they were abundantly clear in the Second World War and central to the very special task he was called on to undertake; they remained obvious as time moved on and the survivors of the wartime generation increasingly showed the great respect and affection in which most of them had always held him. Then there was his professionalism. Not only was he a fine aviator but he was always turning his practical mind to how to do the job better and insistent on the importance of efficient and effective training and of good, firm discipline. Coupled with this was his determination, his utter insistence on pursuing his ideas and plans to completion. At the same time he never failed to recognise his personal responsibility for making the key decisions and accepting the consequences, a burden which he bore with great courage throughout his time at Bomber Command in the knowledge that things were bound to go wrong from time to time.

Inevitably there was another side to the coin. Harris's firmness could easily be seen by others as stubbornness and obstinacy; his single-mindedness could come across as an inability to see others' points of view or to appreciate the wider political and military constraints; his all too frequent exaggerations, usually intended as a means to emphasise his views, were often considered as lapses of judgement. There is truth in such criticisms, and despite his good work in his two Air Ministry tours of duty he was never cut out for top level staffwork, as he himself knew. He was essentially the sort of commander who emerges in a crisis, one for which his knowledge and experience happen to have particularly prepared him. The parallel with Churchill is obvious. But for the war and the critical roles each was called upon to play both would probably have ended their careers in relative obscurity. In the event both proved to be the men for the moment and in Harris's case, if there was to be a strategic bomber offensive, his particular qualities were essential to direct it and bear the inescapable strains.

Yet all too often Harris continues to be portrayed as the hard, insensitive man, totally concentrated on using his bombers to beat the enemy by destroying his homeland, and unconcerned about the implications for the human beings involved. This is far from the truth. Certainly he could be remote and difficult at times but the many who knew him, especially away from the immediate business, found him kind, generous, humorous, compassionate, amply possessed of the human touch. He did care for people, and never more than the men who served under him – including, most importantly, those who came from the nations of the Commonwealth and elsewhere. Towards the enemy, while he hated the slaughter involved, his feelings were dominated by the conviction that the war must be won as quickly as possible, in their interests as much as in those of his own compatriots.

So what of his achievements and those of the Command he led? For over three years he directed its immense build-up and endeavoured ceaselessly to ensure its efficiency; he inspired not just the aircrew but also the hundreds of thousands in other roles whose tasks were essential to its support; he fought endless battles on their part at many different levels of command; and he did his utmost to publicise and explain their work. At the same time, while always subject to the frequent directives he received from above, he made virtually all the key operational decisions. On top of all this he gave unstinted help and encouragement to his United States colleagues – and in the process helped lay the foundations of the close ties between the Royal Air Force and the United States Air Force which have been of such importance ever since. True, there were disputes over policies and methods, not surprisingly with such a forceful, independently minded Commander-in-Chief. So, also not surprisingly, he had at times to be overruled, but once the arguments were over he obeyed his orders, and most notably when supporting the invasion operations and earning the undying gratitude of Eisenhower and his top-level commanders. It was over Harris's primary role, the bombing of Germany itself, that the main disputes arose, particularly in the final months of the war, yet while there will always be debate over the specific targets which he selected at different times his total achievements and those of his Command are clear. They rightly took the war to the enemy in the only way possible in the earlier days, they and their American comrades-in-arms forced his air forces on to the defensive, which was all-important for the great sea and land campaigns waged by the Allies; they caused massive diversion of his resources of all kinds; and they steadily wrecked his economic structure. It was a unique offensive carried out in a unique war, and for his conduct of it Sir Arthur Harris deserves to rank among the great high commanders of modern history.

Notes

1. Except where stated, this chapter is based on scrapbooks and other papers held by the Harris family.
2. Richards, *Portal of Hungerford*, p.406; Misc Folders 11, 20.
3. Misc Folder 19/2.
4. Misc Folders 7, 19/2; CAS folder, AHB.
5. Misc Folders 16/1, 16/2.
6. Information from Lady Mary Pawle.
7. Misc Folders 11, 18. Cochrane did not date his letters, but these must have been written in the late 1960s. He died in 1977.
8. Misc Folder 18; family documents. Saward's tapes are now held by the Bomber Command Association and are referred to occasionally in earlier notes.
9. Misc Folder 5; Speer Archives, Koblenz.
10. *Reading Evening Post*, 14 April 1972.
11. Misc Folder 16/2.
12. *Ibid.*
13. At this time Harris urged upon CAS the award to Cheshire of a 'K', both for his amazing war record and for his wonderful humane effort in starting the Cheshire Homes. Later, in 1980, Harris also pleaded the case for Bennett, whose omission from the post-war honours list was a frequent source of complaint by old members of the PFF.
14. Dean, *op.cit.* p.311; discussion with Ray Callow; family papers; Marshal of the Royal Air Force Sir Michael Beetham.
15. Sidney Ricketts, *The Aircrew Association and Intercom; How it all began.*
16. One of these was Wing Commander Peter Squire, now Air Chief Marshal and Chief of Air Staff.
17. Reprinted in full in Laddie Lucas, *Wings of War*, pp.380–1.
18. Misc Folder 20. The Canadian publishers, with Harris's permission, published his letter (which included comments on Operation Tractable) in the second edition of Peden's book. They told Harris that Dr Frankland had echoed his sentiments about it.
19. Misc Folder 19/2. Discussions after Harris's death about such a reappraisal led in part to John Terraine writing *The Right of the Line*, which devoted considerable attention to Bomber Command.
20. Misc Folder 21; Dean, *op.cit.* pp.289–97; Mason interview (see chapter 15, note 11).
21. Misc Folder 16/2; *The Goebbels' Diaries – the Last Days*. Harris insisted on giving the author extracts when we met in 1979.
22. *Ibid.*
23. Family papers.
24. The Battle of Britain and Bomber Command Museums were later renamed Halls as integral parts of the RAF Museum.

Postscript

One Sunday in 1989, as they were leaving the Church of St Clement Danes, Group Captain Ken Batchelor, Chairman of the Bomber Command Association, turned to Marshal of the Royal Air Force Sir Michael Beetham, its President. Might it not now be time, he suggested, to give the bomber men their due alongside those of Fighter Command, who were already so properly represented by the statue of their Battle of Britain Commander, Lord Dowding? Sir Michael took no persuading. The ideal site for a statue of Sir Arthur Harris was there in front of them and many of his old lags and other well-wishers would surely back the venture. The idea was born.[1]

Key figures in the Association quickly put their heads together and Sir Michael soon obtained the backing of the Chief of Air Staff and the Air Force Board. Then in December he followed up Batchelor's private soundings in letters to Sir Anthony Harris and Jacqueline Assheton, as representing the Harris family; Lady Harris had died two years earlier. He explained the object quite simply. It was 'to commemorate outside the RAF Church both the man who saved us from defeat in the Battle of Britain and the man who subsequently paved the way for victory.' The planned date of completion was 1992, the 50th Anniversary of Harris's taking over Bomber Command and the centenary of his birth. The project would be directed by a committee chaired by Air Marshal Sir Harry Burton, who would greatly value their support. Needless to say, this was immediately forthcoming.

The planning proceeded over the next 18 months, albeit with little publicity outside the Bomber Command Association. Faith Winter, who had already made her name in RAF circles with her statue of Lord Dowding, agreed to undertake the task and began her work, negotiations were set in hand with the various planning authorities whose approval was required, and measures to meet the cost were carefully considered. Fund-raising began on an informal basis very early on, and ultimately most of the money was provided by the members through functions and donations and by benefactors to whom Sir Michael and Air Marshal Sir Ivor Broom had written personally. Also of great importance were the arrangements for the unveiling, and in March 1991 Sir Michael wrote formally to the Queen Mother inviting her to perform the ceremony. Soon afterwards Sir Harry Burton told the family that Her Majesty had agreed to officiate on Sunday 31 May 1992, a date she had chosen as the most suitable for her.

416

The storm broke in September 1991 when the Appeal went public and the press seized upon the news. Here for the media was yet another opportunity to ventilate the many arguments about the wartime work of Bomber Command and its C-in-C, and the battle lines were quickly drawn. Several newspapers, including *The Times* and the *Independent*, called the policy of which Harris was so outspoken an advocate a serious blot on Britain's war record and urged the abandonment of a project which could only reopen old wounds; the symbolism was hurtful and misguided. Others, such as the *Daily Telegraph* and *Daily Mail*, were supportive, representing the arguments for the bomber offensive and stressing that the statue was being entirely paid for by private subscription as a tribute both to Harris and to the 55,000 men of Bomber Command who had lost their lives. The correspondence columns indicated similar divisions, with notable churchmen such as Donald Soper, Bruce Kent and Paul Oestreicher heavily opposed and other writers such as Lord Cheshire, Sir Bernard Lovell and historian Andrew Roberts arguing firmly for the statue. Similarly contrasting opinions were aired abroad, for example in the USA, Canada and Australia, but not surprisingly the strongest views, nearly all against, came from Germany.

The Mayors of Dresden and several other cities which had been heavily bombed in the final months of the war were sharply critical, as was the Mayor of Cologne, who accused the organisers of the unveiling with being particularly insensitive in choosing to hold the ceremony on 31 May, the 50th Anniversary of the thousand bomber raid on his city. In fact he went so far as to write directly to the Queen Mother appealing to her not to take part. Consequently there were political overtones in the final weeks before the unveiling, and the widespread objections that arose in Germany are not difficult to understand. The fact remains that the statue was not publicly financed, its unveiling was a private Royal Air Force occasion, and the Queen Mother was there because of her deep respect and admiration for Harris – 'a wonderful man', she called him – and his boys.

So on the appointed day Her Majesty attended the dignified Service of Reconciliation and Remembrance in a packed St Clement Danes. Among those utterly determined to attend was Leonard Cheshire, who (in his own words) 'would have gone even if I had to be carried on a stretcher'. He came in a wheelchair, against medical advice, only two months before his death.[2] Another particularly well-known public figure also had no doubt where she had to be that day – the recently displaced Prime Minister Margaret Thatcher. Afterwards all moved outside for the Queen Mother to address them and unveil the statue. Hardly had she begun to speak than she was interrupted by a small number of protesters. Uncertain whether to continue she turned briefly to Sir Michael Beetham for reassurance and as the shouting ceased she carried on undaunted:

As Patron of the Bomber Command Association I am very pleased to join you today on this memorable occasion. The Service we have just attended was a fitting prelude to my unveiling the Statue commemorating Sir Arthur Harris and the crews of Bomber Command who lost their lives in the service of our country. Western Europe has been at peace for over 45 years but it is right that we should not forget those dark days of war when we were in grave danger and Bomber Command gave us hope and the means of salvation. Sir Arthur Harris was an inspiring leader who carried a heavy burden of responsibility for more than three years. There could be nowhere more fitting to honour him and those brave crews – more than 55,000 of whom died defending our freedom – than outside the Royal Air Force Church of St Clement Danes, itself a victim of the bombing, and beside Lord Dowding whose statue I was pleased to unveil four years ago. We remember them today with pride and gratitude, but let us remember too those of every nation and background who suffered as victims of the Second World War.

Many have been the comments since on the statue and its symbolism. One of these seems to provide a specially fitting conclusion to the Harris story. On 30 August 1944 Flying Officer Denis Gay, a bomb aimer of 619 Squadron, failed to return from a raid on Königsberg when his Lancaster was shot down. His daughter Sally was born on 29 May 1945 and as she grew up became utterly determined to try to establish his final resting place. She never did, and in 1996 she died after an extremely long illness borne with exceptional bravery. When her mother later went through Sally's papers she found a 'jotting' which her daughter had written in 1992:

> When the statue of Bomber Harris is unveiled I shall be thinking of a father I never met, but have always loved. The father who, when I was a child, I would pray would return so that I could be like other children. This statue is long overdue and I feel that the Mayor of Cologne should also erect a memorial plaque in honour of the boys who sacrificed their futures to free Europe from Nazism. Did they not liberate Germany from oppression and enable it to rise from the Ashes of Destruction? On 31 May we are remembering, through Bomber Harris, his forgotten and much maligned crews and I for one will be very very proud. Let's not forget.
>
> Just a few thoughts jotted down, not very well. Hope it helps. Sally.[3]

Arthur Harris would have approved.

Notes

1. This account is based on family documents and advice from Sir Michael Beetham.
2. Morris, *op.cit.* p.427.
3. Letter to author from Mrs M.V. Gay.

Appendix

RFC and RAF promotions and appointments

1915	1 October		Brooklands
	6 November	2nd Lieutenant, RFC	
	28 November		Central Flying School, Upavon
1916	29 January	Flying Officer, RFC	
	15 February		19 Reserve Squadron Detachment, Northolt
	24 March	Temporary Captain	
	18 April		39 Squadron Detachment, Suttons Farm
	14 July		38 Squadron, Castle Bromwich
	27 September		70 Squadron, Fienvillers
	1 October		(Hospital)
1917	2 March		51 Squadron, Norfolk
	18 June		45 Squadron, Ste-Marie-Cappel
	6 November		Joyce Green, for training duties
1918	1 January	Temporary Major	OC 191 Night Training Squadron, Marham
	8 June		OC 44 Squadron, Hainault Farm
	19 December		OC 50 Squadron, Bekesbourne
1919	1 August	Permanent Commission as Squadron Leader	
	29 July		2 Group
1920	26 April		OC 3 Flying Training School
1921	26 January		OC 31 Squadron, India
1922	28 July		Group Headquarters, Basra
	20 November		OC 45 Squadron, Iraq
1925	17 February		Student, Army Senior Officers' School, Sheerness
	25 May		OC 58 Squadron, Worthy Down
1927	1 July	Wing Commander	
1928	21 January		Student, Army Staff College, Camberley
1930	3 January		Deputy Senior Air Staff Officer, AOC Middle East Command
1932	3 October		Flying Boat Pilots' Course, Calshot

419

1933	21 March		OC 210 Squadron
	11 July		Deputy Director of Operations and Intelligence, Air Ministry
1934	3 April		Deputy Director Plans, Air Ministry
1935	1 July	Group Captain	
1937	12 June	Air Commodore	AOC 4 Group
1938	1 July		AOC Palestine and Transjordan
1939	1 July	Air Vice-Marshal	
	11 September		AOC 5 Group
1940	25 November		Deputy Chief of Air Staff
1941	27 May	Air Marshal (Acting)	Head of British Air Staff, Washington
1942	22 February		AOC-in-C Bomber Command
1943	18 March	Air Chief Marshal (Acting)	
1945	15 September		Appointment relinquished
1946	1 January	Marshal of the Royal Air Force	

Medals and decorations

Officer of the Order of the British Empire

Air Force Cross

1914–1915 Star

War Medal 1914–1918

Victory Medal

India General Service Medal 1908–1935 with clasp Waziristan 1921–1924

General Service Medal 1918–1962 with clasps for Palestine and Kurdistan and Mention in Despatches 1939

Silver Jubilee Medal 1935

Coronation Medal 1937

1939–1945 Star

France and Germany Star

Defence Medal

War Medal 1939–1945 with Mention in Despatches 1941

Coronation Medal 1953

Silver Jubilee Medal 1977

King Feisal's War Medal (Iraq)

Distinguished Service Medal, Army (USA)

Officier of the Légion d'Honneur (France)

Croix de Guerre 1939 with Mention in Army Despatches (France)

Knight Grand Cross of the Order of the Bath, Badge and Star

Knight Commander of the Order of the Bath, Badge and Star

Chief Commander of the Legion of Merit, Star (USA)

Order of Suvorov, 1st Class, Star (USSR)

Order of Polonia Restituta, 1st Class, Badge and Star (Poland)

Grand Officer of the Légion d'Honneur, Star (France)

Order of the Southern Cross, Badge and Star (Brazil)

Bibliography

All books published in London, unless otherwise indicated.

Arnold, General H.A., *Global Mission* (Harper, New York, 1949; Hutchinson, 1951)

Ashton, J. Norman, *Only Birds and Fools* (Airlife, 2000).

Attlee, Earl, *A Prime Minister Remembers* (Heinemann, 1961).

Barker, Ralph, *The Thousand Plan* (Chatto and Windus, 1966).

Bennett, Air Vice-Marshal D.C.T., *Pathfinder* (Muller, 1958).

Bennett, Ralph, *Behind the Battle: Intelligence in the War with Germany, 1939–45* (Sinclair-Stevenson, 1994).

Bergander, Götz, *Dresden im Luftkrieg* (Böhlau Verlag, Köln, 1978).

Boyle, Andrew, *No Passing Glory: The Full Authentic Biography of Group Captain Leonard Cheshire* (Collins, 1962).

Boyle, Andrew, *Trenchard, Man of Vision* (Collins, 1962).

Bryant, Sir Arthur, ed., *Triumph in the West, 1943–1946: Completing the War Diaries of Field Marshal Viscount Alanbrooke* (Collins, 1959; Doubleday, New York, 1959).

Carrington, Colonel Charles, *Soldier at Bomber Command* (Leo Cooper, 1987).

Churchill, Winston, *The Second World War*, vols.IV–VI (Cassell, 1951–4).

Cochran, Jackie, *The Stars at Noon* (Robert Hale, 1955).

Cole, Christopher, & Cheesman, E.F., *The Air Defence of Great Britain 1914–18* (Collins, 1959).

Collins, Diana, *Partners in Protest* (Gollancz, 1992).

Collins, Canon John, *Faith under Fire* (Leslie Frewin, 1966).

Colville, John, *The Fringes of Power – Downing Street Diaries* (Hodder & Stoughton, 1985).

Copp, Pete, *Forged in Fire* (Doubleday, New York, 1982).

Cox, Sebastian, ed., *Sir Arthur Harris – Despatch on War Operations* (Frank Cass, 1995).

Cox, Sebastian, ed., *Official Report of the British Bombing Survey Unit* (Frank Cass, 1998).

Craven, W.F., & Cate, J.L., *Official History of the Army Air Forces in World War II*, 2nd edition (Office of Air Force History, Washington, DC, 1983).

Cumming, Michael, *The Starkey Sacrifice, The Allied Bombing of Le Portel 1943* (Sutton, 1996).

Dean, Sir Maurice, *The Royal Air Force and Two World Wars* (Cassell, 1979).

De Groot, Gerard J., *Liberal Crusader – The Life of Sir Archibald Sinclair* (Hurst & Co, 1993).

Douglas, Marshal of the Royal Air Force Lord, *Years of Command* (Collins, 1953).

Dyson, Freeman, *Disturbing the Universe* (Harper & Row, New York, 1979).

Embry, Air Chief Marshal Sir Basil, *Mission Completed* (Methuen, 1957).

Frankland, Noble, *The Bombing Offensive Against Germany* (Faber, 1965).

Frankland, Noble, *History at War* (Giles de la Mare, 1998).

Franks, Norman, *First in the Indian Skies* (Life Publications, Lincoln, 1981).

Furse, Anthony, *Wilfrid Freeman, the Genius behind Allied Survival and Air Supremacy 1939 to 1945* (Spellmount, 2000).

Gibson, Guy, *'Enemy Coast Ahead'* (Michael Joseph, 1946).

Gilbert, Sir Martin, *The Coming of War – Winston Churchill 1922–39* (Heinemann, 1976).

Gilbert, Sir Martin, *Finest Hour – Winston Churchill 1939–41* (Heinemann, 1983).

Gilbert, Sir Martin, *Road to Victory – Winston Churchill 1941–45* (Heinemann, 1986).

Gilbert, Sir Martin, *Never Despair – Winston Churchill 1945–65* (Heinemann, 1988).

Goulding, Squadron Leader A.G., *Uncommon Valour* (Goodall, Air Data Publications, Manchester, 1985).

Greenhous, Brereton, et al, *The Crucible of War 1939–1945* (RCAF Official History, University of Toronto Press, 1994).

Gwyer, J.M.A., *Grand Strategy*, vol.3, part 1 (HMSO, 1964).

Harriman, Averell, *Special Envoy* (Random House, New York, 1975).

Harris, Marshal of the Royal Air Force Sir Arthur, *Bomber Offensive* (Collins, 1947; republished by Greenhill, 1990).

Hastings, Max, *Bomber Command* (Michael Joseph, 1979; Dial Press, New York, 1979).

Herington, John, *The Air War against Germany and Italy, 1939–43*, Australian Official History (Australian War Memorial, Canberra, 1962).

Herington, John, *Air Power over Europe, 1944–45*, Australian Official History (Australian War Memorial, Canberra, 1963).

Hinsley, Sir Harry, *Official History of Intelligence*, abridged edition (HMSO, 1993).

Horne, Alastair, ed., *Memoirs of Field Marshal Lord Montgomery* (Collins, 1958; World, New York, 1958).

Howard, Sir Michael, *Grand Strategy*, vol.4 (HMSO, 1972).

Hyde, H. Montgomery, *British Air Policy between the Wars 1918–1939* (Heinemann, 1976).

Irving, David, *The Destruction of Dresden* (Kimber, 1963; revised as *Apocalypse 1945*, Veritas, 1995).

Ismay, Lord, *The Memoirs of General the Lord Ismay* (Heinemann, 1960).

Jefford, Wing Commander C.G., *The Flying Camels* (Gresham Press, 1995).

Johnson, Group Captain Peter, *The Withered Garland* (New European Publications, 1995).

Jones, H.A., *The War in the Air*, vol.III (Oxford, 1931).

Jones, Professor R.V., *Most Secret War* (Hamish Hamilton, 1978).

Keegan, John, *The First World War* (Hutchinson, 1998).

Lawrence, W.A.J., *No 5 Bomber Group, RAF* (Faber, 1951).

Lehmann, Captain Ernst, *Zeppelin* (Longmans, 1937).

Le Roux, Willie, *A History of Safmarine* (Safmarine, Cape Town, 1996).

Lewis, Julian, *Changing Direction* (Sherwood Press, 1988).

Lochner, Louis, ed., *Goebbels Diaries 1942–43* (Hamish Hamilton, 1948).

Longmate, Norman, *The Bombers* (Hutchinson, 1983).

Lovell, Sir Bernard, *Echoes of War – The Story of H2S* (Hilger, 1991).

Lucas, Wing Commander Laddie, *Wings of War* (Hutchinson, 1983).

Lucas, Wing Commander Laddie, *Out of the Blue* (Hutchinson, 1985).

Macmillan, Wing Commander Norman, *Into the Blue*, revised edition (Jarrolds, 1969).

Messenger, Charles, *Harris and the Strategic Bombing Offensive, 1939–1945* (Arms and Armour Press, 1984).

Middlebrook, Martin, *The Nuremberg Raid* (Allen Lane, 1973).

Middlebrook, Martin, *The Battle of Hamburg* (Allen Lane, 1980; Scribners, New York, 1982).

Middlebrook, Martin, *The Peenemunde Raid* (Allen Lane, 1983).

Middlebrook, Martin, *The Bomber Command War Diaries* (Viking, 1985).

Middlebrook, Martin, *The Berlin Raids* (Viking, 1988)

Morpurgo, John, *Barnes Wallis* (Longmans, 1972).

Morris, Richard, *Cheshire: The Biography of Leonard Cheshire, VC, OM* (Viking, 2000).

Musgrove, Gordon, *Pathfinder Force* (Macdonald & Janes, 1976).

Neillands, Robin, *The Bomber War* (John Murray, 2001).

Orange, Dr Vincent, *A Biography of Sir Keith Park* (Methuen, 1984).

Overy, Professor Richard, *Why the Allies Won* (Jonathan Cape, 1995).

Overy, Professor Richard, *Bomber Command 1939–45* (Harper Collins, 1997).

Parton, James, *Air Force Spoken Here – The Life of General Eaker* (Adler & Adler, 1986).

Pelly-Fry, Group Captain James, *Heavenly Days* (Crecy Books, 1994).

Probert, Air Commodore H.A., *High Commanders of the RAF* (HMSO, 1990).

Probert, Air Commodore H.A., *The Forgotten Air Force* (Brasseys, 1995).

Revie, Alastair, *The Lost Command* (David Bruce & Watson, 1971).

Richards, Denis, *Portal of Hungerford* (Heinemann, 1978).

Richards, Denis, *The Hardest Victory* (Hodder & Stoughton, 1994).

Richards, Denis, & Saunders, H.St.G., *The Royal Air Force 1939–45*, vols.1–3 (HMSO, 1954).

Saward, Dudley, *The Bomber's Eye* (Cassell, 1959).

Saward, Dudley, *Bomber Harris* (Buchan & Enright, 1984).

Searby, Air Commodore John, ed. by Martin Middlebrook, *The Everlasting Arms* (Kimber, 1988).

Shores, C.; Franks, N.L.R.; & Guest, R., *Above the Trenches* (Grub Street, 1990).

Slessor, Marshal of the Royal Air Force Sir John, *The Central Blue* (Cassell, 1956).

Speer, Albert, *Inside the Third Reich* (Weidenfeld and Nicolson, 1970; Macmillan, New York, 1970).

Speer, Albert, *Spandau: The Secret Diaries* (Collins, 1976).

Sweetman, Professor John, *Operation Chastise* (Janes, 1982).

Swinton, Lord, *I Remember* (Hutchinson, 1946).

Tedder, Lord, *With Prejudice: The War Memoirs of MRAF Lord Tedder* (Cassell, 1966).

Terraine, John, *The Right of the Line* (Hodder & Stoughton, 1985).

Thetford, Owen, *Aircraft of the RAF since 1918* (Putnam, 1995).

Thomas, Hugh, *John Strachey* (Eyre Methuen, 1973).

Trevor-Roper, Professor Hugh, ed., *Goebbels Diaries – The Last Days* (Secker & Warburg, 1978).

Van der Spuy, Major General, *Chasing the Wind* (Books of Africa, 1966).

Verrier, Anthony, *The Bomber Offensive* (Batsford, 1968).

Warner, Philip, *The Story behind the Tragic Victory of 1917* (Sidgwick & Jackson, 1987).

Webster, Sir Charles, & Frankland, Noble, *The Strategic Air Offensive against Germany*, vols.1–4, British Official History (HMSO, 1961).

Wells, Mark, *Courage and Air Warfare* (Frank Cass, 1995).

ROYAL AIR FORCE HISTORICAL SOCIETY

The following editions of the Society's Proceedings (now the Journal) record several significant discussions and personal recollections:

Volume 5: Lectures and discussion on the RAF roles in support of the Special Operations Executive, 31 October 1988.

Volume 6: Lectures and discussion on Portal, Harris and the Bomber Offensive, 13 March 1989.

Volume 9: Joint Seminar on the wartime relationships between the RAF and USAAF, 29 October 1990.

Special Edition: *Reaping the Whirlwind*, Symposium on the Strategic Bomber Offensive, held at the RAF Staff College, 26 March 1993.

Volume 14: Lecture by Professor Sir Michael Howard on Ethics, Deterrence and Strategic Bombing, 4 July 1994.

PERSONAL PAPERS

Marshal of the Royal Air Force Sir Arthur Harris: Most of Harris's official and private papers are held at the RAF Museum, Hendon. They comprise files containing much of his wartime correspondence (referred to in the footnotes as Folders H1, H2, etc) and folders of miscellaneous items covering his whole life and particularly the post-war years (referred to as Misc Folders 1, 2, etc). His Safmarine papers are also there. Other items, including numerous photograph albums and scrapbooks, remain in the possession of his youngest daughter, Jacqueline Assheton.

Marshal of the Royal Air Force Lord Portal: Portal's official papers are held in the Library at Christ Church, Oxford.

Air Chief Marshal Sir Edgar Ludlow-Hewitt: These papers are housed in the Air Historical Branch (RAF).

Wing Commander John Lawrence: A small number of letters are held by his widow, Mrs Ann Lawrence.

Squadron Leader Peter Tomlinson: He bequeathed his papers and other material to Mr Oliver Knesl, in South Africa.

Mr Ian Elliot: His personal memoir, never published, is in the possession of his daughter, Mrs Vivienne Lloyd.

Index

(Note: Officers are accorded the ranks they finally held)